Enlightening the Mystery of Man

Enlightening the Mystery of Man

Gaudium et spes Fifty Years Later

Edited by Antonio López

HUMANUM ACADEMIC PRESS

Pontifical John Paul II Institute for Studies on Marriage and Family
The Catholic University of America
McGivney Hall 307
620 Michigan Avenue, NE
Washington, DC 20064
202-526-9691

Distributed by:
The Catholic University of America Press
c/o HFS
P.O. Box 50370
Baltimore, MD 21211
800-537-5487
Library of Congress Control Number: 2017964034

Text and cover design: Kachergis Book Design
Cover Image: *The Descent into Limbo*; Unknown; Nicaea, Turkey; early 13th century–late 13th century; Tempera colors and gold leaf on parchment; Ms. Ludwig II 5, fol. 191v. Courtesy of the J. Paul Getty Museum, Los Angeles.
Printed in the United States of America.
ISBN: 978-1-948195-00-3

CONTENTS

ABBREVIATIONS

AAS — *Acta Apostolicae Sedis*. Vatican City: Typis Polyglottis Vaticanis, 1909–.

AG — Second Vatican Council. *Ad gentes*. Decree on the Missionary Activity of the Church. December 7, 1965.

AL — Francis. *Amoris laetitia*. On Love in the Family. March 19, 2016.

ART — assisted reproductive technology

CSEL — *Corpus Scriptorum Ecclesiasticorum Latinorum*. Vienna: Austria Academy of Sciences, 1866–2006.

CV — Benedict XVI. *Caritas in veritate*. Charity in Truth. July 7, 2009.

DN — Dionysius the Areopagite. *The Divine Names*.

DV — Congregation for the Doctrine of the Faith. *Donum vitae*. Instruction on Respect for Human Life in Its Origin and on the Dignity of Procreation. February 22, 1987.

ECC — William of St. Thierry. *Expositio super Cantica Canticorum*.

EE — John Paul II. *Ecclesia de Eucharistia*. The Church from the Eucharist. April 17, 2003.

FC — John Paul II. *Familiaris consortio*. The Fellowship of the Family. November 22, 1981.

GS — Second Vatican Council. *Gaudium et spes*. Pastoral Constitution on the Church in the Modern World. December 7, 1965.

HV — Paul VI. *Humanae vitae*. Of Human Life. July 25, 1968.

IVF — in vitro fertilization

Abbreviations

LG	Second Vatican Council. *Lumen gentium*. The Dogmatic Constitution on the Church. November 21, 1964.
LS	Pope Francis. *Laudato si*. On Care for Our Common Home. June 18, 2015.
SCG	Thomas Aquinas. *Summa contra Gentiles*.
ST	Thomas Aquinas. *Summa theologaie*.
VS	John Paul II. *Veritatis splendor*. The Splendor of the Truth. August 6, 1993.

Enlightening the Mystery of Man

Introduction

ANTONIO LÓPEZ

At the close of the jubilee year of 2000, St. John Paul II wrote in his apostolic letter *Novo millenio ineunte* that the Second Vatican Council was "the grace bestowed on the Church in the 20th century" and that with the Council "we find a sure compass by which to take our bearings in the century now beginning."[1] The Washington, DC, session of the Pontifical John Paul II Institute for Studies on Marriage and Family at the Catholic University of America has shared this perception of its founder, even while acknowledging that the conciliar documents are not lacking in inner tensions that have resulted in a complex history of contrasting interpretations. This is why the reception, elucidation, and communication of the wealth that God gave the Church at the Second Vatican Council have always been considered one of our most important tasks. Part of this endeavor has been the hosting of a series of annual conferences dedicated to some of the Council's most significant documents. In 2012, a conference titled "Keeping the World Awake to God: The Challenge of Vatican II" sought to provide an authoritative *grille de lecture* for approaching the Council as an integral whole, one significant for both the Catholic Tradition and for the contemporary "signs of the times."[2] Because during this

1. John Paul II, *Novo millennio ineunte*, "At the Beginning of the New Millennium," January 6, 2001, no. 57.

2. The conciliar documents, when taken as a whole, point to a hermeneutical center radiating outward from the central doctrinal claims of *Dei verbum* and *Lumen gentium*. This "center" illuminates the entirety of the Council's teaching, informing all its statements on mission, interreligious dialogue, modernity, religious freedom, and the like. Briefly stated,

time there was also great controversy in North America surrounding the topic of religious freedom, in 2013 attention was devoted to the Council's declaration *Dignitatis humanae*.[3] The Council's dogmatic constitution on the mystery of the Church was the focus of the following year, with a conference titled "*Lumen gentium*: The Church as Sacrament of Trinitarian Communion." Here attention was paid to the teaching of *Lumen genti-*

---

what the Second Vatican Council sought to highlight was an often overlooked aspect of the Tradition, namely, the Catholicity of God's self-revelation in Christ. Christ is "catholic" insofar as he reveals God in revealing man, and vice versa. John Paul II's encyclical *Dives in misericordia* reads the Council's Christological integration of God-centeredness and man-centeredness as proposed by *Gaudium et spes* 22. Christ, the final Adam, by the revelation of the mystery of the Father and his love, fully reveals man to himself and makes his supreme calling clear. John Paul II, *Dives in misericordia*, "Rich in Mercy," November 30, 1980, no. 1. For John Paul II, then, the novelty of the Council is in its rereading of the Tradition in light of its "catholic" form, something that is not merely "formal" but a unity of form and content (i.e., Christ as the Incarnate Word of the Trinitarian God; see *Dei verbum*, no. 2). For published essays from this conference, see "'Keeping the World Awake to God': The Challenge of Vatican II," *Communio: International Catholic Review 39* (Spring-Summer 2012).

3. Titled "*Dignitatis humanae* and the Rediscovery of Religious Freedom," the conference's task was to explore the theological, metaphysical, and anthropological grounds of human dignity. John Paul II, for his part, forcefully indicated that "the curtailment of the rights of religious freedom of individuals and communities is not only a painful experience but it is above all an attack on man's very dignity, independently of the religion professed or of the concept of the world which these individuals and communities have. The curtailment and violation of religious freedom are in contrast with man's dignity and his objective rights" (*Redemptor hominis*, no. 17). Also aware of the gravity of our historical circumstances, Benedict XVI reiterated the critical importance of our understanding and promoting of religious liberty at an address given to the bishops of the United States on January 19, 2012: "[the] Church's witness is of its nature public … The legitimate separation of Church and State cannot be taken to mean that the Church must be silent on certain issues, nor that the State may choose not to engage, or be engaged by, the voices of committed believers in determining the values that will shape the future of the nation … It is imperative that the Church comes to realize the radical secularism which finds increasing expression in the political and cultural spheres … Of particular concern are certain attempts being made to limit that most cherished of American freedoms, the freedom of religion." It is man's dignity, in other words, as one created in the image of the Triune God and called to filial participation in divine life, that establishes and defines his right to religious freedom. Every understanding of freedom is thus inseparable from its relation to truth (i.e., the truth of God, man, the world, and their relation), and every juridical right, including that of religious freedom, always then rests and expresses a specific metaphysics and anthropology. For essays from this conference, see "*Dignitatis Humanae* and the Rediscovery of Religious Freedom," *Communio: International Catholic Review* 40 (Summer-Fall, 2013). For a comprehensive, historical, and critical investigation of the text of *Dignitatis humanae*, see David L. Schindler and Nicholas J. Healy, *Freedom, Truth, and Human Dignity: The Second Vatican Council's Declaration on Religious Freedom* (Grand Rapids, MI: Eerdmans, 2015).

um on the inner nature and universal mission of the Church as a sign and sacrament of communion, grounded in the Trinitarian mystery of God, concretized in eucharistic fellowship, and expressed ever anew through the life together that Christians are given to share.[4] Finally, having approached the Christological and Trinitarian center that radiates and gives life to the Church, the institute dedicated a conference to the pastoral constitution on the Church in the modern world, *Gaudium et spes*, in the year of the fiftieth anniversary of its promulgation (1965).

With *Gaudium et spes*, the Church spoke to the entire world or, more precisely, to every human being in both "his tragedies and his triumphs" (no. 2:2). She spoke to modern men and women knowing both the questions that constitute them deeply (nos. 4, 10, 21, 41) and the challenges that they face as a result of the atheistic culture that a global and technocratic democracy continues to embrace and foster. She thus spoke as one aware of just how much we have become enthralled by the power of freedom and of lives seemingly content with a finite, historical existence deprived of a transcendental horizon.

To grasp what the Church said in *Gaudium et spes*, it is good to recall what John Paul II, who played an important role in its redaction, clarified on the thirtieth anniversary of its publication: The "joyful and hope-filled" message of this conciliar document is that "the nature and destiny of the human being and of the world can be definitively revealed only in

4. To a significant degree, the pressing question concerning the Church has become how she can be ameliorated, unburdened of her clerical and bureaucratic weight, and humanized. Because the Church is both a human and a divine reality, this is undoubtedly a legitimate concern, but the desire to improve the Church must always be preceded by an understanding of her nature. Only action informed by what something is and by its *telos* bears fruit. Thus the guiding question of this conference was simply "What is the Church?" or, perhaps more aptly, "*Who* is the Church?" See Hans Urs von Balthasar, "Who Is the Church?," in *Explorations in Theology*, vol. 2, *Spouse of the Word*, trans. A. V. Littledale (San Francisco: Ignatius Press, 1991). Contemplating the nature of the Church must be done without either letting the concern for action inform one's thinking or falling into the trap of resolving controversies according to preconceptions so as to distance oneself from what Henri de Lubac describes as the "wealth of contrasting aspects"; see his *The Church: Paradox and Mystery*, trans. James R. Dunne (Staten Island, NY: Alba House, 1969). The Church is a "real paradox," and yet, rather than simply being an "object" of study, she is at the same time "our mother"; in her and through her we are born to a new life. She is always present to us, educating us, accompanying us through life, healing us, correcting, and comforting us. Some of the essays can be found in "*Ecclesiam Unam*," *Communio: International Catholic Review* 41 (Winter 2014).

the light of the crucified and risen Christ. . . . [This] is the message that makes the Pastoral Constitution on the Church in the Modern World—the last of the documents promulgated by the Second Vatican Council and the most extensive of all—in a certain sense the *apex of the Council's journey*."[5] Thus the Church's task of dialoguing with and entering into the modern world, of taking on the joy and the anguish of humanity, and of bearing the message of salvation that is intended for all consists in a genuine assumption of the world and human history into Christ's eucharistic love. Such an "assumption" does not seek to absorb the world into the Church, but rather presupposes that the world's own naturally given creaturely integrity is fulfilled only in and through Christ's eucharistic sacrifice. Yet, given the uniquely areligious times in which we live, the Council Fathers recognized that the articulation and proposal of such a message could not be a straightforward repetition of the Church's dogmatic content or its metaphysical underpinnings. By selecting what questions to raise, what themes to approach, and the kind of dialogue to be adopted, *Gaudium et spes* addressed modern man by both challenging his culture and most basic epistemological assumptions, and by seeking to retrieve what in modern culture is not antagonistic to the truth. *Gaudium et spes* thus provides the Church's most comprehensive official statement regarding her relation to the modern world.

As the essays gathered here show, the conciliar constitution carries out its reflection primarily in terms of a distinctive anthropology conceived in inner openness to the revelation of God in Jesus Christ. The anthropology of *Gaudium et spes* is best understood against the background of Chalcedonian Christology, with its affirmation that, in Jesus Christ, God truly assumes (*assumpta*) but does not absorb (*preempta*) human nature. As Joseph Ratzinger puts it: "The human nature of all men is one; Christ's taking to himself the one human nature of man is an event which affects every human being; consequently human nature in every human being is henceforward Christologically characterized."[6]

5. See John Paul II, "Only Christ Can Fulfill Man's Hopes," *Communio: International Catholic Review* (Spring 1996): 122–28.

6. See *Commentary on the Documents of Vatican II*, ed. Herbert Vorgrimler, trans. Walter M. Abbott (New York: Crossroad, 1989), 160.

Before outlining the themes of the following essays, I call to mind that the fruitfulness of any study or debate on conciliar documents hinges on our capacity to read them within a "hermeneutics of reform," that is, "of renewal within the continuity of the one subject-Church that the Lord has given us."[7] This hermeneutics, then, is thought in terms of a "newness" located within the continuity of the Christian Tradition. The Second Vatican Council represents a true reform precisely because it offers "newness" within the context of continuity. During her two-thousand-year history, the Church has faced many dire crises. She has also seen new syntheses or reforms replace old ones. It is important here to realize that reform within the Church is always a process that stretches both forward and backward. Her reform tends forward because it takes new elements from the peoples she meets or from the internal changes that have taken place within the civilizations she already knows. At the same time, however, the Church's reform also tends toward the past because it re-presents in a new form the principle of her origins: the event of the incarnation, death, resurrection, and glorification of the beloved Son of the Father, who are one in the Holy Spirit. True reform, therefore, is one that allows us to see the truth of God's love as though for the first time. It is "fresh" and "novel" precisely because it re-presents the eternal Triune love of God in a particular historical context. In this sense, the newness of the reform is always a reacquaintance with the definitiveness of the whole in the particularity of "today." Our liberal and technological Western culture makes us think that a reform is to efficaciously pattern the dogmatic content of the Church according to some private interpretation of Christ's truth and of the current state of affairs, however much this may be done with the best of intentions, such as to ease Christianity's reception. This mind-set, however, tends either to bracket history—and thus anchor oneself in the past—or to adapt Christian doctrine and life to the current worldly standards and principles—thereby denaturing Christianity altogether. Rather, a genuine reform enables us to become acquainted anew with the event that lies at the origin of the Church, as something that is thoroughly pertinent to our current circumstances precisely because of, and not in spite of, its eternity.

7. See Pope Benedict XVI's Christmas address to the Roman Curia, December 22, 2005. *AAS* 98 (2006): 45–53, at 46.

It is in this sense that the conciliar documents sought to renew the life of the Church and her mission in the world.

Because the event of Christ, the person-Truth, is the icon of the Father's love, to become familiar anew with the truth of God and man so as to interpret, by that light, what it means to live in a state of life engaged in human, social, scientific, economic, and politics affairs, involves entering into the dramatic interplay between truth and freedom. This interplay is best grasped when we recall that Christ—who receives the truth he is from the Father (Jn 8:26) and leads all those who receive him to it through the Holy Spirit—reveals himself as the truth through the medium of his person (Jn 14:6). Christ, as truth-in-person, calls forth the inescapable human response to man's most essential question: "Who do you say that I am?" (Mt 16:15). It is precisely this dramatic nature of truth that not only allows the "synthesis" of newness and continuity to take place, but also requires that this "placing together" (*syn-tithenai*) of God and man occur first and foremost in the life of a saint. Of course, that the saint is the privileged expositor of the synthesis between truth, eternity, and history does not mean that every single word a saint says must be canonized, nor does it make a specific saint the only voice through which the Spirit of the beloved Son of the Father renews the life of the Church at a given time. The saint's existence, as the unconditional "yes" to Christ's preceding offer of himself for him, is where the wealth of the past is brought together and expressed in a new way for both his or her contemporaries and for succeeding generations. This takes place without the saint seeing, or even been concerned with seeing, the fruitfulness that his or her life will bring to the Church and the world. In light of this, rather than taking our bearings from a specific ideology articulated by one or other "school" of thought, it is more fitting to attempt to see, appropriate, clarify, and creatively deepen the conciliar documents in light of the lived synthesis of one of the saints given to the Church by God this past century.

The essays gathered in this volume were thus written under the light radiating from St. John Paul II's lived synthesis, and were presented at a conference held in November 2015, commemorating the fiftieth anniversary of *Gaudium et spes* titled "The Church in the Modern World: Fifty

Years Later." They do not offer an exegesis of the late pope's interventions during the Council or of his studies published after its conclusion. Rather, in conversation with some of the most significant authors and interpreters of the Council, these essays have a guiding principle in the insight that, according to St. John Paul II, it is Jesus Christ who is the kernel of the conciliar constitution, for only he "remains present as *the Light of the World that enlightens the mystery of man* not only for Christians, but also for the entire human family; he reveals man to himself; he calls all to one and the same destiny, and, through the Holy Spirit, to the possibility of 'being made partners' with his definitive victory over death (*GS*, no. 22)."[8] Christ's revelation of the Father's love in the Spirit unveils that man "who is the only creature on earth which God willed for itself cannot fully find himself expect through a sincere gift of himself" (*GS*, no. 24). Thus, while dealing with many different themes found in the conciliar document, the following essays also seek to deepen the Trinitarian and Christological anthropology called forth by the Second Vatican Council. However undeveloped such an anthropology may be, it is nonetheless the case that the Council perceives man—created in the image of God and called to communion with him—in terms of how God's own being is revealed by Christ, namely, as *gift*.[9]

Besides the common interpretative horizon that enables genuine personal creativity, the following essays build on and enrich each other. Thus, although they can be read separately, one will derive much more fruit if they

8. John Paul II, "Only Christ," 128.

9. "In his intimate life, God 'is love,' (1 Jn 4:8, 16), the essential love shared by the three divine Persons: personal love is the Holy Spirit as the Spirit of the Father and the Son. Therefore, he 'searches even the depths of God,' (1 Cor 2:10) as uncreated Love-Gift. It can be said that in the Holy Spirit the intimate life of the Triune God becomes totally gift, an exchange of mutual love between the divine Persons and that through the Holy Spirit God exists in the mode of gift. It is the Holy Spirit who is the personal expression of this self-giving, of this being-love (cf. Aquinas, *ST* I, q. 37–38). He is Person-Love. He is Person-Gift. Here we have an inexhaustible treasure of the reality and an inexpressible deepening of the concept of person in God, which only divine Revelation makes known to us. At the same time, the Holy Spirit, being consubstantial with the Father and the Son in divinity, is love and uncreated gift from which derives as from its source (*fons vivus*) all giving of gifts vis-a-vis creatures (created gift): the gift of existence to all things through creation; the gift of grace to human beings through the whole economy of salvation." John Paul II, *Dominum et vivificantem*, "On the Holy Spirit in the Life of the Church and the World," May 18, 1986, no. 10.

are read sequentially. The essays are ordered into three parts. The first are authored by David L. Schindler, Antonio López, and Adrian J. Walker, and offer the metaphysical, anthropological, and theological underpinnings of the constitution. The following three, by Nicholas J. Healy Jr., Mathew Levering, and Paolo Prosperi, speak on the relation between Church, sacrament, and the world. The final four texts, by David S. Crawford, Margaret Harper McCarthy, Andrew V. Abela, and D. C. Schindler, provide reflections on two contexts in which this relation is most vividly played out: in the family and in human work.

Part I begins with David L. Schindler's "'Disenchantment' and the End of Modern Civilization: The Symbolical, the Neutral, and the Diabolical," an essay that lays the ontological grounds for the ensuing reflection. In dialogue with Max Weber and John Paul II, he explains how the rightful autonomy of creatures involves an intrinsic reference to and revelation of God. The claim, then, is that the contemporary "forgetfulness" of God obfuscates the genuine intelligibility of the creature's natural integrity. Such a modern ontology, while claiming to be "neutral" with respect to natural "objects," in fact replaces the symbolic constitution of finite beings—that is, what is required by their nature of being as gift—with the "diabolical," an ontology that presents the original power of God who is love under the guise of a love that instead is nongratuitous and restless power. The essay thus seeks to help us in "seeing things as they are at once *in themselves and as related to God*, and in unfolding this 'seeing' into *an integrated way of life* that is *engaged with the whole of reality*."

Antonio López's "Man's Highest Calling: The Theological Anthropology of *Gaudium et spes*" elucidates why the Second Vatican Council wished to present a Trinitarian and Christological anthropology as part of the main content of the Church's dialogue with the world. After explaining some of the internal tensions of the document, the essay develops the Council's anthropology by presenting an account of the mystery of the human person in terms of being as gift. It thus seeks to show how this ontology brings the metaphysical reflection of *esse* as the perfection of all perfections together with the scriptural revelation of the Triune God in Christ and the contemporary perception of the human spirit.

Adrian J. Walker's "*Sincerum sui ipsius donum*: The Trinitarian Ground of *Gaudium et spes*'s Anthropology" argues for how a "sincere gift of self" is the best way of grasping the mystery of actuality in God, who in Christ reveals himself as Triune love (*GS*, no. 24). In dialogue with St. Augustine's reflection on the Trinity, Walker seeks to show that "the communion personified by the Holy Spirit is the paradigm of a sincere gift of self," a communion that "builds something like a sincere gift of self into the very heart of being." The institution that Walker points to as anticipating and foreshadowing this divine and created actuality is also one the conciliar document invites us to consider, namely, the natural institution of marriage. In this fashion, marriage is upheld not so much in its ethical role but for its ontological and symbolic dimension—marriage is an "epiphany of being."

Part II begins with Nicholas J. Healy's "Eucharistic Ecclesiology and Eschatology: On the Church's Relation to the World," which proposes that the eschatological nature of the Church outlined in *Lumen gentium* "sheds light on the pastoral program of *Gaudium et spes* and the purpose of Vatican II." The author elucidates that, contrary to what many contemporary and widely recognized historians of the Council have proposed, "the connection between the Church and the Eucharist is the hidden center of the Council's teaching on the Church-world relation." Therefore one does not adequately grasp why the Church is interested in dialoguing with the world until it is recognized how the Church's missionary character—her being for the world and contributing to the world's salvation—is informed by her sacramental character, which is "the relation to the Eucharist at the heart of the Church."

Matthew Levering's "Nature and Grace in *Gaudium et spes*: The Status of the Theory of the Natural Desire for the Supernatural" approaches the issue of the relation between creature and the creator in terms of the former's *iusta rerum terrenarum autonomia*, or "rightful autonomy of worldly affairs" (*GS*, no. 36). This the essay does from the point of view of the relation between nature and the supernatural. After showing the extensive influence of Henri de Lubac's thought on *Gaudium et spes*, Levering argues that the conciliar document does not positively or negatively answer the question of de Lubac's specific theory on nature and grace. Levering argues that "*Gaudium et spes* can hardly be expected to settle the finer ontological points regarding natural desire for God, particularly given its intention to operate from within the existential conditions of a world in which humans have never lacked a supernatural end."

Paolo Prosperi's "This Mystery Is Great: Reflections on the Fittingness of the Nuptial Analogy in Trinitarian Theology" argues for the appropriateness of interpreting *Gaudium et spes* 22 by way of an analogy to human married love. A close and profound reading of St. John's Gospel and the Song of Songs, buttressed by the contribution of some of the Greek Fathers, is presented to ground certain essential features of nuptiality. Besides speaking to the need of integrating desire with nuptial love, and of how the body is an integral part of this analogy, the author also illustrates why an understanding of the nuptial gift in terms of a self-denying freedom is a diabolical parody of self-giving love. This parody, inasmuch as it opposes nature to freedom, undermines the desire of both spouses and tragically misrepresents divine and human freedom in a manner that undermines all love.

The first essay of Part III, David S. Crawford's "Discerning the Signs of Our Times: *Gaudium et spes*, Contraception, and Some Cultural Implications for Marriage and the Family as Natural Communities," shows why the Church's teaching regarding birth control is "crucially necessary for sustaining an anthropologically adequate and sustainable sense of the family, such as the one so richly developed by *Gaudium et spes*." Contraception, precisely because it represents the "domination and reordering of nature," decisively alters the human subject and entails the "displacement of the symbolic order inscribed in the body and marriage and family as natural communities with an alternative anthropology." The contemporary conception of man, considered primarily as *homo technicus*, transforms natural, constitutive relations into legal ones that, once socially established, cannot but accelerate the demise of the anthropology that produced it.

Margaret Harper McCarthy's "In Dialogue with the World: The Church and the Evanescence of the Family," revisits what it means for the Church to have a genuine and realistic (rather than naïvely optimistic) dialogue with the world. She shows how an inadequate sense of worldliness consists in conceiving creatureliness in abstraction from its constitutive relation with God. The most glaring instantiation of this anthropological abstraction, one that ever more shapes our contemporary Western culture, is that of the modern family. An insightful study of several early modern philosophers shows how the paradigm of the "orphan" came to fuel a systematic rejection of childhood, fatherhood, and motherhood. The call of *Gaudium et spes* to rediscover the truth of married love, and the beauty of the family, thus proves not to be a tangential issue, but one of the Church's and humanity's most urgent endeavors.

The final two essays deal with another crucial aspect of the Church-world relation that stems from man's being created in the image of God: the engagement with the world through work. Andrew V. Abela's "*Gaudium et spes* Fifty Years Later: On Human Work and the Economy" illustrates that an economy that takes seriously *Gaudium et spes*'s anthropology would operate for the sake of the common good and consider man to be "the source, the center, and the purpose of all economic and social life" and not the other way around. After an examination of many of the assumptions of a liberal economy, the author makes his proposal concrete by offering seven imperatives for developing a more humane theory of economics.

Lastly, D. C. Schindler's "Redeeming Work: On *Technē* as an Encounter between God, Man, and the World" asks the question of man's work in a manner uncharacteristic of its more common utilitarian, pragmatic, and technological sense. Instead, the essay claims that work "has the form of an encounter between man and world that opens up *naturally* to God." A just dialogue between the Church and the world therefore requires more than simply a social critique of the meaning of work. What is needed is a rediscovery of the sense in which work, as a task in which the gift of being human is contained, "brings into contact the inner of the essence of the world and the inner essence of the Church."

Heeding the courageous proposal of *Gaudium et spes* that "only in the mystery of the Incarnate Word does the mystery of man take on light" (*GS*, no. 22), the following reflections thus wish to carry out the task called for by the conciliar documents: to elucidate, deepen, and ground our understanding of God, world, the human person, and their relations, in terms of *gift*.

I

Creation, Gift, and God

I

“Disenchantment” and the End of Modern Civilization

The Symbolical, the Neutral, and the Diabolical

DAVID L. SCHINDLER

Introduction

The conclusion of the well-known paragraph of *Gaudium et spes* titled *De iusta rerum terrenarum autonomia* (“On the rightful autonomy of earthly affairs”) states:

> if the expression, the independence (*autonomia*) of temporal affairs, is taken to mean that created things do not depend on (*non pendere*: do not originate from, or hang upon) God, and that man can use them without any reference to their Creator (*ut . . . ad Creatorem non referat*: without bringing or carrying them back to their Creator), anyone who acknowledges (*agnoscit*) God will see how false such a meaning is. For without the Creator the creature would disappear (*evanescit*). For their part, however, all believers of whatever religion always hear (*audierunt*) His revealing voice in the discourse of creatures (*in creaturarum loquela*: in creatures' own speech). When God is forgotten (*per oblivionem Dei*), however, the creature itself grows unintelligible (*ipsa creatura obscuratur*).[1]

My use of the terms “symbolical” and “diabolical” takes its inspiration from and is much indebted to D. C. Schindler, *Freedom from Reality: On the Diabolical Character of Modern Liberty* (Notre Dame, IN: University of Notre Dame Press, 2017).

1. Second Vatican Council, *Gaudium et spes*, Pastoral Constitution on the Church in the Modern World, December 7, 1965, no. 36. The first part of the paragraph describes the rightful autonomy of creation in the following terms: “If by the autonomy of earthly affairs

Other essays in this volume have much to say that is pertinent to this text from *Gaudium et spes*. The aim of this chapter is to reflect on the rightful autonomy of the world in light of what has been called the "disenchantment" of modern culture. This term is taken from the early twentieth-century German sociologist of religion Max Weber (1864–1920), who, in his well-known work on religion and the development of economic culture in Anglo-America, argues that the logic implicit in Calvinist-Puritan theology led to *die Entzauberung der Welt*, the elimination of the sacred or mystical or "magical" from the world, and hence to the world's "disenchantment."[2] A century earlier, German philosopher-poet Friedrich Schiller (1759–1805) had used the phrase *die entgötterte Natur* to describe the elimination of the gods from nature in the modern world.[3] Morris Berman, in *The Re-Enchantment of the World*, says that for both Weber and Schiller this idea means that "the history of the West ... is the progressive removal of the mind, or spirit, from phenomenal appearances."[4]

---

we mean that created things and societies themselves enjoy their own laws and values which must be gradually deciphered, put to use, and regulated by men, then it is entirely right to demand that autonomy. Such is not merely required by modern man, but harmonizes also with the will of the Creator. For by the very circumstance of their having been created, all things are endowed with their own stability, truth, goodness, proper laws and order.... Indeed whoever labors to penetrate the secrets of reality with a humble and steady mind, even though he is unaware of the fact, is nevertheless being led by the hand of God, who holds all things in existence, and gives them their identity."

2. Max Weber, *The Protestant Ethic and the Spirit of Capitalism*, trans. Talcott Parsons (New York: Scribner, 1958), 105. See also idem, "Science as a Vocation," in *The Vocation Lectures*, ed. J. G. Burke (Berkeley: University of California Press, 2004), 12–13: "Thus the growing process of intellectualization and rationalization ... means that in principle ... we are not ruled by mysterious, unpredictable forces, but that, on the contrary, we can in principle *control everything by means of calculation*. That in turn means the disenchantment of the world."

3. Friedrich Schiller, "Die Götter Griechenlands," in *Sämtliche Werke*, ed. Gerhard Fricke and Herbert Göpfert (Munich: Hanser, 1962), 1:173. For an English translation, see "The Gods of Greece," in *Complete Poems of Schiller*, ed. Henry D. Wireman (Philadelphia: Kohler, 1879), 64–69.

4. Morris Berman, *The Re-Enchantment of the World* (Ithaca, NY: Cornell University Press, 1981), 69. Charles Taylor begins *A Secular Age* (Cambridge, MA: Harvard University Press, 2007) by asking what happened in Western society between 1500 and 2000. He frames his answer in terms of enchantment and disenchantment, expressly evoking Weber's use of the term as an apt description of our modern condition. According to Taylor, there are three features characteristic of the Western world prior to 1500:

> (1) The natural world [people] lived in ... testified to the divine purpose and action; and not just in the obvious way ... that its order and design bespeaks creation; but also

In this essay, I propose a reading of the idea of disenchantment of the modern world in light of *Gaudium et spes* 36, together with a reading of the theological anthropology and cosmology of *Gaudium et spes* more generally. This essay concerns the "end of civilization." By "end" I mean, first and most essentially, the basic order and finality of modern civilization, particularly that of America. This discussion of "end" in the sense of finality, however, also implies coming to terms with those ways of being and acting that undermine the realization of this finality, and that so far lead to the "end"—that is, the death—of civilization as such.

A quote from Hans Urs von Balthasar brings us to the heart of the question regarding modernity and rightful autonomy. In his book on Reinhold Schneider, Balthasar writes: "the man who follows Christ to the

---

> because the great events in this natural order, storms, droughts, floods, plagues ... were seen as acts of God. (2) God was also implicated in the very existence of society.... A kingdom could only be conceived as grounded in something higher than mere human action in secular time. And beyond that, the life of the various associations which made up society, parishes, boroughs, guilds, and so on were interwoven with ritual and worship.... One could not but encounter God everywhere. (3) People lived in an "enchanted" world.... I am invoking here [the] negation [of] Weber's expression "disenchantment" as a description of our modern condition.... I'm going to use its antonym to describe a crucial feature of the pre-modern condition. The enchanted world in this sense is the world of spirits, demons, and moral forces which our ancestors lived in. (25–26)

Taylor is quick to clarify that this does not mean that everyone prior to the year 1500 believed in God. The point is simply that "in the outlook of European peasants in 1500, beyond all the ambivalences, the Christian God was the ultimate guarantee that good would triumph or at least hold the plentiful forces of darkness at bay.... God is there, acting in the cosmos, founding and sustaining societies, acting as a bulwark against evil" (26). Atheism as such was inconceivable within this framework.

For Taylor, the disappearance of these three features of the world is significant, but it is nonetheless only part of the explanation of what has happened over the last five centuries. We should not read modernity too simply as a story of loss and subtraction. Indeed, Taylor insists that the distinctive features of the world that emerge in the modern period (e.g., modern science) come from Christian motives and signal a distinctive kind of fullness—or, in his words, "alternative possible reference points for fullness" (27).

It seems to me that Taylor is right: we cannot conceive modernity simply in terms of loss and subtraction. There have been genuine gains in the modern period. At the same time, it is important to see that these gains have not been made simply by way of addition. Recognizing the genuine achievements of modernity, in other words, is consistent with deep criticism of the ambiguity lying at the heart of these achievements—even when the achievements are inspired by Christian motives. For more regarding modern achievements and their ambiguity, see the section on "The Neutral and the Diabolical" below.

full ... can never, ever be a 'bourgeois.' He is not himself (as the bourgeois is): he is the image of Another.... He defends the form (*die Form*) but never the boundary [or limit] (*die Grenze*) (like the bourgeois)."[5] The bourgeois person, in other words, is just himself, while the one who follows Christ is himself *only in being at once the image of another*. This idea is helpful for distinguishing between a false sense of creaturely autonomy and a true or legitimate sense (in the language of *Gaudium et spes*, a *iusta autonomia*). In a falsely conceived autonomy, the creature is understood to be simply itself; as such, it lacks the inner reference to the Creator that would enable us to hear God's voice *within* the language of the creature. It is precisely in this false sense of creaturely autonomy that we find the key for understanding the disenchantment of the modern world.

The argument of this essay, in other words, focuses on what it means to say that the rightful autonomy of creatures involves reference to and revelation of God. As *Gaudium et spes* incisively sees, the denial of this reference to God not only expresses a forgetfulness of God, but also obscures the intelligibility of the creature itself. To deny this reference is thus to change the meaning of both creature and Creator, as well as the meaning of the relation that exists between them. This claim, which goes to the root meaning of disenchantment, leads directly to the core problem of modernity, especially as it takes form in America, and thus to the core of the cultural controversies that occupy the Church with ever greater intensity.

What informs Balthasar's statement regarding the bourgeois, and what I take to be the heart of a false autonomy, is the idea that the creature in his original identity lacks inner reference to the Creator. The creature no longer images its transcendent Source. A rightful sense of autonomy, by contrast, requires an original unity of creaturely identity and reference to the Creator God. *Iusta autonomia* in this sense expresses a symbolical idea of worldly reality.

The argument unfolds as follows. The first section begins by explicating the meaning of the term "symbolical." In its root or ontological sense,

5. Hans Urs von Balthasar, *Tragedy under Grace: Reinhold Schneider on the Experience of the West* (San Francisco: Ignatius Press, 1997), 248; *Nochmals: Reinhold Schneider* (Freiburg: Johannes Verlag, 1991), 264.

"symbolical" signals a being that, in the original constitution of its own identity, bears relation to the Creator—and in a certain sense thereby to all other creaturely beings—in a way that involves an implicit imaging of God. The following section describes Weber's notion of disenchantment (*Rationalisierung* or *Entzauberung*), showing how this rationalizing, disenchanting process not only shapes the economic aspects of Puritan life, but also provides a methodical unity, or "ethos," for the whole of life. The next two sections seek to frame the main principles that undergird this rationalizing "logic" of disenchantment. I argue that this logic can and does survive its original Puritan context, and that it is this logic that displaces the symbolical in modern culture. Today, this displacement takes the form of an allegedly "neutral" idea of being. This would-be neutral idea of being, however, is not empty of an image of God; on the contrary, it logically unfolds into a counterfeit image that is best termed "diabolical." The final section concludes with a discussion of the "authentic theology of integral human liberation" articulated by popes John Paul II and Benedict XVI. Here I clarify the sense in which "integral" human liberation demands that we approach modern culture as, at root, a struggle between a symbolical and a diabolical vision of man and the cosmos. What the preceding pontificates articulate as "structural sin" unmasks the way in which modern economic, political, and academic institutions, in their vaunted, merely methodological "neutrality," in fact imply a counterfeit image of the power of the Creator. This counterfeit image conceives of creation primarily in terms of an arbitrary and forceful power that is properly termed "diabolical," rather than in terms of the inherently generous power of being as symbol of God.

The Symbolical

The Greek verb *symballō* means, literally, to throw or come together, hence to join or unify. The noun *symbolon* referred originally to the *tessera hospitalis*, or token of hospitality, which was one half of an object broken in two and handed over to the safekeeping of a guest while the host retained the other half for himself.[6] The term is also used in refer-

6. Schindler, *Freedom from Reality*, 151–52.

ence to the Nicene Creed, the "symbol of faith," indicating the unity of faith that binds all Christians together.

More generally, a symbol is a sign: it points to a meaning that is other than itself, while relating to that meaning in a distinct way. As D. C. Schindler says, the meaning of a sign, while other than itself, "is nevertheless manifest *in* the symbolic reality, the *thing*, so that the meaning cannot be simply detached from the thing in which it resides."[7] In ontological terms, we may say that "the form of the symbol [is] a description of the nature of things generally." "The classical conception of the cosmos," for example, "may be appropriately described as 'symbolical'": the cosmos is "'an ordered whole that has its foundation in a transcendent cause, understood as most perfect and so as most essentially generous.'"[8] As Plato put it: "the heavens and the earth, gods and men, are bound together ontologically by fellowship and friendship ... and for this reason [wise men] call the sum of things the 'ordered' universe (*kosmon*) ... not the world of disorder (*akosmian*)."[9] The "'parts' of the cosmos" are "so many symbols, which is to say that things are *signs* of the good that is their always prior principle of unity."[10] What is important to note here is that "an order founded on goodness is *essentially* symbolical," and that, conversely, the very notion of the symbolical presupposes and demands the goodness of things.[11]

In light of these considerations, I understand "symbolical" to indi-

7. Schindler, *Freedom from Reality*, 153. A symbol "*makes present* a meaning that cannot be simply translated into other terms, that is, replaced by a concept or a set of concepts.... One who 'reads' a symbol, then, does not simply record the information it indicates, but instead enters into the symbol; he is *assimilated* to its essentially latent sense, so that he can be said to 'indwell' the meaning and 'live' in it" (153). The symbol thus "communicates meaning in a *generous* form; the unity of the meaning that it contains, which is not grasped in abstraction as a discrete, explicit concept, but is rather assimilated through what can be called a concrete indwelling, generates a kind of boundless wealth of significance" (153). For the idea of symbol as a manifestation that is irreducible to concepts in any simple way, Schindler also draws on Paul Ricoeur, *The Symbolism of Evil* (New York: Harper and Row, 1967), 11–17.

8. Schindler, *Freedom from Reality*, 155 (citing Plato, *Timaeus* 29e).

9. Plato, *Gorgias*, 507e, 508a, in Schindler, *Freedom from Reality*, 156.

10. Schindler, *Freedom from Reality*, 156.

11. Schindler, *Freedom from Reality*, 156. In Thomistic terms, this speaks to the way in which the good is both self-communicating (*bonum est diffusivum sui*) and that which all things seek (*id quod omnia appetunt*).

cate an ontological view of cosmic reality according to which things and persons are true and good in themselves, in their natural integrity. Every being in the cosmos, in its own self-identity—or in its own intrinsic truth and goodness—symbolizes the Creator God who originates and sustains this reality. Only a symbolical understanding of reality provides for consistent recognition of an intelligent, loving Creator God on the one hand, and the intrinsic intelligibility, truth, and goodness of cosmic realities—human and nonhuman—on the other. Further, a symbolical understanding of reality implies an ordered cosmos and genuine community among all its "parts." On this understanding, things are intrinsically related not only to God but also, by virtue of this relation, to each other. The identity of each inherently involves reference, and so far "transparence," to all others. This reference of creaturely beings to one another implies a generous presence opening to the unity of all things together, such that they form a cosmos or universe, a many-turned-toward-one. In a word, what we are calling the "symbolical" indicates the nature of all things as inherently good and generous, such that each can *be in itself*, or *represent itself*, only as at once *referring to* and *representing others*, above all God.

Failure to recognize this link between the inherent intelligibility and worth of things (i.e., their original self-identity) on the one hand, and their being fraught with the symbolism of God on the other, leads inexorably to a cosmic utilitarianism in which nothing is finally worth knowing or doing for its own sake. Such failure leads, in other words, to the "nihilating" of civilization in any "legitimate" sense. It is in light of this claim that I situate the discussion of what Weber calls the "disenchantment" characteristic of Anglo-American culture.

Weber on the Disenchantment of Anglo-American Culture

Weber introduces the idea of disenchantment (*Entzauberung*) in the context of his argument regarding the rise of the "spirit of capitalism" in the modern world. According to Weber, the first beginnings of this movement can be traced to Luther, in whose thought we find a profound shift regarding the nature of *Beruf*, or "worldly calling." Luther rejected the traditional idea of a division between two calls to holiness or two states of life. According to this idea, the higher or more perfect state was the life of the evangelical counsels (*consilia*), which Luther understood as entailing solely the "heavenly" activity of contemplative prayer and withdrawal from the world. The less perfect state was the life of marriage, or the living of the commandments (*praecepta*) while remaining in the world. Rejecting the first state, Luther stressed the importance of "worldly" activity, the everyday work of the world. It was in the world, and not in any presumptuous flight from the world, that God and holiness of life were to be found.[12]

Calvin, for his part, agreed with this new conception of "worldly calling," while simultaneously transforming it in his own theology. Key to this transformation was Calvin's idea of sin and predestination: only a small number of human beings were chosen for eternal grace and salvation, while the rest were destined for damnation. God's will in the matter of the ultimate destiny of the human being is inscrutable.

> To assume that human merit or guilt play a part in determining this destiny would be to think of God's absolutely free decrees, which have been settled from eternity, as subject to change by human influence, an impossible contradiction. The Father in heaven of the New Testament, so human and understanding, who rejoices over the repentance of a sinner … is gone. His place has been taken by a transcendental being, beyond the reach of human understanding, who with His quite incomprehensible decrees has decided the fate of every individual and regulated the tiniest details of the cosmos from eternity. God's grace is, since His decrees cannot change, as impossible for those to whom He has granted it to lose as it is unattainable for those to whom he has denied it.[13]

The consequence of this vision, according to Weber, is an "unprecedented inner loneliness of the single individual." Each person has to follow his own path of salvation. No one can help him: no priest, no sacraments, no Church.[14] Even God could not help, because "Christ had died only for the elect, for whose benefit God had decreed His martyrdom from eternity."[15] Weber concludes:

12. Weber, *Protestant Ethic*, 79–81.

13. Weber, *Protestant Ethic*, 103.

14. The sacraments "are not a means of grace, but only the subjective *externa subsidia* of faith," while "the external Church included the damned." Weber, *Protestant Ethic*, 104.

15. Weber, *Protestant Ethic*, 104.

> This, the complete elimination of salvation through the Church and the sacraments (which was in Lutheranism by no means developed to its final conclusions), was what formed [Calvinism's] absolutely decisive difference from Catholicism.... That great historic process in the development of religions, the elimination of magic from the world (*die Entzauberung der Welt*) which had begun with the old Hebrew prophets and in conjunction with Hellenistic scientific thought, had repudiated all magical means to salvation as superstition and sin, came here to its logical conclusion.[16]

How is this spirit of disenchantment, which takes full form in Calvinism, related to the "spirit of capitalism"?[17] According to Weber, the key to the capitalistic spirit in its modern sense is a rationalistic economic life: the acquisition of capital through rational calculation.[18] This rationalizing of economic life is "essentially dependent on the calculability of the most important technical factors. But this means fundamentally that it is dependent on the peculiarities of modern science, especially the natural sciences based on mathematics and exact and rational experiment."[19]

According to Weber, there is a crucial link between this rationalistic spirit of capitalism and the religion of Calvinism. Weber is well aware that there are differences between the seventeenth-century English-speaking Calvinism on which he focuses and the thought of Calvin himself: re-

16. Weber, *Protestant Ethic*, 104–5.

17. I do not wish to enter here into the various controversies surrounding Weber's interpretation of the rise of capitalism. He did not hold that capitalism appeared for the first time with Calvinism or the English Puritans of the seventeenth century, as though the "impulse to acquisition, pursuit of gain, of money" began decisively at this time or with this people. On the contrary, "this impulse ... has been common to all sorts and conditions of men at all times and in all countries of the earth, wherever the objective possibility of it is or has been given." Weber says that "it should be taught in the kindergarten of cultural history that this naïve idea of capitalism must be given up once and for all. Unlimited greed for gain is not in the least identical with capitalism, and is still less its spirit." *Protestant Ethic*, 17.

18. According to Weber, the conditions necessary to account for this are free labor, the separation of business from the household, and rational bookkeeping. *Protestant Ethic*, 21–22.

19. Though it must be said at the same time that "the development of these sciences and of the techniques resting upon them now [also] receives important stimulation from these capitalistic interests in its practical economic application." See Weber, *Protestant Ethic*, 24. In the 1930s, Robert Merton, one of the founders of the sociology of science, developed a thesis similar to Weber's, on the relationship between Puritanism and the rationalizing methods of modern science: *Science, Technology, and Society in Seventeenth-Century England* (New York: Howard Fertig, 1970).

garding the pursuit of profit and the acquisition of wealth, for example, and the detrimental effects it can have on one's spiritual life. Weber's purpose here, however, is to make the more fundamental point that Calvinism's "real moral objection" to wealth is an objection to

> relaxation in the security of possession, the enjoyment of wealth with the consequence of idleness and the temptations of the flesh, above all of distraction from the pursuit of a righteous life. In fact, it is only because possession involves this danger of relaxation that it is objectionable at all. For the saints' everlasting rest is in the next world.[20]

The positive burden of Weber's argument, then, is to identify the cause of the peculiar restlessness of the human spirit that characterizes the Puritan conception of worldly activity, a restlessness that implies a change in the nature of both earthly life and heaven.

Weber focuses on what he calls the "ethos" of Calvinistic theology in his attempt to discover what could reasonably account for the development of rationalized capitalism among Calvinists in (post-)seventeenth-century England and America. He argues that such rationalized activity, which is given its paradigmatic form in modern capitalistic economics, expresses an entire logic of life. While this logic emerged from within the religious piety of Puritanism, Weber shows that essential elements of this logic continued to operate *even when this piety waned* and life took on a more secular form in subsequent ages.[21]

The main features of this rationalization are expressed in the vast variety of activities that made up the Puritan way of life: intense worldly activity as the means of being confident of one's salvation; good works as signs (not causes) of salvation; the rejection of the idea of mystical union with God, since absolute transcendence precludes the possibility of God's penetrating the human soul (*finitum non est capax infiniti*).[22] Further-

20. Weber, *Protestant Ethic*, 157.

21. That is why there is no inconsistency in the fact that Weber selected Benjamin Franklin as a salient example of the logic of Calvinistic faith, despite Franklin's not living this faith in particularly pious fashion. Aphoristic principles like "time is money," for example, continued to characterize the ethos of the American way of life even when its practitioners had long ceased to take conscious inspiration from Puritan faith in God. For Weber on Franklin, see *Protestant Ethic*, 124 and 180.

22. Weber, *Protestant Ethic*, 112–15. Weber notes how Lutherans "have again and

more, because "the God of Calvinism demanded of his believers not single good works, but a life of good works combined into a unified system," there was "no place for the very human Catholic cycle of sin, repentance, [and sacramental confession]."

> The moral conduct of the average man was thus deprived of its planless and unsystematic character and subjected to a consistent method for conduct as a whole. . . . For only by a fundamental change in the whole meaning of life at every moment and in every action could the effects of grace transforming a man from the *status naturae* to the *status gratiae* be proved.[23]

For the Calvinist, then, "the world was . . . dominated entirely by the aim to add to the glory of God on earth."[24] "Hence the utilitarian character of Calvinistic ethics": the world becomes an instrument to be rationalized for the sole purpose of giving glory to God.[25] In this regard, Weber says that "Descartes's *cogito ergo sum* was taken over by the contemporary Puritan with this ethical reinterpretation. It was this rationalization which gave the Reformed faith its peculiar ascetic tendency, and is the basis . . . of its [distinct] relationship to . . . Catholicism."[26] The disappearance of the *consilia evangelica* was thus accompanied by the "transformation of asceticism into activity within the world."[27] Medieval asceticism was less systematic, and for the monk "the holiest task was . . . to surpass all worldly activity." For the Calvinist, by contrast, *every* Christian must now be a monk: "The spiritual aristocracy of predestined saints in the world replaces the spiritual aristocracy of the monks outside of the world."[28] But in becoming "worldly," the nature of the spiritual life of the saints is

again accused . . . the Reformed Churches . . . of reversion to the doctrine of salvation by works" (115).

23. Weber, *Protestant Ethic*, 117–18. In his introduction to Weber's *Sociology of Religion* (Boston: Beacon Press, 1993), Talcott Parsons states that, for Weber, "rationalization concerns in the first instance the systematization of a pattern or program *for life as a whole*, which is given meaning by an existential conception of the universe, and within it the human condition in which this action is to be carried out" (xliii).

24. Weber, *Protestant Ethic*, 118.

25. Weber, *Protestant Ethic*, 109.

26. Weber, *Protestant Ethic*, 118. For more on the similarities and differences between Reformed and Catholic asceticism, see 117–22.

27. Weber, *Protestant Ethic*, 120.

28. Weber, *Protestant Ethic*, 121.

radically transformed: "the end of [Puritan] asceticism was to be able to lead an alert, intelligent life: the most urgent task [was] the destruction of spontaneous, impulsive enjoyment, the most important means was to bring order into ... conduct."[29] "Not leisure and enjoyment, but only activity serves to increase the glory of God." Thus "inactive contemplation" is valueless, or "even directly reprehensible if it is at the expense of one's daily work. For it is less pleasing to God than the active performance of His will in a calling."[30] It is noteworthy that Weber himself, in his summary judgment on Puritanism and its effects, expresses reservations about the nature and future consequences of this new way of life:

> No one knows who will live in this iron cage (*stahlhartes Gehäuse*: steel-hard casing) in the future, or whether at the end of this tremendous development entirely new prophets will arise, or there will be a great rebirth of old ideas and ideals, or, if neither, mechanized petrification, embellished with a sort of convulsive self-importance. For of the last stage of this cultural development, it might well be truly said: "Specialists without spirit, sensualists without heart; this nullity imagines that it has attained a level of civilization never before achieved."[31]

The Rationalizing Logic of Disenchantment

The central principles informing the "disenchantment" of the world in the Reformed faith may be summarized as follows: (1) the utter transcendence and inscrutability of God, and thus the lack of God's immanent

29. Weber, *Protestant Ethic*, 119.

30. Weber, *Protestant Ethic*, 157–58. As the German philosopher Jürgen Habermas has noted, the rationalization of the world in modern times has affected the orders of the economy and the state, thereby dissolving traditional forms of everyday life: "What Weber depicted was not only the secularization of Western *culture*, but also and especially the development of modern *societies* from the viewpoint of rationalization. The new structures of society were marked by the differentiation of the two functionally intermeshing systems that had taken shape around the organizational cores of the capitalist enterprise and the bureaucratic state apparatus. Weber understood this process as the institutionalization of purposive-rational economic and administrative action. To the degree that everyday life was affected by this cultural and societal rationalization, traditional forms of life—which in the early modern period were differentiated primarily according to one's trade—were dissolved." Habermas, "Modernity's Consciousness of Time and Its Need for Self-Reassurance," in *The Philosophical Discourse of Modernity: Twelve Lectures* (Cambridge: Polity Press, 1987), 2.

31. Weber, *Protestant Ethic*, 181–82.

presence in the world and in man; (2) the sinfulness of man and a world judged to be under the power of sin, which imply a loss of the integrity of nature, both human and nonhuman; (3) the loss of a sacramental sense of the world and of the Church, and the consequent isolation of the individual. Each of these features is situated within a horizon weighted by a deep sense of (double) predestination.

These principles imply a life that is deeply centered on God, indeed a God-centered existence that embraces every aspect of the believer's life. But note the paradoxical character of this God-centeredness. God-centeredness, for Puritanism, takes the form of preoccupation with God's absence, with his "negative" presence, so to speak. God is not effectively present, in a generous way, in man and in the cosmos. Although the rationalizing of worldly activity can serve as a "sign" of God's favor, the human being is never an intrinsic participant in that favor: he can never intrinsically share in God's own goodness. He will always remain a worldly human subject to whom God's goodness is *imputed*, entirely *from outside*. This goodness, in fact, is not imputed to all human beings, but only to an inscrutably chosen few.

Similarly, the things of the world that the human subject rationalizes never transcend the status of pure instrumentality. They remain, in themselves, essentially "dumb," and hence apt solely for use. They are thus understood to be "good," not in themselves and as given (by God), but only insofar as they are subject to the extrinsic, controlling, and forceful activity of human agents. This rationalized control of things turns everything into an instrument for the realization of the *otherworldly*, even as this rationalizing activity itself becomes the sole sign of God's favor (which, again, remains purely adventitious). In a word, neither things nor human beings are, or ever can be, considered intrinsically good—which means that neither can ever be a symbol of the good God.

In light of the foregoing, we may say that worldly being, human and nonhuman, is no longer conceived as gift in its original givenness *qua* being, that is, in its original and continual *being-given*. Being ceases to be, in itself, an intrinsic bearer of the generosity of God, and thereby ceases to participate in the generosity of God as a genuine sign of this generosity. In other words, being ceases to be true and good *in itself*. To use the language of Aquinas, things lose their "transcendental" meaning as true, good, and beautiful.[32]

In summary, rationalizing disenchantment consists above all in a God-centeredness tied to negative transcendence: God is pervasively "present" in the world only through the influence of his "absence." God is placed beyond and outside the world, so that the world is principally understood in terms of its separation from God. Or better: the world is understood apart from any positive relation to God, a relation that now makes no difference *to* things and *in* things in their original givenness. Things are just "there," beyond and outside the divine, "dumb" and

32. The affirmation of the generosity of the Creator, which entails an original order of mind and will operating in creatures, and the affirmation of creatures as true and good in their inmost order and thus being *in themselves gifts* stand and fall together. What Aquinas calls the "transcendental" character of being bears an intrinsic relation to the creative intellect and will of God, which in turn establishes being as true and good in itself. See Aquinas, *De veritate*, q. 1, a. 10: "Each thing . . . is related to the divine intellect in one way, as what is measured to its measure . . . and in another way, as what is known to the one who knows. . . . Therefore everything is true in its relation to the divine intellect (*in comparatione ad intellectum divinum vera est*). . . . Yet because, as we have noted, this relation to the divine intellect is essential to the thing, in this respect the thing is said to be true in itself (*per se dicitur vera*)." The genuine in-itself-ness of a creature, we might say, as an *immanent order*, always implies relation to an original ordering intelligence. At the same time, such in-itself-ness, hence also interiority—which is manifest in the human person as intelligence and freedom—is the necessary condition for a creature's acting in and through itself, and not simply by virtue of "force" initiated from without.

We are thus ultimately confronted with a choice between an understanding of being as gifted to itself by a creative and loving intelligence (Aquinas), and an understanding of being as intrinsically dumb and without meaning, a mere matter of the interplay of "chance and necessity" (Jacques Monod). For Aquinas, created being, as true and good in itself, implies an intelligence built into the very act whereby being is at all. For Monod, by contrast, the creative reason of God is excluded from any account of the world, so that being's own intrinsic truth and goodness reduce ultimately to dumbness: to an "objectivity" whose "projectivity" (or "teleonomy," in the language of Monod: the inner law of purpose) is ultimately explicable in terms of a randomness that evolves over time into "invariance," or mechanical necessity. According to Monod, "all properties of living beings rest on a fundamental mechanism of molecular invariance. . . . the same source of fortuitous perturbations, of noise, which in a nonliving (i.e., nonreplicative) system would lead little by little to the disintegration of all structure, is the progenitor of evolution in the biosphere and accounts for its unrestricted liberty of creation, thanks to the replicative structure of DNA: that registry of chance, that tone-deaf conservatory where the noise is preserved along with the music." *Chance and Necessity* (New York: Vintage, 1972), 116–17. Monod's book has the merit of pursuing to its very foundations a vision of a world accounted for wholly without a Creator. He thereby demonstrates "empirically," as it were, the truth of the Council's statement that "when God is forgotten, the creature itself grows unintelligible" (*GS*, no. 36).

"mute" in themselves, awaiting the human rationalizing power that will instrumentalize them *ad maiorem Dei gloriam*.

This rationalizing logic of disenchantment goes to the heart of modernity, especially in the form it has taken in Anglo-American culture, which has been so deeply influenced by Puritan Protestantism. But what if anything remains of this disenchantment in a culture for which Puritan piety has ceased to provide any (conscious) common horizon? In Puritanism, the negative transcendence of God and the instrumentalized autonomy of worldly being were enfolded in a deeply Christian piety. As Weber rightly notes, however, even as Puritan piety has waned, its ethos has nonetheless remained, while taking on a new and secularized form. The central features of this piety—its "onto-logic," as it were—survived the gradual loss of belief in a worldly reality trapped in the power of sin and a transcendent God who inscrutably assigns vast numbers of human beings to an eternity of hell. The distant God of Calvin, that is, continues to remain distant, even without the explicit motivating force of Calvinist piety. Worldly things likewise continue to remain "dumb" and "mute," able to become "true" or "good" only insofar as they are subject to the rationalizing power of human beings.

The hallmark of Weber's argument is that the main features of a capitalistic economy predated seventeenth-century Protestantism, which served rather as a watershed religious moment that galvanized these earlier elements into a distinct rationalizing way of life. Similarly, what I am proposing is that, although key theological and ontological principles of this rationalizing process predate Puritan Protestantism, the latter nonetheless galvanized these principles into an ethos that continues to define modern culture today, even as Puritan piety has long ceased to exercise any explicit inspiration. Pious moderns and secularized moderns occupy largely the same space, insofar as they both partake of the modern ethos in its particular sense of the God-world relation. The modern believer, of course, acts with an explicit reverence for God and a deep sense of sin, while the secularized modern acts with no such reverence or fear. Yet both act in a way that presupposes an absent God, and both operate with a common ontological sense of what constitutes the world's "legitimate autonomy." Both conceive the legitimate autonomy of the world, whether consciously or unconsciously, in terms of things that bear no interior reference to God in their original givenness.

Whether in its theistic or anti-theistic form, then, modernity perpetuates a worldview in which things are no longer symbols of their Creator. In typical "bourgeois" fashion (to refer back to Balthasar), worldly being is assumed to be "mute" in itself. Things are considered only as apt for rationalization, whether in the interest of enhancing comfort and advancing the (secular) human estate, or, if one is more religiously inclined, as a sign of God's imputed favor. But in either case, worldly being is considered to be merely "neutral" in itself, to be raw material waiting to be made into what is (instrumentally) "true" and "good." Modern believers and secularizers do differ, of course, but fundamentally they differ only in terms of *how they use* the things of the world, and *with what intention*. In a word, believers and secularizers alike see worldly being, in its original reality as given, as bearing no image of the Creator. The relation of things to God is no longer understood to reach to the heart of what each thing is in itself.

The Neutral and the Diabolical

What is the best way to characterize this loss of the symbolical? The apparent alternative to a symbolical understanding of the world would seem to be modernity's "neutral" idea of being.[33] According to this understanding, worldly being has an original identity in itself, and so far an initial self-reference, to which reference or relation to the Creator may subsequently be *added*, without significantly altering the meaning of this original self-referential identity or its relation to God. Yet to affirm that being is first simply itself, and that relation to God is added *after* the fact, is to miss the very *ratio* of the symbolical, namely, that being in its original constitution *in itself* bears an intrinsic reference to the Creator. The crucial point here is that the original identity of being is realized only in community, a community ordered from and toward God, such that each being is understood as gift in the very act of its coming to be.

33. "Neutral" comes from the Latin *ne-uter* (literally, "not either"), meaning not one or the other (of two), or neither.

But why does the rejection of this symbolical understanding of reality implied by being as gift necessarily lead to the "diabolical," rather than simply to the neutral? Such a claim may seem precipitous, and thus reductive. Two considerations are important for understanding the nature of the claim: first, how does the idea of neutrality undermine the idea of gift, such that what is assumed to be "neutral" is revealed rather to be *logically exclusive of* gift? Second, why does this inherent exclusion of gift necessarily take the form of a *"diabolical" opposition to* gift?

To answer the first question, we need only ponder further the implications of the logic of disenchantment set forth above. Being is assumed to exist without any inner relation or original reference to the Creator and consequently to be, by nature, indifferent or "neutral" with respect to God. Modernity's supposedly "neutral" idea of being, in other words, implies an original self-identity that is mute and dumb. By failing to take account of the generous "givingness" of the Creator implicit in the very act whereby the creature *is* in the first place, modernity changes the nature of the creature's original *givenness*. Things turn out not to be truly *given* at all, except as just brutely "there," or as matters of bare fact, so that any inherent order of truth or goodness becomes a matter of what is given by the creature to itself. Original givenness is thus reduced to an indifference fraught with restlessness: insofar as being is not *originally given to* itself as true and good, it becomes structurally restless for construction into what is true and good. But if being is conceived as indifferent or "neutral" in its original constitution, then such constructed "truth" and "goodness" can only ever be arbitrary and forced, because it is not rooted in an *anteriorly given order* of truth and goodness. In sum, the would-be "neutral" idea of being transforms worldly action into sheer power, a power that necessarily takes the form of constructive, arbitrary force, rather than that of participatory gift-giving, or a giving that is innerly receptive. Worldly being, in a word, becomes at root mere mechanical energy, which of its essence displaces the generous power of love.

It is important to note that this rejection of being's purported "neutrality" does not call into question the "in-itselfness," or abiding self-identity and self-reference, of the creature. The burden of my argument, in fact, is that only a creature that is given as a gift from God can be said to be true and good in its own original constitution as such. To conceive of the creature as lacking such constitutive giftedness is to reduce the creature to a bare givenness without interiority that is by definition always on the way toward, and so restless for, its own "truth" and "goodness," which are ever still-to-be-constructed.[34]

Regarding the question of being's neutrality, then: what is typically claimed to be neutral *appears* not to represent God, or even to imply such representation. Yet such neutrality, which would appear to drain the world of its symbolism of God, *does* in fact "symbolize" God in his relation to the world, albeit in a paradoxical way. The world now signifies God as a being that exists utterly outside the world. The world thus "speaks" of an absent God, a God whose distance is exclusive of his nearness and immanence.[35] Worldly being represents God as "negatively" transcendent, which implies not only that the God who exists is by nature indifferent to the world, controlling it arbitrarily and from the outside, but also that it is not possible for God to be present *in* the world.[36]

34. The implication of my argument is that a being conceived as originally neutral or indifferent with respect to its Creator lacks self-identity, as true or good *in itself*. Such a being thus remains always in search of its own identity as true or good, ever restless for and never achieving this identity. If modernity can be defined by the original neutrality of (self-)identity, postmodernity signals the endless restlessness implied by modernity's would-be neutral identity. The point here is that the putatively neutral identity characteristic of modernity and the dissolution of identity characteristic of postmodernity do not stand in opposition to each other so much as they merely emphasize different aspects of a commonly (if unconsciously) held view of the given as created and related to God. This essay, in contrast, insists that a right understanding of the creature's identity—as its own interior center of truth and goodness—on the one hand and of the creature's relation to God on the other stand and fall together. On this, see note 32 above regarding the absence of God and the ontological link between random process and mechanical identity (Monod), and note 50 below regarding Hans Jonas's claim that the true meaning of Nietzsche's "God is dead" is the loss of the vision of the good and the beautiful as being.

35. A God who is (simply) outside or beyond the world thus implies a world *without* God: a-theism or anti-theism.

36. That God's relation to the world is not "indifferent" does not imply that God must necessarily create. The fact that creation is in no way necessary for God—which is tied to the gratuitous gift-character of creation—accounts for why Aquinas, for example, says that "creatures are really related to God, whereas in God there is no real relation to creatures" (*Summa theologiae* I, q. 13, a. 7). The crucial point is that God is infinitely generous for all eternity *in se*; his generosity is already complete in itself because he is of his essence expressed in a tri-unity of divine persons. While creation is therefore not necessary in order for God to be the fullness of self-communicative Trinitarian love, when such a God creates,

There is no place, in this worldview, for a God who is generously present in the world; such a God does not exist. Modernity's "neutral" idea of being, in other words, simultaneously implies the existence or presence of a God of forceful power and the nonexistence or absence of the God of power-as-creative-intelligence-and-love. In neither sense does the neutral idea of being succeed in avoiding the implication of an image of God and of his power in the world, and of the worldly power that images this God. On the contrary, in each case we end up with what is but a counterfeit image of divine power, and of a world made in this image.[37]

Now, my argument is that it is this *counterfeit* image of God lying hidden in the neutral idea of being that logically unfolds into a "diabolical" vision of the world and its power. It is significant that the etymological opposite of "symbolical" is "diabolical." *Dia* means "through" or "across," and when used as a prefix in compound words, it means "in different directions" or "asunder." Thus *dia-ballō* means both "to throw over or across" and "to set at variance." In its more extended meaning, the term includes "to slander," "to misrepresent," and "to deceive by false accounts." The noun *diabolos*, of course, is used in reference to the devil.

The key feature of the diabolical is its *assimilation* of God's unoriginated power as love, concurrent with the *transformation* of this power as love. The diabolical subsumes what is originally and objectively given in and as love *into itself*, making itself the source or origin of love. It thereby creates an appearance of love that destroys love's proper meaning. The one who thinks and acts diabolically undermines the nature of God's worldly power as gratuitous love, a love that is always *given* to the world

we can say ("after the fact," as it were) that he "necessarily" creates generously, as befits his (triune) being.

37. The understanding of God implied by modernity's "neutral" idea of being, then, expresses not no image of God, nor simply a false image, but what is most properly conceived as a *counterfeit* image. The God of power as force is a "counterfeit double" of the God of power as creative intelligence and love. On this last point, see D. C. Schindler's discussion in *Freedom from Reality*, 158–71, which refers also to William Desmond's *Hegel's God: A Counterfeit Double?* (Burlington, VT: Ashgate, 2003), 9–10. Regarding why precisely this image is a counterfeit, the relevant point here is that modernity's efforts to affirm what is true and to do what is good (acts which seem so far to image God) in fact express what is already, for the creature, a false power, because it is precipitously constructive and controlling. Such acts thereby counterfeit God's originally generous power, which creates through "letting things be (in themselves)."

for its own sake, thereby constituting the world, and every being in the world, as inherently true and good.

One who thinks "diabolically" thus recognizes an original difference between God and the self (and the world) while simultaneously, *in* this recognition, rejecting the radical ontological dependence that this difference entails. The result is a change in the nature of worldly power. Power is no longer something first *given as gift*, the presence of which invites reception and thereby participation in gift-giving. On the contrary, power now becomes restless, because it is always a matter of precipitous grasping, of constructing for the purpose of controlling. The truth and goodness of things in themselves are no longer first a matter of *ens* (being) but of *factum* (what is made or done, or on the way to being made or done).[38] This is aptly captured in the claim of Goethe's *Faust*: "In the beginning was the deed."[39] Refusing first to attend to the order of the world as it is articulated by God, and by the world itself, in its originally given reality as true and good—thus refusing the primacy of the *logos*, of contemplation or "theory"—the diabolical turns everything into an object of originally orderless constructive power, or "practice." In short, the world, under the power of the diabolical, becomes a vast collection of *restless relations of instrumentalized constructive power*, whose imaging of God parodies the divine power of a love that brings into being through generously letting be. The diabolical thus always intends *to imitate the symbolical*, even as it can only do so *deceptively*. This is what it means for the diabolical to be a counterfeit image of God and of originary power.

Toward an "Authentic Theology of Integral Human Liberation"

The foregoing argument is illuminated further by what John Paul II calls, in his encyclical *Centesimus annus*, an "authentic theology of integral human liberation," whose meaning is developed at length in the Congregation for the Doctrine of the Faith's *Instruction on Christian Freedom*

38. See Joseph Ratzinger, *Introduction to Christianity* (San Francisco: Ignatius Press, 2004), 57–66.

39. See Johann Wolfgang von Goethe, *Faust* I, verse 1237: "*Im Anfang war die Tat.*"

and Liberation.[40] These documents conceive the Christian's liberating presence in the world in "radical" terms (from *radix*, "root"): on the one hand, the ultimate source of liberation is the creative-redemptive love of God; on the other hand, the most basic cause of worldly disorder in need of liberation is sin. Accordingly, John Paul II interprets the failures of modern social and cultural institutions to liberate humanity as failures of love ultimately rooted in sin.[41] By this, the pope means personal sin, but in a sense that includes a social, and indeed "structural" or "objective," dimension as well. Sin is social insofar as persons are by nature embodied, and thus cannot but extend their being and influence into the space and time of the culture. Social sin, however, is also "structural," insofar as it entails objective disorder.[42] In this way, sin takes on an institutional form that is irreducible either to an individual's sin or to the sum of individual sins, even as it always remains tied to these.[43]

40. John Paul II, *Centesimus annus*, Encyclical on the One Hundredth Anniversary of *Rerum Novarum*, May 1, 1991, no. 26; Congregation for the Doctrine of the Faith, *Instruction on Christian Freedom and Liberation*, March 22, 1986, no. 63.

41. The pope notes that "Pope Pius XII had already declared that 'the sin of the century is the loss of the sense of sin,' and [that] this loss goes hand in hand with the 'loss of the sense of God.'" John Paul goes on: "In fact, God is the origin and the supreme end of man, and man carries in himself a divine seed. Hence it is the reality of God that reveals and illustrates the mystery of man. It is therefore vain to hope that there will take root a sense of sin against man and against human values, if there is no sense of offence against God, namely the true sense of sin." *Dominum et vivificantum*, Encyclical on the Holy Spirit in the Life of the Church, May 18, 1986, no. 47, citing *Reconciliatio et paenitentia*, Apostolic Exhortation on Reconciliation and Penance, December 2, 1984, no. 18.

42. General confusion and resistance to the idea of "social" or "structural" sin are characteristic of liberal societies, which operate with a conception of the individual that lacks a sense of the objective social or bodily *order* of the human being. See here the pertinent statement of John Paul II in *Dominum et vivificantum*, no. 56: "the resistance to the Holy Spirit which St. Paul emphasizes in the *interior and subjective dimension* as tension, struggle and rebellion taking place in the human heart finds in every period of history and especially in the modern era its external dimension (*rationem exteriorem*), which takes concrete form as the content of culture and civilization, *as a philosophical system, an ideology, a program* for action and for the shaping of human behavior" (emphasis added). It is sin in its "exterior" or "objective" dimension, as a tissue of metaphysical assumptions, that gives sin its "structural" form.

43. On the relation between personal sin and the social or structural form personal sin takes, see the Congregation for the Doctrine of the Faith, *Instruction on Christian Freedom and Liberation*, nos. 42, 74–75, as well as John Paul II, *Reconciliatio et paenitentia*, no. 16, and *Sollicitudo rei socialis*, Encyclical on the Twentieth Anniversary of *Populorum Progressio*, nos. 35–40. This last text discusses in a thematic way what is involved in situating social-economic-political problems within their deepest context, i.e., relation to God and sin. This differs from contem-

It is persons, therefore, who are the proper subjects of liberation; yet they are so in a way that always includes their assumptions (whether conscious or unconscious) regarding the nature of the creature before God, as these assumptions have taken shape *in*—and in a significant sense also *as*—the institutions in which these persons live and work. Insofar as these assumptions are not properly ordered (i.e., in terms of an adequate sense of the relation between the creature and God, and the relations among creatures as related to their common Creator), institutions informed by these assumptions take on the character of sin in its structural sense. Transformation of the order of these institutions thus becomes integral to the liberation of the persons who indwell them.

The argument to this point has been that the basic problematic of modernity concerns whether the originary power in the world is the power of gratuitous love or the power of instrumentalizing construction. In light of this problematic, I now assess three modern institutions—the economy, the polity, and the academy—in accordance with the perspective offered by John Paul II's "theology of integral human liberation." With respect to the economy, issues regarding wealth and poverty today are typically approached first in terms of what people have or do not have (i.e., food, possessions, and the money necessary to secure these). With respect to the polity, citizens are understood first in terms of negatively conceived rights, that is, as individual agents demanding immunity from coercion by others. With respect to science and the academy, knowledge is conceived primarily as power, with the result that things are approached first technologically, as instruments apt for control in the interests of human health and comfort.

Now, to be sure, it is good to address the needs of hunger and homelessness, to recognize, protect, and uphold human rights, and to control things for the purposes of accurate study. The problem, however, when seen in light of the above argument, is that each of these goods is understood *first in terms of a power that is wrongly conceived*. They are understood, that is, in terms of a primacy of "having" over "being," of self-centered, mutually "coercive" relations, and of external, forceful control. What is lacking in each case is the inherent symbolism of God proper to the human subject and to

porary society's tendency to conceive such problems in terms of social, economic, or psychological conditions abstracted from such theological considerations.

every creaturely thing.[44] What is lacking, in other words, is "integral" *relation*: above all to God, but inclusive of relations to all other creatures. The liberation of contemporary economic, political, and academic institutions must be a matter of these constitutive relations that reach to the heart of the human being, and indeed all of nature. Truly "integral" liberation, in the case of each of these institutions, therefore requires a vision of worldly being as gift, and of worldly power as made in the image of gift receiving and gift giving, in which all creatures share, proportionately and analogically.

The basic order of relations indicated here is precisely articulated in *The Compendium of the Social Doctrine of the Church*, in its description of creation and the "original sin" of human beings:

> In Israel's profession of faith, to affirm that God is Creator … [means] grasping the original extent of the Lord's gratuitous and merciful action on behalf of man. In fact, God freely confers being and life on everything that exists. Man and woman, created in his image and likeness (cf. Gn 1:26–27), are for that very reason called to be the visible sign and the effective instrument of divine gratuitousness in the garden where God has placed them as cultivators and custodians of the goods of creation.
>
> *It is in the free action of God the Creator that we find the very meaning of creation, even if it has been distorted by the experience of sin*. In fact, the narrative of the first sin (cf. Gn 3:1–24) describes the permanent temptation and the disordered situation in which humanity comes to find itself after the fall of its progenitors. Disobedience to God means hiding from his loving countenance and seeking to control one's life and action in the world. Breaking the relation of communion with God causes a rupture in the internal unity of the human person, in the relations of communion between man and woman and of the harmonious relations between mankind and other creatures. *It is in this original estrangement that are to be sought the deepest roots of all the evils that afflict social relations between people, of all the situations in economic and political life that attack the dignity of the person, that assail justice and solidarity.*[45]

44. "There will be no cure if God is not recognized as the structural core of our whole existence." Joseph Ratzinger, *A New Song for the Lord* (New York: Crossroad, 1996), 28. See also St. Athanasius: "The Word of God, incorporeal, incorruptible and immaterial, entered our world. Yet it was not as if he had been remote from it up to that time. For there is no part of the world that was ever without his presence; together with his Father, he continually filled up all things and places." *On the Incarnation of the Word*, nos. 8–9.

45. Pontifical Council for Justice and Peace, *The Compendium of the Social Doctrine of the Church, April 2, 2004*, nos. 26–27, emphasis added.

This last line makes it clear that in order for liberation to be "integral," it must follow the original order of creation, and understand the dis-order of sin in this light. The beginning and root of sin is the original disobedience to God that involves taking precipitous control over one's life and action. This can be typified as a refusal to accept one's original meaning as gift from another, and thus as a child of God. This refusal first fractures "the original unity of the person" in his integrity as related to God, and then the "relations of communion between man and woman" and "between mankind and other creatures." It is in this "original estrangement" that we find "the deepest roots of all the evils that afflict" people in their social relations, and that "attack the dignity of the person" and "assail justice and solidarity."

My point here is basic: characteristically modern approaches to "liberation" as they concern the economy, the polity, and the academy overlook the original order of creation and the original disorder of sin, failing to take account of the integrity of nature in its wholeness as given. This is a failure to account for the wholeness of nature in its intrinsic creaturely relation to God, for the social relations that are included within this original relation to God (above all, filial and spousal relations), and for the relation between mankind and other creatures.

The primary concern here is not that conventional approaches to economic, political, or academic liberation *consciously reject* the relations that are constitutive of the wholeness of creatures in their natural givenness, but that these approaches initially *abstract* from this wholeness. Current approaches to liberation, that is, typically isolate certain aspects of the person for attention while bracketing other aspects. For example, contemporary economics treats want, hunger, and poverty as merely material or bodily concerns, while questions of the body-soul relation, or of the human being's relation to God and the family, are set aside to be dealt with by others, if at all. Such relations are thus treated as essentially extrinsic aspects of the person that can be safely addressed "later on," without detriment to the integrity of what is either included in the abstraction (material and bodily concerns) or excluded and to be added later (relation to God and family). It is assumed, in other words, that such abstraction can be made without detriment to the integrity of the person himself *as created*. In fact, this original abstraction fragments the nature of physical hunger and poverty, since hunger and poverty among human beings are inseparable from the desire for meaning, that is, for God and for the love that alone satisfies and enriches in a truly human fashion.[46]

There is much more that could be said regarding modern approaches to liberation. My concern, however, is simply to say enough to indicate the deeply different ideas of worldly power operative in John Paul II's understanding of integral liberation on the one hand, and in the "liberationist" approaches implied by the prevalent logic of modern liberal institutions on the other. Key to this difference is the nature of modern abstraction, which each institution expresses in its own way. Such abstraction is intrinsically fragmented in a way that implies a false conception of worldly power, one that is expressed and reinforced by the very act (and nature) of the abstraction itself.

Note, though, that the peculiar genius of modern liberal institutions is their purported ability to abstract from questions of content or ideology in a merely methodological way. In this light, the alternative drawn above between the symbolical and the diabolical seems precipitous and reductive. Modern economic, political, and academic institutions, it is said, mean only to abstract for specific methodological, *as distinct from ontological*, purposes. Each of these institutions, in other words, intends by the abstraction peculiar to its sphere to focus on a particular aspect of human, social, or cosmological reality so as to understand that aspect in a more precisely detailed and accurate way. The problem, however, is that the distinction between "methodological" and "ontological" is rendered moot, insofar as the eventual relating of the particular aspect focused on in the abstraction to what is left out by the abstraction—ultimately, the

46. Something similar could be said with regard to liberation as it concerns political and academic-scientific institutions. Abstracting human rights as immunities from the person's positive relation to God and other persons implies a shift away from a conception of the person as naturally social and religious, and thereby reconfigures the nature of human society and the common good that is its end. Knowledge and science likewise change insofar as they begin in an act of power that abstracts from the nature of things in their given wholeness. Knowledge becomes a matter primarily not of seeing or attentive experience, but of experimental manipulation for control. Science thus becomes essentially technological, contrary to the ancient sense of the word *techne*, which began by working *with* the given order and rhythms of nature.

wholeness of the creature in its relation to the Creator—is conceived simply in terms of *addition*, rather than integration.

The example of Descartes is helpful on this point. The Cartesian way of making distinctions is informed by the primacy Descartes gives to abstract geometric lines.[47] Akin to the way in which a line cleanly divides two quadrants of a grid, Descartes distinguishes body and soul as two separate entities that are united only through extrinsic addition. The *way* he distinguishes thus determines (as well as tacitly presupposes) the *content* of what is distinguished. Clarity, for Descartes, demands the distinguishing of *x* and *y* after the manner of two entities that exist originally outside of one another. In the case of the body-soul relation, this involves a radical shift away from the classical Thomistic understanding of body and soul as a distinction-within-unity, a shift that entails a radical change in the nature of both the soul and the body. Each are now conceived as first indifferent to the other, such that any "subsequent" relation of soul to body becomes of its essence extrinsic, and so coercive: solely a matter of arbitrary, forceful activity from the outside.[48]

Similarly, modern institutions "methodologically" abstract their limited object of concern from the relations initiated naturally in the creation of the human being, above all the relation to God, in a way that presumes that these relations can be added back later without loss. The upshot is that each institution takes itself to have its own proper logic separate and apart from these relations, a logic that is so far indifferent or neutral with respect to them. Relations that are naturally established by God in the act of creation are treated as merely "additive." In this way, modern institutions proceed in a Cartesian fashion and end up with the same result as Descartes: a change in the nature of both the content of what is abstracted and the relations subsequently added back in. The problem, in a word, lies in the putative neutrality characteristic of modern institutions in their original abstraction from God. Such neutrality in the name of abstraction in fact *changes the nature of worldly power* at

47. See René Descartes, *Discourse on Method*, Part II, in *The Philosophical Writings of Descartes* (Cambridge: Cambridge University Press, 2009), 1:120–21.

48. Such activity is "forceful" because, being merely "efficient," it does not form, or give final order, from within.

work in the logic of these institutions, and in the approaches of those who would liberate them.

There is, then, a need to distinguish two ways of approaching liberation theology in the present age. The prevalent approach begins by accepting the logic of modern institutions, and thus by abstracting from the relation between mankind and God (as well as between man and woman, and mankind and the rest of creation).[49] This approach thereby fails to place the question of liberation in its sufficiently "radical" context. Liberation means, first and above all, liberation from sin, in which sin is understood in its original disorder, which consists in the creature's primitive abstraction from the relations that constitute him in his nature as *given* by God. By failing to attend to the original relation of the creature to God, modern liberation takes the form of action that is insufficiently imbued with the power of God and of creaturely being itself as love. This action, in other words, comes (logically) too late, in the sense that it lacks integration by and into the love that is first given by God and carried in being itself as gift. Such action, in a word, is able to provide only adventitious and extrinsic moral inspiration for institutions that are themselves *structurally disordered*, by virtue of their being originally abstracted from the power of God's love, in which creatures participate by virtue of the act of creation.

The point here is not to reject moral and social efforts to ameliorate the conditions of modern life. Rather, it is a matter of *integrating* these efforts *by and into the power of the given*—of what is always first given by God as gift. Modern liberal institutions, and prevalent approaches to their liberation, begin with an original "methodological" abstraction that reduces nature as given to what is neutral with respect to the Creator. Such abstraction is blind to the nature of the first and original sin, which consists in the creature assuming just such an original posture of indifference with respect to the Creator. John Paul II's "integral" liberation, by contrast, begins with nature as concretely *given*, and thus as already initially related to God, and so entails an awareness of the first sin that

49. For more on this point, see David L. Schindler, *Ordering Love: Liberal Societies and the Memory of God* (Grand Rapids, MI: Eerdmans, 2009), 65–132 (on politics), 154–218 (on economics), and 383–429 (on the academy).

would abstract the creature from his originally given positive relation to God. The former approach, in sum, begins with a confusion of the natural with the neutral, and proceeds to moralize relation to God in a way that is inevitably instrumentalist, that is, arbitrary, extrinsic, and precipitously constructive. In this way, the modern approach to liberation falls, logically, into the power of the diabolical.[50] Genuine liberation, by contrast,

50. This instrumentalist and prematurely constructive activity characteristic of modern liberationist approaches expresses itself in a variety of related forms, which can in fact be identified as heresies: Pelagianism, e.g., signals the precipitous nature of a worldly power first abstracted from the Creator; nominalism indicates the individualistic power of one who first contracts relations to God and others rather than finding himself enabled by a community always already begun by God; voluntarism indicates the arbitrary nature of a power uninformed by any originally given relation to divine intelligence; rationalism indicates the controlling and possessive nature of a power that is first grasped from God, rather than received. What these heresies have in common is their original abstraction from what is the first and ultimate power of God's gift of love to the world, participated in via the orders of creation and redemption.

Relevant to this idea of heresy as a fundamental key for social-cultural discernment is Hans Jonas's reflection on Gnosticism and religion in the modern period, as found in his "Gnosticism and Modern Nihilism," *Social Research* 19, no. 4 (December 1952): 430–52. Jonas states that the "loss of eternity is the disappearance of the world of ideas and ideals, in which Heidegger sees the true meaning of Nietzsche's 'God is dead': in other words, the absolute victory of nominalism over realism. Therefore the same cause which is at the root of nihilism is also at the root of the radical temporality in Heidegger's scheme of existence, in which the present is nothing but the moment of transience [a later edition has "crisis"] from past to future. If values are not beheld in vision as being (like the Good or the Beautiful of Plato), but are posted by the will as projects, then indeed existence is committed to constant futurity ... and a merely formal resolution to be, without a nomos for that resolution, becomes a project from nothingness into nothingness" (450). This essay can be found with some changes in both Jonas's *The Gnostic Religion* (Boston: Beacon, 2001) and his *The Phenomenon of Life* (Evanston, IL: Northwestern University Press, 2001) under the title "Gnosticism, Existentialism, and Nihilism." In his essay, Jonas discusses the modern depreciation of the concept of nature—now understood as "indifferently extant," or as what is merely "there"—as well as the corresponding loss of what the ancients understood as looking at "what is there ... as it is in itself," which was "called by the name of contemplation, *theoria*" (449).

The point here is that we must come to see the extent to which contemporary moral-social liberationist efforts are interiorly structured by theological-ontological disorder, as identified in these heresies. Engaging cultural problems most basically as moral issues, or issues of economic and political policy, inevitably leaves intact the "theoretical" vision that informs the problems at their root—the theological-ontological disorder properly called heresy. Terms that often appear to name only abstruse doctrinal errors are in fact indispensable for identifying the core problems with respect to modern institutions' intended ameliorations of the suffering of the human condition. Each institution assumes, in its own way, a

begins with the natural in its concrete reality as related to the Creator. Beginning in this way with worldly being understood as gift, it is logically governed by the power of the symbolical.

The distinction between worldly being understood first as abstracted from and neutral to God, on the one hand, and worldly being understood concretely as in itself related to God, on the other, is scarcely trivial. On the contrary, its significance becomes apparent in the profound ambiguity that is characteristic of modern liberal institutions and their efforts to liberate various spheres of life. Undoubtedly, the liberal free market has created the greatest abundance of quantitative wealth in human history, and the liberal welfare state has provided more extensively for the poor than any previous state in history. At the same time, the free market and the welfare state, by their own inner logic, have arguably undermined the integrity of organic communities as much as any society in history, particularly communities such as the family or religions that take man to be religious by nature (*homo religiosus*). The free market, *qua* market, knows no relations among human beings that are not primarily useful, that is, for profit and enhanced comfort. The liberal polity has attended more extensively to the rights of individuals than any prior state in history, but this same polity is arguably guilty of as many homicides of the most vulnerable as any polity in history, be they at the beginning or end of life. The liberal state cannot recognize the worth of a human life whose power and dignity reside only in its being *qua given*. The liberal academy and its technological science have done more to control and eliminate disease and physical disorders than any earlier forms of technology and science ever could. But this same technological (or technocratic) science arguably represents the gravest threat to human being and consciousness in history, by undermining the human capacity for contemplation and paying attention, and by weakening the organic sense of time, space, matter, motion, and place that is necessary for the formation of community among creatures as well as for prayerful-liturgical community with God.[51]

world that is first logically indifferent to the Creator God and remains so until improved via human action. Being is no longer given as true and good and beautiful, and so must now be constructed and controlled to be such.

51. Modern technocratic science is also implicated, of course, in the destruction of

This profound ambiguity lying at the heart of modern liberal institutions should not surprise us. On the contrary, it is of the very nature of what is taken to be first neutral with respect to the generous power of God, and with respect to the gifted power of the creature that participates in this generosity, to take the form finally of the counterfeit power of the diabolical. Modernity, as we have articulated it, is most basically a struggle between a symbolical and a diabolical vision of man and the cosmos—a struggle that passes through what is thought to be a merely "neutral" vision of being.

The task of an "integral" liberation, then, consists above all in recuperating the symbolical, understood in terms of contemplation. The task consists in *seeing things* as they are at once *in themselves and as related to God*, and in unfolding this "seeing" into *an integrated way of life* that is *engaged with the whole of reality*. Liberation, in a word, consists in sustaining the primacy of the theoretical, of *theoria*, in its definitive meaning: in acknowledging that "in the beginning was the *Logos*," that the Logos became flesh, and that "all things came into being through him" (Jn 1:1–3, 1:14). It is in this context that we see why the proper creaturely meaning of the theoretical and of liberation begins with Mary's *Fiat*—with letting being be—and with the *Magnificat* that actively deepens and increases the being that is always first given and received.[52] As ever, Mary is the first creaturely-symbolical response to the power of the diabolical.

Finally, the sustaining of a symbolical view of being and the task of promoting integral human liberation demands the renewal of what Catholics understand as a "sacramental" vision of things, founded upon the reality of the God who is, in Jesus Christ, at once Creator and Redeemer of the world. This sacramental vision includes what may be called

human life at its beginning and end, in practices such as artificial reproductive technology, cloning, and the like. Arguably, these problems are likewise tied to the inability to pay attention—to see things in their intrinsic depth and worth.

52. See John Paul II, *Redemptoris Mater*, no. 37, where the pope cites from the Congregation for the Doctrine of the Faith, *Instruction on Christian Freedom and Liberation*, no. 97: "Mary is totally dependent upon God and completely directed towards him, and at the side of her Son, she is the most perfect image of freedom and of the liberation of humanity and of the universe. It is to her as Mother and Model that the Church must look in order to understand in its completeness the meaning of her own mission."

the "pre-sacramentality" of nature and the proper sacramentality of the Church, whose sum and summit is the Eucharist.[53] Given the foregoing diagnosis of the key principles operative in the ethos of disenchantment, the task for the Church in the face of modernity is to renew the sacrament of God's power as love in herself and all of creation. Only through such a renewal can things be restored to their rightful autonomy (*iusta autonomia*). Only in this light can we thus truly address in its root meaning what *Gaudium et spes* 36 implies regarding false autonomy: "Creatura ... sine Creatore evanescit.... Immo, per oblivionem Dei ipsa creatura obscuratur."[54]

53. Nature refers to what may be called the "infallible" effective presence of God in natural things. Nature, that is, is enduring and unerring in the sense that it bears the mark of universality and necessity, even within and under the burden of its historical distortions through sin. It thus symbolizes the generous mind and love of the Creator that becomes effective in and through creatures in the act of creation. The Eucharist, in an infinitely greater but intrinsically related way, sacramentalizes the love of God revealed in Jesus Christ, infallibly effecting the real presence of that love in the Church for the sake of the world.

54. "Without the Creator, the creature disappears.... Indeed, when God is forgotten the creature itself becomes unintelligible."

2

Man's Highest Calling

The Theological Anthropology of *Gaudium et spes*

ANTONIO LÓPEZ

Introduction

In the conciliar constitution *Gaudium et spes*, the Church wished to speak humbly and boldly to a world that, in her estimation, had severed itself from the Church, claiming to exist rather well without her.[1] She thus engaged in an open dialogue with the world on crucial matters including work, culture, economics, and science, all of whose historical instantiations, as the document wisely acknowledges, are in a "constant state of development."[2] This perception of ongoing development, along with the

1. *AAS* 58 (1966): 1025–120. The English translation can be found on the Vatican website: http://www.vatican.va/archive/hist_councils/ii_vatican_council/documents/vat-ii_const_19651207_gaudium-et-spes_en.html. All quotations from *Gaudium et spes* reflect this translation, though in some cases modifications have been made to more faithfully translate the Latin original. The Church's "speaking humbly" refers to her acknowledgment of her role in the rise of atheism (*GS*, no. 19), not the pastoral nature of the constitution.

2. As its famous footnote 1 explains, *GS* is a "pastoral" constitution because it seeks to express how the Church's theological principles guide the way she relates to the world and shape what she has to offer to the world. While the constitution first presents the main tenets of an incipient theological anthropology (nos. 11–45) in order to then tackle some problems of special urgency (nos. 46–90), the first part of the document does not set forth a doctrinal framework bereft of pastoral intention, nor does the second part unveil a "pastoral program" wanting in doctrinal principles. It is helpful to bring to mind the constitution's main content. Part I consists of four chapters: (1) "The Dignity of the Human Person," nos. 12–22; (2) "The Community of Mankind," nos. 23–32; (3) "Man's Activity throughout the World," nos. 33–39; and (4) "The Role of the Church in the Modern World," nos. 40–45.

"immense variety of situations and forms of human culture in the world," provoked the deliberate decision to offer a program that remained "general ... in several of its parts" (*GS*, no. 91). It is not surprising, then, that the document calls for its exposition "to be followed up and amplified" (*GS*, no. 91). Undoubtedly, these last fifty years have brought stark changes in many different fields. Yet all these changes appear to stem from a single source already indicated by the conciliar constitution: an atheistic culture that enshrines man and his freedom as the origin and destiny of history.[3] If a certain view of man thus stands at the root of many contemporary issues facing the Church and the world, then the called-for "amplification" should first be a deepening of the constitution's main anthropological proposal. This chapter, however, neither addresses the issue of atheism directly nor offers a genealogy of the liberal understanding of human freedom and of the immanent and historical subjectivity that grounds it. Instead, taking its bearings from the theological anthropology that *Gaudium et spes* put forward, it explores and deepens the theological concept of human personhood in terms of gift, that is, in terms of the

Part II comprises five chapters: (1) "Fostering the Nobility of Marriage and the Family," nos. 47–52; (2) "The Proper Development of Culture," nos. 53–62; (3) "Economic and Social Life," nos. 63–72; (4) "The Life of the Political Community," nos. 73–76; and (5) "The Fostering of Peace and the Promotion of a Community of Nations," nos. 77–90. For an account of the meaning of "dialogue," see Karol Wojtyła, *Sources of Renewal: The Implementation of Vatican II*, trans. P. S. Falla (San Francisco: Harper and Row, 1979); Angelo Scola, "*Gaudium et spes*: Dialogo e discernimento nella testimonianza della verità," in *Il Concilio Vaticano II: Recezione e attualità alla luce del Giubileo*, ed. Rino Fisichella (Cinisello Balsamo: Paoline, 2000), 82–114.

3. These changes include globalization, the dominating presence of technology, the totalitarianism of contemporary democracy, the development of biotechnological sciences, the cultural disappearance of the family, and religious relativism. The main texts recounting the history of the complex and laborious redaction of *GS* are Yves M.-J. Congar and Michel Peuchmaurd, eds., *L'Église dans le monde de ce temps: Constitution pastorale "Gaudium et spes,"* 3 vols. (Paris: Éditions du Cerf, 1967)—including two chapters of special note, Philippe Delhaye, "Histoire des textes de la Constitution pastorale," 1:215–77 and Roberto Tucci, "Introduction historique et doctrinale à la Constitution pastorale," 2:33–127—Charles Moeller, "History of the Constitution," in *Commentary on the Documents of Vatican* II, vol. 5, *Pastoral Constitution on the Church in the Modern World*, ed. Herbert Vorgrimler, trans. W. J. O'Hara (New York: Herder and Herder, 1969), 1–76; René Latourelle, ed., *Vatican II: Bilan et perspectives; Vingt-Cinq ans après (1962–1987)*, 3 vols. (Paris: Éditions Du Cerf, 1988); and John Paul II, "Only Christ Can Fulfill Man's Hopes," *Communio: International Catholic Review* 23 (Spring 1996): 122–28.

person's "call to communion with God" ("Dignitatis humanae eximia ratio in vocatione hominis ad communionem cum Deo consistit," *GS*, no. 19)—which constitutes his call to be a person—and of his mission in history. To this end, the essay begins by elucidating why the Council was interested in presenting an anthropology to the modern world and by identifying the causes of that anthropology's internal tensions. It then examines the main features of *Gaudium et spes*'s Christological and Trinitarian anthropology. Finally, this theological anthropology serves to ground an approximation to the mystery of the human person in terms of gift.

Man's World

Why is "man himself, whole and entire, body and soul, heart and conscience, mind and will" the "focal point" of *Gaudium et spes* 3? Why is a Christian anthropology the content of the Church's dialogue with the world when the declared purpose is "to explain to everyone how it conceives of the presence and activity of the Church in the world of today" (*GS*, no. 2)? It is true that "nothing genuinely human fails to raise an echo" in the hearts of the followers of Christ" (*GS*, no. 1). Yet it suffices to recall the witness of the saints to realize that this spirit of communion between Christians and all men and women has belonged to the Church since her inception, not only since the Second Vatican Council.[4] Nor is mortal man's perennial need to understand himself the main reason for the document's decision to offer a theological anthropology, though it is undoubtedly a factor (*GS*, nos. 9–10). Instead, the source of this decision—which is also the originality of the document—is that the Church recognizes the new self-awareness that characterizes modern man and acknowledges it as the cause of both his triumphs and the dire state in which he finds himself. The Church therefore has the urgency to present to contemporary man his highest calling and his true dignity, since it is only with Christ that the nature of the human person is discovered. The Church, however, must present Christianity's unique content in a way

4. Mario Vittorino said this much: "When I encountered Christ, I discovered myself to be a man." "In epistolam Pauli ad Ephesios," 4.14, in *Marii Victorini Opera: Pars II, Opera exegetica*; CSEL 83.2.

that incorporates what is of value in this modern self-awareness without absorbing its ambiguities and faulty presuppositions.

Gaudium et spes acknowledges that modern man's self-awareness is new in two inseparable respects. First, man sees himself as a subject historically situated in an ever more globalized world that seems to be entirely at his disposal. Second, he thinks he can account for his being in the world and his actions without God (*GS*, nos. 19–20). This self-awareness drives man to consider the doctrine of creation a negligible theory, Christian religion a matter only of morality, and the memory of man's eschatological salvation a surrender of worldly responsibility. Modern man considers himself to be an areligious subject by nature, and his world, too, is without theological significance.[5] "Atheism," *Gaudium et spes* says, "must be accounted among the most serious problems of this age" (*GS*, no. 19).

The anthropology undergirding atheism most radically contradicts

5. This perception of the human subject may give the impression that, for modern man, the world regards a space or a time that encompasses his existence. This is not the case. The world, for modern man, is not simply the overarching place that he inhabits along with all that is, as it was for the Greeks. The modern understanding of the world is burdened by a radical sense of immanence unknown to the Greeks. It is not, as Christianity holds, the reality created from nothing to enjoy God's life, a reality whose glorious *telos* will be disclosed at the end of history. "World" instead refers mainly to man and to his historical existence. Undoubtedly, this anthropomorphic and historical-dynamic sense of "world" has its roots in Scripture (Gn 1–3; Ps 8). Yet it differs from the Judeo-Christian account in that it is conceived without its theological horizon of meaning. God is no longer a reality with which man must grapple or essential for his living an authentic human existence. It is true that, as has been noted already, the Council's perception of the meaning of "world" merits clarification. Yet the Church's recognition of the modern understanding of the world as historical and anthropocentric is of great value because it calls for a deepening of the meaning of man's freedom and responsibility for his own existence. It can thus be said that when addressing the world, the Church is in fact speaking to the complex and unified totality that can function as a partner in dialogue. This totality, rather than being a hypostasis, is modern culture as it orders and gives meaning to the historical existence of singular men and women. Perhaps the clearest expression of the meaning of "world" is that given in *GS*, no. 2. By "world," *GS* refers to "the world of men, the whole human family along with the sum of those realities in the midst of which it lives; that world which is the theater of man's history, and the heir of his energies, his tragedies and his triumphs; that world which the Christian sees as created and sustained by its Maker's love, fallen indeed into the bondage of sin, yet emancipated now by Christ, Who was crucified and rose again to break the strangle hold of personified evil, so that the world might be fashioned anew according to God's design and reach its fulfillment." Cf. Joseph Ratzinger's commentary on the first chapter of *GS* in Vorgrimler, *Commentary on the Documents of Vatican II*, 5:115–63; Johann B. Metz, *Lexicon für Theologie und Kirche Herder Verlag* (2017), vol. 10, s.v. "Welt."

man's original nature. *Gaudium et spes* clarifies that to consider man a subject in the modern sense means that freedom defines his identity.[6] "Never before," says the constitution, "has man had so keen an understanding of freedom" (*GS*, no. 4). Freedom, for modern man, is not the property of the will that expresses itself in the capacity to choose or to dismiss the true good. It is not the capacity for God. Rather, it defines man's essence as a being that has its own *telos*. This anthropology is not wrong, but it is one-sided. The modern conception of freedom is built upon the rejection of the existential evidence, recorded also by Scripture, that man is not his own (Jer 10:23; 2 Cor 3:5). Modern culture does not want to recognize that man's autoteleology—as Karol Wojtyła calls it—is given to him.[7] Through its denial of constitutive creatureliness, modern, atheist culture understands freedom simply as man's capacity to be "an end unto himself, the sole artisan and creator of his own history" (*GS*, no. 20).[8] The further realization that the freedom that defines human nature is historically situated does not mean solely that, for modern man, history has priority over nature. It also implies that the human being sees himself as endowed with an extraordinary capacity to make always new and better things and, as technical and scientific findings illustrate, to mold the world as he sees

6. Departing from typical modern usage, *GS* does not employ the term "subject" when it speaks about the human being. Although the term is thus absent from the conciliar text, the modern anthropology underpinning such usage is the one that the Council Fathers seem to have critically in mind. "Subject" does not retain for modern thinkers its Aristotelian meaning, "subject of being." Rather, it indicates the abstract and disembodied self that for modernity grounds truth and perceives beings in the world as objects, i.e., as material deprived of intrinsic meaning and open to scientific and technological manipulation. It goes without saying that *GS* does not delve into these terminological considerations, but its clarification of the concern for the "whole man" and the themes it treats of in Part II justify our description in the present essay of "man" as "subject." Cf. Kenneth L. Schmitz, *The Texture of Being: Essays in First Philosophy*, ed. Paul O'Herron (Washington, DC: Catholic University of America Press, 2007), 149–241.

7. Karol Wojtyła, "The Person: Subject and Community," in *Person and Community: Selected Essays*, trans. Theresa Sandok (New York: Peter Lang, 1993), 219–61, at 228–32; Karol Wojtyła, *Persona e atto*, trans. Giuseppe Girgenti and Patrycja Mikulska (Milan: Bompiani, 2001), 261–443.

8. What is true for man is also the case for human affairs and the created world, all of which are autonomous with respect to God. *GS*, of course, seeks to defend what is true of this "autonomy" and to show why it does not entail opposition to God. See, e.g., nos. 36 and 59.

fit. This conception of freedom thus transforms reason from the capacity to recognize and affirm the truth into technological reason, that is, a reason that measures and manipulates the given. Man is inebriated by freedom's power: "Mankind is stricken with wonder at its own discoveries and its power" (*GS*, no. 3).[9] The historical development of the last five decades amply confirms that "the sense of power which modern technical progress generates in man" (*GS*, no. 20) strengthens his awareness of being a free, autonomous subject.

Nevertheless, if it is true, as Heidegger says with Hölderlin, that "where danger is, grows / The saving power also," then it is crucial to look at man and his freedom anew.[10] The modern sense of freedom can be the opportunity to gain a deeper, truer perception of the mystery of man and his freedom. As *Gaudium et spes* indicates, the ambiguous results of man's exercise of freedom and of scientific discoveries elicit in him questions regarding how to steer his accomplishments toward society's good—questions overshadowed and made more urgent by the fact that "the magnified power of humanity threatens to destroy the race itself" (*GS*, no. 37). More importantly, however, the deepest questions that these findings elicit in man regard his very person, who he is (*GS*, no. 10).[11] Man "remains ... an unsolved puzzle (*quaestio*)" (*GS*, no. 21). Because the spirit of modern times hinges upon and fosters this specific anthropology of freedom and power, *Gaudium et spes* proposes a Christian anthropology before it explains how man ought to order his being in the world. By prioritizing this anthropology, the Church hopes to show modern man how "Christ, who died and was raised up for all (2 Cor 5:15), can through His Spirit offer man the light and the strength to measure up to his supreme destiny (*suae vocationi*)."[12] The Church undertakes this task with

9. We find in *GS* other similar expressions: "Man extends his power in every direction" (no. 4); he is dominated by a "sense of power which modern technical progress generates in" him (no. 20).

10. Martin Heidegger, *Basic Writings: From "Being and Time" (1927) to "The Task of Thinking" (1964)*, ed. David Farrell Krell (New York: HarperCollins, 1993), 340.

11. Man's question regarding himself also involves the question of what it means to hand on to his children an understanding of life and time (*GS*, no. 7), to be called to a communion of persons (no. 12), and to avoid a conflictual relation with the sexually differentiated other who most naturally corresponds to him (no. 8).

12. For the recent history of the term "Christian anthropology," see Angelo Scola, Gil-

the certainty "that in her most benign Lord and Master can be found the key (*clavem*), the focal point (*centrum*) and the goal (*finem*) of man, as well as of all human history" (*GS*, no. 10).

What Anthropology?

Gaudium et spes seeks to present the conception of man that the Church received from Christian revelation as a truer and more profound account than that of modern subjectivity. Its "introductory statement" (*GS*, nos. 4–10) concludes by affirming that the Church finds in Christ "image of the invisible God and firstborn of every creature" (Col 1:15), the light to illumine the mystery of man (*GS*, no. 10). One would then expect that *Gaudium et spes* would begin with an elucidation of what Christ reveals of the human being. Instead, chapter 1 of the document gives us a theological anthropology that follows the first three chapters of Genesis, according to which man is created in the image of God as man and woman (*GS*, no. 12) but rejects God's offer of grace (*GS*, no. 13). In light of Genesis, *Gaudium et spes* proceeds to offer a philosophical anthropology that deals with man's dual unity of body and soul (*GS*, no. 14), the greatness of reason and knowing (*GS*, no. 15), the defense of the existence of moral conscience (*GS*, no. 16), the greatness of human freedom (*GS*, no. 17), the mystery of death (*GS*, no. 18), and the challenge of atheism (*GS*, nos. 19–21). The first reference to creation in Christ comes only at the end of the chapter (*GS*, no. 22),[13] and it does so abruptly.[14] The order of exposition, as well

fredo Marengo, and Javier Prades López, *La persona umana: Antropologia teologica* (Milan: Jaca Books, 2000), 25–67.

13. "The truth is that only in the mystery of the incarnate Word does the mystery of man take on light. For Adam, the first man, was a figure of Him Who was to come, namely Christ the Lord. Christ, the final Adam, by the revelation of the mystery of the Father and His love, fully reveals man to man himself and makes his supreme calling clear. It is not surprising, then, that in Him all the aforementioned truths find their root and attain their crown" (*GS*, no. 22).

14. This structure repeats itself throughout *GS*: no. 38, which deals with the perfection of human action in the paschal mystery, is the penultimate section of chapter 3. In chapter 4, we find two references to the relation between Christology and anthropology. The first occurs in no. 41, which deals with the help that the Church offers to every man and which indicates that whoever follows Christ, the perfect man, becomes more human. The second reference occurs in the chapter's final section, no. 45, where Christ is again spoken of as the "perfect man" and as "the Alpha and Omega," in whom all men may be saved.

as the fact that most passages dealing with man's creation do not speak of creation in Christ, represents the tacit disclosure that some Council Fathers still perceived the Christological meaning of man as an addition to the purportedly self-sufficient philosophical anthropology elucidated in *Gaudium et spes* 12–21. Why is the sought-after Christological anthropology presented in such a timid way?

Undoubtedly, the need to speak to an atheistic world favored a certain apologetic approach. This apologetic recognizes that, for modern sensibilities, faith often comes across as an obtrusive element, and it considers the fact that a world blind to God's presence cannot see what Christ reveals of man's nature. It thus deems it more fitting to address the spirit of modern times by first laying out what remains within the reach of pure reason—presuming that creation can be considered accessible to pure reason. Only after this is done can one propose a Christological anthropology for whose elaboration faith is needed. Giuseppe Colombo has ably shown that behind the apologetic approach governing some sections of *Gaudium et spes*'s theological anthropology lies the theology of the manuals, which had its inception in the seventeenth century and which considered Genesis the sufficient scriptural text for an adequate Christian anthropology. Christological references, in this view, do not affect man's essence, mainly because creation is understood as a nature deprived of its metaphysical and scriptural character of *mysterion*. Bereft of its character of *mysterion*, nature lacks an intrinsic openness and reference to Christ. As seen in those treatises on grace, Christology is not thought of together with the account of creation and vice versa. The creature is only graciously elevated to the realm of the divine.[15] Yet, we may ask, how is it possible to understand that the union with God does not violate human freedom—as modern culture believes it does—if this union is not mediated and enabled by Christ, himself the "perfect man"?[16] How can one

15. Giuseppe Colombo, "La teologia della *Gaudium et spes* e l'esercizio del magistero ecclesiastico," in *La ragione teologica* (Milan: Glossa, 1995), 265–303, at 274–77. For an account of the theology of the manuals, see his chapter in the same work, "La teologia manualistica," 305–35. It was M. Scheeben who reintroduced into Catholic theology the intrinsic relation between creation and *mysterion*.

16. *GS* describes Christ as the perfect man four times. See Luis Ladaria, *Jesus Christ, Salvation of All*, trans. María Cristina Herrera and María Isabel Reyna (Miami: Convivium

root obedience in man's nature—and hence account for its human reasonableness—if this listening entrustment of oneself in which obedience consists is not a participation in the eternal Logos who alone hears what the Father says (Jn 5:30) and speaks to man?[17] Even if *Gaudium et spes*'s anthropology is burdened by these internal tensions between a Christological anthropology and a philosophical anthropology harmonious with the scriptural account of creation, it is still the case that in several key places it presents, at least *in nuce*, the main features of a Christological and Trinitarian anthropology.[18] As the 1985 Synod contended, this is the anthropology that is at the heart of *Gaudium et spes* and that the Church must develop fully if she is to communicate Christianity's newness. Let us now focus on the key passages of *Gaudium et spes* 22 and 24.

Theological Anthropology

To look at man in the light of Christ requires seeing that the incarnate Logos, the image of the invisible God (Col 1:15), was prefigured in Adam (*GS* no. 22). With this vision, *Gaudium et spes* indicates that man's nature needs to be conceived in terms of "mystery." Man is a "mystery" not so much because he is a transient creature or because he does not know who he is. He is a mystery because he is part of God's eternal design to communicate his love to man in Christ.[19] Man therefore is called from the

---

Press, 2008); Marcello Bordoni, *Gesù di Nazaret: Signore e Cristo; Saggio di Cristologia sistematica*, vol. 1, *Problemi di metodo* (Rome: Herder-PUL, 1982–86), 186–219.

17. A. Scola adduces as a further reason for the constitution's timid Christological anthropology the fact that Christocentrism was not yet fully proposed and welcomed in the Church. This development's later success was aided by the work of Karl Barth, Romano Guardini, Erich Przywara, and Michael Schmaus, among others, as well as by renewed reflection on the Fathers of the Church, the retrieval of Scripture, the integration of Scripture with theological reflection, and the articulation of personalist philosophies.

18. The most significant sections with regard to *GS*'s Christological anthropology are nos. 10, 22, 32, 38–41, and 45. Parallel passages in other conciliar documents include *Ad gentes* 8, *Nostra aetate* 5, and *Lumen gentium* 50.

19. Mystery can be an "epistemological" category because it is first a sacramental one: it refers primarily to Christ and in him to man. The element of the "unknown" regards, on the one hand, the gratuitous and free insertion of man in God's design, which will be fulfilled in the eschaton, and, on the other hand, the personal relation between God and man, both of whom are inexhaustible, personal wholes. See Matthias J. Scheeben, *The Mysteries of Christianity*, trans. Cyril Vollert (London: B. Herder, 1946), 733–96.

very beginning to this communion with God in Christ, and he is created free in order to participate in it (*GS* no. 19). If man is not created in and for Christ, then, once the perception of creation and of being as gift is rejected—as it has been since the early modern period—it is difficult not to conceive of human freedom as antagonistic to God.[20] If God is all in all (Eph 4:6) but the relation with him is not one of being and love, then one lacks the grounds to answer what it means for a finite freedom to be. Instead, it is only in Christ that man's constitutive religiosity, the natural desire to see God and be one with him, acquires its full meaning.[21]

To correct the modern fear that communion with God entails an elimination of freedom, *Gaudium et spes* 22 brings together the more static Chalcedonian Christology with a more dynamic, kenotic Christology.[22] That Christ's humanity is complete means, among other things, that he is given to himself; that is, he is free. It is at the Council of Chalcedon that the Church offers the theological grounds for the defense of the integrity of human freedom. If, as we see throughout Christ's life and most particularly at the moment of his internal passion in Gethsemane (Mk 14:32–42; Mt 26:36–46; Lk 22:39–46), the divine and human natures are united in the one person of Christ without division, confusion, separation, or change, then human freedom is not evacuated. But we are not to think that the preservation of Christ's human freedom means that it exists parallel to his divine freedom, as if they were juxtaposed. Rather, as Ratzinger clarifies in his explanation of why the Third Council of

20. Kenneth L. Schmitz, *At the Center of the Human Drama: The Philosophical Anthropology of Karol Wojtyła/Pope John Paul II* (Washington, DC: Catholic University of America Press, 1993), 121–46; Kenneth L. Schmitz, *The Gift: Creation* (Milwaukee: Marquette University Press, 1982), 118–30.

21. The filial relation between God and man that Christ enables, inasmuch as it is recognized and lived, is religiosity. Natural religiosity (the natural desire to see God, or the desire for happiness, freedom, truth, justice) is an inchoative expression of what grace makes unforeseeably and gratuitously possible. See Luigi Giussani, *The Religious Sense*, trans. John Zucchi (Montreal: McGill-Queen's University Press, 1997); Henri de Lubac, *The Discovery of God*, trans. Alexander Dru (Grand Rapids, MI: Eerdmans, 1996); Henri de Lubac, *The Mystery of the Supernatural*, trans. Rosemary Sheed (Grand Rapids, MI: Eerdmans, 1998); Hans Urs von Balthasar, *The Glory of the Lord: A Theological Aesthetics*, vol. 1, *Seeing the Form*, trans. Erasmo Leiva-Merikakis (San Francisco: Ignatius Press, 1982).

22. *GS*, no. 22 refers to Constantinople II, 7 (DH 219), Constantinople III (DH 291), and Chalcedon (DH 148).

Constantinople fulfills Chalcedon, the two freedoms dwell in each other.[23] What the spatial image intends to say, as Maximus eloquently shows, is that the motion most naturally corresponding to Christ's (and every) human freedom is precisely that of his divine freedom, that is, his being for the Father.[24] To be free is to be for him who gives life and does not deceive.

This latter aspect of freedom, man's "for-existence," as Ratzinger characterizes it, emerges more clearly in the kenotic Christology, according to which the incarnation encompasses Christ's earthly life, the paschal mystery, and his return in glory to the Father with whom he sends the Holy Spirit.[25] Attentive to this filial aspect, *Gaudium et spes* indicates that Christ's humanity was perfect not only because "he worked with human hands, He thought with a human mind, acted by human choice and loved with a human heart," but also because, through all this, he lived real union with and perfect obedience to the Father (*GS*, no. 22).

Christ is man's archetype and makes it possible for every human being to be human, that is, to be in relation with the Father. He thus reveals that man is defined by his religiosity ("What can man give in exchange for his soul?" Mk 8:37) and enables man to live, in him and thanks to the Spirit, a relation with the Father. Uniting a human nature to himself, Christ, in a way we do not know, united himself with every man (*GS*, no. 22). Yet in order for man to be saved—that is, in order for man not to end up seeking and promoting death under the guise of total freedom—Christ had to do more than assume human nature. In a certain sense, he had to unite himself with every person, with every man in his constitutive and dramatic relation to God. Christ, without committing sin (Heb 4:15), had also to assume responsibility for our sin and for our death—which is perhaps what is most personally ours. Assuming death, Christ makes not only human nature in general his own but also man in his free-

23. Joseph Ratzinger, *Behold the Pierced One: An Approach to a Spiritual Christology*, trans. Graham Harrison (San Francisco: Ignatius Press, 1986), 37–42.

24. Andrew Louth, *Maximus the Confessor* (London: Routledge, 1996); Maximus the Confessor, *The Disputation with Pyrrhus of Our Father among the Saints Maximus the Confessor*, trans. Joseph P. Farrell (South Canaan, PA: St. Tikhon's Seminary Press, 1990).

25. Joseph Ratzinger, *Introduction to Christianity*, trans. J. R. Foster (San Francisco: Ignatius Press, 2004), 251–54.

dom, responsibility, and condemnation. Assuming the death of everyone (2 Cor 5:14), he assumes all the ambiguities of human freedom and all its possibilities—whose origin and resolution modern man is particularly at pains to fathom. Had Christ not borne responsibility for man's sins and died on the cross, he would have remained foreign to man (*GS*, no. 22).[26]

Gaudium et spes elucidates the positive content of man's salvation from sin as the gift of divine filial adoption.[27] Admittedly, the constitution does not fully develop the dimension of filiation. This lack, as Piero Coda indicates, is probably because *Gaudium et spes*'s Christology does not adequately integrate its Chalcedonian perspective with the paschal, kenotic perspective proper to Scripture. *Gaudium et spes* does, however, indicate three crucial aspects regarding divine sonship.[28] The first is that man, contrary to what moderns think, is always dependent on someone. Autonomy and dependence are not dialectically opposed terms. The former, autonomy, is to be understood in light of the latter. The human being, as our experience teaches us, is himself only because he is generated. He is himself only inasmuch as he receives life, and he lives a genuine existence only inasmuch as he welcomes God. When *Gaudium et spes* states that "by the free shedding of His own blood" the innocent Lamb freed us from "bondage to the devil and sin" and "merited for us life" (*GS*, no. 22), it clarifies that, while dependence on God is the original and most primordial dependence, man can, however, become a son of Satan (Jn 8;

26. The assumption of our responsibility is what the mystery of Christ's baptism represents. If at his birth the Logos assumes our mortal flesh, at the baptism in the Jordan, Christ assumes, for our sake, our moral responsibility before God. At his baptism, he is revealed as the beloved Son of the Father on whom the Spirit descends (Mk 1:11). In this mysterious way, because he is baptized on behalf of all mankind, he also gains for each man the possibility of receiving at the appropriate time the Holy Spirit and thereby enjoying divine, adoptive sonship—i.e., being—in Christ, a beloved son of the Father.

27. This is seen in the constitution's indication that the divine vocation is always mediated through Christ, who is the Son of the Father, and in its citations from Scripture: Rom 8:5; Gal 4:6, Jn 1:12; 1 Jn 3:1–2. It does not, however, cite 1 Cor 15:45–49, leaving the link between protology and eschatology implicit. Because for the Council the revelation of God's paternity is coincident with his offer of divine adoptive sonship, anthropology has in Christology its foundation and crown (*GS*, no. 22).

28. Piero Coda, "L'uomo nel mistero di Cristo e della Trinità: L'antropologia della *Gaudium et spes*," *Lateranum*, n.s., 54 (1988): 164–94, at 184; Piero Coda, "Antropologia teologica e agire umano nel mondo nella *Gaudium et spes*," *Lateranum*, n.s., 55 (1989): 176–207.

1 Jn 3:3–9). These two ways of living sonship (being generated by God or by a creature who opposes him) do not stand on equal footing, yet both are the only two real possibilities. The question, therefore, is to discover the constitutive relation of dependence that allows man to be himself.

The second aspect of *Gaudium et spes*'s teaching on divine filiation is its reminder to modern man that only when he receives the unforeseeable gift of the Son does he become truly human, that is, a son of God. Thus adoptive sonship, being children of God in Christ through the Holy Spirit, is the way man enters into and lives communion with God. In winning for him divine adoptive sonship, Christ reveals and, through the gift of the Holy Spirit, enables man's life-giving dependence on God, the loving relation with him. It is only this dependence that establishes personal distinction from the paternal origin.[29] It is not irrelevant that the Council's emphasis on the gift of divine filiation is not Christomonistic but refers to all of the divine persons: being sons in the Son is a gift of the Father merited by the Son and communicated through the Spirit. The Council's Christological anthropology is fully Trinitarian.

The third decisive aspect of *Gaudium et spes*'s Trinitarian anthropology is the clarification that adoptive filiation is a relation of love bearing the form of the new commandment given by Christ and that it is a participation in the way the person of the Son enjoys the one divine being, which is love (*GS*, no. 22).[30] In the new commandment, love has a twofold directionality: on the one hand, being brought to his dignity in the Son, man can call God "Father" (*GS*, no. 22). He can love God; that is, in Christ, he can enjoy the Father's love, let love be generated in him, and, through the Spirit, respond to the Father's love. God not only speaks to man, as Israel knew well, but also allows man to speak to him. In this way, Christ makes possible the mysterious depth of man's highest calling: be-

29. Theologically speaking, it can also be said that the incarnation of the Son would not be real—i.e., he would not be a real man—if this act were not also the elevation of man to God. Since the one God whose being is love (1 Jn 4:8) is not just a Plotinian One but a communion of persons, and since the relations that constitute God as a triune God cannot be multiplied, for man to participate in the divine communion is for him to be a person through graced incorporation into the relation that constitutes the Logos as second person of the Trinity.

30. It is postconciliar theology—particularly the work of Balthasar, John Paul II, Ratzinger, and Giussani—that will develop this Christian anthropology.

ing the least of God's creatures, he is still allowed to be himself in being for God and to enter into a real unity with God.

On the other hand, in the Spirit of both Christ and the Father, man can love other men and thus enjoy already in a certain sense the unity proper to divine charity. This does not simply mean that man, because he is in Christ and for Christ, is himself when he lives for those who are part of Christ's own body—the baptized and every man (Mt 25:40). Because this being for another is at the service of the other's being given the gifts of faith, hope, and charity, it is also, through the Spirit, a participation in Christ's mission. We could thus say that, in a way analogous to the Son's divine fruitfulness, which is the spiration of the Spirit with the Father, the fruitfulness of the baptized consists in allowing the Spirit of Christ to expose the truth and love of God through the transfiguration of the believer's own flesh, which is one with the crucified and risen body of Christ. In this way he also contributes to the growth of the personal existence of other men, that is, to their filial relation to the Father and their incorporation in Christ's body. Just as being son in the Son secures both unity with and distinction from God, so being children of God brings men to a new, sacramental unity, a social reality in which man's singularity is not dissolved.[31]

Gaudium et spes describes this unity—which will be fully realized in the eschaton but is already present in the world through the Church—with the words of that other passage that, along with paragraph 22, represents the heart of the document's Christological anthropology: "When He prayed to the Father, 'that all may be one ... as we are one' (Jn 17:21–22)," Christ "opened up vistas closed to human reason, for He implied a certain likeness between the union of the divine Persons, and the unity of God's sons in truth and charity. This likeness reveals that man, who is the only creature on earth which God willed for itself, cannot fully find himself except through a sincere gift of himself" (*GS*, no. 24).

31. This point is also important for the historical, totalitarian context that governed the twentieth century and that, under a different form, remains in force today. See Karol Wojtyła, "Participation and Alienation," in *Person and Community*, 197–207; David Crawford, "*Evangelium vitae*, the Rhetoric of Freedom, and Roe v. Wade's Totalitarian Implications," *Nova et Vetera* 13, no. 4 (2015): 1209–28.

Commenting on this passage, Karol Wojtyła wrote that "while it is true that this text seems to refer primarily to a certain order of activity (*operari*), which consists in the giving of oneself, this order of activity is itself rooted in the order of existence, in the personal being (*esse*) of the human being. In this sense, activity always follows being (*operari sequitur esse*). If the 'gift of oneself' characterizes human activity, human conduct, it does so always because of this personal *esse*, which is capable of a disinterested gift of itself."[32] The ability to give, in fact, depends upon a divine creative act that not only allows finite beings to be but also enables them to be generous givers like God himself. Creatures' finite giving flows from the gift of their being. Whereas at the subhuman level this further giving on the part of the creature is for the most part natural spontaneity, at the human level—that is, at the level of an enfleshed spirit—natural giving is also a free act. The concluding sentence of this famous section of *Gaudium et spes* therefore invites us to think of the category of personal being in terms of gift. Further, this passage offers a fitting alternative to the fictitious unity of a technological and globalized world, a unity that is ultimately unable to embrace human otherness. *Gaudium et spes* speaks instead of a unity within which one can both be affirmed as an end in oneself and live a true existence in the gift of oneself. This unity is, first and foremost, that of the family, but it also regards "the unity of God's sons in truth and charity" (*GS*, no. 24).[33] Now, following the suggestion of *Gaudium et spes* itself and in light of the theological anthropology here outlined, I offer an exploration of the meaning of person in terms of gift. I will leave for another occasion an elucidation of the type of unity God's love generates and its capacity to image the divine triune mystery.

32. Karol Wojtyła, "The Family as a Community of Persons," in *Person and Community*, 315–28, at 318–19. A similar passage is found earlier in the same collection: "The words of Vatican II cited above [*GS*, no. 24] seem chiefly to accentuate the axiological aspect, speaking of the person as a being of special intrinsic worth, who is, therefore, specially qualified to make a gift of self. Beneath this axiological aspect, however, we can easily discern a deeper, ontological aspect." "The Personal Structure of Self-Determination," 187–96, at 193–94.

33. John Paul II, *Letter to Families*, no. 11. In *GS*, no. 24, the Council proposes a theological account of God's unity in terms of a communion of persons, and in this way it offers theological grounds for what it stated earlier regarding the creation of man as male and female (*GS*, no. 12).

Approaching the Mystery of the Person

To give a preliminary account of what the category of gift reveals of the mystery of the person, we must have a sense of the meaning of "person." Few words are as slippery as this one. To find a word to name what is both unrepeatable and common is an arduous task. On the one hand, the word "person" situates the human being as a member of the species to which it belongs. In this sense, a person is simply an individual, an instance of human being. On the other hand, "person" also signals the uniqueness of each human being. In this sense, despite appearances to the contrary, "person" is not a common name but a proper noun, and to use it for every member of the same species constitutes a semantic transgression. These two different connotations must be held together. In fact, when "individuality," membership in the species, is detached from personal uniqueness, the person dissolves into the realm of natural or ontological necessity, and freedom is reduced to the arbitrary exercise of power that only a few have the right to implement. Conversely, if personal uniqueness is severed from the belonging to a common ground, then the person is isolated and unable to realize that his belonging to a larger whole precedes his own choice. Everyone knows from his own experience that the separation of these two meanings is untrue: every human person is both one among many beings and a unique, unrepeatable being.[34]

To view the person as an individual is to consider him on the basis of what is common. This approach was the one taken by Aristotle, among others, who characterized man as *zoon noetikon*, *animal rationale*, and who further specified man's being and activity by recurring to the hylemorphic theory.[35] Man is just an animal whose rational soul puts him in a category of his own. For Aristotle, the rational soul fulfills simultaneously a

34. According to Aristotelian logic, the first transcendental is "one," in the sense that what is one cannot be divided in itself but is separate from others ("one" means "indivisum in se, et divisum a quolibet alio"). Cf. Thomas Aquinas, *De veritate,* q. 1, a. 1. The categories "universal," "particular," and "singular" are quantitative in Aristotelian logic; that is, they refer to the extension of a given subject of a proposition: all the members (Greeks), some (Athenians), a single member (Plato). "Person," instead, does not regard a quantity but a quality; that is, it indicates that a given being is a someone.

35. Aristotle, *De anima* 3.4–5.429a10–430a25.

twofold task: it indicates man's *logos* and his unrepeatable uniqueness, his being a "this." The soul, or form, is thus responsible for every man's being a man and for his being "this" concrete man. Boethius's famous definition of "person"—"person is the individual substance of a rational nature" (*persona est rationalis naturae individua substantia*)—follows this route, although his definition accounts for the human being not from its most proximate genus, animal, as was the case in Aristotle, but from the most comprehensive category of being, substance.[36] Man is therefore a self-standing being whose principle of life, movement, and rest is a rational soul. This so-called metaphysical understanding of person shows that one cannot ponder the mystery of the person without addressing the daunting metaphysical question "What is being?" As indispensable as this is, however, personal uniqueness is not sufficiently elucidated when personhood is reduced to a common being circumscribed by a specific difference. Every human being who belongs to a common species, who knows himself to be a rational, embodied soul, and who desires more than what he can obtain still cannot fully answer the question "Who am I?" In other words, recognizing the person as a being endowed with reason and freedom still leaves untouched the question regarding the embodied "self" that does the thinking, choosing, and desiring.

The metaphysical understanding is therefore enriched by a theological reflection on person that, taking its bearings from Scripture, sheds further light on the mystery of the person by means of a paradox: the singular self-standingness of each person derives from, most fundamentally, his relation with God. This coincidence of self-standingness and relation is the paradox of filiation. As the Old Testament recounts, man knows that he is not just one animal among many—even if the most noble—precisely because God speaks *and* listens to him.[37] The mysteries of language and relation belong together. Because God loves, creates, chooses, and takes care of his people, Israel knows that God is not an apersonal God and that man is a person called to nuptial relation with God.[38] It is

36. Boethius, *Contra Eut.* 3.1–6.

37. Within this dialogue, God entrusts man with the responsibility to fill the earth, subdue it, rule over it, and name all that is (Gn 1:28–30; 2:19–20).

38. Divo Barsotti, *La rivelazione dell'amore* (Bologna: Edizioni Dehoniane, 1955).

this relation that both distinguishes Israel from and binds it to all other peoples. Because this call is for all the peoples (through Israel), it also teaches man that every person has his specific identity in that relationship with God. Christ reveals a God who can speak to man, belong to him, and wait for an adequate response without thereby ceasing to be God; the God of Jesus Christ must therefore be a God who knows an eternal dialogue in himself because he is a tripersonal communion of love. The Son is the Word whom the Father eternally breathes in the Spirit and who, taking flesh from Mary, says himself to man and man to God. Christian revelation therefore helps us see that the mystery of the "self," the mystery of the person, regards the possibility of participating in this eternal dialogue whose content cannot but be that of God's very being, that is, love (1 Jn 4:8). In light of this, we need to acknowledge that the anthropology proper to human nature is always a dramatic anthropology, one that conceives man's freedom in a constitutive dialogue with divine freedom.

The only category left in our vocabulary to convey the mystery of the human person in a way respectful to both Scripture and man's original experience is that of relation. This is the case for both divine and human persons. The second person of the Trinity, as Son and Logos, is sheer relation to the Father, and the Father is never anything but his begetting of the Son and with him the giving further of the Spirit.[39] By virtue of being totally from and for the Father, the Son, through his incarnation, can be totally for man, the one who saves every man.[40] Relation also de-

39. Christ, throughout his existence, continuously discloses that he receives everything from the Father. His entire essence, as the name "Son" indicates, comes from the Father. Whatever he is he has from the Father (Mt 11:27). It is of his very being, of his essence as Son, says Balthasar, "to receive life (Jn 5:26), insight (3:11), spirit (3:34–35), word (3:34; 14:24), will (5:30), deed (6:9), doctrine (7:16), work (14:10) and glorification (8:54; 17:22, 24) from another, from the Father." Hans Urs von Balthasar, *A Theology of History* (San Francisco: Ignatius Press, 1994), 30. This reception, let us not forget, has no beginning. It is eternal: "He was in the beginning with God" (Jn 1:2). Once incarnate, Christ continues to live this absolute, constitutive dependence on the Father. Christ does only the Father's will (Jn 6:38; Lk 22:42). The Father's will is his only food (Jn 4:34). Without the Father, he cannot do anything (Jn 5:30). He loves the Father and what the Father has given him to the end (Jn 13:1). This being from the Father and being for him constitutes his human existence and, as Aquinas suggests, is a communication ad extra of the eternal generation of the son by the Father.

40. Precisely because in eternity he is everything from and for the Father, the Word that says without redundancy all that the Father is, he can live his being-gift in being every-

fines human persons in an analogous way. Relation with God determines every level of human existence. In fact, creation is the original, permanent, and constitutive relationship with God, who calls man out of nothingness and fashions him in Christ as male and female. Lived religiosity, the natural desire to see God, and the actual and ongoing search for and recognition of God, is the living out of this original, ontological relationship with God. Finally, the specific place and unique task that the lived belonging to God entails for every man is also a relationship. The "place" of each man's belonging to God and to other human persons must be concrete, for man is gift as an embodied soul and is called to participate in the fruitful giving that constitutes him. This giving takes the forms of sonship, nuptiality, fatherhood, motherhood, and brotherhood. These forms themselves exist only within a larger whole, a communion: Church, family, and the communities in which consecrated celibacy is lived. Using "person" in this theological sense centered on the category of relation, we see that it is an analogical term: it indicates what is most proper to God's being, and, because God creates man in his image and speaks to him, it also regards what man is. Theologically speaking, then, the term "person" indicates the highest perfection in the order of being because it is said of a spiritual being who is given to participate in language.[41] In God, language is not something he does; it is what he is. In man, on the contrary, language is a participation in God's being that requires him to enact what he is. Therefore a theological anthropology that wishes to take Scripture into account is always a dramatic anthropology. "Person," then, refers most properly to God's being and analogically to man's, because God creates man in his image and speaks to him.[42]

---

thing for man. He is man's light (Jn 8:12), his door to the Father (Jn 10:9), his good shepherd (Jn 10:11), his teacher (*didaskalos*), his lord (Jn 13:13), and his way, life, and truth (Jn 14:6). He is man's friend (Jn 15:15), his servant (Mt 20:28), and his brother (Heb 3:10–13). He is man's very food and drink (Jn 6:53–58). He is the resurrection (Jn 11:25). Christ is pure relation of love for man. As Son of the Father, he is all for man and in man (Jn 15 and 17) and hence allows man to live his constitutive religiosity, his dependence on the Father.

41. In this sense, the account of person as a spiritual, rational being who can act of himself calls for a deeper understanding of the relation between action and language. Thomas Aquinas, *Summa theologiae* (*ST*) I, q. 29, aa. 1 and 3.

42. "Nomen persona quantum ad rem significatam, prius et verius est in Deo quam in creaturis, unde est in illis analogice; sed quantum ad modum significandi et impositionem

The theological reflection prior to high scholasticism offered an account of the meaning of person that tried to hold together both its scriptural and metaphysical meanings.[43] It is good to recall that in Trinitarian theology, Richard of St. Victor undertook the task of elucidating the Trinitarian meaning of person by correcting Boethius's definition, understanding person anew as the "incommunicable existence of a spiritual nature."[44] Aquinas instead adopted and modified Boethius's elucidation, famously defining "person" as *relatio ut subsistens* or *subsistens relativum*.[45] All these authors emphasized in different ways that the individuality of the divine persons, their "self-standingness," is given by the incommunicable way they enjoy all of the divine being in an eternal relation with the correlative persons. Unity and personal distinction belong together.[46]

While these accounts did preserve the metaphysical meaning when describing each divine person's irreducibility to the others, they lack an organic reference to Scripture and to the anthropological implications of the concept of person.[47] This lack is perhaps because they did not deem it necessary to think the Trinitarian meaning of person on the grounds of its Christological meaning. During these centuries, in fact, the Christological elucidation of person was circumscribed to the unique identity of

---

nominis familiarius convenit creaturis." Thomas Aquinas, *Comm. Sent.*, bk. 1, d. 25, q. 1, a. 2; *ST* I, q. 29, a. 3, ad 2.

43. The English term "person" translates the Latin *persona* and the Greek *prosopon* and *hypostasis*. *Prosopon* ("what I have before my eyes") refers to the individual inasmuch as it stands before another as a face, a figure, a mask (in the Greek tragedies). *Hypostasis* means, in Aristotelian language, "what lies underneath." *Persona*, in Stoic philosophy, indicates the single individual that has a social role. See, among others, Carl Andresen, "Zur Entstehung und Geschichte des trinitarischen Personbegriffes," *Zeitschrift für die neutestamentliche Wissenschaft* 52, no. 1–2 (1961): 1–39.

44. Richard of St. Victor, *De Trinitate* 4.22: "Persona divina est divinae naturae incommunicabilis existentia."

45. Thomas Aquinas, *ST* I, q. 29, a. 4, and a. 3, ad 2; Bonaventure, *In Sent.* I (Quaracchi: College of St. Bonaventure, 1832–39), 431, 439, 441.

46. The formal principle that accounts for personal distinction in God is given in terms either of the spiritual faculties of knowing and willing or of God's very *esse* understood in light of Scripture as eternal charity.

47. This has already been noted by, among others, Joseph Ratzinger, "On the Understanding of 'Person' in Theology," in *Dogma and Preaching: Applying Christian Doctrine to Daily Life*, trans. Michael J. Miller and Matthew J. O'Connell (San Francisco: Ignatius Press, 2011), 181–96.

Christ as the personal union of divine and human natures and thus was not used to ground an analogical sense of person. The anthropological account of person was thus given in parallel to the theological; in his treatise in the *Summa*, for example, Aquinas adopted Aristotle's hylemorphic theory without reference to the concept of person he laboriously elucidated in his account of the Trinitarian dogma.

With the arrival of Protestantism, the theological reflection on person came to a halt and limited itself to reiterating the metaphysical account. Modern philosophy gradually severed its ties with theology to focus exclusively on the human subject, which was conceived, starting with Descartes, in terms of hypostasized consciousness. For modern man, consciousness is viewed as the source of evidence for truth and of the subject's activity. The body, according to this perception of the subject, is understood mechanistically, that is, as an object ready at hand for the (positive or negative) manipulation of the subject.[48] Along with consciousness, freedom is given great importance and is explained as either an expression of rationality itself (as in Hegel) or as opposed to rationality (as in Schopenhauer). Although it does not form an organic whole with the body, consciousness, or the subject, is endowed with a historical and dialogical existence: the subject exists in time fulfilling his possibilities and is always with others.

Thus focused on finite subjectivity, the modern reflection on person followed a path divorced from that of Trinitarian theology. Whereas the latter dealt with person in God, the former occupied itself with a human person no longer seen in constitutive relation with God. Here again, the separation of theological and anthropological reflections on person indicates a failure to take Christology sufficiently into account. Insofar as both the traditional, theological-metaphysical reflection on person and modern philosophy lack adequate Christological grounds, they display weaknesses that mirror one another. Modernity did not deal with the Trinitarian question aside from projecting into the Trinity the understanding of God as subject, and Christian theology did not develop an adequate anthropology.

48. Heidegger attempts to correct this perception of the subject, as do many postmodern thinkers.

At this point, both theological-metaphysical and anthropological reflections on person find themselves at an impasse. On the one hand, there are elucidations of the meaning of person that rightly want to preserve its metaphysical dimension. On the other hand, there are those that try to take stock of the modern emphasis on the subject and wish, *mutatis mutandis*, to integrate into the theological notion of person the four elements that characterize the modern perception of human subjectivity: awareness, freedom, time (as history), and interpersonal relations. These approaches, the one tending toward a metaphysical account and the other based on conscious subjectivity, seem to be running on parallel tracks. In addition, a renewed and deeper approach to Scripture has brought other authors to emphasize the indispensability of kenotic love and reciprocity for an adequate understanding of both divine and human persons. It is at this juncture that the category of gift becomes relevant for an account of person, since this category seems to be the crossroads where these three paths—the scriptural, the theological-metaphysical, and the modern philosophical-anthropological—meet.

Person as Gift

Within the context of an elucidation of the meaning of person, "gift" refers neither to a subcategory of the transcendental good, as if gift were simply an instance of the good's self-diffusiveness, nor to a philosophical category, as if gift were only a particular being whose fundamental raison d'être was to be an object that a giver and receiver could freely exchange. If gift merely flows forth from the good as such, the personal and epistemological dimensions of gift are lost—or at least it is difficult to account for them. Likewise, if gift is reduced to an object, it loses its metaphysical nature; that is, it no longer refers to being as such. There is, of course, a sense in which giving and receiving witness to the self-diffusive nature of the good, and a sense in which a gift is a being that can be exchanged—like presents given to honor someone. These partial senses, however, reach their full meaning only in light of Christ. Gift, properly understood, is a Christological category that illuminates God's tripersonal being, man's personal nature, and the meaning of being as such. It is from this Christological center that we will be able to elucidate the meaning of gift and its intrinsic unity with the mystery of person.

Contemplating Christ, we can say that gift refers to that mysterious property of personal being according to which the person has his own being, though not from himself: what is most his own has its origin in another. "What the Father gives," says Hans Urs von Balthasar, explaining the meaning of divine Sonship revealed in Christ, "is to be a self (*Selbstsein*), freedom, and thus autonomy, but an autonomy that can be understood only as owning-oneself-as-borne-in-another (*Übereignung*)."[49] This is most properly the case for the Trinitarian persons, each of whose personal existence is totally relative to that of the other two. The paradox of the gift—that is, of being oneself only by eternally having given all of one's being to another and owning all of oneself in another, in short, being for another and in another—characterizes not only the Father and the Son ("All mine are yours, and yours are mine," Jn 17:10) but also the Holy Spirit ("He will glorify me, for he will take what is mine and declare it to you. All that the Father has is mine; therefore I said that he will take what is mine and declare it to you," Jn 16:14–15). Through Christ, therefore, we are brought to see that the being of each of the divine persons is their eternally ordered donation, reception, and reciprocation of God's one being-love. Every divine person is gift in being sheer relation to the correlative persons.[50]

49. Hans Urs von Balthasar, *Unless You Become Like This Child*, trans. Erasmo Leiva-Merikakis (San Francisco: Ignatius Press, 1991), 44, translation modified.

50. Christian revelation suggests that the beginning is triune love (1 Jn 4:8, 4:16) that is coextensive with being (Ex 3:14; Jn 8:28). This coextensiveness means that it is inadequate to think that God is first eternal, simple, perfect, and self-identical being (*ipsum esse subsistens*) and then that he is love (*caritas*), or that he first is and then loves. Rather, God's being is a perfect act as triune love, and this triune love is what being is. To think of divine love without being or of divine being before love is to anthropomorphize the beginning without beginning that God is. The first separation (love without being) understands love sentimentally as sheer intimacy and asks of history the impossible task of either constituting being or sustaining it in existence. The latter (being before love) reduces love to an effect of the will and, since truth is a transcendental property of being, also separates truth from love. When being is placed before love in this way, the subsequent identification of being and love (as willing) tends to transform God into an incomprehensible, absolute, and arbitrary will. How can the claim of being and love's coextensiveness be upheld? Only by Christ's revelation, which sets before our gaze the inexhaustible mystery that the eternal *being* of God is love precisely because the Father of Jesus Christ is the fount of all divinity and, as Father, eternally is so only in relation with the Son and the Spirit. In Christ we discover that the

Christ, who reveals the coextensiveness of being and love, allows us to see that man's being (*ousia*) consists in his having what is most proper to himself, that is, his own substance—in Greek, *ousia* means the inalienable property without which one is not oneself—as received from and given over to another.[51] Additionally, in Christ we discover that the human being, who is created in Christ, is given to be himself (to be a child) only through the gift of self.[52] Creation in time introduces into the structure of human being a diastasis between man's being and its actualization in freedom: on the one hand, the receiving of himself from and the giving of himself to another determine his very being (man is himself, and he is himself as inevitably oriented to his divine origin and to others); on the other hand, this very being is in constant need of actualization (in freedom, man has to accept the gift of himself and reciprocate it). Gift therefore indicates the way one enjoys the being that one is, in the case of God, or the being that one has, in the case of man.[53]

Gift, in retaining the scriptural and metaphysical dimensions of person, goes beyond simply reiterating in new terms the twofold connotation of relation. The category of gift is indeed capable of indicating both the directionality of relation (and hence the dynamic proper to love) and the state of being in relation. Yet it also deepens our understanding of relation. With regard to relation's directionality, gift expresses the mystery

Father never holds on to divinity (love-being) for himself. Rather, beyond any dialectics of freedom and necessity, the Father is always the perfect and total gift of self without remainder to the Son, and with and through him to the Spirit. Because God is eternal, this also means that the Father's giving (his begetting of the Son) is coincident with his receiving of the Son's gratuitous response, which is fruitful in the Holy Spirit. This beautiful mystery entails both that the Son and Spirit share the same being and that they have it differently. Every divine person, therefore, is "itself" only inasmuch as it is for the others and in the others. For the clearest available elucidation of this issue, see Hans Urs von Balthasar, *Theo-logic: Theological Logical Theory*, vol. 2, *Truth of God*, trans. Adrian J. Walker (San Francisco: Ignatius Press, 2004). See also Hilary of Poitiers, *De Trin.*, bk. 9, no. 61; CCSL 62A.

51. Plato, *Meno* 72B; Aristotle, *Met.* 1038b25–28, 1039a1–3.

52. What is the case for human beings is also valid, albeit in a lesser degree, for the subhuman. See von Balthasar, *Theo-logic*, 1:61–78.

53. A satisfactory account of the coextensiveness of being and love in the human being requires elucidating the meaning of gender and the different ways in which man, as male and female, is called to participate in the giving of himself. I approach this topic in "God Opens His Love to Man: The Family as the Human Path to Communion with God," *Anthropotes* 31, no. 1 (2015): 125–62.

of personal being as posited by another: the Son as posited by the Father, the Spirit by the Father and the Son, and the Father as the one who is made perfect by the Son and the Spirit—man as created and redeemed by God in Christ and hence belonging to him in the communion of the Church, body of Christ. It is also the case that the gift of the person regards the permanence of the relation constituting those who are bound by it. In this twofold sense, to see the mystery of person in terms of gift is to retrieve and confirm the metaphysical category of relation. Additionally, gift indicates more clearly than the term "relation" the unity proper to those who are in relation, which is one of indwelling ("that they may be one, even as we are one," Jn 17:11). The giver is in the receiver and vice versa without this indwelling entailing the dissolution of its members. Person-gift therefore renders more explicit the truth that to be a person is to be from, for, and in another.[54] Furthermore, along with securing the scriptural and metaphysical senses of person, gift is also able to integrate the positive elements of modern subjectivity without absorbing its negative presuppositions.

The category of gift can help us integrate a proper sense of "selfhood" into the understanding of the human person in three different respects. The first recognizes that because the created gift is totally given, it is given to itself. "Man … is the only creature on earth which God willed for itself (*propter seipsam*)" (*GS*, no. 24). Giving a gift to itself, so that it can be "for itself," requires that the giver posit a conscious self with the capacity to be aware of the giving, of the giver, and of itself as given. Gift in this sense not only includes rationality but also brings awareness and self-awareness

54. A comprehensible misunderstanding normally arises here, namely, that of thinking that sheer relativity entails the dissolution of self. If we look at Christ, we see that this is not the case: receiving all from the Father and doing only his will, being for every man (*GS*, no. 22), does not mean that Christ's person-gift is pure relativity without "self." He receives everything in himself (Jn 5:26), and this "everything" is to be a free self that owns itself in another. To be free—to be for oneself, which is an essential aspect of what it means to be a person—is to be given to be oneself as the (total) gift of oneself to another (beyond any dialectics of necessity and freedom), first to God, the original giver, and then, in that reciprocation to God, to every man. This is why Christ's person is life (Jn 1:3), why he can dispose of his life as his own, and why he can dispose of it only by giving it without remainder: "No one takes it from me, but I lay it down of my own accord. I have power to lay it down, and I have power to take it again" (Jn 10:18).

to the forefront. More importantly, it accounts for these in light of the self's constitutive relation to the original giver. To be given to oneself, to be a "self," is therefore to be able to perceive the inexhaustible whole that one is, to perceive that one is a unique, unrepeatable whole in relation to the generous giver. This awareness of one's own wholeness arises precisely because one is in constitutive relation to the original giver and not because one can fully grasp one's own being (or others', for that matter). In this way, the category of gift allows us to retrieve a nonconceptualistic, nontechnological understanding of reason and knowing, since, seeing beings as given (not as data) by a generous and paternal origin, one avoids the risk either of thinking that human language is a perfect expression of divine language (as in Hegel) or of considering reality to be a heap of fragments that can be manipulated at will (as in a technological epistemology devoid of wonder). That the person-gift is given to itself, to be for itself, discloses both the rationality of the person—understood here as both awareness and self-awareness—and that this rationality is a participation in a constitutive dialogue that precedes one's own existence. Rationality—that is, wonder-filled awareness of the meaning of beings and self-awareness of oneself as gift—is a seeing in being-seen.[55]

In the second respect, we see that to be given to oneself is to be placed at one's own disposal, that is, to be free. The modern conception of freedom as self-determination is inadequate because it forgets man's

55. Rationality, as the confirmation that the person is given to himself in order to participate in the dialogue that God is, also offers the ultimate justification for understanding prayer as the utmost consciousness of oneself. Prayer, in other terms, is the (loving) awareness of one's constitutive dependence. "Life," says Luigi Giussani, "expresses itself... as consciousness of the relationship with he who made it, and prayer is the realization that in 'this' very moment, life is 'made.' Devout wonder, respect, loving subjection are all contained in this act of awareness: this is the soul of prayer. Reality perceived as fascination (*fascino*) is the very first level of this mystical attitude, which is the most natural to man, the most elementary aspect of our awareness." Giussani continues, "Prayer is not a separate act. Rather, it realizes the primary dimension of every action. The act of praying will be necessary to train ourselves to such a consciousness of every action. For this reason, the height of prayer is not ecstasy, that is, such a profound consciousness of the depths that one loses the sense of the ordinary. Rather, it is seeing the depths as if they were everyday things." *At the Origin of the Christian Claim*, trans. Viviane Hewitt (Montreal: McGill-Queen's University Press, 1998), 90. Jesus's prayer, says Ratzinger, is the true origin of the term "Son." Joseph Ratzinger, *Jesus of Nazareth: From the Baptism in the Jordan to the Transfiguration*, trans. Adrian J. Walker (New York: Doubleday, 2007), 344.

creatureliness, not because it claims that man determines himself to action. Our reflection on person as gift allows us to deepen this claim. That being given to oneself is to be at one's own disposal means, of course, that the human being is not simply confined to the created world, to his own bodiliness (or to his limited way of knowing). For man, we must affirm two things at once: because the soul is the form of the body, he cannot be himself without his body, yet he is not identical with his body. If his bodiliness (and hence nature) were to perfectly encompass his being, he would not be able to oppose natural instincts and would, in the end, be nothing more than the outcome of fate or biological (or cosmic) necessity. But even as he transcends this necessity, man's bodiliness entails that his being free is not represented well in terms of independence. Man, for example, still depends on the air he breathes to keep on living. Instead, the account of person in terms of gift allows us to express the nature of freedom, of man's being for himself, through the paradox of beginning.

Man can be a beginning: he can set beginnings in place; he can take initiative. This is a paradox that, like every paradox, brings together a continuity and a discontinuity. To begin something is to posit what was not there before; beginning as such is a discontinuity, a newness, that for the human being is also a continuity. This point may be clearer if we think of the mystery of birth: the child is a new beginning and yet is the fruit of a parental love that preceded him. Man's initiative is real—that is, it originates in him as something new—precisely because it arises out of his prior being given. In other words, man's own beginning is given to him, and if this were not the case, he would not be able to begin anything (or to give birth). To put it more formally, I alluded above to the mystery of person in terms of the person's being an individual in a species and being a unique singular. Individuality regarded his being, or substance (as gift), and singularity regarded his being himself in relation to the original giver. It is this distinction between the individual (substance) and the person—or between substance and subject, to speak with Hegel—that helps us elucidate freedom's paradox. If man were simply personal singularity, he would be the beginning without beginning; that is, he would be God and not man. Yet if he were simply an individual instantiation of his nature, he would not be able to take initiative, to posit any genuine beginning. He, again, would be fully circumscribed by his finite nature, and procreation would be just another case of reproduction. But man is an individual in order to be a person—that is, in order to take the initiative to respond from himself to the original and ever-preceding giver—and hence to fully participate in the divine language.[56] He would not be able to respond gratuitously if his answer could not come from himself. In fact, gratuity is a quality of human action that reflects the original (divine) initiative. That man is at his own disposal means, therefore, that with the gift of his own self comes the permanent possibility of positing new beginnings, the most important of which is the ongoing reception of the gift of himself. This reception, as such, is the gratuitous response to the original giver. To posit new beginnings, to be free, is the fulfillment of the original gift that man is. It is in this paradox of the beginning that we see that man is given to himself in order to be a person.[57]

Lastly, along with awareness and freedom, the perception of person in terms of gift integrates selfhood by rescuing bodiliness from opaque, mechanistic extension and restoring it to the category of organism. This restoration, however, is not simply the reproposal of a lost anthropology. After the modern rejection of interiority, retrieving bodiliness through the category of gift requires that one perceive it more clearly as an integral part of the language in which man is created and in which he is called to participate. With this we do not simply mean that the person needs the body to respond to God's call, and that all of his somatic structure is informed by language, but also that the body is an integral part of language because the body itself is a sacrament of the person. In this way we confirm and secure the perception of *mysterion* (sacrament) that *Gaudium et spes* retrieved for theological reflection. Man is created in Christ as male and female so that he can enjoy at his own level the dimensions proper to love: filiality, nuptiality, paternity/maternity, and communion (which includes brotherhood and friendship). In light of gift, we can thus indicate that the body, sacrament of the person, brings together anew the person-

56. Claude Bruaire, *L'être et l'esprit* (Paris: PUF, 1983), 75–83.

57. As Aquinas would say following Aristotle, the first act is for the sake of the second operation. Aristotle, *De anima* 2.1; Thomas Aquinas, *Summa contra Gentiles* (*SCG*) 1.45.6; *SCG* 3.113.1; *ST* I, q. 105, a. 5; *ST* I-II, q. 3, a. 2.

al and the substantial dimensions of man and hence reminds man of his own being-gift and of his call to be a person through the gift of himself. The body places man in history and keeps him bound to it, and yet it does not make man a purely passive entity in the flow of history, because through the body man's fulfillment takes place. Man's incarnate freedom is moved by other beings (themselves also gift) to find its fulfillment in another. This fulfillment, which our corporeal existence allows us to see, is not merely the appeasing of a natural thirst but personal fruitfulness. The gift of self to another, while representing the desired unity with the other, brings into existence another being who will also be an agent of generosity.[58]

When we see these three senses in which the category of gift restores some of the elements of modern subjectivity to the understanding of person, it is perhaps easier to realize why autonomy and dependence are not dialectical opposites. Positively stated, we see why autonomy is being for oneself as being for another and why dependence is the being for another that makes one be. Viewed through the category of gift, freedom cannot be interpreted as random arbitrariness, and dependence cannot be perceived as pantheism in disguise. The eccentric nature of the inseity of the human person, which rests on the identity of being and love revealed by Christ, does not eliminate the integrity of the human person. On the contrary, it allows him to be a free and conscious self who shares in the fruitfulness of God, the beginning without beginning.

58. The perception of man's embodied (self-)awareness and freedom—his being given to himself in order to be a person, to posit new beginnings, and thus to participate in the mystery of his own birth—strengthens further both the difference and the similarity between God's tripersonal being and man's being a person. This is not only because of the real distinction between man's being and his essence—which, as we know, cannot be found in God—or the fact that the divine persons' self-disposal, their being themselves in being for another, is absolute, whereas man's self-disposal takes place in time and is limited. It is also because God calls man to be a person by introducing him, through gratuitous incorporation into his Son's risen body, into the eternal dialogue that God is. The "not" being a person like God is, once again, a matter of relation with God. Further, man's positing new beginnings, as in the fruitfulness of marriage, is a participation in God's creativity. Here again, the difference between the way God is tripersonal and the way man is personal in a communion of persons is determined not so much by man's finitude as by his imaging God, that is, by his being in relation with him. Of course, God is not fruitful in the way man is fruitful, but sonship, communion, fatherhood (and motherhood) are primordially said of God and, in light of him, of man.

The paradox of autonomy and dependence is not freed from a logic of dialectic opposition until we realize the historical dimension of gift more deeply. Pondering the mystery of the person in terms of gift, the distinction between individuality and singularity both allows and requires that the person posit new beginnings and participate in the beginning that he is, that is to say, in his own begetting. As *Gaudium et spes* 24 indicates and as I have articulated here, this assumption of the gift of self in freedom entails a gratuitous response, a lived belonging to the original source by means of the historical gift of oneself to others. In light of Christ, we can see more clearly that the human person's historicity is not generic but has a meaning unique to each person. To better grasp this uniqueness, I conclude this reflection on the person as gift by recalling two other terms: vocation and mission. Being a human person means that, in addition to being called to exist and to dwell in time as a unique response to this call, one is destined to participate in the eternal dialogue of love that God is. This dialogue is ultimately a work of the Spirit of Christ, the one sent by the Father (Jn 5–7). Reflecting the work of the Spirit and Son, the call that constitutes man as a person is double-pronged: it has a permanent origin in God and is thus a *vocation*, and it is given as a task to be carried out in time, rendering it also a *mission*. In this sense, vocation and mission are the two terms that best account for the historical existence of the person-gift. Because Christ's personal identity is in an analogous way best characterized in terms of mission, as some have indicated, the human being reaches his true personal singularity when the constitutive relation with God becomes explicit participation in Christ's mission to let the glory of the Father be seen ("Quicumque Christum sequitur, Hominem perfectum, et ipse magis homo fit," *GS*, no. 41).[59]

Christ's revelation offers an elucidation of person in terms of gift that brings together the theological-metaphysical, the scriptural, and the modern senses of person. This synthesis allows us to appropriate more deeply the mystery of man's constitutive freedom, which modernity so treasures,

59. For a full development of this thesis, see Hans Urs von Balthasar, *Theo-drama: Theological Dramatic Theory*, vol. 2, *The Dramatis Personae: Man in God,* and vol. 3, *The Dramatis Personae: The Person in Christ,* trans. Graham Harrison (San Francisco: Ignatius Press, 1990–92); Giussani, *Origin of the Christian Claim.*

without embracing modern atheistic presuppositions. Freedom's paradoxical nature—described here as the belonging together of individuality and singularity, of substance and person, of autonomy and dependence, and of filiation and unoriginated beginning—does not condemn the human being to conflictual relations with God and others, precisely because God calls each human being to participate through Christ in the eternal dialogue that he is. God, a jealous lover and a merciful Father, can receive from man only a gratuitous response. This response is a genuine initiative only when, through the Spirit, man speaks the Father's love as other from him, that is, when he becomes in the Logos a word that says only what the Father is and, thus abiding with the Father, remains ever himself.

3

Sincerum sui ipsius donum

The Trinitarian Ground of *Gaudium et spes*'s Anthropology

ADRIAN J. WALKER

Triune Actuality

According to *Gaudium et spes* 24, "man cannot find himself fully apart from a sincere gift of his very own self."[1] This is because man is made to participate in the "union of the divine persons," which contains the original paradigm of the sincere self-gift.[2] It is on this original paradigm of self-gift in God that I focus in this essay.

Why should it matter that there is self-gift in God? What is at stake? Imagine what would happen if the Father, in generating the Son, did not give himself to the only-begotten, or if his generative act did not engage the whole of his self, his ipseity, his "I am who I am." Would he not fail to communicate the whole of his deity to the Son? But if the Father failed to communicate the entire Godhead to the Son, he would also fail to pos-

For Martin Bieler. The following account of the triune life owes much to his masterful account of Trinitarian theology in light of the Father's innascibility. See his *Freiheit als Gabe: Ein schöpfungstheologischer Entwurf* (Freiburg: Herder, 1991), 166–209.

1. Second Vatican Council, *Gaudium et Spes*, Pastoral Constitution on the Church in the Modern World, December 7, 1965, no. 24: "hominem ... plene seipsum invenire non posse nisi per sincerum sui ipsius donum." This and all other translations mine.

2. "Immo Dominus Iesus, quando Patrem orat ut 'omnes unum sint ... sicut et nos unum sumus' (Jn 17:21–22), prospectus praebens humanae rationi impervios, aliquam similitudinem innuit inter unionem personarum divinarum et unionem filiorum Dei in veritate et caritate."

sess himself fully as the principle he is. He would remain in potency, either wholly or partly, to his own principiality. But if "the Principle" were only imperfectly "principle," then what comes first in the order of reality would not be superabundant fullness (i.e., would not be actuality), but lack and want. How could such an imperfectly principial principle have the wherewithal even to create, let alone to beget a co-equal Son?[3] The eternal generation of the Son is the a priori, eternal actuality in which all becoming must participate in order to be actual *as* becoming: "without him, not a single thing came to be" (Jn 1:3). What is at stake in saying that there is self-gift in God? The answer is the nature of actuality in itself. I spend the rest of this section fleshing out this claim.

We wrongly tend to think of God as an exceptional phenomenon that tells us nothing about the nature of being as such. But this is to get things backward. If anything is an exception, it is us. The real question is not whether God exists, but how anything can exist other than God.[4] In any case, even if the universe suddenly relapsed into nonentity, God would continue to exist undiminished. Consequently, if we wanted to get the fullest possible picture of what being *qua* being "looks like," as it is in itself, we would have to see God as he is in himself. Does not Aquinas tell us that the divine essence is identical with the subsistent plenitude of what he calls the *actus essendi*, the very beingness of being?[5] God, then, is the first principle of all reality who guarantees a "place" for actuality

3. This is not a deduction of the Trinity by unaided reason, but an unfolding of the implications of the scriptural teaching concerning the eternity and necessity of the generation of the Son. Just as God cannot fail to be, the Father cannot fail to generate the Son; the two necessities stand and fall together: "Ad quintum dicendum quod necessarium dicitur aliquid per se, et per aliud. Per aliud quidem dupliciter. Uno modo, sicut per causam agentem et cogentem, et sic necessarium dicitur quod est violentum. Alio modo, sicut per causam finalem, sicut dicitur aliquid esse necessarium in his quae sunt ad finem, inquantum sine hoc non potest esse finis, vel bene esse. Et neutro istorum modorum divina generatio est necessaria, quia Deus non est propter finem, neque coactio cadit in ipsum. Per se autem dicitur aliquid necessarium, quod non potest non esse. Et sic Deum esse est necessarium. Et hoc modo patrem generare filium est necessarium." Thomas Aquinas, *Summa theologiae* (*ST*) I, q. 41, a. 2, ad. 5.

4. Although I do not directly address this question here, the reflection on the Trinity that follows can be read as an implicit answer to it.

5. Augustine agrees: "Et ideo sola est incommutabilis substantia vel essentia, quae Deus est, cui profecto ipsum esse, unde essential nominata est, maxime et verissime competit." *De Trinitate* V, ii, 3.

to realize its entire nature all at once, before any entity woven together with act and potency, essence and *esse*, form and matter, and the like, can participate in it. Now, God necessarily does this as Father, Son, and Holy Spirit. If God failed to be Trinity, he would also fail to be the entire simple, complete, and subsistent fullness of actuality in himself, and would thus fall short of his own role as first principle. In this sense, we cannot contemplate being *qua* being apart from the union of Father, Son, and Holy Spirit, whose circumincession defines the concrete *Gestalt* of the divine being. "For in that Trinity," Augustine writes, "is the highest origin of all things, and the most perfect beauty, and the most blessed delight. Those three, then, are both seen (*videntur*) to be determined one by the other and infinite in themselves."[6]

The point I am driving at, then, is this: if God guarantees actuality a place to be fully itself—to be at its "being-most"—he cannot do so while bypassing his own Trinitarian *Gestalt*. We need to avoid the trap of placing the divine actuality entirely on the side of the divine essence, as if the three persons, and their circumincession, were accidental to its act-character. This is to forget that the divine actuality is manifested only in the interplay between unity and trinity in God. As Maximus the Confessor puts it, "the Triad is truly a Monad, because this is the form in which [the Triad] has essential being (*esti*), and the Monad is truly a Triad, because this is the form in which [the Monad] subsists hypostatically (*hyphestêken*)."[7]

If, therefore, we wanted to look into the very heart of actuality, realizing itself as such, we would have to behold that privileged "moment" (which of course is not a moment at all, but eternal life) when the Father begets the Son and, in begetting him, gives him to co-spirate the Holy Spirit—the moment Augustine describes in the following passage from book XV of his *De Trinitate*:

6. "In illa enim Trinitate summa origo est rerum omnium et perfectissima pulchritudo et beatissima delectatio. Itaque illa tria et a se invicem determinari videntur et in se infinita sunt." Augustine, *De Trinitate* VI, v, 12. Within the triune *Gestalt*, the Word plays a role corresponding to that of form. He is a "forma simplex et simpliciter aequalis ei de quo est, et cui mirabiliter coaeterna est." Augustine, *De Trinitate* XV, xvi, 24.

7. Maximus Confessor, *Ambiguum* 1 (PG 91:1036c).

The Father alone, in fact, is not from another, and so he alone is called "unbegotten." The Son, however, is born of the Father, while the Holy Spirit proceeds principially from the Father and, the Father giving [this] without any interval of time, commonly from both.[8]

In another, longer passage from the same book, Augustine observes that the Spirit's simultaneous procession *principaliter a Patre* and *communiter ab utroque* underscores his identity as "the common gift" belonging equally to both begetter and begotten:

The reason I have added "principially" is that we find that the Holy Spirit proceeds from the Son as well. But this, too, is something the Father has given him. Not, of course, as if he did not yet exist or did not possess [what he was to receive]. Rather, whatever he has given to the only-begotten Word, [the Father] has given in the very act of generating him. It follows, then, that he has generated [the Word] in such a way that the common Gift should proceed from him, too, and that the Holy Spirit should be of both.[9]

8. "Pater enim solus non est de alio, ideo solus appellatur ingenitus.... Filius autem de Patre natus est: et Spiritus Sanctus de Patre principaliter, et ipso sine ullo temporis intervallo dante, communiter de utroque procedit." Augustine, *De Trinitate* XV, xxvi, 47.

9. "Ideo autem addidi, Principaliter, quia et de Filio Spiritus Sanctus procedere reperitur. Sed hoc quoque illi Pater dedit, non iam exsistenti et nondum habenti: sed quidquid unigenito Verbo dedit, gignendo dedit. Sic ergo eum genuit, ut etiam de illo Donum commune procederet, et Spiritus Sanctus spiritus esset amborum." Augustine, *De Trinitate* XV, xvii, 29. In this sense, the Council of Florence was perfectly right to declare the substantial equivalence of the Augustinian *filioque* and the Eastern *dia tou hyiou*. When an Eastern theologian like Maximus the Confessor denies that the Son is the *aitia*, or "cause," of the Holy Spirit, he is not repudiating the substance of the *filioque*, but offering a key to its orthodox interpretation. Like Augustine, the Confessor knows that the absolute first principle, the Father of Jesus Christ, does not regard his firstness (which is what Maximus means by "causality" here) as a treasure to be clung to jealously, but shares it unreservedly with the Son. Maximus's concern, then, is simply to underscore the extent to which the Son spontaneously makes himself totally transparent to the Father as the unoriginated origin both of himself, the Son, and of the Holy Spirit. Nevertheless, the Confessor is no less aware that the Son must manifest the Father's primal causality *as unstinting personal gift* (i.e., the very gift hypostatized in the person of the Holy Spirit). The Son is accordingly never more transparent to the Father's firstness than when he, the Son, participates coequally in the Father's active spiration of the *Pneuma*. It goes without saying that the Son does not exercise this undiminished participation in the same mode as the Father, but in the mode proper to himself as the consubstantial image, Word, and Son; hence the *dia*, which reflects the unique character of the only-begotten as the "middle person" in the Godhead. Cf. Maximus Confessor, *Opuscula Theologica et Polemica*, 10 (PG 91:136a–b), where he writes concerning the "Roman Fathers" and Cyril that they "knew that the Father is the one cause of Son and Spirit, of the former by begetting and of the latter by

According to Scripture, the Holy Spirit is the eschatological gift that Christ, exalted to heavenly glory, receives from his Father to pour out upon all flesh (cf. Acts 2:33). Yet the exalted Christ is not administering an alien good when he bestows this gift on humanity, since, as Scripture also teaches, the gift is nothing other than the charity that he, the Son, has in common with his Father.[10] Christ's communication of the Spirit to us manifests *ad extra* his full involvement in the eternal production of the Third Person *ad intra*:

> But this is a way of teaching that [the Spirit] proceeds from both. For the Son himself says "He proceeds from the Father." And when he had risen from the dead and appeared to his Apostles, he breathed on them and said "receive the Holy Spirit," so that he might show that [the Spirit] proceeds from him as well.[11]

Now, the Son's involvement in the production of the Holy Spirit is significant for this discussion because it sheds light on the character of the Father's principiality. It shows that he is never first principle apart from, or prior to, his communion with the only-begotten Son, which it is the Spirit's privilege to personify. This brings us to next section of my essay, where I propose that the Son's co-spiration of the Third Person places communion at the heart of the Father's principiality and, therefore, at the core of actuality as such.

---

procession, but [they affirm the "from the Son"] in order to show the going-forth through [the Son] and in this way to set forth the conjunction and invariance of the essence."

10. "Dilectio igitur quae ex Deo est et Deus est, proprie Spiritus Sanctus est, per quem diffunditur in cordibus nostris Dei caritas, per quam nos tota inhabitet Trinitas. Quocirca rectissime Spiritus Sanctus, cum sit Deus, vocatur etiam Donum Dei. Quod Donum proprie quid nisi caritas intellegenda est, quae perducit ad Deum, et sine qua quodlibet aliud donum Dei non perducit ad Deum?" (Augustine, *De Trinitate* XV, xviii, 32). The gift-character of the Spirit does not reduce him to the status of a thing that is given without his own involvement in the giving. On the contrary, he is the gift that gives itself, and therefore he who lets himself be given in order to express both his concord with the Father and the Son and their concord with each other: "Nec quia illi dant, ipse datur, ideo minor est illis. Ita enim datur sicut Donum Dei, ut etiam se ipsum det sicut Deus. Non enim dici potest non esse suae potestatis, de quo dictum est: Spiritus ubi vult spirat: Et apud Apostolum quod iam supra commemoravi: Omnia haec operatur unus atque idem Spiritus, dividens propria unicuique prout vult. Non est illic conditio dati et dominatio dantium, sed concordia dati et dantium" (Augustine, *De Trinitate* XV, xix, 36).

11. "De utroque autem procedere sic docetur; quia ipse Filius ait: De Patre procedit. Et cum resurrexisset a mortuis et apparuisset discipulis suis, insufflavit et ait: Accipite Spiritum Sanctum, ut eum etiam de se procedere ostenderet" (Augustine, *De Trinitate* XV, xviii, 32).

Societas Dilectionis

As we learn by contemplating the order of the cosmos, actuality is both a proper good and a common one at the same time.[12] The principle of this actuality must therefore guarantee both dimensions at once; if not, he will fail to guarantee the a priori completion of act. For if the true a priori is not the completion of act, but its deficiency, how can act be *absolutely* prior to potency? Moreover, without this absolute priority, how can the divine principle suffice to account for the very existence of potency or of matter *ex nihilo*? A first principle worthy of the name must guarantee that the interplay of the proper and the common always belongs to actuality in its absolute firstness. Such a principle, therefore, must possess actuality while sharing it as well. Communion-in-actuality must define the shape of his principiality *ab initio*.

Now, in accordance with Nicene orthodoxy, the one who is principle cannot possess and share actuality in the requisite manner if there was ever a time when the Son was not. Unless this principle is eternal-

12. *Societas dilectionis* is my adaptation of a phrase from Augustine, *De Trinitate* IV, ix, 12: *dilectionis societatem*. According to Aristotle, the very existence of the cosmos as an ordered whole depends on the fact that the first aspiration of all cosmic entities—considered singly and collectively—is to imitate the divine goodness. Things accomplish this by enjoying their respective proper perfections in the very act of diffusing them, and vice versa. Consider the following passage: "It is now time, then, to inquire in which way the nature of the whole has the good and best, either as something separate, existing just as itself on its own, or by reason of the order [within it]. Or is it in both ways, as in the case of an army? For the good (*to eu*) of the army is in its order and is its general. Indeed, it is principally the general, since he is not on account of the order, but the order is on account of him. Now, all things are set together in a certain order. They are not, however, ordered in the same way, but there are swimming things, and flying things, and growing things. But neither are things so constituted that the one has nothing in relation to the other. The contrary is the case, since all things are set in order together in relation to one, but [it is] as in a household, [where] the free members have the least permission to do any random thing, but all or most of what they do follows a prescribed order, whereas the slaves and the beasts make but a small contribution to the common good, while much of what they do is at random. For nature is a source of this kind for each of them. I mean, for example, that all things necessarily end up decomposing. And the other things in which all commune in view of the whole are like this as well" (Aristotle, *Met.* XII, 10:1075a11–25). This contemplation of cosmic order is only deepened by the knowledge that the primal aspiration of cosmic entities is itself a (receptively structured) response to, and a participation in, the creative self-gift of the Divinity. On my reading, Aristotle already implicitly glimpses God's creative act.

ly and intrinsically "the God and Father of our Lord Jesus Christ" (Eph 1:3), he has not yet communicated the whole of his deity, and if he has not yet communicated the whole of his deity, he can never have actually possessed the whole of it in the first place. Now, it is at this point that Augustine reenters the scene to carry the Nicene teaching to its logical conclusion. He does this by, among other things, highlighting the interplay of the principial and the common in the procession of the Third Person. This interplay is the irrefutable proof that the first principle is always entirely and unreservedly Father; it is the definitive confirmation that he has committed himself once and for all to communion with the Son, without the slightest temptation to take back what he has given.

I discuss the ontological implications of this commitment toward the end of this essay. For the time being, however, consider the following analogy. In offering the covenant to Israel, God commits himself to being nameable as the God of Abraham, the God of Isaac, and the God of Jacob. This gracious offer is a temporal analogue of what the Father eternally does when he begets the Son *in divinis* and so commits himself to being nameable—to being named through and through—as the Father of this Son. If the covenant involves God in a sincere self-commitment that reveals his sovereign freedom rather than compromising it, will not the covenant's intradivine prototype (i.e., the Father's generative act) involve a self-commitment that is infinitely more revelatory of his sovereign "I AM!" precisely because it is infinitely more complete and definitive than the covenant could ever be? Could there ever be a time when the Father was anything but the God and Father of our Lord Jesus Christ? Moreover, if the Holy Spirit is the bond of this intradivine covenant, does it not make sense that he should proceed principially from the Father, who initiates the covenantal binding, but also commonly *ab utroque*, since the covenant in question here must be bilateral in its very initiation if there was never a time when the Son was not? Let us highlight this bilaterality with another text from Augustine's *De Trinitate*:

> There is absolutely no way in which either Father or Son can be said to be such by himself alone, since the former is always and inseparable with the Father, and the latter is always and inseparably with the Son, not so that both may be Father or

both Son, but because, the one always being into the other in reciprocity, neither is ever by himself alone: *semper in invicem, neuter solus.*[13]

Now, Augustine clearly uses the expression *in invicem* to characterize the circumincession of Father and Son. But the expression also carries the unmistakable connotation of a vis-à-vis starting simultaneously from two different points of view. This vis-à-vis is characterized by what Scholastic theology calls an "opposition of respects," in that each faces the other from an opposite direction. This opposition, moreover, is characterized by a certain asymmetry because the Son receives the divine substance from the Father, rather than the other way around. Nevertheless, the Father's commitment to communion is such that the Son cannot enact his self-reception without reciprocating that commitment vis-à-vis, which he does by participating fully in the Father's generative act, albeit in the mode of one receiving himself from his begetter. This participation culminates in the Son's reception of the authority to co-spirate the Spirit with the Father.

The foregoing suggests that the procession of the Word *per modum intellectus* involves Father and Son in a mutual, asymmetrical nuptial knowing, in which both truth and goodness, intellect and will, are always fully present in their circumincessive interplay: "No one knows who the Son is except the Father, and who the Father is except the Son" (Lk 10:22). Note that Jesus pronounces these words while rejoicing before his Father in the Holy Spirit (cf. Lk 10:21). Christ's joy here is, perhaps, an irradiation of the splendor of the beautiful that pervades the interplay of the true and the good in his procession from the Father.

Now, amid enjoying their circumincessive vis-à-vis, Father and Son jointly communicate it to the Holy Spirit. The enjoyment of their "ineffable embrace," in other words, coincides with their enjoyment in giving over both the embrace and the fruition to the Spirit, so that he can embody both of these things in himself.[14] The Holy Spirit is thus both *condi-*

13. "Non invenitur quomodo dici possit aut Pater solus, aut Filius solus cum semper atque inseparabiliter, et ille cum Filio sit et ille cum Patre, non ut ambo sint Pater aut ambo Filius, sed quia semper in invicem neuter solus" (Augustine, *De Trinitate* VI, vii, 9).

14. "Ille igitur ineffabilis quidam complexus Patris et Imaginis non est sine perfruitione, sine caritate, sine gaudio" (Augustine, *De Trinitate* VI, x, 11).

lectio and *condilectus*, a mutual fruition and its undivided fruit, a personally subsistent charity whose fullness not only exceeds every opposition between what we call *eros* and *agape*, but also between joy and kenosis, enstasy and ecstasy, and the like:[15]

The Holy Spirit, therefore, is a common otherness (*commune aliquid*) belonging to the Father and the Son, though it is not easy to say what this reality is. Or let us say that he is consubstantial and coeternal communion itself. There would be no objection to calling this communion "friendship," if the term is fitting, but it is more aptly called "charity." And charity, for its part, is substance, because God is substance and "God is charity," as Scripture says.[16]

I conclude this section with a brief commentary on this inexhaustibly rich passage. The circumincession of Father and Son is not a purely formal interchangeability lacking any content beyond the (empty) structure of the *in invicem*. No, the entire space of their circumincessive vis-à-vis is filled up with a common theme, just as every good friendship is filled with common themes that friends find joy in talking about (or doing) together. In one sense, the theme that Father and Son enjoy together is simply the subsistent fullness of actuality itself. Their enjoyment is to realize together what Augustine calls the inexhaustibly "multiple simplicity or simple multiplicity" of the divine being.[17] In another sense, however, their theme is also their friendship, which, as in the case of human friendships, colors both the content of the theme (in this case, the inexhaustible richness of being) and the friends' mode of realizing it together. In a word, the Father and the Son co-realize the divine actuality in the

15. It is not anachronistic to find a foreshadowing of Richard of Saint Victor's *condilectus* doctrine in Augustine. For the Bishop of Hippo, in fact, the Holy Spirit is a kind of personal "with" *for* the Father and the Son. He gives them, in other words, a shared reference point so that they can be one principle with respect to him without sacrificing their mutuality, which is an abiding co-cause of their unity vis-à-vis the Spirit. Of course, the Spirit is not just *for* the Father and the Son, but *with* them as well: he is *simul substantia cum Patre et Filio* (Augustine, *De Trinitate* VI, vi, 7).

16. "Spiritus ergo Sanctus commune aliquid est Patris et Filii, quidquid illud est, aut ipsa communio consubstantialis et coaeterna; quae si amicitia convenienter dici potest, dicatur, sed aptius dicitur caritas; et haec quoque substantia, quia Deus substantia et Deus caritas, sicut scriptum est" (Augustine, *De Trinitate* VI, vi, 7).

17. "Deo autem hoc est esse quod est potentem esse aut iustum esse, aut sapientem esse et si quid de illa simplici multiplicitate vel multiplici simplicitate dixeris quo substantia eius significetur" (Augustine, *De Trinitate* VI, iv, 6).

mode of friendship, even as their friendship is essential to the actuality they realize.

To the extent that a good is truly common, it also "wants" to be appreciated in common. This common appreciation takes the form of communion or friendship, and such friendship is inherently fruitful. This is *a fortiori* true in the case of the Trinity, whose third member personifies the fruitfulness of the *communio* uniting the other two. The Spirit, then, performatively demonstrates that the common good *par excellence* (i.e., infinite actuality) never lacks the common appreciation due to it and vice versa; he shows that the *bonum commune* and the *communio personarum* are as inseparable within infinite being as the monad and triad within the divinity. The Spirit thus represents the quintessence of the entire deity, which is also the quintessence of the really real: the coincidence of actuality and communion-in-friendship. Put another way, he personifies the charity that is (divine) being and the being that is (divine) charity.[18] "[For] if the charity by which the Father loves the Son, and the Son loves the Father, ineffably demonstrates the communion of both, what is more

18. This suggests that love is above all a form of being in and as society, whose unity both causes difference and, in another sense, is caused by it. Is this account of charity as a form of society contradicted by Augustine's identification of love with will ("Nam quid est aliud caritas, quam voluntas?" Augustine, *De Trinitate* XV, xx, 38)? No, because divine will, for Augustine, is a shared fruition of the divine being: "Pater et Filius, non tantum aequalitate substantiae, sed etiam voluntate unum sunt" (*De Trinitate* IV, ix, 12). The will, understood as love, is anything but blind; it is the *eros* of knowing, an *eros* that shares in, and joins together, both the insight stored in the memory and the expression of that insight in the intellectual word: "Numquid dicturi sumus voluntatem nostram, quando recta est, nescire quid appetat, quid evitet? Porro si scit, profecto inest ei sua quaedam scientia, quae sine memoria et intellegentia esse non possit. An vero audiendus est quispiam dicens, caritatem nescire quid agat, quae non agit perperam? Sicut ergo inest intellegentia, inest dilectio illi memoriae principali, in qua invenimus paratum et reconditum ad quod cogitando possumus pervenire; quia et duo ista invenimus ibi, quando nos cogitando invenimus et intellegere aliquid et amare, quae ibi erant et quando inde non cogitabamus: et sicut inest memoria, inest dilectio huic intellegentiae quae cogitatione formatur; quod verbum verum sine ullius gentis lingua intus dicimus, quando quod novimus dicimus; nam nisi reminiscendo non redit ad aliquid, et nisi amando redire non curat nostrae cogitationis intuitus: ita dilectio quae visionem in memoria constitutam, et visionem cogitationis inde formatam quasi parentem prolemque coniungit, nisi haberet appetendi scientiam, quae sine memoria et intellegentia non potest esse, quid recte diligeret ignoraret" (Augustine, *De Trinitate* XV, xxi, 41). Note that the identification of charity with will (understood as a social "thirdness" linking mind and word) is itself relative to the identification of charity with the actuality of (spiritual) being *simpliciter*.

fitting than that 'charity' be given as a proper name to the One who is the Spirit common to both?"[19]

I thus return to the earlier point that a first principle worthy of the name must guarantee the simultaneity of the proper and the common within actuality. The Father fulfills this condition in the most consistent possible way. While remaining the unique principle in the divinity, he shares his principiality with the Son, communicating to him the authority to spirate the Third Person in his, the Father's, name.[20] The simplic-

19. "Et si caritas qua Pater diligit Filium, et Patrem diligit Filius, ineffabiliter communionem demonstrat amborum; quid convenientius quam ut ille dicatur caritas proprie, qui Spiritus est communis ambobus?" (Augustine, *De Trinitate* XV, xix, 37). For Augustine, God cannot be substance unless the substance he is is charity, but his substance cannot be charity unless the Holy Spirit has "charity" as his proper name: "Et ideo non amplius quam tria sunt: unus diligens eum qui de illo est, et unus diligens eum de quo est, et ipsa dilectio. Quae si nihil est, quomodo Deus dilectio est? Si non est substantia, quomodo Deus substantia est?" (Augustine, *De Trinitate* VI, vi, 7). Why does Augustine say this? The property of the Holy Spirit is to be the mutual charity common to both Father and Son: "Quia enim est communis ambobus, id vocatur ipse proprie quod ambo communiter" (Augustine, *De Trinitate* XV, xix, 37). If, however, the Spirit were not this common mutual charity—if we could not call him "charity" and mean his proper name—then the Father and Son would not commune in everything. Their being, affected by an uncommunicated residue, would both fail to coincide with charity and fall short of its own perfect simplicity. As it is, just the opposite is the case: "Qui Spiritus Sanctus secundum Scripturas sanctas, nec Patris solius est, nec Filii solius, sed amborum: et ideo communem, qua invicem se diligunt Pater et Filius, nobis insinuat caritatem" (Augustine, *De Trinitate* XV, xvii, 27).

20. According to Augustine, the Father and Son form a single principle of the procession of the Third Person: "Si ergo et quod datur principium habet eum a quo datur quia non aliunde accepit illud quod ab ipso procedit, fatendum est Patrem et Filium principium esse Spiritus Sancti, non duo principia, sed sicut Pater et Filius unus Deus, et ad creaturam relative unus Creator et unus Dominus, sic relative ad Spiritum Sanctum unum principium; ad creaturam vero Pater et Filius et Spiritus Sanctus unum principium sicut unus Creator et unus Dominus" (Augustine, *De Trinitate* XIV, xv, 15). Note that Father and Son can constitute a single, simple principle of spiration only if the Son is the pure mediation of the Father's spirative act, while his mediating transparency goes hand in hand with his unabridged involvement in the production of the Third Person. As Bonaventure suggests in the following gloss on the Augustinian *principaliter a Patre*, "Spritus sanctus dicitur procedere a Patre principalitr et per se: principaliter, quia auctoritas est in Patre; per se, quia non tantum mediante Filio, sed etiam immediate. Non tamen pleinus procedit a Patre nec perfectius, quia plenius ponit gradum perfectionis. Ponit etiam compositionem substantiae in producto, quorum neutrum est in divinis" (Bonaventure, *In Librum Sententiarum* I, d. XII, art. unic., q., 2, *corpus responsionis*). The identity between Father and Son as a single principle of the Third Person is not only compatible with but also positively requires their abiding distinction; it calls for their vis-à-vis in the "opposition of respects," so that asymmetrical, fruitful mutuality is internal to the principiality of the principle *ab initio*.

ity of the principle—and the subsistent fullness of actuality—coincides with the communion in charity that both unites begetter and begotten and underscores their abiding distinction. This brings us back to the main thesis, which is that the communion personified by the Holy Spirit is the paradigm of a sincere gift of self. Before returning to this point in the conclusion of the essay, I first offer four critical clarifications.

Four Clarifications

1. The position one adopts regarding the nature and possibility of self-gift in God depends entirely on one's understanding of what classical theology calls the "innascibility" of the Father, which is his unique property of being underived from any other divine Person. There is a stark either-or here. Either innascibility is understood in an Arian manner, which excludes self-gift from the intrinsic constitution of divine actuality, or it is read in light of Nicene orthodoxy, which builds self-gift, and indeed a communion-in-charity, into God's *actualitas* itself.

If innascibility is interpreted in an Arian manner, as if the Father first existed and then decided to become Father, we implicitly reduce his fontal power to a kind of reserve, or preserve, of sheer possibility, whose purity would be somehow defiled by actuality. Note that this account of innascibility implicitly subordinates actuality to possibility, as if actuality were a hindrance to freedom understood purely as the power to begin entirely *a se*. In this sense, Arianism is intellectually akin to the "possibilist" ideal of freedom inherited (arguably) from medieval theology that underlies the modern notion of rights. The point here is not that potentiality, power, and possibility are bad things, but that the commitment to a voluntaristic *possibilism* is the improper way of doing justice to what is good in them.

On an orthodox reading, by contrast, innascibility cannot mean that there was ever a time when the Father was anything other than the Father that he is. For orthodoxy, the Father cannot fail to generate the begotten and to spirate the Spirit with and through him; he is Father in virtue of his own inmost nature, which is identical with eternal actuality. Of course, insofar as his nature is truly *his*, he is not subordinate to its exigencies as if he were a creature subject to some alien or anonymous law. Borrowing an expression from Plotinus, we can say that if the Father wills to be what he is, he is also what he wills to be.[21] Of course, we must keep in mind what Plotinus (not to mention Augustine and Maximus the Confessor) means by "will," namely, not aggressive self-assertion, but ontological delight, in which being enjoys its full presence to itself, just as its presence to itself is the fullness of joy.

Nevertheless, even if there is a sense in which the Father gives himself paternity by generating, we must immediately add that he also gives himself *to* it at the same time.[22] The very perfection of divine actuality requires that he can never fail to have done so already. There is never a time when the Father has not already given himself away into his paternal role, which thus becomes the a priori form of his entire self-possession. This self-given a priori, far from blocking the Father's access to his fontal power, is the very thing that puts it entirely in his hands as the intimate expression of his own "hyperdeterminate" actuality.[23]

2. The Father's self-commitment to paternity is no mere "altruistic" self-sacrifice. Rather, the very generosity of his self-gift finds expression in a desire for the Son's reciprocation of it.[24] This desire is not a sign of

21. The Father generates by virtue of his own nature. The act of begetting, then, is neither imposed on him from without nor, again, is it the fruit of a particular decision. The *generatio activa* is prior to the either/or between constraint and choice; it is "necessary" in that there is nothing other for the Father to be than Father, but it is also free in that the Father is glad to be the Father that he is. See Plotinus, *Enneads* VI, 8.

22. Considered as a relation, paternity follows upon the generative act. Considered as an internal constituent of the Father's person, however, it precedes the generative act as well: "proprietas personalis patris potest considerari dupliciter. Uno modo, ut est relatio, et sic iterum, secundum intellectum, praesupponit actum notionalem; quia relatio, inquantum huiusmodi, fundatur super actum. Alio modo, secundum quod est constitutiva personae, et sic oportet quod praeintelligatur relatio actui notionali, sicut persona agens praeintelligitur actioni" (Thomas Aquinas, *ST* I, q. 40, a. 4).

23. I owe the term "hyperdeterminate" to a private conversation with Kenneth Schmitz.

24. If we thought of the Father's self-gift as an expression of gratuity, we would have to say that the Son's receptive reciprocation of the gift manifests the same gratuity in turn. Nevertheless, we must immediately add that the bilateral gratuity of the gift not only does not exclude any sense of debt or obligation, but also positively includes it. How could the gratuity of the mutual gift involve a real, permanent, covenantal self-binding of Father and Son unless it included something like the acknowledgment of a prior claim that each naturally has on the other?

lack or want, but of pure actuality. Precisely for this reason, it is always accompanied by the Son's actual, and not merely wished for, presence. The Father's generosity goes so far as to presuppose that the Son already has (and is) what he receives from the paternal begetter:

> For [the Son] receives (*accepit*) what he has from the Father in such a way that [the Son] has received it in being born and that [the Father] has given it [to the Son] in begetting him. For [the Son], too, is life, and he received life precisely in being born, and not because he existed beforehand but lacking life. After all, the Father, too, has life, and he is what he has, yet he has not received it, because he is not from another. The Son, however, has received while the Father, from whom he is, was giving: and he himself also is what he has, for he has life and he is life.[25]

It is as if the Father's active begetting and the Son's passive being begotten were two poles of a single co-act, a single event of mutual giving and receiving in which both begetter and begotten jointly realize the divine actuality as charity.[26] Clearly, this co-act would be incomplete without the co-spiration of the Holy Spirit, who personifies the charity that Father and Son have in common. Note that the co-spiration of the Third Person recapitulates the same pattern we see in the generative event, since in both cases the Father presupposes what he gives. In this instance, what the Father presupposes is the Son's full participation in the production

25. Here is the entire passage, including the parts omitted in the above citation: "Ita enim a Patre quod habet accepit, ut nascendo acceperit, dederitque illi gignendo. Nam et vita est, et accepit vitam utique nascendo, non prius sine vita existendo. Quia et Pater habet vitam, et quod habet est: nec accepit tamen, quia non ex aliquo est. Filius autem accepit vitam, dante Patre a quo est: et ipse quod habet, est; habet enim vitam, et vita est. Ipsum audi loquentem: Sicut habet, inquit: Pater vitam in semetipso, sic dedit et Filio vitam habere in semetipso. Numquid existenti, et non habenti dedit? Sed eo dedit quo genuit, qui vitam genuit, et vita genuit vitam. Et quia parem genuit, non imparem vitam; ideo dictum est: Sicut habet ipse vitam in semetipso, sic dedit et Filio vitam habere in semetipso. Vitam dedit, quia gignendo vitam, quid dedit, nisi esse vitam? Et quia aeterna est ipsa nativitas, nunquam non fuit Filius qui est vita, nunquam fuit Filius sine vita; et sicut est nativitas aeterna, sic est qui natus est vita aeterna. Ita et mandatum non quod Filius non habebat, Pater dedit; sed, sicut dixi, in Sapientia Patris, quod est Verbum Patris, omnia mandata sunt Patris. Dicitur autem mandatum datum, quia non est a seipso cui dicitur datum: et hoc est dare Filio sine quo nunquam Filius fuit, quod est gignere Filium qui nunquam non fuit" (Augustine, *In Evangelium Ioannis Tractatus* LIV, 7).

26. I owe the term "co-act" to D. C. Schindler. See "Freedom beyond Our Choosing: Augustine on the Will and Its Objects," *Communio: International Catholic Review* 29, no. 4 (2002): 618–53.

of the Holy Spirit, who thus shows beyond all doubt that communion is not an afterthought in God, but defines the very *Gestalt* of the divine actuality:

> When the Son says "as the Father has life in himself, so, too, has given the Son to have life in himself," this doesn't mean that the Father has given life to the Son as if [the Son] already existed without life. No, it means that [the Father] has timelessly begotten him in such a way that the life that the Father has given to the Son in begetting him might be coeternal to the life of the Father who has given it. If someone can understand this, then let him also understand that, as the Father has it in himself that the Holy Spirit should proceed from him, so, too, he has given to the Son that the same Holy Spirit might proceed from him as well, and both without time. And that, when the Holy Spirit is said to proceed from the Father, the point is that his proceeding also from the Son is something that the Son has from the Father. For if whatever the Son has, he has from the Father, he surely also has it from the Father that the Holy Spirit should proceed from him.[27]

Now, by letting the Son co-spirate the Spirit, the Father confirms that the Son's so-called "passive generation," his being begotten, does not place him on a lower ontological level with respect to the paternal deity. In this sense, the *filioque* valorizes the Son's self-reception as a distinct yet fully equal way of being the one God. The Spirit confirms that the Son's receiving is a positive perfection, which is anchored in a corresponding feature of the Father's fontal generosity: his ability to presuppose and let himself be defined by the only-begotten in the very act of generating him.[28] In this sense, the Spirit's procession *ab utroque* underscores that

27. "Et qui potest intellegere in eo quod ait Filius: Sicut habet Pater vitam in semetipso, sic dedit Filio vitam habere in semetipso; non sine vita exsistenti iam Filio vitam Patrem dedisse, sed ita eum sine tempore genuisse, ut vita quam Pater Filio gignendo dedit, coaeterna sit vitae Patris qui dedit: intellegat sicut habet Pater in semetipso ut de illo procedat Spiritus Sanctus, sic dedisse Filio ut de illo procedat idem Spiritus Sanctus, et utrumque sine tempore; atque ita dictum Spiritum Sanctum de Patre procedere, ut intellegatur, quod etiam procedit de Filio, de Patre esse Filio. Si enim quidquid habet, de Patre habet Filius; de Patre habet utique ut et de illo procedat Spiritus Sanctus" (Augustine, *De Trinitate* XV, xxvi, 47).

28. Despite (or perhaps because of) the asymmetry in the Father-Son relation, it cannot be the case that whatever "happens" between them goes only in one direction, i.e., from the Father to the Son and never from the Son to the Father. The Father is as really related to the Son as the Son is really related to the Father; neither could be without the other in the

divine actuality is superior to any necessary choice, tradeoff, or synthesis between the absolute and the relative, or between autonomy and heteronomy, individuality and community, and so forth, for it always comprehends the good in each without having to sacrifice the good in the other.

3. Clearly, innascibility cannot mean that the Father first exists and then decides to give himself, as if he fully possessed his productive power before resolving to use it to bring forth the Son and the Holy Spirit. If the Father is to have complete mastery of his own productive power, then he can do so only insofar as he has always already fully expressed this power in act. Now, to express one's power in act is also to give it, as we see in the case of a composer who, in publishing a score, entrusts his creation to the interpretation of the pianists who plays it in his name. This is all the more true in the case of the Father, who, as Augustine says, "would not have said himself wholly and perfectly, if there were anything less or more in his Word than [there is] in himself."[29]

If "the Father loves the Son and shows him all that he himself does" (cf. Jn 5:22), he will not fail to initiate the only-begotten into the secret of his own fontal authority. The Son, therefore, will recapitulate the entire productive self-expressivity of the Father in an equally original way. It is not that Word becomes the paternal *archê*, or that the paternal *archê* becomes the Word; it is that the Word, who is always in the *archê*, embodies, expresses, and "mak[es] luminously manifest (if it is licit to speak thus) the inmost ground of the paternal goodness."[30] Or, as Bonaventure elsewhere puts it, "the Word expresses the Father as a principle principiating of itself (*principium principians de se*), and in this way [the Word] exists in explicating and representing the production of the Holy Spirit and of himself."[31]

---

way that, say, God could be without the creature, or the column without my standing to the right of it. The conclusion that I draw from this fact is that the Son's act of self-reception is internal to the Godhead to such an extent that the Son's existence, while resulting from the Father's *activa generatio*, is also an internal condition of the generative act.

29. "Proinde tamquam se ipsum dicens Pater genuit Verbum sibi aequale per omnia. Non enim se ipsum integre perfecteque dixisset, si aliquid minus aut amplius esset in eius Verbo quam in ipso" (Augustine, *De Trinitate* XV, xiv, 23).

30. Maximus Confessor, *Quaestiones ad Thalassium*, 60 (PG 90:621B).

31. "Et Verbum exprimit Patrem ut principium principians de se, et sic est explicans et repraesentans productionem Spiritus sancti et suam" (Bonaventure, *Collationes in Hexaemeron* III, 7).

The Father's actuality as principle goes hand in hand, then, with his exercise of an infinite productive power that is always fully in act. This active productivity involves an unreserved self-expression, just as this self-expression involves, in its turn, an unreserved self-communication. In a word, the Father's perfect actuality coincides with his total self-gift to the Word and, through and with the Word, to the Holy Spirit.

In one sense, we can think of the Trinitarian communion as the articulation of the Father's principial self-gift. Nevertheless, this articulation presupposes the Father's way of being the principle in the Godhead. At one and the same time, he originates the entire triune *communio* and is—or better, *always already was*—a member of it along with the Son and the Spirit. Similarly, in giving himself, the Father performs (or, once again, has *always already performed*) his self-gift in communion with the Son, which is to say, "in the unity of the Holy Spirit." Divine self-gift is both the proper self-expression of the Father and the common good of the whole Trinity. It is at once the Father's deed and a co-act involving all three persons in the shared realization of being-as-charity.

Although each *hypostasis* remains incommunicable, this incommunicability is not a barrier to unreserved communication among all three. It is by remaining perfectly distinct in themselves that each person can let the other two participate fully in their respective hypostatic property, without obliging them to become the other and without the fear that the other might become them. In a word, the incommunicability of each *hypostasis* enables a "circumincessive communication of idioms" among Father, Son, and Holy Spirit.[32] This circumincession of propreties is the very thing that *Gaudium et spes* calls "the union of the divine persons" (no. 24).[33]

4. I return to the initial claim that the union of the divine persons embodies the paradigm of self-gift. Does this thesis imply a rejection of Augustine's analogy of the Trinity as a triad of memory, intellect, and will

32. I owe this idea to a private conversation with Paolo Prosperi.

33. Why, then, must there be a first Person to play the unique role of an unoriginate origin in the Deity? The answer is that the firstness of the first frees the other two persons to enjoy the full perfections corresponding to their respective roles within the Trinitarian *taxis*—perfections that are no less internal to the one *actus purus* than the primity of the first. The other two persons are co-original with the first, precisely because their own unique originality is coordinated with, and yet never reducible to, the first's way of being the origin.

that structures the human mind? Not at all. We do not need to choose between an "interpersonal" and an "intrapersonal" approach to the Trinity, as if the one ruled out the other. The two approaches, far from being mutually exclusive, are two sides of the same theological coin.[34]

This latter claim finds corroboration in an attentive reading of Augustine's *De Trinitate*, where the Bishop of Hippo approaches the Trinity in terms of *two* triads, not just one. In addition to the abovementioned mental triad of *memoria*, *intellectus*, and *voluntas*, Augustine also uses what I would call a "social triad" consisting of lover, beloved, and love itself, in which love plays the role of a jointly beloved third.[35] Now, Augus-

34. In one respect, the Father is like a living substance endowed with a natural tendency to bring forth from itself a product that is like itself in every respect. This natural emanation does not, however, bypass the Father's knowledge or love, and, insofar as it does not, it is as much a reciprocated self-gift as it is a *naturalis emanatio*. There is no opposition here: the natural generative event (looked at in the simultaneity of its active and passive sides) is substantially identical with reciprocal (and asymmetrical) self-gift, just as reciprocal self-gift is substantially identical with the natural generative event. Augustine seems to hint at this when he writes: "quod autem dictum est: Filii caritatis suae, nihil aliud intellegatur, quam Filii sui dilecti, quam Filii postremo substantiae suae. Caritas quippe Patris quae in natura eius est ineffabiliter simplici, nihil est aliud quam eius ipsa natura atque substantia, ut saepe iam diximus, et saepe iterare non piget. Ac per hoc Filius caritatis eius nullus est alius, quam qui de substantia eius est genitus" (Augustine, *De Trinitate* XV, xix, 37). This identity is confirmed and guaranteed by the commonality of the Spirit's production *in divinis*. In co-spirating the Holy Spirit, in fact, Father and Son fully express *both* their natural consubstantiality *and* their personal reciprocity—bringing both aspects together into a single, simple co-act directed toward one and the same *condilectus*. By virtue of this co-act, they jointly reveal and constitute the divine being as a perfect unity of substance and charity equally present in both of them at once. And not just in both of them. The very *ratio* of their spirative co-act, after all, is to communicate that same unity to a third *Hypostasis*, so that he might embody in his own person, as it were, the identity of substance and charity, of natural emanation and personal self-gift, *in divinis*: "Ut scilicet in illa simplici summaque natura, non sit aliud substantia et aliud caritas; sed substantia ipsa sit caritas, et caritas ipsa sit substantia, sive in Patre, sive in Filio, sive in Spiritu Sancto, et tamen proprie Spiritus Sanctus caritas nuncupetur" (Augustine, *De Trinitate* XV, xvii, 29).

35. "Quid est autem dilectio vel caritas, quam tantopere Scriptura divina laudat et praedicat, nisi amor boni? Amor autem alicuius amantis est, et amore aliquid amatur. Ecce tria sunt: amans, et quod amatur, et amor. Quid est ergo amor, nisi quaedam vita duo aliqua copulans, vel copulari appetens, amantem scilicet, et quod amatur? Et hoc etiam in extremis carnalibusque amoribus ita est. Sed ut aliquid purius et liquidius hauriamus, calcata carne ascendamus ad animum. Quid amat animus in amico, nisi animum? Et illic igitur tria sunt: amans, et quod amatur, et amor. Quid est ergo amor, nisi quaedam vita duo aliqua copulans, vel copulari appetens, amantem scilicet et quod amatur? Et hoc etiam in extremis carnalibusque amoribus ita est" (Augustine, *De Trinitate* VIII, x, 14). Augustine is fully aware

tine introduces the mental triad precisely in order to explain how the social triad illumines the Trinity.[36] He can do this because, on his account, the mental triad *is* the social triad, and vice versa. The social pattern of lover, beloved, and love is inscribed in the very self-recursion of the human mind. Put more concretely, Augustine's point is that the mind's loving self-apprehension is not an ontological egoism, but the ineradicable memory of being-as-communion; communion not only with God, but also with one's fellow men, who are all partakers of the same *sociale quiddam* that is human nature.[37] Hence Augustine's insistence that the individual cannot love himself wisely unless he loves God more than his own person and his neighbor as himself.[38]

that that the Holy Spirit, who personifies divine love, represents the principle of "thirdness" required for the coupling of the One and the Other in God. What Augustine says in the following passage about the mind applies, *mutatis mutandis*, to God as well: "Haec autem duo, gignens et genitum, dilectione tertia copulantur" (Augustine, *De Trinitate* IV, vi, 8). In this sense, his account of the Holy Spirit as *condilectio*, the joint love of Father and Son, opens itself to a Richardian understanding of the Spirit as their *condilectus*, or jointly beloved third.

36. Augustine thinks of the social triad as a kind of original phenomenon in which the intelligibility of the Trinity first becomes manifest: "Deinde per veritatem quae intellecta conspicitur, et per bonum summum a quo est omne bonum, et per iustitiam propter quam diligitur animus iustus ab animo etiam nondum iusto, ut natura non solum incorporalis, verum etiam incommutabilis quod est Deus, quantum fieri potest, intellegeretur admonui: et per caritatem, quae in Scripturis sanctis Deus dicta est, per quam coepit utcumque etiam Trinitas intellegentibus apparere, sicut sunt amans, et quod amatur, et amor" (*De Trinitate* XV, iii, 5).

37. Augustine, *De Bono Conjugali* I.1. We could further elaborate on this by developing the implications of the centrality of the *verbum* or "word" to the mental life. If the word stands at the center of the mental life, does not communication *ad intra* immediately imply communication *ad extra*, and vice versa?

38. "Haec igitur trinitas mentis non propterea Dei est imago, quia sui meminit mens, et intellegit ac diligit se: sed quia potest etiam meminisse, et intellegere, et amare a quo facta est. Quod cum facit, sapiens ipsa fit. Si autem non facit, etiam cum sui meminit, seque intellegit ac diligit, stulta est. Meminerit itaque Dei sui, ad cuius imaginem facta est, eumque intellegat atque diligat. Quod ut brevius dicam, colat Deum non factum, cuius ab eo capax est facta, et cuius particeps esse potest; propter quod scriptum est: Ecce Dei cultus est sapientia, et non sua luce, sed summae illius lucis participatione sapiens erit, atque ubi aeterna, ibi beata regnabit" (Augustine, *De Trinitate* XIV, xii, 15). Augustine later continues: "Non dixit: 'Ego et ipsi unum,' quamvis per id quod Ecclesiae caput est et corpus eius. Ecclesia posset dicere: 'Ego et ipsi' non unum sed 'unus,' quia caput et corpus unus est Christus. Sed divinitatem suam consubstantialem Patri ostendens (propter quod et alio loco dicit: Ego et Pater unum sumus), in suo genere, hoc est in eiusdem naturae consubstantiali parilitate, vult esse suos unum, sed in ipso quia in se ipsis non possent dissociati ab invicem per diversas voluntates et cupiditates et immunditiam peccatorum; unde mundantur per Mediatorem

Once again, the two triads imply each other. Human nature cannot be a *sociale quiddam*—a specific instance of being-as-society—unless the social triad is inscribed in the mind, just as the mental triad makes no sense without an at least implicit social horizon. But if this is true of God's image, it is even truer of God himself. So much so, in fact, that the one divine mind loving itself *is* the Father and the Son loving each other by the Spirit, and vice versa. This is because in God the mental triad is a simple, undivided common good whose proper appreciation and appropriation requires a communion of three, that is, a social triad. Note that each member of this social triad reflects the entire mental triad, both in themselves and in relation to all others, albeit with a unique accent on memory, intellect, or will, according to the order of the processions.

If three divine persons jointly possess the same mind—the same mental triad—and reflect its pattern in their circumincessive interplay, the converse is also true: God's loving self-apprehension, articulated in the "I am who I am" of Exodus 3, requires the mutual indwelling of the Father and the Son for its enactment. God's "I AM," even when considered as a property of the divine nature, is a co-act uniting all the virtues of singular self-consciousness and all the virtues of mutual love. The divine self-consciousness—and the divine self, for that matter—exists only in the interplay between Trinity and unity in God, which comprehends all the perfection of individuality and all the perfection of community in one and the same simple fullness of act:

Neither can we say that, as the image—namely, man who has [memory, intellect, and will]—is one person, the [divine] Trinity is one person, too. Rather, it

ut sint in illo unum; non tantum per eamdem naturam qua omnes ex hominibus mortalibus aequales Angelis fiunt, sed etiam per eamdem in eamdem beatitudinem conspirantem concordissimam voluntatem in unum spiritum quodam modo caritatis igne conflatam. Ad hoc enim valet quod ait: Ut sint unum sicut et nos unum sumus, ut quemadmodum Pater et Filius, non tantum aequalitate substantiae, sed etiam voluntate unum sunt, ita et hi inter quos et Deum Mediator est Filius, non tantum per id quod eiusdem naturae sunt, sed etiam per eamdem dilectionis societatem unum sint. Deinde idipsum quod Mediator est per quem reconciliamur Deo sic indicat: Ego, inquit, in eis et tu in me ut sint consummati in unum" (Augustine, *De Trinitate* IV, ix, 12). What Augustine presents here as a fruit to be attained through conversion from sin is also the graced fulfillment of nature, the completion of the image of God in our likeness to him. In this sense, the fruit of conversion is also the full realization in history of the social kind of being that we always already are by nature.

is three persons: the Father of the Son, and the Son of the Father, and the Spirit of Father and Son.... In the image of the Trinity [memory, intellect, and will] are not one man, but are properties of one man. It is not like this in in the supreme Trinity whose image [man] is. These things are not properties of the one God, but are the one God himself, and what we find [in him] is not one person, but three. We thus have this wondrously ineffable or ineffably wondrous phenomenon: Although this image of the Trinity is one person, while that supreme Trinity is three, the latter Trinity of three persons is more inseparable than the former trinity [of faculties] belonging to one.[39]

What does all this imply for the claim that triune communion is the paradigm of self-gift? To this question I now turn in the conclusion.

39. "Nec rursus quemadmodum ista imago quod est homo habens illa tria una persona est, ita est illa Trinitas: sed tres personae sunt, Pater Filii, et Filius Patris, et Spiritus Patris et Filii ... non tamen, sicut in ista imagine Trinitatis non haec tria unus homo, sed unius hominis sunt, ita in ipsa summa Trinitate cuius haec imago est, unius Dei sunt illa tria, sed unus Deus est, et tres sunt illae, non una persona. Quod sane mirabiliter ineffabile est, vel ineffabiliter mirabile, cum sit una persona haec imago Trinitatis, ipsa vero summa Trinitas tres personae sint, inseparabilior est illa Trinitas personarum trium, quam haec unius" (Augustine, *De Trinitate* XV, xxiii, 43). The divine "I AM" is a co-act that can be proper to each person because it is common to all, and vice versa. This challenges our habitual assumption that inhabiting the first-person perspective means looking out onto the world from the center of an invisible subjectivity. Is this assumption true even in the case of human beings? If a single glance suffices to discern whether someone is looking at us, it would seem to follow that the subjectivity of the act of seeing, far from remaining purely invisible, is somehow evident over the entire surface of the body. How much more will this be true in God, who *is* his very act of seeing, so that the entire subjectivity of his *actus videndi* is visible in the act itself? But where the subjectivity of seeing is itself entirely seen, it is by definition intrinsically common, a good defined through and through by mutual showing and beholding—which is also a mutual giving and receiving. If saying "I" *in prima persona* is not simply a matter of seeing, but also of seeing and of being seen at once, each divine Person *is* this seeing-and-being-seen—though obviously always in and with the other two, as Augustine seems to hint in a passage I cited above: "Itaque illa tria et a se invicem determinari videntur et in se infinita sunt" (Augustine, *De Trinitate* VI, x, 12). Far from being an essentially solitary prison relieved only by a narrow window onto "otherness," the divine "I AM," in its very singularity, is an unobstructed interchange between self and society that naturally calls to be unfolded in the form of Trinitarian communion. This is not an option for "interpersonal categories" over "ontological" ones; it is an argument for abandoning the notion that we must opt for one at the expense of the other in order to do Trinitarian theology. I owe this train of thought to a personal conversation with Jordan Miller.

Conclusion: The Paradigm of Self-Gift

In the preceding pages, I have highlighted what I take to be an implication of the revelation of the Trinity: communion—the interplay between the common and the proper, and so between the *principaliter a Patre* and the *communiter a Patre Filioque*—defines God's way of possessing the perfection of the divine nature, and therefore of actuality per se. Now, insofar as this communion involves giving and receiving, which it clearly does, it builds something like a sincere gift of self into the very heart of being. When the authors of *Gaudium et spes* say that the union of the divine persons is the paradigm of the *sincerum sui ipsius donum*, they are not simply saying that the Trinity is the model of ecclesial charity. They are also saying that the Trinity is the model of the really real *tout court*—whose full manifestation is of course the privilege and burden of the Church. The Church, for its part, is nothing other than the "one Christ loving himself," because "when the members love one another, the body loves itself."[40]

We glimpse an earthly foreshadowing of this truth in the natural institution of marriage, whose very existence shows that self-gift is not a contradiction, but an actuality woven into the texture of our richest experiences of what it means *to be*. Within marriage, in fact, each spouse is a giver to the same extent that he, or she, is also a gift—where gift means an offering placed once and for all at the disposal of the nuptial communion and of all its members. Far from being an impossible self-division, self-gift is the realization of what it means to be a "self" in the first place: to represent, by dint of a kind of vicarious substitution, both the society to which one belongs and all the others who belong to it as well.[41]

40. "Qui diligit Filium, diligit et filios Dei. Quos filios Dei? Membra Filii Dei. Et diligendo fit et ipse membrum, et fit per dilectionem in compage corporis Christi; et erit unus Christus amans seipsum. Cum enim se invicem amant membra, corpus se amat" (Augustine, *In Epistolam Ioannis* X, 3).

41. This is an implication, for example, of Maximus's account of the *thelêma physikon*, of which three points can be raised. First, the deepest sense of our will is to receive our being from our creator. We cannot receive being, however, unless we also appropriate it. This appropriation generates the self, placing it at the heart of the receptive exercise of being. There is never a time, then, when we are simply substance without also being a self, i.e., a self-relation that simultaneously relates to itself again as such. Selfhood, as the completion of

But can we go beyond the letter of Augustine to claim marriage as an analogue of the triune communion?[42] Yes, but only if we keep in mind that marriage is an epiphany of *being*.[43] Thanks to this epiphanic character, the

our reception of the gift of being, is itself part of the gift given *ab initio*. Second, the reflexive self-reception I have just described is an ontological concomitant of our very existence *ab initio*. It thus begins—and has already begun—by nature, and it operates day and night whether we are awake or asleep, whether we realize it or not. Its existence and operation are necessary, both in the sense that it stands or falls with our being, and in the sense that our being stands and falls with it. At the same time, we must not imagine natural will as a kind of foreign object that precedes us that we must finally approve or ratify, because, after all, it is a good thing on balance. No, the natural will would not even be natural to us if it operated in this way. Rather, it must operate in us from the beginning as the very basis of our affirming the gift that we are, or, rather, as having already begun affirming the gift that we are. Third, our reflexive self-possession remains the receiving of a gift, a gift in which the Creator is present as a giver. In this sense, the self (i.e., the reflexively grasped substance that we are) is always more than itself, always the representative of the good of being, which does not belong exclusively to it. Our self-possession, then, is not only a self-reception from the Creator, but also a co-reception with all other creatures. In giving myself *to* myself *as* a self in the core of my being, I find myself at the same point as every other creature who performs an analogous act in its own proper way. Here we are all present to one another *magis intime*, yet without the slightest confusion. The very form of our self-possession, then, is defined by something in the order of nature that anticipates the mystery of vicarious substitution in the order of grace.

42. This claim may not be entirely beyond the letter of Augustine. There is, e.g., a striking parallel between "connection" and the conjugal act that forms a "society"—i.e., an indivisible joint act or "one-flesh-union"—involving the mutual love of male and female. The child is this *connexio societatis* (Augustine, *De Bono Conjugali* I, 1). This is why, almost in the next breath, Augustine calls the child the "one honest fruit" (*unus honestus fructus*; Augustine, *De Bono Conjugali* I, 1) of the conjugal embrace, by which he means that the child is the parents' union, received by God and handed over in its very fruition to be given back in the form of a substantial, personal fruit. We see here, by the way, why Augustine and the Church teach that only a sexual act that is "open to new life" can be properly nuptial, i.e., express the eucharsitic form of the nuptial vow without diminution or distortion: "Concubitus enim necessarius causa generandi inculpabilis et solus ipse nuptialis est" (Augustine, *De Bono Conjugali* X, 11).

43. Augustine draws attention to this epiphanic character when he defines marriage as "the first bond of natural human society": "Prima naturalis humanae societatis copula vir et uxor est" (Augustine, *De Bono Conjugali* I, 1). Marriage, then, is much more than the "elementary building block" of society. It is nothing less than the original self-expression of man as a social being, the primordial "place" where human nature first becomes fully visible (also to itself) in its inherently social form. Augustine says this both as an interpreter of the creation accounts set forth in the first chapters of Genesis and as an observer of what he calls "this condition of being born and dying which is the one we actually know" (as opposed to one that might have existed had man not sinned: *istam conditionem nascendi et morendi, quam novimus*; *De Bono Conjugali* III, 3).

exchange of marital vows—which is a specific form of self-giving—offers us an image, however imperfect and time bound, of the mutual love of the Father and the Son in the Holy Spirit. *That* love is God's way of fully possessing and realizing his divine being in the one form that alone fully expresses all its inner riches: the form of communion-in-charity. The Trinity *is* the one God amid realizing the fullness of actuality as charity.[44]

The aim here is neither to deduce the form of the Trinity from an analysis of marriage nor to deduce the form of marriage from an analysis of the Trinity. I am merely offering an analogy to explain the sense in which the union of the divine persons represents the original paradigm of sincere self-gift. The purpose of the analogy is to help elucidate how a giving of oneself involves a living life wholly within the context of a certain community—be it the community of marriage or of the Trinity. This comparison is of course imperfect, for while husband and wife are not born spouses but become such by virtue of their marital consent, there was never a time when the three divine persons were not perfectly in communion. From all eternity, Father, Son, and Holy Spirit have found themselves together *by nature* and have consented to be together *by conscious desire*. The eternal communion of divine persons rests on both nature and consent, which are two inseparable dimensions of the same superabundant "firstness" of divine actuality. Far from reducing "self-gift" in God to the status of mere metaphor, the difference just highlighted implies that God's being eternally contains the archetypal fullness of every *sincerum sui ipsius donum*. A glimpse of this triune archetype can be seen in marriage, though this appreciation is not an exclusive one. Self-gift, in one form or another, is the lifeblood of every true community, whether we are talking about the consecrated life or the Church, the *polis*, or the cosmos.

The three eternally divine persons commune both by nature and consent. Each of these dimensions is foundational for the perfection of the other. There is, in other words, something nature-like about the divine persons' consent to communion, just as there is something consent-like

44. This communion has all the virtue of a natural given belonging to the original fullness of being together with a free commitment to embody the love that always already belongs to this fullness *an sich*. Here, ontology and action, nature and morality, the a priori and the a posteriori, are one without confusion or separation. In a word, it is as Trinity that God wills to be the good he is and that he is the good he wills to be.

about their naturally existing as *communio*. This interplay between nature and consent is bound up with an analogous interplay between being and charity. Augustine's teaching about the procession of the Holy Spirit implies just this sort of interplay, for if the Holy Spirit proceeds commonly from Father and Son, and so presupposes the generation of the Word, then charity is the fruit of the loving apprehension of being.[45] But if the Spirit proceeds *principaliter a Patre*, there is another sense in which charity—or love—constitutes the very *ratio* of being in its indemonstrable firstness.[46] This twofold Augustinian insight brings us to what I take to be the deepest ontological entailment of Vatican II's teaching about self-gift in God. Love, the conciliar teaching implies, is not only the highest fruit of actuality, but also its most original principle. Love coincides with the ontological perfection that shines through the entire network of the transcendentals—a perfection consisting in the unity of indwelling fullness and an expansive communicativity between what is proper and common, for which the Trinity stands as the primordial archetype.

45. This is why we must affirm the enduring (relative) validity of the ordering of the transcendentals underlying Thomas's account of the Trinity of persons in God (first being, then the true, then the good), while also acknowledging Thomas's sensitivity to the complex, circumincessive interplay of the true and the good, and of intellect and will, that is at the heart of the Trinitarian life. This Augustine expresses in the following passage: "Verbum est igitur, quod nunc discernere et insinuare volumus, cum amore notitia. Cum itaque se mens novit et amat, iungitur ei amore verbum eius. Et quoniam amat notitiam et novit amorem, et verbum in amore est et amor in verbo, et utrumque in amante atque dicente" (*De Trinitate* IX, x, 15).

46. On the indemonstrable firstness of being, see the following text: "Nam illud quod primo cadit in apprehensione, est ens, cuius intellectus includitur in omnibus quaecumque quis apprehendit" (Thomas Aquinas, *ST* I-II, q. 94, a. 2, co.). Now, as Thomas tells us in *De Veritate*, *ens sumitur ab actu essendi* (I.1). In other words, *ens* (both the name and the reality) is taken or derived from the act of being. It is this *ens*, as fullness of actuality, that is saturated with the richness of all the other transcendentals: *res*, *unum*, *aliquid*, *verum*, *bonum*, and, I would add, *pulchrum*, which "first falls into the apprehension." What is absolutely first in itself is also absolutely first for us as well, even though we initially grasp it only implicitly in apprehending the quiddities of material things, which form the proper object of our specifically human intellect.

II

Church, Sacrament, and World

4

Eucharistic Ecclesiology and Eschatology

On the Church's Relation to the World

NICHOLAS J. HEALY JR.

The Church and the World

"I am convinced," writes Gregory of Nazianzus, "that every assembly of bishops is to be avoided, for I have never experienced a happy ending to any council ... only ambition and wrangling about what was taking place."[1] These words, written by the great Cappadocian father shortly after the First Council of Constantinople (381), are cited by both John Henry Newman and Joseph Ratzinger in order to illustrate the fact that the period following an ecumenical Council is often characterized by confusion, turmoil, and discord.[2] The high-water point of the Arian crisis occurred some thirty years after the solemn confession of the Council of Nicaea that Jesus Christ is *homoousios* with the Father. The period immediately following the Council of Trent witnessed new challenges and resistance to the reforms undertaken by the Council.

We should not be too surprised, then, that the past fifty years have been marked by turmoil and a general crisis of faith. But there does seem to be a unique feature or characteristic of the current discord within the

1. Gregory of Nazianzus, Epistle 130, "Ad Procopium," in *Gregor von Nazianz: Briefe*, GCS 53, ed. Paul Gallay (Berlin: Akademie-Verlag, 1969).

2. Cf. Joseph Ratzinger, *Principles of Catholic Theology: Building Stones for a Fundamental Theology* (San Francisco: Ignatius Press, 1987), 368; John Henry Newman, *The Arians of the Fourth Century* (London: Longmans, Green, 1890), 451.

Church. The novelty consists in the fact that there is considerable confusion and deep disagreement concerning the basic aim or purpose of the Second Vatican Council. Unlike earlier ecumenical Councils, Vatican II was not convened in order to address a specific doctrinal crisis, at least not in any obvious sense. In the apostolic constitution *Humanae salutis*, which officially convoked the Council, Pope John XXIII indicated that the Council was called in order to "give the Church the possibility to contribute more efficaciously to the solution of the problems of the modern age."[3] In his opening address to the Council on October 11, 1962, John XXIII said that the Council was tasked with guarding and handing on more efficaciously the sacred deposit of faith: "The substance of the ancient doctrine of the deposit of faith is one thing, and the way in which it is presented is another."[4] To be faithful to Christ's gospel, an updating, or *aggiornamento*, was necessary. In short, Vatican II was conceived as an essentially pastoral Council.

As many others have noted, this is a remarkably open-ended program. For some Catholic theologians, the pastoral emphasis of Vatican II represents a radically new beginning, the most significant event in the life of the Church since Pentecost. Other theologians, citing the same texts of Pope John XXIII, draw the opposite conclusion: because Vatican II was only a pastoral Council, the Council's teaching contains nothing of significance in terms of the deposit of faith.

The preeminent English-language historian of the Second Vatican Council John O'Malley has argued that conflicts over the interpretation of the Council revolve around the question of what the real aim or goal of the Council was. It is highly instructive to consider O'Malley's own account of the purpose of Vatican II:

> A fair, but not exhaustive, list of the aims of the Council would go something like this: to end the stance of cultural isolation that the Church was now seen as having maintained; to initiate a new freedom of expression and action within

3. John XXIII, *Humanae salutis*, Apostolic Constitution for the Convocation of the Second Vatican Council, December 25, 1961, no. 6, in *The Documents of Vatican II*, ed. Walter M. Abbot (New York: Guild, 1966), 705.

4. John XXIII, Address on the Occasion of the Solemn Opening of the Most Holy Council, October 11, 1962, in *Documents of Vatican II*, 715.

> the Church that certain Vatican institutions were now interpreted as having previously curtailed; to distribute more broadly the exercise of pastoral authority, especially by strengthening the role of the episcopacy and local churches vis-à-vis the Holy See; to modify in people's consciousness and in the actual functioning of the Church the predominantly clerical, institutional and hierarchical model that had prevailed; to affirm the dignity of the laity in the Church; to establish through a more conciliatory attitude, through some new theological insights and through effective mechanisms a better relationship with other religious bodies, looking ultimately to the healing of the divisions in Christianity and the fruitful "dialogue" with non-Christian religions; to change the teaching of the Church on "religious liberty" and give new support to the principle of "freedom of conscience"; to base theology and biblical studies more firmly on historical principles; to foster styles of piety along the lines I indicated above; to affirm clearly that the Church was and should be affected by the cultures in which it exists; finally, to promote a more positive appreciation of "the world" and the relationship of the Church to it, with a concomitant assumption of clearer responsibility for the fate of the world in "the new era" that the Council saw opening up before its eyes.[5]

Notice what is missing from O'Malley's lengthy articulation of the purposes of Vatican II. There is not a single reference to the figure of Jesus Christ, or to the saving mystery of divine love mediated by the Church, or to the Church's responsibility to hand on the faith received from the Apostles, or to the Church's mission of proclaiming the gospel to every creature.

In order to grasp the significance of this lacuna, it is necessary to focus attention on the final item in O'Malley's list, which seems to sum up and recapitulate the other aims. The purpose of Vatican II, he writes, was "to promote a more positive appreciation of 'the world' and the relationship of the Church to it."[6] At one level, this claim is undeniably true. There is ample evidence to support this thesis in the writings of John XXIII and Paul VI, and in the conciliar documents themselves.[7]

5. John W. O'Malley, "Vatican II: Historical Perspectives on Its Uniqueness and Interpretation," in *Vatican II: The Unfinished Agenda; A Look to the Future*, ed. Lucien Richard with Daniel T. Harrington and John W. O'Malley (New York: Paulist, 1987), 26. Cf. John W. O'Malley, *What Happened at Vatican II* (Cambridge, MA: Belknap Press, 2008).

6. O'Malley, "Vatican II: Historical Perspectives," 26.

7. John Paul II also concurs with O'Malley's judgment regarding the Church's "open-

At the same time, O'Malley's formulation calls for further discernment and reflection. *Why* did the Second Vatican Council seek a more positive relationship with the world? What is meant by the concept of "world"? What is the source and measure of the Church's relation to the world? In light of the distinction between nature and grace, and given the tragedy of sin, what is the ideal form of the Church's relation to the world?

An adequate answer to these questions on the Church-world relation would engage all sixteen of the conciliar texts and require interpreting them in the context of the Catholic tradition. The aim here is more limited. Specifically, I focus on an aspect of the Council's eschatology—its teaching on the last things. I would suggest that a better understanding of what *Lumen gentium* calls "the eschatological nature of the pilgrim Church" sheds light on the pastoral program of *Gaudium et spes* and the purpose of Vatican II as a whole. The Council's teaching on the eschatological nature of the Church is inseparable from its teaching on the mystery of the Eucharist. The Church's eschatological mission, which aims at the recapitulation of all things in Christ, is realized in and through her eucharistic communion with Christ. It is this sacramental mode of transmission of the Church's faith that best helps us understand the Council's pastoral program.

Joseph Ratzinger, among others, has argued that the Second Vatican Council is deeply indebted to Henri de Lubac's rediscovery of the inseparable connection between the Church and the Eucharist.[8] Christ's Eucharist is the innermost heart of the Church. As *Lumen gentium* teaches,

---

ness" to the world: "The Council," he writes, "opened itself widely to the contemporary world, as is clearly seen from the important Conciliar Constitutions *Gaudium et spes* and *Lumen gentium*." John Paul II, *Dominum et vivificantem*, Encyclical on the Holy Spirit in the Life of the Church and the World, May 18, 1986, no. 26.

8. Joseph Ratzinger, "The Ecclesiology of the Second Vatican Council," in *Church, Ecumenism and Politics: New Essays in Ecclesiology* (New York: Crossroad, 1988), 7. "De Lubac made it clear in a splendid work of comprehensive scholarship that the term 'mystical body' originally meant the holy Eucharist and that for Paul as for the Fathers of the Church the idea of the Church as the body of Christ was indissolubly linked with the idea of the Eucharist in which the Lord is bodily present and gives us his body as food. Thus there now arose a eucharistic ecclesiology which people also liked to term an ecclesiology of communion. This ecclesiology of communion became the real core of Vatican II's teaching on the Church, the novel and at the same time the original element in what this Council wanted to give us."

it is "the source and summit of the whole of Christian life,"[9] the mystery by which "the unity of all believers who form one body in Christ is both expressed and brought about."[10] The corollary thesis that I explore is that the connection between the Church and the Eucharist is the hidden center of the Council's teaching on the Church-world relation. The Eucharist is not only the source and summit of the Church's life; it is also the deepest and fullest expression of the world itself in its original goodness and in its eschatological perfection. It follows that the Church's pastoral and missionary opening to the world finds its source, measure, and fulfillment in the life, death, and resurrection of Christ, which is summed up and communicated in Church's liturgy.

My argument unfolds in two steps: the first summarizes in broad strokes de Lubac's account of the relationship between the Church and the Eucharist, while the second develops the significance of eucharistic ecclesiology for the Church's relation to the world. I conclude by revisiting O'Malley's observation that at the Second Vatican Council the Church sought a more positive relationship with the world.

Corpus Mysticum

In his seminal book *Corpus Mysticum*, published at the height of World War II, Henri de Lubac demonstrated that the term "mystical body" originally referred to the Eucharist.[11] For St. Paul, for St. Augustine, and for early medieval theologians, the Eucharist corresponds to the Church as cause to effect, or as sign to reality. Christ instituted the Eucharist in order to build up his body, the Church, and for this reason the Church was described as *corpus Christi verum*—the true body of Christ. Within this great tradition, the relation between Church and Eucharist is one of reciprocal causality. In the words of de Lubac, "Each has been entrusted

9. Second Vatican Council, *Lumen gentium* (*LG*), Dogmatic Constitution on the Church, November 21, 1964, no. 11.

10. *LG*, no. 3.

11. Henri de Lubac, *Corpus Mysticum: The Eucharist and the Church in the Middle Ages*, trans. Gemma Simmonds with Richard Price and Christopher Stephens, ed. Laurence Paul Hemming and Susan Frank Parsons (Notre Dame, IN: University of Notre Dame Press, 2006).

to the other, so to speak, by Christ; the Church produces the Eucharist, but the Eucharist also produces the Church."[12] Centuries of theological reflection thus celebrated the inseparable unity between the Eucharist and the Church, which, "like the Eucharist, is a mystery of unity—the same mystery, and one with inexhaustible riches. Both are the Body of Christ—the same Body. If we are to be faithful to the teaching of Scripture, as Tradition interprets it, and wish not to lose anything of its essential riches, we must be careful not to make the smallest break between the Mystical Body and the Eucharist."[13]

To gain a deeper understanding of this mystery of reciprocal causality, it is helpful to reflect on the unity-in-distinction of the threefold body of Christ. First, there is the historical body of Jesus of Nazareth, born of the Virgin Mary, crucified for our sake and risen from the dead. Second, there is the sacramental body that is the Eucharist, the body and blood of Christ that comes to be through the transubstantiation of bread and wine in the Church's liturgy.

Third, there is the ecclesial body that is the Church—the unity of believers with Christ and with one another. The supreme mystery of our faith, which is confirmed and communicated by the Holy Spirit as the fruit of Christ's going to the end of love on the cross and rising to new life, is that this threefold body of Christ is one. It follows that each mode of Christ's bodily existence presupposes and reveals something essential about the other two. Let me elaborate this claim by reflecting on each aspect of the threefold body.

1. Beginning and remaining with the historical body of Jesus Christ is the key to realizing the abiding concreteness of God's gift of love. "What we value most in Christianity," writes Vladimir Solovyov, "is Christ himself—in his Person. All comes from him, for we know that in him dwells all fullness of the Godhead bodily."[14] The crucial point is that Christ's body, precisely as historical, is eucharistic and ecclesial from beginning

12. Henri de Lubac, *The Splendor of the Church*, trans. Michael Mason (San Francisco: Ignatius Press, 1986), 133.

13. De Lubac, *Splendor*, 156.

14. Valdimir Solovyov, "A Short Story of the Anti-Christ," in *War, Progress and the End of History* (Hudson: Lindisfarne, 1990), 183–84.

to end. Christ's historical body is ecclesial in the sense that his coming into the world depends on Mary's faith and Mary's body. His historical body is also ecclesial by virtue of being totally and irrevocably given to his bride, the Church, in order to establish a new and eternal covenant. Christ's historical body is already the sign and instrument of communion between God and creation.

Christ's historical body is eucharistic in the sense that the whole of Christ's incarnate life is a thanksgiving to the Father and an offering of himself back to the Father and to the Church. The form of Christ's historical life is a grateful and obedient reception of his existence from the Father coincident with an offering of his life back to the Father. In this sense, the Eucharist does not simply come at the end of Christ's life, but is the deepest expression of his identity as the eternal Son, who became man for our salvation. In the words of Hans Urs von Balthasar:

> The Son's form of existence, which makes him the Son from all eternity, is the uninterrupted reception of everything that he is, of his very self, from the Father. It is indeed this receiving of himself which gives him his "I," his own inner dimension, his spontaneity, that sonship with which he can answer the Father in a reciprocal giving.[15]

> The Son is obedient to the Father in his spontaneous surrender. And he understands this obedience as a permission, because he owes himself and everything that comes to him from the Father, including the possibility of his self-surrender, to the Father. In this sense he is, as Son, the Eucharist: that is, thanksgiving absolutely.[16]

2. As the historical body is both eucharistic and ecclesial, so the sacramental body, precisely as sacramental, is historical and ecclesial. As Catholics, we confess that in the gift of the Eucharist, Christ communicates the very substance of his life. "The Church has received the Eucharist from Christ her Lord," writes John Paul II, "not as one gift—however precious—among so many others, but as the gift par excellence, for it is the gift of himself, of his person in his sacred humanity, as well as the gift

15. Hans Urs von Balthasar, *A Theology of History* (San Francisco: Ignatius Press, 1994), 30–31.

16. Hans Urs von Balthasar, "Spirit and Institution," in *Explorations in Theology*, vol. 4, *Spirit and Institution*, trans. Edward T. Oakes (San Francisco: Ignatius Press, 1995), 230.

of his saving work."[17] To say that Christ communicates his substance or his being is another way of saying that he communicates the totality of his human and divine life. The saving mysteries of Christ's historical life—especially his dying on the cross and his rising from the dead—are included in the Sacrament. When we receive the Sacrament in faith, the Holy Spirit brings us into communion with the historical and bodily existence of Jesus of Nazareth.

In giving the Eucharist to the Church, Christ communicates more than the substance of his life; he bestows the gift of unity or communion with all of the faithful in heaven and on earth. As *Lumen gentium* teaches, "Partaking of the body of the Lord in the breaking of the Eucharistic bread, we are taken up into communion with Him and with one another."[18] The Eucharist is the abiding source of the Church; hence her words in the Second Eucharistic Prayer, "Humbly we pray that, partaking of the Body and Blood of Christ, we may be gathered into one by the Holy Spirit."

3. The ecclesial body of Christ—the community of believers—is historical and sacramental. Paul writes to the Corinthians: "The bread which we break, is it not a participation in the body of Christ? Because there is one bread, we who are many are one body" (1 Cor 10:16–17). The Church, as it were, is Christ's body extended in history through the mediation of the Holy Spirit. "One should not believe," writes Augustine, "that Christ is in the head but not in the body; rather he is complete in the head and in the body"—*Christus totus*.[19]

By virtue of her unity with Christ, the Church is a sacrament of communion. *Lumen gentium* describes the Church as "a sacrament or as a sign and instrument both of a very closely knit union with God and of the unity of the whole human race."[20] The ecclesial body of Christ—*corpus mysticum et verum*—is a real symbol and cause of communion between God and creation. Insofar as she continually receives her life from Christ's Eucharist, the form and fruit of ecclesial unity is a covenant—a reciprocal

17. John Paul II, *Ecclesia de Eucharistia* (*EE*), Encyclical on the Eucharist in Its Relationship to the Church, April 17, 2003, no. 11.

18. *LG*, no. 7.

19. Augustine, *In Iohannis evangelium tractatus* 28.1 (PL 35.1622).

20. *LG*, no. 1.

exchange of life and love. Drawing on the letter to the Ephesians, Ratzinger explains:

> The Church is the Body [of Christ], not by virtue of an identity without distinction, but rather by means of the pneumatic-real act of spousal love. Expressed in yet another way, this means that Christ and the Church are one body in the sense in which man and woman are one flesh, that is, in such a way that in their indissoluble spiritual-bodily union, they nonetheless remain unconfused and unmingled.[21]

In summary, I draw two conclusions from these reflections on the inseparable connection between the Eucharist and the Church. The first is to note that each modality of the threefold body of Christ accomplishes and bears witness to a true union between God and creation. The historical, sacramental, and ecclesial body of Christ is the archetype of the relationship between nature and grace and of the relationship between the Church and the world. In other words, the Church-world relation begins in the womb of Mary. The unabridged humanity of Jesus Christ, together with Mary's *fiat*, represents the deepest truth of the world or creation itself. Jesus Christ is the alpha and the omega, the one in whom and for whom all things were made. By revealing the mystery of the Father and his love, Christ "fully reveals man to man himself."[22] He is, we might say, the personal and living unity of nature and grace without confusion or separation. The concern of *Gaudium et spes* to uphold the "rightful autonomy of earthly affairs"[23] is grounded both in the doctrine of creation and in the Church's confession that Jesus Christ, the only begotten Son "is to be acknowledged in two natures without confusion, change, division, or separation … The distinction between the natures was never abolished by their union, but rather the character proper to each of the two natures was preserved as they came together in one person and one hypostasis."[24] The integrity or autonomy of Christ's human nature is real-

21. Joseph Ratzinger, *Called to Communion: Understanding the Church Today*, trans. Adrian Walker (San Francisco: Ignatius Press, 1996), 39.

22. *Gaudium et spes* (*GS*), no. 22.

23. *GS*, no. 36.

24. Council of Chalcedon (451): DS 301. Cf. John Paul II, *Fides et ratio*, no. 80: "The mystery of the Incarnation will always remain the central point of reference for an understanding of the enigma of human existence, the created world and God himself.… The

ized and perfected within the hypostatic union. Analogously, the realities of the created order (i.e., "earthly affairs") attain their deepest integrity or autonomy within the mystery of the Church.

The second point concerns the dynamic unity of the historical, sacramental, and ecclesial body of Christ. Undergirding the mystery that these three are one is the plan of God to gather up all of creation into union with Christ. The eternal Son of the Father entered history and assumed a historical body in order to communicate or share his life by giving himself eucharistically. The Eucharist was instituted by Christ in order to build up the Church as a mystery of communion. The Church, continually born from the pierced side of Christ, is the "universal sacrament of salvation."[25] Her mission is to gather the entire human family and ultimately all of creation into communion with Christ's body.

Again, this Christocentric vision finds confirmation in the documents of the Second Vatican Council. The conciliar constitution proclaims that "Christ, who died and was raised up for all ... is the key, the focal point and the goal ... of all human history."[26] The decree on the laity similarly teaches the centrality and the catholicity of Christ: "God has willed to gather together all that was natural, all that was supernatural, in a single whole in Christ, 'so that in everything he would have the primacy' (Col 1:18)."[27] The eschatological gathering of creation into a single whole in Christ is prefigured and accomplished in the eucharistic offering of the Church. By offering this sacrifice in which "the building up of the Body" is made complete, "the Church both prays and labors in order that the entire world may become ... the Body of the Lord and the Temple of the Holy Spirit, and that in Christ, the Head of all, all honor and glory may be rendered to the Creator and Father of the Universe."[28] This final

intimate essence of God and of the human being become intelligible: in the mystery of the Incarnate Word, human nature and divine nature are safeguarded in all their autonomy, and at the same time the unique bond which sets them together in mutuality without confusion of any kind is revealed."

25. *LG*, no. 48.

26. *GS*, no. 10.

27. Second Vatican Council, *Apostolicam actuositatem*, Decree on the Apostolate of the Laity, November 18, 1965, no. 7, in *Vatican Council II: The Conciliar and Post Conciliar Documents*, ed. Austin Flannery (Northport: Costello, 1975).

28. *LG*, no. 17.

text from *Lumen gentium* leads to the second step in my argument, on the significance of the Eucharist for the Church's missionary opening to the world.

Christ's Eucharist and the Eschatological Nature of the Pilgrim Church

One of the basic aims of *Gaudium et spes* was to unfold and develop the teaching of *Lumen gentium* on the "eschatological nature of the pilgrim Church."[29] Accordingly, the first part of *Gaudium et spes* culminates with a reflection on Jesus Christ as "the Alpha and the Omega":

> The Church has a single intention: that God's kingdom may come, and that the salvation of the whole human race may come to pass. For every benefit which the People of God during its earthly pilgrimage can offer to the human family stems from the fact that the Church is "the universal sacrament of salvation," simultaneously manifesting and exercising the mystery of God's love.
>
> For God's Word, by whom all things were made, was Himself made flesh so that as perfect man He might save all men and sum up all things in Himself. The Lord is the goal of human history, the focal point of the longings of history and of civilization, the center of the human race, the joy of every heart and the answer to all its yearnings.... Enlivened and united in His Spirit, we journey toward the consummation of human history, one which fully accords with the counsel of God's love: "To reestablish all things in Christ, both those in the heavens and those on the earth" (Eph 11:10).[30]

The form of this world is passing away, and the Church is called to bear witness to the eschatological kingdom of God, which transcends the confines of history by reaching beyond death in the hope for eternal life with God. At the same time, the authors of *Gaudium of spes* were concerned to show that the expectancy of a "new dwelling place and a new earth where justice will abide" (cf. 2 Cor 5:2) does not diminish the Church's responsibility for the world:

> While we are warned that it profits a man nothing if he gain the whole world and lose himself (cf. Lk 9:25), the expectation of a new earth must not weak-

29. Cf. *LG*, nos. 48–51.
30. *GS*, no. 45.

en but rather stimulate our concern for cultivating this one. For here grows the body of a new human family, a body which even now is able to give some kind of foreshadowing of the new age. Hence, while earthly progress must be carefully distinguished from the growth of Christ's kingdom, to the extent that the former can contribute to the better ordering of human society, it is of vital concern to the kingdom of God.[31]

Without confusing "earthly progress" and the kingdom of God, the Council Fathers presented anew the social and cosmic dimension of Christ's saving mission. The Church is "called upon to save and renew every creature, that all things may be restored in Christ."[32] The pastoral concern of *Gaudium et spes* to enter into dialogue with the modern world on questions such as marriage and the family; the development of culture, economic, and social life; and the political community all stems from the saving mystery of Jesus Christ. In order to grasp the significance of this Christocentric vision of the kingdom of God, it is helpful to have a sense of how eschatology was conceived and taught in the decades prior to the Second Vatican Council.

Eschatology, or *De Novissimis*, as it was often titled, was usually a chapter or section of dogmatic theology that considered the four last things: death, judgment, heaven, and hell. For the most part, neoscholastic reflections on the last things turned on differing accounts of how (after death) an individual human soul can attain (or suffer the loss of) a vision of the divine essence.[33] It was essentially and almost exclusively concerned with the afterlife, that is, with questions concerning what happens to a soul after death. The limitations, or one-sidedness, of this eschatology stem from a certain abstraction from, or forgetfulness of, the eschatological significance of Christ's incarnation, death, resurrection, and Eucharist, and from this abstraction, several consequences follow.

First and foremost, there was a tendency to conceive salvation in essentially individualistic terms. Citing *Lumen gentium*, *Gaudium et spes* corrects this imbalance by confirming anew the central truth of Catholic

31. *GS*, no. 39.

32. Second Vatican Council, *Ad gentes*, Decree on the Mission Activity of the Church, December 7, 1965, no. 1.

33. Cf. Reginald Garrigou-Lagrange, *Life Everlasting and the Immensity of the Soul* (Rockford, IL: Tan Books, 1991).

eschatology: God does not want to save us alone, for the salvation he offers in Jesus Christ involves a communion with all the blessed in heaven and on earth: "As God did not create man for life in isolation, but for the formation of social unity, so also 'it has pleased God to make men holy and save them not merely as individuals, without bond or link between them, but by making them into a single people, a people which acknowledges Him in truth and serves Him in holiness.'"[34]

Second, the theme of eschatology was removed from history and became almost exclusively about the afterlife. There was a corresponding tendency to therefore overlook the presence of the eschaton in history. Responding to this deficiency, *Lumen gentium* teaches that "already the final age of the world has come upon us and the renovation of the world ... is already anticipated in some kind of a real way."[35] This same idea is taken up and deepened in the final chapter of *Lumen gentium*: in the person of Mary, assumed into heaven, "the Church has already reached ... perfection."[36]

Third, neoscholasticism tended to view the Church and the sacraments of the Church in instrumental terms. This point is illustrated well by a text from Abbot Vonier's influential book *A Key to the Doctrine of the Eucharist*. Vonier writes:

> There is ... in the Catholic sacramental system a certain transitoriness which it is very important to remember. Saint Thomas never tires of alluding to the instrumental character of the sacraments. They are the tools of God to bring about definitive results, and when those ends are completely achieved the tools will be laid aside by the divine Artificer. Sacraments belong to the work which Christ does here on earth; they are not permanent glories of the everlasting triumph.... There will be no Eucharistic sacrifice in heaven.[37]

34. *GS*, no. 32.

35. *LG*, no. 48.

36. *LG*, no. 65.

37. Abbot Vonier, *A Key to the Doctrine of the Eucharist* (Bethesda, MD: Zaccheus, 2003), 171–72. In a luminous essay, "The Eucharist and Transubstantiation," in *Christian Faith and Human Understanding: Studies on the Eucharist, Trinity, and the Human Person* (Washington, DC: Catholic University of America Press, 2006), 98, Robert Sokolowski presents an alternative account of the eschatological dimension as the Liturgy:

> As we say in the Eucharistic Canon, we join the angels and saints and take part in the celestial Eucharist, the glory given to the Father by the Son who redeemed the world, the

For Vonier, the Eucharist provides the means to help us attain our end—union with God in the beatific vision. It is a tool that will be laid aside.

Again, the Second Vatican Council qualifies this one-sided view of the sacramental economy:

In the earthly liturgy we take part in a foretaste of that heavenly liturgy which is celebrated in the holy city of Jerusalem toward which we journey as pilgrims.[38]

Celebrating the Eucharistic sacrifice . . . we are most closely united to the Church in heaven. . . . [We partake] in foretaste the liturgy of consummate glory.[39]

The Lord left behind a pledge of this hope and strength for life's journey in that sacrament of faith where natural elements refined by man are gloriously changed into His Body and Blood, providing a meal of brotherly solidarity and a foretaste of the heavenly banquet.[40]

In his final encyclical, *Ecclesia de Eucharistia*, John Paul II confirms and develops the Council's rediscovery of the eschatological significance of Christ's Eucharist. He describes the Eucharist as "a straining towards the goal, a foretaste of the fullness of joy promised by Christ (cf. Jn 15:11); it is in some way the anticipation of heaven, the 'pledge of future glory.'"[41] He writes further: "Those who feed on Christ in the Eucharist need not wait until the hereafter to receive eternal life: *they already possess it on earth*, as the first-fruits of a future fullness which will embrace man in his totality. . . . With the Eucharist we digest, as it were, the 'secret' of the resurrection."[42]

Finally, by focusing so exclusively on the question of how an individual soul abstracted from the material cosmos can attain the beatific

---

Lamb presented in heaven as slain, the Mystic Lamb, so profoundly depicted by Jan van Eyck in the Ghent Altarpiece. Our worldly Eucharist joins the celestial. Dr Eric Perl, who is a member of the Orthodox Church, once said that he was asked by a student in religion class whether there would be a Eucharist in heaven; he said that he answered, "There won't be anything else." The angels and saints in heaven participate in the action of the Son toward the Father, and we now in our Eucharist join in their participation.

38. Second Vatican Council, *Sacrosanctum Concilium*, Constitution on the Sacred Liturgy, December 4, 1963, no. 8.

39. *LG*, nos. 50–51.

40. *GS*, no. 38.

41. *EE*, no. 18.

42. *EE*, no. 18.

vision, neoscholastic reflection tended to overlook the significance of creation within our final union with God in heaven. The result was an eschatology without the fullness of the created world or the cosmos as a whole. Pope Benedict XVI seems to target this unfortunate development when he writes in *Spe salvi*:

> Modern Christianity, faced with the successes of science in progressively structuring the world, has to a large extent restricted its attention to the individual and his salvation. In so doing it has limited the horizon of its hope and has failed to recognize sufficiently the greatness of its task—even if it has continued to achieve great things.[43]

The root cause of this limitation of Christian hope was an inadequate understanding of the catholicity or universality of Christ's saving mission. There was, we might say, a failure to be guided by the unsurpassable teaching of St. Paul that the world was created in, through, and for the incarnate Son, that creation itself is groaning for redemption (cf. Rom 8:19, 8:22), and that "all things hold together" in Christ, who is "the first-born from the dead" (Col 1:17).

Instaurare Omnia in Christ

The Church, born from the sacrifice of Christ, exists in order to save the whole world. Drawing on both the New Testament and Catholic tradition, the Second Vatican Council presented anew the breadth and depth of Christian hope: "The Church is called upon to save and renew every creature, that all things may be restored in Christ."[44] Her mission is of universal scope, for "creation itself will be delivered from its slavery to corruption into the freedom of the glory of the sons of God."[45] On account of the breadth of God's plan, "the faithful … must learn the deepest meaning and the value of all creation as well as its role in the harmonious praise of God.… In this way the world may be permeated by the spirit of Christ."[46]

43. Benedict XVI, *Spe salvi*, Encyclical on Christian Hope, November 30, 2007, no. 25.
44. Second Vatican Council, *Ad gentes*, Decree on the Mission Activity of the Church, December 7, 1965, no. 1.
45. *LG*, no. 9.
46. *LG*, no. 36.

How, then, can creation be saved? How can the temporal order in all of its distinct dimensions and legitimate autonomy—cultural, economic, and political—be brought into union with the body of Christ? A partial answer to this question requires thinking more deeply about the lay dimension of the Church's mission. In the ordinary living within a family and working in various occupations toward the common good, the laity are called to offer spiritual worship to God (Rom 12:1). Through this worship, the laity consecrate the world itself to God:

> For all their works, prayers and apostolic endeavors, their ordinary married and family life, their daily occupations, their physical and mental relaxation, if carried out in the Spirit, and even the hardships of life, if patiently borne-all these become "spiritual sacrifices acceptable to God through Jesus Christ" (1 Pt 2:5). Together with the offering of the Lord's body, they are most fittingly offered in the celebration of the Eucharist. Thus, as those everywhere who adore in holy activity, the laity consecrate the world itself to God.[47]

Thinking about the lay dimension of the Church also goes hand in hand with a renewed understanding of the cosmic dimension of the Church's liturgy. In *Ecclesia de Eucharistia,* St. John Paul II teaches:

> the Eucharist is always in some way celebrated *on the altar of the world.* It unites heaven and earth. It embraces and permeates all creation. The Son of God became man in order to restore all creation, in one supreme act of praise, to the One who made it from nothing. He, the Eternal High Priest who by the blood of his Cross entered the eternal sanctuary, thus gives back to the Creator and Father all creation redeemed.[48]

The transubstantiation of bread and wine is an anticipatory and effective sign of the eschatological transformation of the entire material cosmos. Bread and wine symbolize God's good creation as received and cultivated by human beings. In the Church's liturgy, the gifts of creation are acknowledged and offered back to God in gratitude. Through the words of institution and the work of the Holy Spirit, these created gifts are changed into the body and blood of Christ. The bread and wine are not annihilated, but transubstantiated and fulfilled by becoming signs of Christ's real

47. *LG,* no. 35.
48. *EE,* no. 8.

presence among us. The accidents of bread and wine that remain are not an embarrassment but a sign of Christ's sacrificed and risen humanity, which is our true food and drink. Christ gives himself to the Father and to us in all that he is and all that he does. In his Eucharist he includes the material order of creation, as well as human work and human celebration, within this exchange of gifts. Nothing of creation is disdained or lost in the reciprocal sacrifice of eucharistic communion. Beyond the confines of death, the world itself is invited to share in the eternal love between the Father and the Son.

Conclusion

Let me conclude by returning to Fr. O'Malley's claim that the purpose of the Council was "to promote a more positive appreciation of 'the world' and the relationship of the Church to it."[49] These words, or some variation on these words, continue to be echoed by countless theologians. Richard Gaillardetz argues that "Vatican II remains a fundamental turning point in the history of the Catholic Church.... Its teaching represents an important shift in the stance of the Catholic Church from one of isolation, fear, and condemnation to one of humble openness and willingness to learn through dialogue with other Christians, with other religions, and with the wider world."[50] "*Gaudium et spes*," writes Maureen Sullivan, "expresses the most profound change from being a church in conflict with the world to being a church in dialogue with the world"—a Church that, "despite a history of mistrust, disdain, often outright condemnation, ... had reconciled with the world."[51]

What is missing from these reports of a new "appreciation," "dialogue," and "reconciliation" is a reflection on *why* the Church is interested in the world. What does it mean to have an essentially pastoral Council? In seeking an answer to this question, it is helpful to return to Pope Paul VI's words at the start of the second session:

49. O'Malley, "Vatican II: Historical Perspectives," 26.

50. Richard R. Gaillardetz and Catherine E. Clifford, *Keys to the Council: Unlocking the Teaching of Vatican II* (Collegeville, MN: Liturgical, 2012), 189–90.

51. Maureen Sullivan, *The Road to Vatican II: Key Changes in Theology* (New York: Paulist, 2007), 40 and 45.

> From what point, dear brethren, do we set out? ... What is the road we intend to follow? What is the goal we propose to ourselves? These three very simple and at the same time very important questions have, as we well know, only one answer, namely, that here at this very hour we should proclaim Christ to ourselves and to the world around us; Christ our beginning, Christ our life and guide, Christ our hope and our end.... Let no other light be shed on this Council but Christ the light of the world![52]

Guided by this vision, *Gaudium et spes* sought "to explain to everyone how it conceives of the presence and activity of the Church in the world of today"[53] and to enter into a dialogue with the contemporary world on "a number of ... urgent needs characterizing the present age, needs which go to the roots of the human race."[54] The Church exists in the midst of the world—with its joys and sorrows—as a sign and instrument of God's plan to recapitulate all things in Christ. The source and the goal of the Church's pastoral dialogue with the contemporary world is the figure of Jesus Christ, who is the Alpha and Omega of creation. In giving the substance of his life and love to the Church, Christ has bestowed his catholicity upon the Church. Her sacramental character—the relation to the Eucharist at the heart of the Church—determines her missionary character. In other words, the Church is missionary because of Christ's love. From beginning to end, the aim of the Church in her relation to the world is to bear witness to the saving mystery of Christ's love, which seeks to heal and renew all of God's creation.

In an inspired book written on the eve of the Second Vatican Council, Hugo Rahner uncovers the hidden center and the astonishing breadth of the Church's relation to the world. He writes:

> The very fact that it is the flesh of the Logos become man that ultimately defines the limits of Christian humanism contains the possibility of almost explosively extending those limits to what is really a limitless degree. Now we may dare—indeed dare we must—to take up with an all-embracing gesture into this pattern of the Christian man whatever in the long perspectives of history or in the depths

52. Paul VI, Speech at the Beginning of the Second Session of the II Vatican Council, September 29, 1963.

53. *GS*, no. 2.

54. *GS*, no. 46.

of the soul is true and noble in thought or deed. All that is good and true has proceeded from the Logos and has its homing-point in the incarnate God.... For the humanist Christian there is only one possible attitude that he can take towards the world: he must love. Yet one can only love a person, and that is why the Christian humanist loves the human in every shape and form but only in him of whom St. Paul says "*panta eis auton ektistai*—all things were created in him."[55]

In the same spirit, J. R. R. Tolkien described the Blessed Sacrament as "the one great thing to love on earth."[56] Christ's Eucharist is the one thing to love because in loving this Sacrament we are given a share in God's own incarnate love. We learn to love what he loves and to love in the way that he loves—with love that is ready to die but that reaches beyond death in hope for the resurrection. At the school of Mary, we learn to say "yes" and "amen"—to receive this gift of Christ's presence in the Blessed Sacrament as an invitation to offer our lives and the entire created order back to God in gratitude.

55. Hugo Rahner, *Greek Myths and Christian Mystery*, trans. B. Battershaw (New York: Harper and Row, 1963), xiv–xv.

56. "Letter to Michael Tolkien, March 6–8, 1941," in *The Letters of J. R. R. Tolkien*, ed. Humphrey Carpenter (Boston: Houghton Mifflin, 2000), 53–54.

5

Nature and Grace in *Gaudium et spes*

The Status of the Theory of the Natural Desire for the Supernatural

MATTHEW LEVERING

Introduction

As Susan Wood has observed, Henri de Lubac drew a "clear connection ... between his own work on the supernatural and themes developed in *Gaudium et spes*."[1] De Lubac's work on the nature-grace relationship sought to articulate the intimacy of the relationship between created nature and the divine gift of grace so as to prevent grace from being conceived as a mere add-on to a fundamentally self-sufficient human na-

A version of this essay was previously published as chapter 4 of my *An Introduction to Vatican II as an Ongoing Theological Event* (Washington, DC: Catholic University of America Press, 2017).

1. Susan K. Wood, SCL, "Henri de Lubac and the Church-World Relationship in *Gaudium et Spes*," in *The Legacy of Vatican II*, ed. Massimo Faggioli and Andrea Vicini, SJ (Mahwah: Paulist, 2015), 227. For a helpful introduction to and contextualization of the development of de Lubac's thinking on nature and grace, see Raul Berzosa Martinez, *La teología del sobrenatural en los escritos de Henri de Lubac: Estudio historico-teologico (1931–1980)* (Burgos: Aldecoa, 1991). See also Georges Chantraine, SJ, "The Supernatural: Discernment of Catholic Thought According to Henri de Lubac," in *Surnaturel: A Controversy at the Heart of Twentieth-Century Thomistic Thought*, ed. Serge-Thomas Bonino, OP, trans. Robert Williams (Ave Maria, FL: Sapientia Press, 2009), 21–40; and Henry Donneaud, OP, "*Surnaturel* through the Fine-Tooth Comb of Traditional Thomism," in *Surnaturel*, 41–57. For further background, see Bernard Comte, "Le père de Lubac, un théologien dans l'Église de Lyon," in *Henri de Lubac: La rencontre au coeur de l'Église*, ed. Jean-Dominique Durand (Paris: Cerf, 2006), 35–89.

ture. This was, according to John Paul II, a central aim of the Council, to show how it is Christ alone who reveals "the inward mystery of man," his "heart," and true desire for communion with God, and that it is only through Christ that "man finds again the greatness, dignity and value that belong to his humanity."[2]

In the first paragraph of his encyclical *Dives in misericordia*, John Paul II refers to *Gaudium et spes* 22, stating that "man cannot be manifested in the full dignity of his nature without reference—not only on the level of concepts but also in an integrally existential way—to God." The pope continues by beautifully drawing together a central conviction shared by both Henri de Lubac and *Gaudium et spes*, that "the more the Church's mission is centered upon man—the more it is, so to speak, anthropocentric—the more it must be confirmed and actualized theocentrically, that is to say, be directed in Jesus Christ to the Father" (*DM*, no. 1). For John Paul II, the reality that human nature is fueled by the desire for loving communion with God is "one of the basic principles, perhaps the most important one of the Second Vatican Council."[3]

Although de Lubac describes working on the text of *Gaudium et spes* "only in its later stages," he was a member of the Mixed Commission, which in 1963 drafted what would eventually become the Council's pastoral constitution.[4] Many members of this commission, including then Archbishop Karol Wojtyła, were deeply influenced by de Lubac and knew well his writings on nature and grace. As his *Carnets du Concile* records, de Lubac spoke openly about nature and grace with respect to the commission's draft of what would later become *Gaudium et spes*.[5] In *Entretien autour de Vatican II*, he observes that with the writing of *Gaudium et spes* "the Council broke away from extrinsicism which [was] the illness of modern Catholicism 'which had misunderstood the full character of the

2. John Paul II, *Redemptor hominis*, nos. 8 and 10.

3. John Paul II, *Dives in misericordia*, no. 1.

4. See Henri de Lubac, *Entretien autour de Vatican II: Souvenirs et reflections* (Paris: Cerf, 1985), 45. See also his posthumously published *Carnets du Concile*, 2 vols. (Paris: Cerf, 2007), as well as his *At the Service of the Church: Henri de Lubac Reflects on the Circumstances That Occasioned His Writings*, trans. Anne Elizabeth Englund (San Francisco: Ignatius Press, 1993), chap. 7 and Appendix 7.

5. See de Lubac, *Carnets du Concile*, 2:271, cited in Wood, "Henri de Lubac and the Church-World Relationship in *Gaudium et spes*," 236.

desire of nature' (Congar) purposefully avoiding the vocabulary of the two 'orders.'"[6] One need not fully agree with this viewpoint to appreciate the importance of reading *Gaudium et spes* in light of de Lubac's work. David Schindler, for example, does not exaggerate when he states that "once we have clarified what is basic to de Lubac's theological 'project,' we can see that it has been vindicated. Indeed, we need only recall the text from *Gaudium et spes* with which we began this Introduction: 'Christ the Lord, Christ the new Adam, in the very revelation of the mystery of the Father and of his love, fully reveals man to himself and brings to light his most high calling' (no. 22)."[7] This text, as Schindler points out, is a paraphrase of a central passage from de Lubac's book *Catholicism*. Schindler notes that the "organic relationship" between anthropocentrism and theocentrism is both "the most fundamental principle taught at Vatican II" and "likewise the most fundamental principle in the life-work of Henri de Lubac."[8] Each shares the conviction that the mystery of man can only be understood through the mystery of the saving God.

The first section of this essay focuses on *The Mystery of the Supernatural*, a book published by de Lubac in 1965, which de Lubac seems to have written at least partly in response to a speech made on the floor of the Council criticizing his position on nature and grace in the context of the Council Fathers' discussion of the working document known as Schema 13.[9] The book develops "point by point" themes introduced by an ear-

6. De Lubac, *Entretien autour de Vatican II*, 28, cited in Wood, "Henri de Lubac and the Church-World Relationship in *Gaudium et spes*," 237. Wood's translation.

7. David L. Schindler, "Introduction," in Henri de Lubac, SJ, *The Mystery of the Supernatural*, trans. Rosemary Sheed (New York: Crossroad, 1998), xi–xxxi. See also for the same position Schindler's "Christology and the *imago Dei*: Interpreting *Gaudium et spes*," *Communio: International Catholic Review* 23 (1996): 156–84.

8. Schindler, "Introduction," xxvii.

9. See Karl Heinz Neufeld, SJ, "In the Service of the Council: Bishops and Theologians at the Second Vatican Council (for Cardinal Henri de Lubac on His Ninetieth Birthday)," trans. Ronald Sway, in *Vatican II: Assessment and Perspectives: Twenty-Five Years After (1962–1987)*, vol. 1, ed. René Latourelle, SJ (Mahwah, NJ: Paulist, 1988), 74–105. Neufeld states that during discussions on Schema 13, which would later become *Gaudium et spes*, "A speaker launched into an offensive against ideas that he attributed to de Lubac in *Surnaturel* concerning the relationship between nature and the supernatural, or, more precisely, against the signification he gave to the 'natural desire' of man for God. What was at stake here was nothing less than the basic idea underlying the subsequent text of *Gaudium et spes*: the question of the correct understanding of being a Christian in the world." In response, says Neufeld, de

lier article published under the same title in 1949.[10] After summarizing the main principles that inform de Lubac's position, I offer a brief response to the book's thesis, before then turning to specific texts from *Gaudium et spes*. In my view, the influence of de Lubac's ideas on the text of *Gaudium et spes* is extensive; the question is only whether his specific theory on the relationship between nature and grace is mandated by *Gaudium et spes* and given the weight of a magisterial teaching. Although I argue that the answer to this question is ultimately negative, it is undoubtedly true that the relationship of nature and grace is of critical importance for *Gaudium et spes* on account of its aim of emphasizing the strong interconnection of Church and world.

Gaudium et spes agrees with de Lubac's assessment that whenever nature and grace are sharply separated, it will seem as though the world does not need the Church, or the Church the world. At the same time, as de Lubac himself warned in a letter distributed to various participants at the Council during the drafting of *Gaudium et spes*, there is a similar danger in any instance where nature and grace are too tightly joined together.[11] It was the intent of *Gaudium et spes* to avoid these extremes by seeking out what de Lubac would later describe as a difficult-to-establish "doctrinal equilibrium."[12] In his 1968 commentary *Athéisme et le sens de l'homme: Une double requête de Gaudium et Spes*, which as William McDonough says "remains perhaps the most helpful interpretation of *Gaud-*

Lubac produced "two new volumes, which appeared in 1965 and which attempted to give a clearer presentation of his position: *Augustinisme et théologie moderne* and *Le Mystère du surnaturel*. Had these two works been read attentively, there should have been no further misunderstandings concerning this question. Naturally, de Lubac also did what he could to exclude such misunderstandings as far as possible from the drafted text of *Gaudium et spes*" (91–92).

10. De Lubac, *At the Service of the Church*, 123. See also de Lubac's "Le Mystère du surnaturel," *Recherches de science religieuse* 36 (1949): 80–121, which appears in English as "The Mystery of the Supernatural," trans. Anne Englund Nash, in de Lubac, *Theology in History* (San Francisco: Ignatius Press, 1996), 248–80.

11. See de Lubac, *At the Service of the Church*, 341: "Others, going farther, construct theories according to which there would no longer even be any true evangelization in view for the future, the so-called 'profane' world being already Christian in reality, independent of any evangelical revelation."

12. Henri de Lubac, SJ, *Athéisme et le sens de l'homme: Une double requête de Gaudium et spes* (Paris: Cerf, 1968), 126.

ium et spes,"[13] de Lubac rightly insists that in the document "everything ... was placed under the sign of the Word of God made flesh, who as 'a perfect man has entered into the history of the world, assuming it and recapitulating it in himself.'"[14]

The Mystery of the Supernatural

In *The Mystery of the Supernatural*, de Lubac reprises and develops the insights of *Surnaturel*, first published in 1946, and his 1949 article "Le Mystère du surnaturel." He opens the book by arguing that "the traditional idea" of nature and grace is currently under threat from two directions. First, there is the dualist or separatist view of nature and grace, which, while not having many modern adherents, still bears bitter fruit "in the sphere of practical action" by conceiving the secular world as though grace did not exist.[15] Second, there is the immanentist conflation of nature and grace that supposes that the dialectic of history will produce from within itself the transcendence that we desire. To account for how these two extremes arose, and how they may be overcome, de Lubac focuses his attention on what he calls the "new theory" of "pure nature."[16] This theory, according to de Lubac, was entirely lacking among the Greek Fathers, as well in the West until Cardinal Cajetan, and was even criticized by some Baroque commentators such as Francisco Toletus. Scholarship done in the early twentieth century had already contested the histo-

13. William C. McDonough, "The Church in the Modern World: Rereading *Gaudium et spes* after Thirty Years," in *Vatican II: The Continuing Agenda*, ed. Anthony J. Cernera (Fairfield: Sacred Heart University Press, 1997), 113–33, at 114.

14. De Lubac, *Athéisme et le sens de l'homme*, 126, translation mine. McDonough summarizes well the position that de Lubac takes in his commentary: "For de Lubac, *Gaudium et spes* moves beyond its partial interpretations by insisting that neither church nor world has meaning except in its link to the other." "Church in the Modern World," 119. For a commentary from the same period as de Lubac's *Athéisme et le sens de l'homme*, see Gregory Baum, OSA, and Donald Campion, SJ, *De Ecclesia in Mundo Huius Temporis: The Pastoral Constitution on the Church in the Modern World* (New York: Paulist, 1967).

15. Henri de Lubac, SJ, *The Mystery of the Supernatural*, trans. Rosemary Sheed (New York: Herder and Herder, 1967), xi. The translation is exactly the same in the 1967 and 1998 editions, with the exception that the Latin quotations are all translated by John M. Pepino in the 1998 edition.

16. De Lubac, *Mystery of the Supernatural*, 7.

ricity of the theory of pure nature by calling into question the legitimacy of Cajetan's interpretation of Thomas. Even earlier, Théodore de Régnon acknowledged that he could "find no explicit affirmation in St. Thomas of the concrete possibility of a purely natural order—remembering always that this means a complete order, bearing within it its own final end, in the modern sense of the expression."[17]

The problem, however, is that if a purely natural end or "pure nature" is not at least hypothetically possible or conceivable, then the difference between human nature and grace would seem to be incapable of description.[18] Without any concept of "pure nature," we could never know "nature" as something distinguishable from grace. De Lubac argues that the answer to this quandary consists in accepting a paradox. He fully grants that created spirit, as such, is not naturally a supernatural reality: "The fact that the nature of spiritual being, as it actually exists, is not conceived as an order destined to close in finally upon itself, but in a sense open to an inevitably supernatural end, does not mean that it already has in itself, or as part of its basis, the smallest positively supernatural element." Certainly, too, human nature has "its own proper stability and its own definite structure."[19] But, paradoxically, this does not mean that human nature, as graced, has a twofold ultimate end—that is to say, a proportionate natural end identifiable by the postulate of a hypothetical "pure nature" and the graced end of beatific vision.

To explain what he means here, de Lubac appeals to the perspective of the Fathers, which he thinks was shared by Thomas Aquinas.[20] He states: "In the old teaching, which remains for us the traditional one, the argument was based on no such duality of ends. The supernatural, which always represented God's will for the final end of his creatures, put no obstacle in the way of the normal development or activity of nature in its own order."[21] There was never a need to dissociate "the two orders com-

17. As cited in de Lubac, *Mystery of the Supernatural*, 15.

18. De Lubac, *Mystery of the Supernatural*, 15–17.

19. De Lubac, *Mystery of the Supernatural*, 41.

20. According to de Lubac, Aquinas never accepted "a completely natural perfection [of the human person] which can be adequately defined by pure philosophy." *Mystery of the Supernatural*, 49.

21. De Lubac, *Mystery of the Supernatural*, 45.

pletely," because grace permits the activity of nature in such a way that this activity need not constitute an end in its own right.[22] The greatness of grace means that it can never be merely "juxtaposed" with nature as if nature and grace could be "contained in the same genus, of which they form as it were two species."[23] Because grace is infinitely above nature, it does not, therefore, simply work to align a supernatural end with a natural end, as though these were two instances of the same kind of thing, or as if humans could be theoretically perfected without divine assistance. De Lubac's concern is that setting up a natural beatitude alongside a supernatural beatitude inevitably flattens the latter, so that nothing "remains peculiar to the supernatural order, except the word."[24]

Against such a univocal understanding of nature and grace, de Lubac insists that nature cannot produce a "beatitude" in any way comparable to the God-given beatitude for which God made humans. He states that according to his opponents, "the two series—'pure nature' and supernaturalized nature, or nature called to the supernatural—flowed along parallel channels in complete harmony.... Without anything apparently to distinguish them, one is called 'natural,' the other 'supernatural.'"[25] Such a view risks a merely nominal distinction between nature and grace because it presents grace as a "supernatural good" parallel to the "natural good" that nature produces in and of itself. The postulating of God as the "natural good" of humans presumptuously offers God to humans through the work of nature itself and does so in a way that the ancient tradition would never have dared suppose, since, after all, God "dwells in unapproachable light" (1 Tm 6:16).

But what about the distinction between seeing God's essence (i.e., the gift of beatific vision) and seeing God as first cause (i.e., the proportionate end of human nature)? Here, citing Bernard of Clairvaux, de Lubac questions whether this distinction is effectively conceived. What does it mean to be blessed by seeing God without seeing his essence? De Lubac argues that the fact that the soul is an image of the Trinity indicates that the

22. De Lubac, *Mystery of the Supernatural*, 46.
23. De Lubac, *Mystery of the Supernatural*, 48.
24. De Lubac, *Mystery of the Supernatural*, 52.
25. De Lubac, *Mystery of the Supernatural*, 53.

highest aspect of our humanity is our being made for the enjoyment of the Trinity. Any idea, however hypothetical, that suggests human beings could be happy without God's aid, simply by the exercise of their natural powers, strikes de Lubac as not only mistaken, but also as the source of a false view of the sufficiency of natural morality. Furthermore, the central problem with the hypothesis of pure nature is that it leads to a God whose giving of himself to humans is no longer free, but pertains to a natural order that requires it on account of the debt of justice that the Creator God owes himself once he determines to create. Even if the "formal hypothesis" of pure nature were taken as "legitimate," it is so only when devoid of content, pointing to an abstract "human nature" that is utterly inconceivable in light of actually existing nature as we know it.[26]

To support his argument, de Lubac makes use of the following four principles. First, he insists that grace (or the supernatural) must be analogously and radically distinguished from human nature. The supernatural end cannot be conceived as a parallel option; by its very nature, grace has no parallel. Because this is so, it follows that when we speak of "beatitude," only the supernatural end can be meant. This, de Lubac argues, is in accordance with scriptural, patristic, and Thomistic teaching.

Second, grace for de Lubac does not overwhelm natural structures but does imply that human nature has but one supernatural end. The point here is that grace can allow for the fullness of natural human structures without displacing any natural human end. De Lubac's view is comparable to the way Aquinas conceives the personhood of Jesus Christ. Although Jesus has only one divine Person, he is fully human; the full structure of his humanity is present even though he does not possess a human personhood. While it is difficult to conceive how the natural human structures would not require a natural "person" and a natural "end," the suggestion here is that the supernatural can accomplish things that might not otherwise be considered possible.

Third, because the human person is created in the image of the Trin-

26. De Lubac, *Mystery of the Supernatural*, 64. Étienne Gilson, with whom de Lubac was in correspondence and who shared de Lubac's concerns regarding nature and grace, likewise feared that "modern Scholasticism" from Francisco Suárez onward focused on essence (i.e., possible being) rather than on existence (i.e., actual being). See, e.g., his remark in *Being and Some Philosophers*, 2nd ed. (Toronto: Pontifical Institute of Mediaeval Studies, 1952), 119.

ity, the deepest desire of human nature is therefore to be united with the triune God. Given that God's causality is his essence, there can be no distinction between the desire for union with God as first cause and the desire for union with God's essence. Any supposition of a merely natural beatitude would require God to give himself to us in a way that would disregard the utter transcendence of God's "inviolable mystery, so profoundly hidden that, even in a universe ruled by grace, no creature could ever see it direct."[27] By contrast, de Lubac holds that the created natural desire for beatific vision simply speaks to our neediness and our utter dependence upon God's free gift.

Fourth, the limits of theological discourse need to be respected. De Lubac points out that, in the case of grace, one is always dealing with a paradox or mystery. He questions what is to be gained by setting up a system in which the supernatural end of grace is combined with an Aristotelian end rooted in the structures of nature. Although the purpose of such a system may be to help highlight the gratuity of grace and the integrity of nature, in fact, the gratuity of grace was never in question. As for the integrity of nature, it can be better defended by upholding the gift of a supernatural end that radically transcends nature and therefore poses no threat to natural structures. Whenever one tries to explain the natural end by itself, one becomes inevitably tied up in conceptual knots and highly inadequate and implausible explanations, until it becomes clear that a supposedly "pure" natural end is existentially implausible. The only thing that positing a natural end truly does, according to de Lubac, is mark off a sphere of autonomy from God's gifting and open the conceptual door to secularization, with the idea that humans could actually be satisfied by something less than real beatitude.[28] This is the invariably high cost of speculating, even hypothetically, on a natural proportionate end of the human creature.

27. De Lubac, *Mystery of the Supernatural*, 55.

28. Because a natural end requires some kind of union with God by our own resources, and in a way strictly in accordance with natural justice, de Lubac thinks that "the final result is Pelagianism, or Baianism: in either case we arrive at a hypothetical creature who has no kind of relationship of love with God; at a 'beatitude' which the creature requires and which God owes him. In the 'purely natural world' where this creature lives, all idea of God's free gift is lost." De Lubac, *Mystery of the Supernatural*, 62.

But the difficulty that de Lubac's proposal must overcome is that if there is only one end of supernatural beatitude, then this would seem to imply that the spiritual powers belonging to the natural constitution of human beings (i.e., intellect and will) have supernatural beatitude as the end to which they are naturally ordered. If this were so, then it would seem impossible to preserve the gratuity of grace, since the dynamism toward the supernatural end would be built into a human nature whose exigencies would be profoundly and unjustifiably frustrated were grace not available. Yet de Lubac insists that the question of whether grace is freely given cannot concern hypothetical humans who have never existed, but only "the being whose finality is 'already,' if one can say so, wholly supernatural—for such is the case with us.... there is only one end, and therefore I bear within me, consciously or otherwise, a 'natural desire' for it."[29] At our existential core, we do not wait for knowledge of divine revelation and only then experience a desire for supernatural union with God. Rather, supernatural union with God is the only end for which God has made us, and since God has made us for this end, we desire it and we would suffer if we failed to attain it.[30]

In order to show how being animated by such a desire does not result in nature being "owed" a supernatural end, de Lubac proposes that we approach the question from the side of God: does God, having from the outset given humans their ultimate end, give this beatific vision freely, or is God compelled?[31] Reflecting on this question, de Lubac rejects the supposition that "an end cannot be given freely for a definite being, existing here and now, unless there had first of all been a different end for him that was objectively, concretely realizable."[32] Because God never willed any other end for human beings other than beatific vision, humans are wholly constituted by this end and are not abstractable from it. Human finality is deeply "inscribed" in what it means to be human; if humans had a different finality, they would not remain the same qua human.

29. De Lubac, *Mystery of the Supernatural*, 71–72.

30. As de Lubac comments, "if I fail to achieve this which is my end, it may be said that I have failed in everything; if I lose it, I am 'damned'; and to be aware of such a situation is for me the 'pain of damnation.'" *Mystery of the Supernatural*, 73.

31. De Lubac, *Mystery of the Supernatural*, 75–76.

32. De Lubac, *Mystery of the Supernatural*, 88.

To resolve the question of God's freedom in giving the gift of a natural desire for beatific vision, de Lubac suggests we recognize the utter transcendence of God's gift of grace. Although supernatural beatitude must certainly not be conflated with the gift of a created nature, seeing as grace is "wholly distinct" and "wholly super-eminent," the danger lies in seeing creation as a double gift; one of natural being (i.e., creation) and another of finality (i.e., grace).[33] To view created being as strictly preceding its finality leads both to a false extrinsicism and to an anthropomorphic notion of the power of the divine giver. Instead, the radical contingency and freedom of both gifts must be preserved. God gives no "exterior" gifts to us; our being and our finality are given in a twofold way *all at once* and are therefore utterly gratuitous.[34] There are indeed two gifts, but the second gift cannot be conceived as a mere sequel of the first, as though they were on the same ontological level. Grace radically transcends nature.

De Lubac is seeking to undermine the view that a spiritual nature must have an end that corresponds to its powers. The longing or desire for the supernatural present in the first gift of nature expresses a lack, not a possession; thus the natural desire for the supernatural "does not constitute as yet even the slightest positive 'ordering' to the supernatural."[35] De Lubac insists that "man's longing for God is in a category of its own; we cannot apply univocally to it any of the patterns of thought which we generally use to try to define relationships between beings in this world."[36] Because the innate human desire for the supernatural is not a positive power in human nature, God does not owe humanity grace in order to do justice to what he has created. While recognizing its lack and longing for the supernatural, nature cannot rise to the level of grace. Human nature contains "no slightest element of the supernatural in it"; but the supernatural nonetheless (without violating God's freedom) summons human nature through nature's God-given supernatural finality.[37] Thus human nature, for de Lubac, is a paradox, always reaching above itself without thereby be-

33. De Lubac, *Mystery of the Supernatural*, 98.
34. De Lubac, *Mystery of the Supernatural*, 101.
35. De Lubac, *Mystery of the Supernatural*, 111.
36. De Lubac, *Mystery of the Supernatural*, 114.
37. De Lubac, *Mystery of the Supernatural*, 124.

ing divine in any way. Although he grants that we need revelation to know the "gift coming gratuitously from above to raise up that needy nature, at once satisfying its longings and transforming it," he nonetheless maintains that God has inscribed in human nature "a certain innate openness . . . to that superabundance," a supernatural "call within nature," whose roots lie "deeper than any tendency or commitment of man's free will."[38] This call from within nature, because it is not a positive power, does not compel God to satisfy it, even while its being placed within us is because God wills to satisfy it by raising human nature above itself. In recognizing divine revelation, humans come to recognize their "capacity for God and . . . the 'natural' desire corresponding to it."[39]

De Lubac's fundamental proposal involves a rereading of the "obediential potency" for grace that Aquinas locates in humans. His argument is that "obediential potency" is in fact expressive of a "call within nature" for the supernatural, even though this "inscribed" finality is not a positive power in the human spirit.[40] As de Lubac concludes: "The desire to see [God] is in us, it constitutes us, and yet it comes to us as a completely free gift. Such paradoxes should not surprise us, for they arise in every mystery; they are the hallmark of a truth that is beyond our depth."[41] Faced with the seemingly contradictory truths of a naturally, constitutive supernatural end and its status as a free gift, theologians sought to reconcile the two without compromising the gratuitousness of grace. Yet in de Lubac's view, choosing between the two resulted in a failure of understanding, which a better reading of Aquinas could have avoided. The fundamental insight of Aquinas was that an affirmation of the gratuitousness of grace does not require the rejection of the natural desire for the supernatural since the "desire" for God, far from mandating a particular divine response, only becomes clear in the light of God's utterly free gift of self. The revelation of Jesus Christ shows that God's utter freedom in love is at the root of everything. Revelation also shows that the utterly gratuitous "vision of God face to face is the only genuinely final end for any created spirit, since it is

38. De Lubac, *Mystery of the Supernatural*, 168, 170, 177.
39. De Lubac, *Mystery of the Supernatural*, 179.
40. De Lubac, *Mystery of the Supernatural*, 187.
41. De Lubac, *Mystery of the Supernatural*, 217–18.

the only end which can totally satisfy its desires."[42] Ultimately, then, God is *freely* bound by our natural desire, since it is God who willingly "awakens the desire" that reason alone cannot demonstrate.[43] As de Lubac remarks, "Certain depths of our nature can be opened only by the shock of revelation. Then, with a new clarity, deep calls upon deep."[44]

By way of brief evaluation, it can be appreciated how de Lubac insists upon the gratuity of grace. In his view, God's creating human nature with a natural desire for the supernatural does not threaten the gratuity of the movement of grace that answers to this desire, since nothing in God's creative will requires that he do anything in response to this desire. Even so, the question remains how to avoid naturalizing the elevation of the intellect and will. In other words, if there is a "natural desire for the supernatural," how is it that this desire is not already naturally elevated and supernaturalized?[45] De Lubac responds to this problem by depicting the natural desire for the supernatural as a lack rather than a positive volition or ordering. But since a natural hunger must involve a natural appetite, I fear that this results in a positive volition or ordering. If so, then graced elevation of nature would not be necessary for humans to be ordered to the supernatural. Although I concur with de Lubac's wish to go beyond

42. De Lubac, *Mystery of the Supernatural*, 262.

43. De Lubac, *Mystery of the Supernatural*, 272, 289.

44. De Lubac, *Mystery of the Supernatural*, 282; cf. 294: "revelation cannot help at the same time transforming and completing our idea of man and his desire, and ultimately, at least if we consent to it, of the desire itself."

45. For recent discussion of this difficult topic, see Steven Long, "Obediential Potency, Human Knowledge, and the Natural Desire for the Vision of God," *International Philosophical Quarterly* 37 (1997): 45–63; John Milbank, *The Suspended Middle: Henri de Lubac and the Debate Concerning the Supernatural* (Grand Rapids, MI: Eerdmans, 2005); Nicholas J. Healy, "Henri de Lubac on Nature and Grace: A Note on Some Recent Contributions to the Debate," *Communio: International Catholic Review* 35 (2008): 535–64; Servais Pinckaers, OP, "The Natural Desire to See God," trans. Aaron Riches, *Nova et Vetera* 8 (2010): 627–46; Lawrence Feingold, *The Natural Desire to See God According to St. Thomas Aquinas and His Interpreters*, 2nd ed. (Ave Maria, FL: Sapientia Press, 2010); David Braine, "The Debate between Henri de Lubac and His Critics," *Nova et Vetera* 6 (2008): 543–90; Christopher J. Malloy, "De Lubac on Natural Desire: Difficulties and Antitheses," *Nova et Vetera* 9 (2011): 567–624; Edward T. Oakes, SJ, "The *Surnaturel* Controversy: A Survey and a Response," *Nova et Vetera* 9 (2011): 626–56; Reinhard Hütter, *Dust Bound for Heaven: Explorations in the Theology of Thomas Aquinas* (Grand Rapids, MI: Eerdmans, 2012), 129–248; Thomas Joseph White, OP, "Imperfect Happiness and the Final End of Man: Thomas Aquinas and the Paradigm of Nature-Grace Orthodoxy," *The Thomist* 78 (2014): 247–89.

the endless debates over how to conceive of a proportionate or natural beatitude, human nature has natural structures (i.e., powers and capacities) and these natural structures simply must have natural ends or else they could not be distinguished from grace. Lacking any identifiable proportionate ends, they would not be real powers or capacities.

Similarly, de Lubac's critique of "natural beatitude" requiring God's presence does not sufficiently appreciate the arguments in favor of the "debt of nature" that God owes in justice to himself as Creator. Although de Lubac points out that the order of grace can seem to be a merely parallel order to that of nature, rather than being radically and infinitely greater, none of de Lubac's opponents thought univocally in this way. Instead, what was affirmed was an intellectually elicited natural desire to know the divine essence regarded as an expression of the intellect's capacity to exceed itself in wonder. In this light, it was understood that our capacity for engracement is an "obediential potency." Obediential potency need not be understood as something in the human creature, but rather as something bearing on a created nature that has the ontological capacity to embrace a divine actuation leading beyond itself, in a manner that fulfills rather than destroys it. In other words, as rational creatures, we have the obediential potency of being capable of receiving graced elevation. This presupposes a natural desire to know the divine essence, but grace elevates this natural desire and orders it to a supernatural end so that we experience grace as a wondrous fulfillment and elevation of all our desires. The difficulty with de Lubac's proposal is that grace always enables us according to God's own essential mode. An appetitive movement toward supernatural union with the Trinity, therefore, requires a movement according to the divine mode. One cannot put modally supernatural elements into created human nature, as such, without undermining the transcendence of grace that de Lubac insists upon.

De Lubac's position has value if we see it as a description of the existential, historical condition of fallen human nature embedded in a graced economy, rather than as a successful attempt to avoid certain Scholastic metaphysical distinctions. When thinking about human beings in concrete historical terms, one must always hold nature and grace together under the rubric of our supernatural finality. It is this attentiveness to the situation of humanity's historical circumstances that profoundly informs the text of *Gaudium et spes*. But the question we must now face is whether *Gaudium et spes*, in insisting upon the inseparability of nature and grace, explicitly endorses de Lubac's view of a natural desire for God, or whether it in fact leaves this question unanswered.

Nature and Grace in *Gaudium et spes*

In its opening paragraph, *Gaudium et spes* states that "nothing genuinely human fails to raise an echo" in the hearts of Christian believers, and so Christians—as befits those who bear "the news of salvation which is meant for every man"—realize that they are "truly linked with mankind and its history by the deepest of bonds" (no. 1).[46]

But at the same time, Christians are "united in Christ and are led by the Holy Spirit" (no. 1). What, then, distinguishes what is "genuinely human" from what comes from being "united in Christ" and "led by the Holy Spirit"?

Paragraphs 2 and 3 specify that "the world ... as created and sustained by its Maker's love," although "fallen ... into the bondage of sin," has been "emancipated now by Christ, who was crucified and rose again to break the stranglehold of personified evil" (no. 2). The world, therefore, must "be fashioned anew" and brought to its "fulfillment" through the renewal of the "whole" of man and the proclamation of the "noble destiny of man" and "the Godlike seed which has been sown in him" (nos. 2–3). Precisely what this "seed" is and how it relates to what is "genuinely human" are not specified and remain ambiguous.

After some paragraphs that offer a portrait of modern life, *Gaudium et spes* argues that "the imbalances under which the modern world labors are linked with that more basic imbalance which is rooted in the heart of man himself. For in man himself many elements wrestle with one another" (no. 10). We are finite and limited creatures, but we have "boundless ... desires" and feel ourselves "summoned to a higher life" (no. 10). At first glance, this may seem as though the constitution were talking of a

46. Focus here will be on the preface, introduction, and Part I of *Gaudium et spes*, which contain the most relevant texts to our question.

natural desire for the supernatural as de Lubac describes it. *Gaudium et spes* could certainly be read in this way, but it could also be read as simply describing human nature in its historical state, fallen but called from the outset to share in the divine life. *Gaudium et spes* 11 offers a similar rendering of the nature-grace relationship when it proposes to assist the world in finding "solutions which are fully human" (no. 11). These "fully human" solutions are said to be knowable only through faith, which "throws a new light on everything" and "manifests God's design for man's total vocation" (no. 11). This "total vocation" is a supernatural one, and it is only in this light that what is "fully human" can be judged. If one were to separate the supernatural ultimate end from one's understanding of human life, one would arrive at a sadly reduced vision of the human. Arguably, what is at stake here is ascertaining what pertains to humanity given its graced vocation.

Chapter 1 of *Gaudium et spes*, on "The Dignity of the Human Person," begins by observing that divine revelation teaches "man's true situation" (no. 12). The document presents the basic components of this revealed teaching on the human person through an exposition on the economy of salvation, before then going on in paragraphs 14–17 to explore human nature in more detail. These paragraphs describe human nature as a body-soul unity, one that enables the entire material cosmos to participate in worship of God. We are said to possess an immortal, spiritual soul, which manifests in itself a power to know ourselves, to encounter God, and to determine our destiny by free moral choices. Our spiritual capacities have the power to go beyond the limits of sense perception so as to obtain certitude about invisible realities, such as God. Each human person enters "into the depths of reality whenever he enters into his own heart," since "God, Who probes the heart, awaits him there" (no. 14). We experience within ourselves a law of right and wrong, conscience, through which we encounter God. Our natural rational powers can proceed this far, but to know and obey God's plan, we need grace. These paragraphs speak to the distinction between human nature and grace, and there is no mention of a natural desire for the supernatural.

Paragraph 18 addresses the problem of death and underscores that humans possess within ourselves "an eternal seed which cannot be reduced to sheer matter." God has created us for "a blissful purpose" that will not only restore our bodily integrity, but will also establish us "in an endless sharing of a divine life beyond all corruption" (no. 18). The following paragraph makes it clear that the call of grace is not a finality that is added to an already established human nature, but that God, in creating human beings, gave them a graced finality. Here, *Gaudium et spes* grounds human dignity on the supernatural ultimate end that defines all humans from the outset of their existence: "The root reason for human dignity lies in man's call to communion with God. From the very circumstance of his origin man is already invited to converse with God" (no. 19). The text specifies that to live "fully according to truth" requires that humans respond to God in love. A key principle with which *Gaudium et spes* works is that atheism is not the natural condition of human nature despite the fallen human drive for autonomy and self-sufficiency, for it is not present in the human mind from the start.

Gaudium et spes 21 reiterates that human dignity arises both from human intelligence and freedom (i.e., nature) and from the call to share in God's own happiness (i.e., grace), and also affirms that "all men, believers and unbelievers alike, ought to work for the rightful betterment of this world in which all alike live." The final sentences of paragraph 21 emphasize that the message of grace does not impair human nature but instead bestows "light, life, and freedom," since "apart from this message nothing will avail to fill up the heart of man." In this context, the document cites the famous line from book I of Augustine's *Confessions*, "Thou hast made us for thyself, O Lord, and our heart is restless until it rest in thee." But it remains unclear whether the human heart is satisfied by nothing less than the gospel because its spiritual nature is open to what is above itself and that nothing less than the beatific vision can quell *all* desire, or because of a *natural* desire for the supernatural. One challenge to the latter reading would be that the corruption associated with atheism would be further intensified, given that atheists would be unable to ascertain the truth of the natural order itself. This would render it more doubtful that atheists could in fact "work for the rightful betterment of this world." Still, either interpretation is consistent with the paragraph's insistence that only the gospel can satisfy the yearning of the human heart.

Paragraph 22 is of central importance for this discussion, for it states that "only in the mystery of the incarnate Word does the mystery of man truly take on light." This claim echoes paragraph 10's statement that "the key, the focal point, and the goal of man, as well as of all human history" is to be found in its "Lord and Master," and its promise to unfold "the mystery of man" on the basis of the revelation of Jesus Christ. Each of these texts echoes a well-known statement made by de Lubac in *Catholicism*: "By revealing the Father and by being revealed to him, Christ completes the revelation of man to himself. By taking possession of man, by seizing hold of him and by penetrating to the very depths of his being Christ makes man go deep down within himself, there to discover in a flash regions hitherto unsuspected."[47] De Lubac's statement refers clearly, even if implicitly, to the natural desire for the supernatural. But is the same true of paragraph 22? After remarking that Adam, the first human, was a type of Christ, paragraph 22 adds that Christ, "by the revelation of the mystery of the Father and his love, fully reveals man to himself and makes his supreme calling clear." The question is whether Christ "fully reveals man to himself" by bringing to light not only "a supreme calling" but also a natural desire for the supernatural, or by bringing to light a "supreme calling" for which human nature has an obediential potency that has now been actualized. Paragraph 22, as with passages earlier in *Gaudium et spes*, does not make clear which option is correct. The paragraph concludes with a final reference to "the nature and the greatness of the mystery of man as enlightened for the faithful by the Christian revelation."

Chapters 2 and 3 of *Gaudium et spes* continue the emphasis on the existential condition of human nature. Paragraph 23 encourages all humans to undertake a "brotherly dialogue" through the "mutual respect for the full spiritual dignity of the person," while paragraph 24 reiterates that all humans "are called to one and the same goal, namely God himself." Although this text does root the ultimate end in human nature as created in the image and likeness of God, this could mean either that humans are made in the image of the Trinity and possess a natural desire for Trinitarian communion, or that human nature is capable of a supernatural end

47. Henri de Lubac, SJ, *Catholicism: Christ and the Common Destiny of Man*, trans. Lancelot C. Sheppard and Elizabeth Englund (San Francisco: Ignatius Press, 1988), 339.

because the intellect opens upward. For its part, paragraph 24 explicitly distinguishes nature and grace when it comes to Trinitarian and ecclesial communion, stating that Jesus "opened up vistas closed to human reason for he implied a certain likeness between the union of the divine persons, and the unity of God's sons in truth and charity." Without revelation, reason cannot come to know the deepest sense of this communion. Called to communion, man "cannot fully find himself except through a sincere gift of himself" (no. 24). Human nature has to be self-giving in order to find itself, since love must be ecstatic; and so our "true self" is found in the existentially given order revealed by Christ.

Gaudium et spes goes on to make it clear that there has never been a historical instance of "pure nature" (i.e., one lacking the call to the supernatural destiny) and reiterates that the spiritual unity of the human race involves both nature and a supernatural destiny: "All men possess a rational soul and are created in God's likeness; since they have the same nature and origin and have being redeemed by Christ, they enjoy the same divine calling and destiny" (no. 29).[48] Once again, the question of whether a desire for the supernatural destiny is inscribed in the nature of God's image is neither raised nor answered.

It is on the basis of the spiritual equality of all humans that *Gaudium et spes* defends human rights, rules out such things as racism, sexism, and religious discrimination, and criticizes economic disparities. In examining "Man's Activity in the Universe" (nos. 33–39), chapter 3 seeks to affirm the value of human work and innovation insofar as they represent the exercise of God-given intellectual abilities. Work and scientific or technological advances are not ends in themselves, but are good only insofar as they serve the spiritual unity of humanity by cultivating personal development, justice, a universal brotherhood, and genuine social progress. *Gaudium et spes* denies that work, science, or technology can be conceived as autonomous from God, which is consistent with its assertion that human nature is always related to and dependent upon God.

Gaudium et spes is well aware that there is no natural realm or "world" that is not profoundly in need of the healing and elevating power of

48. See also *GS*, nos. 25–28.

grace. The document underscores the necessity of love in every human activity. Love is "the basic law of human perfection and hence of the world's transformation" (no. 38). Here and now, the glorified Jesus at the right hand of the Father is the source of grace that makes the world a better place: "Christ is now at work in the hearts of men through the energy of his Holy Spirit, arousing not only a desire for the age to come but by that very fact animating, purifying, and strengthening those noble longings by which the human family makes its life more humane and strives to render the whole earth submissive to this goal" (no. 38). *Gaudium et spes* also describes various vocations inspired by the Holy Spirit. In every case, grace inspires a willingness "to put aside love of self and bring all earthly resources into the service of human life, in order to devote themselves to that future day when mankind itself will become an offering accepted by God" (no. 38).[49] The profound intertwining of nature and grace, distinct though they are, is the overriding theme here.

The chapter concludes by reflecting upon how the activities that occupy us in this life are related to the full establishment of the kingdom of God in a way that supports the meaningfulness of the work to which most of our lives are devoted. Grace transforms whatever work is necessitated by the needs of nature, so that "after we have obeyed the Lord, and in his Spirit nurtured on earth the values of human dignity, brotherhood, and freedom, and indeed all the good fruits of our nature and enterprise, we will them again, but freed of stain, burnished and transfigured, when Christ hands over to the Father 'a kingdom eternal and universal'" (no. 39).[50] In other words, works done in charity will remain in a transformed way in eternal life, since the works we do for the building up of the human family, in response to its natural needs, will be supernaturally crowned in the final consummation. Thus, far from there being a separation between our natural needs and the life of grace, it is already true that "on this earth the Kingdom is already present in mystery. When the Lord returns it will brought into its flower" (no. 39).

The last chapter of Part I of *Gaudium et spes*, "The Role of the Church in the Modern World," begins with the point that Christ founded the

49. Translation modified.
50. Translation modified.

Church by the eschatological outpouring of the Holy Spirit, and so the Church has "a saving and eschatological purpose which can be fully attained only in the future world" (no. 40). Until Christ comes again in glory, members are to be added to his family; indeed, the spreading of this family of Christ, through the Holy Spirit, is the sole purpose of the Church. The Church serves no worldly or secular purpose, although its members live in the world, share in the movement of history, and are called to be "a leaven and as a kind of soul for human society as it is to be renewed in Christ and transformed into God's family" (no. 40). To be sure, grace does not liberate humans from their natural constitution, nor does it remove them from the world and its various needs. On this basis, paragraph 40 goes on to describe the Church as "pursuing the saving purpose which is proper to her," communicating the divine life to men in a manner that "casts the reflected light of that life over the entire earth, most of all by its healing and elevating impact on the dignity of the person," and in a way that "imbues the everyday activity of men with a deeper meaning and importance."

The subsequent paragraph then specifies the benefits that revelation brings to individual humans by "healing" and "elevating" their natural constitution. The text notes that by revealing the triune God, who is the supernatural finality of human life, the Church "opens up to man … the meaning of his own existence, that is, the innermost truth about himself" (no. 41). The interpretation of this text should be similar to that of paragraph 21 and its citation of Augustine's *Confessions*: "[the Church] knows her message is in harmony with the most secret desires of the human heart … Apart from this message nothing will avail to fill up the heart of man: 'Thou hast made us for thyself, O Lord, and our heart is restless until it rest in thee.'" A possible interpretation is that paragraph 41 means to teach that there is a natural desire for the supernatural. But it is equally possible that the passage is referring simply to the fact that nothing but God can satisfy the human heart, and that we cannot but constantly feel the tug of grace in the actual human existential situation in which we live. In its observance that "man is constantly worked upon by God's spirit" so as never to be "altogether indifferent to the problems of religion," paragraph 41 clearly has in view the supernaturalized economy that is the only situation in which humans have ever existed. Like the earlier paragraphs on atheism, the text is realistic about the extent to which "the deepest longings of the human heart" actually lead to interest in God and how dependent human beings are on the Holy Spirit to stimulate our attention through the giving of grace. Paragraph 41 also underscores that our fallen nature needs to be humanized. A genuine human nature profoundly needs grace, which promises that "whoever follows Christ, the perfect man, becomes himself more a man" (no. 41). Far from overriding the "rightful autonomy of the creature," the Church therefore contributes to the world by making the world more truly the world (no. 41).[51] Although the paragraph appears to be referring to healing grace and the restoration of humanity to itself, this is certainly not done in a way that excludes elevating grace. The precise relationship between human nature and this grace by which we are united to our supernatural end is not specified.

The Church's purpose, which only God can bring about, is the salvation of the world. This does not mean that the Church does not benefit the world, but it does mean that all benefits that flow from the Church are rooted in the gospel of the kingdom. These benefits are not alien to the world, however, because the world was created by and for Jesus Christ. Refuting any separation of nature and grace, *Gaudium et spes* 45 describes the incarnate Word as "a perfect man" and states in accord with paragraph 41: "The Lord is the goal of human history, the focal point of the longings of history and of civilization, the center of the human race, the joy of every heart and the answer to all its yearnings."[52] Does this mean that all natural aspirations or desires are in fact desires for supernatural beatitude? Such an interpretation of the text is possible, but the text could also mean that the gospel, once revealed, fulfills all human desires. The concluding sentences of paragraph 45, which bring to a close Part I of *Gaudium et spes*, emphasize that Christ, along with the Father and the Holy Spirit, is the creative source and ultimate end of all things, "'the Alpha and the Omega, the first and the last, the beginning and the end' [Rv 22:13]." Because this is so, nature and grace must be intimately and, in history, inextricably related.

51. Translation modified.

52. See also *GS*, nos. 10–11, 21–22.

Conclusion

Given what has been shown above concerning the teaching of *Gaudium et spes* 10, 22, and 45, it can rightly be remarked that "to the council's mind, Christ illumines the mystery of man, his truth, by accompanying him."[53] Although there are different emphases at various parts of *Gaudium et spes*, it should be clear that the constitution offers a profound portrait of the goodness of the created world (despite its fallenness) on the one hand, and of humanity's urgent need of the grace of the Holy Spirit through Jesus Christ on the other. Although there are "natural" spheres of life that are not governed by the Church, the document is clear that there is no sphere of strict autonomy from God. Human nature seeks and desires God, and man's true dignity is only known through Christ's conquest of sin and death. But *Gaudium et spes* cannot be expected to settle the finer ontological points regarding natural desire for God, particularly given its intention to operate from within the existential conditions of a world in which humans have never lacked a supernatural end.

Some paragraphs lean strongly in the direction of human nature having its own proportionate ends. For example, paragraph 14 teaches that "by [man's] interior qualities he outstrips the whole sum of mere things," while paragraph 15 proclaims that "steeped in wisdom, man passes through visible realities to those which are unseen." Further examples come from texts that confirm the proper "autonomy of man" (no. 36) and the "rightful autonomy of the creature" and "the rights of man" (no. 41). Of course, proper autonomy does not mean having no relation to the Creator. Human nature has never been conceived by any Christian theologian as lacking a profound ordering to know and love God, even though human nature as such can be conceived as having an ordering to God that is distinct from the gratuitous ordering established by grace. In conceiving of proportionate ends of human nature, which include knowing and loving God, *Gaudium et spes* never imagines that human beings ever have an ultimate end other than the supernatural end that God freely bestows upon us from the outset.

53. Antonio López, "Vatican II's Catholicity: A Christological Perspective on Truth, History, and the Human Person," *Communio: International Catholic Review* 39 (2012): 106.

Other paragraphs lean toward the existence of a natural desire for the supernatural. Paragraph 11, for example, proposes that "faith throws a new light on everything, manifests God's design for man's total vocation, and thus directs the mind towards solutions that are fully human." If the "total vocation" of humanity enables us to identify what is "fully human," this may seem to imply that our humanity contains a natural desire for a supernatural end. Similarly, many paragraphs speak of the harmony of the gospel "with the most secret longings of the human heart" and how only Jesus Christ "fully reveals man to himself and makes his supreme calling clear" (nos. 21–22). Paragraph 41 emphatically observes that "whoever follows Christ, the perfect man, becomes himself more a man," while paragraph 45 describes Jesus as "the answer to all [human] yearnings."

The interpretation of such passages, however, does not necessitate the positing of a natural desire for the supernatural. While they do make clear that grace fulfills nature and that God alone can satisfy nature, even those who hold the hypothetical possibility of a human existence without the supernatural *additum* of grace agree that human beings cannot be satisfied by anything less than knowing and loving God. No one is proposing a self-enclosed human nature with only an extrinsic relation to God. Although it does seem that paragraphs 21 and 41 lean significantly toward de Lubac's position, they do not require it, and I would suggest that they are best understood in light of the actual existential ordering of human nature, by grace, to a supernatural end.

Gaudium et spes offers a vision of the whole world created for Jesus Christ, a world that needs Christ ever more deeply due to its fallenness, and that, both in its wonderfully positive gifts and its deep neediness, calls out for the fulfillment and truth given by the gospel. The Church proclaims to the whole world the Creator who is simultaneously the Redeemer: "The true light that enlightens every man was coming into the world. He was in the world, and the world was made through him, yet the world knew him not … But to all who received him, who believed in his name, he gave power to become children of God; who were born, not of blood nor of the will of the flesh nor of the will of man, but of God" (Jn 1:9–13).

6

This Mystery Is Great

Reflections on the Fittingness of the Nuptial Analogy in Trinitarian Theology

PAOLO PROSPERI

Introduction

Gaudium et spes proclaims that "Christ, the final Adam, by the revelation of the mystery of the Father and His love, fully reveals man to man himself and makes his supreme calling clear" (no. 22). One way in which this now-famous statement has been interpreted—most noticeably by St. John Paul II in his apostolic letter *Mulieris dignitatem* and in his Wednesday catecheses on human love—is through the nuptial analogy.[1] According

1. John Paul II, *Mulieris dignitatem*, Apostolic Letter on the Dignity and Vocation of Women, August 15, 1988, nos. 6–8; John Paul II, *Man and Woman He Created Them: A Theology of the Body*, trans. Michael Waldstein (Boston: Pauline Books and Media, 2006); see also John Paul II, *Gratissimam sane*, Letter to Families, February 2, 1994, nos. 6–7. In *Familiaris consortio*, Apostolic Exhortation on the Role of the Christian Family in the Modern World, November 22, 1981, no. 11, John Paul II interprets the *imago Dei* more broadly in terms of loving communion: "God is love and in Himself He lives a mystery of personal loving communion.... God inscribed in the humanity of man and woman the vocation, and thus the capacity and responsibility, of love and communion." Cf. Benedict XVI, *Caritas in veritate*, Encyclical Letter on Integral Human Development in Charity and Truth, June 29, 2009, no. 54; *Catechism of the Catholic Church*, no. 2205; *Compendium of the Social Doctrine of the Church*, nos. 33–37, 109–11. On the nuptial analogy as a specifically Trinitarian analogy, see Marc Cardinal Ouellet, *Divine Likeness: Toward a Trinitarian Anthropology of the Family*, trans. Philip Milligan and Linda M. Cicone (Grand Rapids, MI: Eerdmans, 2006), 20–37; Marc Cardinal Ouellet, *Mystery and Sacrament of Love: A Theology of Marriage*

to this analogy, Christ reveals to man "his supreme calling" when, in revealing God as a mystery of triune love, he reveals the vocation of man and woman to mirror in and through their fruitful love the life of God himself. The crucial middle term that makes it possible to grasp the reciprocal illumination of the analogy's two extremes—God and man—is the mystery of Christ, considered specifically as a nuptial mystery (*admirabile connubium*). It is only because of the simultaneously *katalogical* and *analogical* character of Christ's revelation that we are allowed to speak of a certain analogy between God's being and the nuptial form of human love: katalogically, Christ truly *reveals the mystery of the Father and his love* in human form, even as, analogically, Christ truly reveals the mystery of the Father and his love *in human form*. This essay meditates on the fittingness of such an analogy and, by more fully unfolding what "nuptial love" is *and* who God is, shows the dynamic, reciprocal illumination between creation and Trinitarian revelation.

Our way of proceeding will necessarily be "rotatory," that is, simultaneously *analogical* and *katalogical*. It will be analogical insofar as our use of nuptial language in relation to the mystery of Christ and even to the mystery of the triune God requires that we begin with a precise understanding of what nuptial love is in God's creation. The method here is the ascending one proper to biblical typology: from Adam and Eve, through Christ and Mary, figure of the Church, up to the triune God. Our path will be katalogical insofar as the nuptial form of divine love as revealed in Christ deepens and transfigures the meaning of human love as such. In this direction, we move from Christ and the Church up to the triune God and then back down to Adam and Eve. Chronological priority must be given, as it is in the process of human knowing, to the analogical; yet this priority requires from the beginning that one allow the objective form of the love revealed in Christ to transfigure and deepen our understanding of the goodness, beauty, and truth of nuptial love *as such* (katalogy). Through this circular method, we hope to further illuminate

---

and the Family for the New Evangelization, trans. Michelle K. Borras and Adrian J. Walker (Grand Rapids, MI: Eerdmans, 2015), 193–313. On the significance and limits of the nuptial analogy for theology as a whole, see Angelo Cardinal Scola, *The Nuptial Mystery*, trans. Michelle K. Borras (Grand Rapids, MI: Eerdmans, 2005), esp. 384–405.

why the nuptial analogy is a particularly fitting key to *Gaudium et spes*'s teaching that Jesus Christ reveals to man his supreme calling.

The Johannine Presupposition

Before delving into the heart of the matter, two indispensable premises must be established. The first consists in a double Johannine foundation, on which the whole of our argument depends; the second, to be taken up in the following section, concerns the very possibility of analogy between nuptial love, divine Trinitarian life, and the relation between Christ and the Church. Grounding our argument in John's gospel, we presuppose on the one hand, according to the katalogical perspective, that Christ truly makes the Father visible *in and through his very flesh*—particularly in his pierced and emptied flesh lifted up on the cross (Jn 12:32, 19:34): "He who has seen me has seen the Father" (14:9). But we presuppose that a genuinely analogical relationship exists between human nuptial love and the paschal mystery of Christ. It is, in fact, on the cross that the divine bridegroom (3:29) consummates his love to the end (13:1, 19:30).

Fully establishing both Johannine presuppositions would require an in-depth biblical study, which this essay cannot offer. Hence I postulate such a study in order to focus attention on the most debated "level" of the analogy: the Trinitarian one.[2] Such contemplation of the Trinity does not mean that either Christology or Scripture can be at any moment bracketed as irrelevant. The opposite is true. Everything that follows is grounded on the Johannine theology of glory (*doxa*): Jesus Christ, through the display of his love to the end (Jn 13:1), explains and makes visible the glory of the Father (1:18). There is real analogy, which means *real* similarity despite infinite difference, between Jesus's act of *laying down his life on the cross*—an act of love *greater* (*meizon*) *than any other* (15:13)—and the eternal act

2. The presence and significance of nuptial symbolism in the Gospel of John have been increasingly studied in recent scholarship. See, e.g., Johns Varghese, *The Imagery of Love in the Gospel of John* (Rome: Gregorian and Biblical Press, 2009); Jocelyn McWhirter, *The Bridegroom Messiah and the People of God: Marriage in the Fourth Gospel* (New York: Cambridge University Press, 2006); Ann Roberts Winsor, *A King Is Bound in the Tresses: Allusions to the Song of Songs in the Fourth Gospel* (New York: Peter Lang, 1999). I dedicate to the importance of nuptial symbolism in the fourth gospel the second section of my forthcoming study *You Are the Fairest of the Sons of Men: An Essay in Johannine Aesthetics*.

of love through which the Father gives all of his being to the Son: "*As* (*kathos*) the Father has loved me, so have I loved you" (15:9). The flesh of Jesus, lifted up on the cross (3:14, 8:28, 12:32), pierced and emptied out at once (19:34), becomes to the eyes of John the concrete epiphany of the glory of God, the apex of the entire history of revelation (19:35). It is here that the one who has eyes purified by the Spirit of truth (16:12–15) can behold what is ultimate, that beyond which there is nothing more to seek—or, to use the expression of *Gaudium et spes* 22, "the mystery of the Father and of His love."[3] Foregoing likewise a thorough exegetical demonstration of the importance of nuptial symbolism in the Johannine narrative of Jesus's death, according to the symbolic theology of the fourth gospel, his display of love to the end (13:1) becomes *also* the act of love of a bridegroom. Through the total gift of his flesh and blood, Christ the bridegroom simultaneously generates his bride and consummates his thirst (19:28) for a fruitful union with her (19:25–27).

From these two presuppositions an important syllogistic conclusion follows: if it is true that Jesus's gift of himself on the cross is for John a nuptial act, and if it is true that this very gift reveals the mystery of the Father, then the mystery of the Father is, according to the evangelist, analogically a mystery of nuptial love. It thus becomes clear why theologians

3. The words of Jesus to Philip, "He who has seen me has seen the Father" (Jn 14:9), are too often taken in a minimalistic sense that loses sight of the full breadth and depth of John's theology of glory. On the debated question of the meaning of the Johannine concept of glory (*doxa*) in its connection to the twofold exaltation of Jesus on the cross and up to the Father, see especially Wilhelm Thüsing, *Die Erhöhung und Verherrliching Jesu im Johannesevangelium*, 3rd ed., Neutestamentliche Abhandlungen 21.1–2 (Münster: Aschendorff, 1979); Rudolf Schnackenburg, *The Gospel According to St. John*, vol. 2, *Commentary on Chapters 5–12*, trans. Kevin Smyth (London: Burns and Oates, 1980), 398–410; Jean Zumstein, "L'interprétation johannique de la mort du Christ," in *The Four Gospels 1992: Festschrift Frans Neirynck*, ed. Frans Van Segbroeck et al. (Leuven: Leuven University Press, 1992), 3:2119–38; D. Moody Smith, *The Theology of the Gospel of John* (Cambridge: Cambridge University Press, 1995), 80–115; Nicole Chibici-Revneanu, *Die Herrlichkeit des Verherrlichten: Das Verständnis der doxa im Johannesevangelium*, Wissenschaftliche Untersuchungen zum Neuen Testament 2.231 (Tübingen: Mohr Siebeck, 2007); Jesper Tang Nielsen, "The Narrative Structures of Glory and Glorification in the Fourth Gospel," *New Testament Studies* 56, no. 3 (2010): 343–66. For an excellent overview of this motif in recent scholarship, see John E. Morgan-Wynne, *The Cross in the Johannine Writings* (Eugene, OR: Pickwick, 2011), 4–209. For a deep Trinitarian account of John's theology of glory, see Hans Urs von Balthasar, *The Glory of the Lord: A Theological Aesthetics*, vol. 7, *Theology: The New Covenant* (San Francisco: Ignatius Press, 2008), 239–63, 374–85.

heavily inspired by Johannine theology, such as Hans Urs von Balthasar, can claim that the witness of Scripture, implicitly yet clearly, ask us to speak in favor of a real analogy between the mystery of nuptial love and the Trinitarian *communio personarum.*[4]

Metaphor or Analogy?

In addition to the double Johannine foundation, we must establish as a second premise the possibility of a properly analogical relation between human nuptial love and divine Trinitarian life. The inspired language of Scripture is often metaphoric and poetic but not strictly analogical. Even though nuptial symbolism plays a significant role in the writings of both Paul and John, no less than in Scripture as a whole, does such evidence sufficiently ground a properly analogical discourse when passing from human nuptial love to the highest mysteries of the Trinity, or even when passing from nuptial love to the fruitful union between Christ and the Church?[5] We must make a few essential observations in response to this important question.

4. For Balthasar's contribution, see especially his work cited in note 3. The analogy is already suggested, although through a different metaphysics, in the Cistercian commentaries on the Song of Songs. As is well known, both Bernard of Clairvaux and, more often, William of St. Thierry allegorically associate the Holy Spirit with the nuptial embrace (*amplexus*) and kiss (*osculum*) of the spouses. Bernard of Clairvaux, *Sermones super Cantica Canticorum* 8; William of St. Thierry, *Expositio super Cantica Canticorum* (*ECC*) 91; William of St. Thierry, *Disputatio adversus Petrum Abelardum* 4; William of St. Thierry, *Speculum fidei* 111; William of St. Thierry, *Epistola ad fratres de Monte Dei* 263. In *ECC* 91, William writes, "Unitas Patris et Filii Dei, ipsum eorum osculum, ipse amplexus, ipse amor, ipsa bonitas, et quidquid in unitate illa simplicissima commune est amborum; quod totum est Spiritus sanctus, Deus caritas, idem donans, idem et donum." In *Expositio super Epistolam ad Romanos* 6.959–62, he calls the Holy Spirit *dilectio, delectatio, felicitas* and *genitoris genitique suavitas* (cf. *ECC* 28). On the Holy Spirit as hypostatic "reciprocity" of the Father and the Son in William of St. Thierry, see Odo Brooke, "The Trinitarian Aspect of the Ascent of the Soul to God in the Theology of William of St. Thierry," *Recherches de théologie ancienne et médiévale* 26 (1959): 85–127.

5. It would be interesting to show how the twentieth-century debate between allegorists and "anti-allegory" interpreters of the Song of Songs latently presupposes the same problem at stake here. Although most scholars today favor human love as the only original (in a historical-critical sense) meaning of the Song, it remains unquestionable that allusions to the covenant of love between Yahweh and Israel fill the imagery of this mysterious book from top to bottom. Ellen F. Davis, *Proverbs, Ecclesiastes, and the Song of Songs*, Westminster Bible Companion (Louisville, KY: Westminster John Knox Press, 2000), 231–302. The question becomes, for the modern exegete, how to explain the reference to covenantal imagery, and the answer usually goes in one of two directions: first, that the covenantal references are the

First, if by analogy we mean analogy of proportionality strictly understood, then we must maintain with the tradition that it is impossible to speak of analogy between the Trinitarian *communio personarum* and the nuptial bond.[6] This kind of analogy entails the alternative between proper and equivocal predication as the only two options. The former is simply not possible with regard to the nuptial mystery in the same way and sense that it is possible with regard to the transcendentals of being. For example, goodness can be as predicated properly of both creaturely and divine being even though the difference in *modus significandi* is infinite. In the case of nuptial love, however, we simply cannot give the name of bridegroom to God the Father in relation to the Son, regardless of whether we conceive the essence of God in terms of fruitful, self-giving love. The sexual difference and the language of the body are essentially constitutive of the polarity bridegroom/bride to leave room for anything like an analogy of proportionality understood *stricto sensu*. It cannot be accidental that the New Testament uses explicitly nuptial language only

result of a secondary intervention by a final redactor who wanted to give a symbolic allure to the whole; second, that the poet or poets who wrote the Song were interested in celebrating not so much the relationship of love between God and Israel through nuptial imagery but the greatness of human love through the analogy with the covenant (see Barbiero, among others). The two perspectives are not mutually exclusive. There are still those—one thinks especially of the French School (Tournay, Robert, Feuillet), but see also Davis, *Proverbs*—who strongly support, in line with the ancient and medieval tradition of the Church, the thesis that the Song had from the start (*intentio auctoris*) a primarily if not exclusively allegorical meaning: the bridegroom would be Yahweh and/or the messianic king, and the bride would be Israel, the daughter of Sion, as in the tradition of the prophets. See on these questions Roland E. Murphy, *The Song of Songs: A Commentary on the Book of Canticles or the Song of Songs* (Minneapolis: Fortress Press, 1990), 11–40; Raymond Jacques Tournay, *Word of God, Song of Love: A Commentary on the Song of Songs* (New York: Paulist, 1988); Othmar Keel, *The Song of Songs: A Continental Commentary* (Minneapolis: Fortress Press, 1994), 1–37; Anne-Marie Pellettier, *Lectures du Cantique des cantiques: De l'énigme du sens aux figures du lecteur* (Rome: Editrice Pontificio Istituto Biblico, 1989); *Cantico dei Cantici: Nuova versione, introduzione e commento di Gianni Barbiero* (Milan: Paoline, 2004), 17–53. In my opinion, the question of the canonical meaning of the Song requires and fosters a more profound approach. The real question at stake is this: is human love *just* a metaphor (allegory) without any possible claim of real participation in divine love, or is it rather a sacramental image of the mysteries of faith?

6. For a good survey of the doctrine of analogy as it crystallized in the Thomistic tradition (following Cajetan), see Bernard Montagnes, *The Doctrine of the Analogy of Being According to Thomas Aquinas*, rev. ed. (Milwaukee: Marquette University Press, 2004). For a more recent treatment, see John R. Mortensen, *Understanding St. Thomas on Analogy* (Boca Raton, FL: CreateSpace, 2007).

in relation to the union between Christ and the Church, which entails the body as means of sacramental union. Moreover, one can make the case from the other side that the polarity Father/Son is centered on the opposition begetting/begotten, which *seems* to be absent from the bridegroom/bride polarity as it is given in worldly existence.

In spite of all this, however, there are good reasons to identify a genuinely participatory relation between the (perfect) form of nuptial love and the life of God. While one may prudently avoid the language of analogy in light of the qualifications just made, the very factor that prevents this analogy from being an analogy of proportionality in Cajetan's sense—the absence of sexual difference in God—is, on a different plane, precisely what makes the analogy fitting.[7] There is in God something *analogous* to the sexual difference, namely, the infinitely greater difference of the *oppositio relationis* between Father and Son. Even more strikingly, there is something *analogous to the role of the body* within the personal gift of self of the divine persons, namely, the *receptive* dimension of the act, the "passion-like" character of the gift *qua gift*.[8] Having specified these analogous elements, it becomes possible to use the language of *quasi-analogy*, which is perhaps able to keep together a certain real participation and the inapplicability of the analogy in every respect.[9]

I have thus far explicated two initial premises: the Johannine foundation for the analogy between human nuptial love and the Trinitarian *communio personarum*, and the more general possibility of such an analogy. At this point we may start our journey *from below* in an analogical contemplation of nuptial love in order to then show *from above* how a katalogical perspective brings more fully to light the "glory" hidden in nuptial love from the beginning.

7. Tommaso de Vio Cajetan, *The Analogy of Names, and the Concept of Being*, trans. Edward A. Bushinski with Henry J. Koren (Eugene, OR: Wipf and Stock, 2009).

8. For further discussion of active passion, see "Yearning Goodness" above.

9. It goes without saying that the possibility of considering nuptial imagery as genuinely analogical, rather than as a vague metaphor "good for praying but not for thinking," depends entirely on what one means by "nuptial." I argue that it is precisely the elusiveness of the concept of nuptial love—i.e., the difficulty of defining its essence with precision—that allows one, with almost equally good reasons, to make a case for or against it. One of the goals of this essay is to approach a description of the nuclear essence of nuptial love as it dynamically unfolds throughout the mystery of creation and redemption taken together.

The Five Characteristics of Nuptial Love

I begin with a brief description of nuptial love in five characteristics. First, the nuptial bond requires a difference that opposes the lovers but also draws them toward each other. This is found in the sexual difference, according to which the masculine person is primarily giver and the feminine person is primarily receiver—though both in every case give and receive, since each of these movements contains within itself the other.

Second, the primary end of nuptial love is total union. Being total, this union excludes nothing: "You shall be one flesh" (*una caro*, Gn 2:24). The end of nuptial love is to become truly one, and this is why we associate nuptial love with that act we call gift of self. Through it, each spouse assumes and receives the other into his or her very self, so that each of them is no longer him- or herself alone but is also in some way the other through the *ekstasis* of dispossession.

Reciprocal dispossession, which is the mode of total union, is the third constitutive element of nuptial love. The lovers' free reciprocal *ekstasis* is the means of their unity even as it entails the abiding, unconfused distinction of personal freedoms. The two lovers become one by way of mutual indwelling (*perichoresis*), yet they remain perfectly distinct from each other (*unitas duorum*). This mutual indwelling is the stable fruit of the gift, that is, of the act of reciprocal dispossession. It is by way of ecstatic dispossession that the lover makes of his person the "dwelling place" of the beloved, so that the beloved no longer lives and suffers in herself, but also *in him* (cf. Gal 2:20). Conversely, it is also by way of dispossession that the lover comes to dwell in the beloved, sharing with her all that is his. "My beloved is *mine* and I am *his*," the bride of the Song repeats three times, and this is also the formula through which the prophets describe the end of the nuptial covenant between Israel and the Lord.[10] Jesus prays similarly to the Father, "All mine are yours, and yours are mine" (Jn 17:10).

Intriguingly, we find the same language of ecstatic self-gift in an author

10. We find the famous formula repeated in the Song of Songs with an intriguing variation of order: "My beloved is mine and I am His" (2:16); "I am my beloved's and my beloved is mine" (6:3); "I am my beloved's, and his desire is for me" (7:10).

who is usually accused of being the least biblical and most unforgivably Neoplatonic among the ancient masters of Christian thought: Dionysius the Areopagite.[11] But he highlights in addition to dispossession the dimension of receptivity that belongs to every genuine self-gift, and it is this receptive dimension proper to giving that constitutes the fourth characteristic of nuptial love. Upholding nuptial love's reciprocal gift, Dionysius writes, "Eros is ecstatic: it does not allow the lovers *to belong to* ("to be of") themselves, but it compels them *to belong to* their beloved."[12] For Dionysius, however, eros is not only ecstatic: in order to be ecstatic, it must also be jealous. Jealousy, or zeal (*zelos*), indicates for Dionysius not only the intensity of one's care for the other's good but also the "drawing" dimension of love, the lover's desire for reciprocation,[13] which is required for the union to be both total and unconfused.[14] Through his desire, the lover does not only

11. It has been too rarely emphasized that if there is a (crucial) difference between the language of Dionysius and Plotinus regarding the union (*henosis*) of intellect with the Supreme One, it lies in the fact that for Dionysius the end of the union is not to become the One but to belong to Him, to be *of* Him. The Christian mystic does not say "I am you" but "I am yours," which is the language of the Song of Songs. Cf. Ysabel de Andia, *Henosis: L'union à Dieu chez Denys l'Aréopagite* (New York: E. J. Brill, 1996); Paolo Prosperi, *Al di là della parola: Apofatismo e personalismo nel pensiero di Vladimir Losskij* (Rome: Città Nuova, 2014), 200–204.

12. Dionysius the Areopagite, *The Divine Names* (*DN*) 4.13.712B.

13. The interpretation of the passage in question is controversial. I offer here my own translation: "This is why those possessed by spiritual insights call him *zelotes* (zealous/jealous), because his zeal for the good of everything is so great (*polun*); because he stirs 'unto zeal' the yearning desire (*erotike ephesis*) [of others] for him, and in this way he shows himself as jealous—he, to whom those who desire him (*ta ephiemena*) are objects of jealousy (*zelota*); and because those for whom he provides become zealous imitators of him" (*DN* 4.13.712B). Divine eros is jealous/zealous (*zelotes* means both) in three different senses: first, because it is zealously eager for the good of its products—zealous, i.e., in its providential activity (*pronoia*); second, because it moves its products to *the zealous imitation* of itself as God's good eros, i.e., to take care of their own good and of others' good; third, because it moves its products back toward itself. "He, to whom the products that yearn for him are objects of jealousy (*zelota*), shows himself to be desirous" (*DN* 4.13.712B). Only according to this last meaning does the name *zelotes* merge with the properly biblical meaning of divine jealousy (in Hebrew, *quineah*). Cf. Bernard Renaud, *Je suis un Dieu jaloux: Évolution sémantique et signification théologique de qine'ah* (Paris: Éditions du Cerf, 1963).

14. For Dionysius, as for Plotinus and Proclus, the ultimate end of eros remains the union of the lover with the beloved (eros is a *dynamis enopoios*, *DN* 4.12.709C). But union, for Dionysius, is attained by way of the combination of two moments: ecstatic dispossession and drawing zeal. Eros is in this way a circle (*kyklos*, *DN* 4.14.712D). Cf. Ysabel de Andia, "*Eros* and *Agape*: The Divine Passion of Love," *Communio: International Catholic Review* 24, no. 1 (Spring 1997): 29–50.

say, "I want to be yours."[15] He also yearns for the beloved's reciprocation. The act of self-giving always already bears within itself a receptive dimension without which nuptial love is not itself.

Recapitulating the first four characteristics of nuptial love, we affirm, first, that this love entails the sexual difference. Second, the desire for total union between the bridegroom and bride is essential to nuptial love. Third, this union takes place by way of reciprocal dispossession, whose end is mutual indwelling. Fourth, this mode of union requires that the lovers desire to both give and receive; that is, the union demands both *ekstasis* and jealousy, without any priority of one over the other.

The fifth and final characteristic of nuptial love is that it is always fruitful. It is inherently "overflowing," as is fully apparent in the birth of the child. The child manifests that fruitfulness is not merely external to the spouses' desire for union but is rather the full accomplishment of the union, as we glimpse through the beautiful somatic fact that most every child resembles both parents. As the fruit of their union, the child as "third" effects a sort of admirable exchange of "idioms": each spouse becomes able to give to the other not only what is his or hers, but even what he or she received from the other, as we see especially in the mother. The bride, in becoming mother, becomes able to give not only what is hers, but also what she has received from the bridegroom enriched through her own gift.

Difference: Bearing the Other within Oneself

Having characterized nuptial love, we now move on to contemplate the Trinitarian mystery, while in no way leaving behind our foregoing reflections. The first and most critical issue we must address in moving from human love to divine love is the lack in God of anything analogous to the sexual difference. Here we must be clear and precise: the lack of body and of the related sexual difference makes it impossible to speak of analogy of proportionality in the traditional Thomistic sense. Yet if with Cardinal Scola we define "difference" as the bearing of the other within one's identity, then it becomes immediately clear that such a difference is not absent but rather present in the highest degree possible in the *oppositio relatio-*

15. Cf. Song 2:13, 6:2, 7:6.

nis between the Father and the Son.[16] Both the Father and the Son in a sense *receive* their respective identities precisely and exclusively through this *relational opposition*. While there is, then, no analogy in terms of the embodied character of sexual difference, we can speak of analogy insofar as the sexual difference—by which male and female bear in their mutual opposition the reference to one another and are each identified through this reference—is a created image of the infinite personal difference between Father and Son.

While we can thus preserve the language of analogy by extending the meaning of difference beyond that inscribed in the sexually differentiated body, the analogy is further secured by its intermediate member: the nuptial difference between Christ and the Church. This difference bridges the other two "couples" because it bears in different respects a greater similarity to both than they do to each other. On the one hand, not unlike the Father in relation to the Son, Christ is simultaneously the bridegroom and the giver who *generates* the Church through the act of self-giving love (cf. Jn 19:34; Eph 5:22–27). The difference between bridegroom and bride in the case of Christ and the Church parallels the *oppositio relationis* between Father and Son in terms of absolute giving and receiving far more precisely than does the relation between human spouses. But the difference between Christ and the Church bears also, from a different perspective, a greater similarity to the sexual difference because it is a fruitful exchange of giving and receiving that happens sacramentally through the body. In this way, the Christ-Church relation serves as a sort of bridge between the two extreme poles of the analogy, revealing the sexual difference as a created participation in that *oppositio relationis* that opposes but also binds together Christ and the Church, Father and Son. It is precisely through the body that the nuptial relationship mirrors the infinitely greater opposition that characterizes these two relationships. The priority that belongs to giving and initiating in the masculine figure is, of course, not as exclusive in human love as it is in the Christ-Church relationship and, on a higher level, in the Father's generation of the Son.[17]

16. Scola, *Nuptial Mystery*, 25, 89–95, 217–21, 364.

17. It is significant in this respect that the deepest biblical development of the analogy, which is found in Eph 5:22–32, deals with Adam and Eve, a couple whose uniqueness

This dissimilarity between the members of the analogy themselves, however, only confirms the analogy as such: a similarity in infinitely greater difference. More importantly, if the difference between Christ and the Church is incomparably greater than the sexual difference—because of both the infinite ontological gap between God and man and the infinitely more radical receptivity of the bride in relation to the bridegroom—it also confirms the goodness of difference as such and especially on the level of human nuptial love. The nuptial difference between Christ and the Church grounds the analogy in terms of both similarity and greater difference relative to the nuptial difference between human spouses and the Trinitarian persons.

In light of this analogical understanding of difference, I propose speaking of the "nuptial" rather than the "sexual" difference in order to hold together the three members of the analogy. This terminology is not intended to deny the constitutive character of the sexual difference in human love; rather, it attempts only to embrace all the members of the analogy: man and woman, Christ and the Church, Father and Son. In what follows, a full account of nuptial difference is possible only in light of its interaction with the other two constitutive factors of nuptial love: union by way of *reciprocal gift of self* and *fruitfulness*.[18] It is precisely this interaction that makes the difference nuptial as opposed to other kinds of difference. In addition, the nuptial difference involves an order between the lovers. An attentive reading of the symbolic structure of the Song of Songs taken as a whole reveals that where love is lived out according to its perfection, the nuptial difference, understood in terms of a hierarchical taxis between a "masculine" giver and a "female" receiver, is not the seal of inequality and subordination. Rather, it opens onto a noncompetitive equality that makes possible a genuine "inversion of roles" by way of an "exchange of properties," without thereby undermining the taxis.

---

depends in part upon the bride's being taken out of the bridegroom's side. As is well known, the Genesis narrative points symbolically and etiologically to the hierarchical structure of the relationship between husband and wife as lived out in Israel. For an in-depth exegesis of Eph 5:22–32, see John Paul II, *Man and Woman*, catecheses 87–102, 465–529.

18. Only if it is seen in unity with these other two elements—union and fruitfulness—can the personal opposition between loving giver and loving receiver legitimately deserve to be called "nuptial."

Yearning Goodness

The second constitutive element of nuptial love that we must address in light of the proposed analogy is union by way of reciprocal gift of self, or reciprocal dispossession. The nuptial analogy is on this point particularly precious, because it allows us to qualify the content of that act that we call gift of self, the act that in the divine triune life coincides with the simple act of being of each divine person. It is nuptiality that allows us to see as intrinsic to self-giving the receptive desire for the beloved's reciprocation, that is, the erotic dimension without which love would not be itself.

Let us consider the divine gift of self in the act of the Father's generation of the Son. It is well known that Hans Urs von Balthasar, following in this matter the Russian theologian Sergei Bulgakov, has gone so far as to describe the Father's generative act as an *Ur-Kenose*, a primal *kenosis* that finds in the historical self-emptying of Christ on the cross its most perfect analogical epiphany.[19] This seems to accord perfectly with the Johannine theology of revelation, although St. John never uses the language of self-denial in reference to the incarnation or cross. There is good reason to see this omission as intentional and, at its prompting, to ask why self-giving cannot be understood exclusively in terms of self-denial.

An initial consideration of the divine gift of self reveals it to be a paradoxical act. At the very moment in which we take seriously the language of kenotic self-giving, we must immediately ask ourselves: What exactly is the content of the Father's will in the act of giving himself away? The answer is necessarily that the Father wills to give all his being away to the Son, letting the Son be through his gift. It becomes evident, however, that this *will to give* requires simultaneously two opposing realities: the Father's *will to be* and the Father's *self-denial*. For a person to give himself away to another, he must possess himself and must want this possession

19. See especially Hans Urs von Balthasar, *Theo-Drama: Theological Dramatic Theory*, vol. 4, *The Action*, trans. Graham Harrison (San Francisco: Ignatius Press, 1994), 313, 323, where Balthasar explicitly recognizes his debt to Bulgakov. On Balthasar's critical appropriation of Russian sophiology, see the important work by Jennifer Newsome Martin, *Hans Urs von Balthasar and the Critical Appropriation of Russian Religious Thought* (Notre Dame, IN: University of Notre Dame Press, 2015). Regarding Bulgakov's treatment of kenosis see, e.g., his *The Lamb of God*, trans. Boris Jakim (Grand Rapids, MI: Eerdmans, 2008), 94–118.

as much as he wants to give himself over. In the spiritual act of total, self-giving love, self-affirmation, and self-denial, the will to be and the desire to give oneself away require each other and must be simultaneous without any succession or precedence of one over the other.

This simple point reveals that the language of self-denial, if understood unilaterally, entails a too "kataphatic"—to use Dionysius's epistemological categories—reduction of the gift to our finite opposition between affirmation and denial, which in our context becomes opposition between "holding" and "giving away," or between one's will to be and one's letting the other be. The problematic task, then, is to determine the content of the giver's will in a way that keeps together both his will to be and his will to give his being away irrevocably—in a way, to speak again with Dionysius, that lies beyond (*hyper*) affirmation and negation as the supereminent unity of both.

How is it possible to uphold this unity without falling into contradiction? How might we maintain both the seriousness of the giving—"I give *away for you*" (cf. the Johannine *tithenai hyper*; Jn 10:17, 15:13) all of my substance—and the necessity of the lover's dwelling within the gift as its source? A possible answer is that "self-emptying" (kenosis) can exhaustively describe the content of the act only if it is qualified as a dynamic unity of giving away and *begging*, because each of these is the flipside of the other. In other words, within the donative dimension of the act of love (letting be), there has to be always already—as the very condition of possibility of the giving itself—receptive desire for the beloved's answer (affirmation of oneself through the other). Begging, then, is the erotic dimension of the nuptial gift of self.[20] The beggar is not only the one who

20. The Byzantine mystic Nicholas Cabasilas gave in his famous "Dionysian" meditation on Christ's "mad eros" what is perhaps the best Christological expression of this unity of begging and gift: "Just as human affection, when it abounds and becomes greater (*otan hyperbalen kai kreitton ginetai*) than its recipients (*ton dechomenon*), draws the lovers out of themselves (*tous erontas existesi to philtron*), in the same way (*tropon*) God's love (*eros*) for men emptied God (*ekenosen Theon*, cf. Phil 2:7). He does not stay in His own place and call the slave, He seeks him in person by coming down to Him. He who is rich reaches the pauper's hovel, and He displays His love by approaching in person. He seeks love in return and does not withdraw when He is treated with disdain. He is not angry over ill treatment, but even when He has been repulsed He sits by the door (cf. Rv 3:20) and does everything to show us that He loves, even enduring suffering and death to prove it." *The Life in Christ*,

has nothing but also the one who, since he has nothing, accepts to rely upon the gratuitous gift of another, honoring him or her as the only possible rescuer of his being.

Only the act that unifies giving and begging—the thanksgiving holocaust (Ps 39) and the entreaty of a contrite heart (Ps 50)—is a perfect sacrifice of love, because only such an act of love allows the lover to be present in the gift as one who has truly given himself over, who truly belongs to the beloved. Without this moment of dependence on the beloved's response, the kenotic act of "self-emptying" would in fact be emptied from within: it would be deprived of its humility, because the lover would not really put his self in the hands of the beloved. He would no longer be present within the being he has given. If perfect love requires a unity of giving and begging, then any moment of denial in the act of love must be understood as one's refusal to be but through the response of the other.

In light of this paradoxical character of the act of love, we can better grasp the sense in which Dionysius claims that God is elevated beyond affirmation and negation. Divine being transcends these opposites because in the purely spiritual Trinitarian exchange, self-affirmation and self-denial are simultaneously present. Richard of St. Victor, at the apex of the so-called century of love (twelfth century), had already glimpsed the importance of including eros in the "perfect goodness" of the Trinitarian relations. Unfortunately, his profound intuitions were not taken seriously by the subsequent developments of Scholasticism and thus remained for a long time undeveloped. In *De Trinitate* the Scottish mystic writes:

> To want to be much loved by him who is much loved is typical of love. If this is not possible, there absolutely cannot be [love]. Therefore, there can be no joyful love that is not also reciprocal.[21]
>
> The very nature of love persuades us that he who loves supremely is not satisfied if the other one, who is supremely loved, does not respond [to this love] with a supreme love.[22]

---

trans. Carmino J. de Catanzaro (Crestwood, NY: St. Vladimir's Seminary Press, 1974), bk. 6, sec. 1, 162–63 (Migne, *PG* 150.644–45), translation modified.

21. Richard of St. Victor, *On the Trinity*, trans. Ruben Angelici (Cambridge: James Clarke, 2012), 118.

22. Richard of St. Victor, *On the Trinity*, 121.

Amongst the delights of charity and of wisdom, the prime difference usually consists of this: while the delights of wisdom can be received—and this is that which happens most of the time—from one's heart, the profound delights of charity-love can be received from someone else's heart. In fact, one who loves profoundly and seeks to be profoundly loved is not happy—but rather he is tormented—when he does not receive the sweetness of love he so vehemently desires from his loved one's heart. The delights of wisdom, instead, give more joy when they come from one's own heart.[23]

Remarkably, the Victorine presents the desire for reciprocation not only as a constitutive dimension of love but also of that which makes of love the most joy-giving good. On this view, the moment of "distance" or "longing" proper to nuptial love, once seen in perfect unity with the simultaneous knowledge of the other's (always already given) answer of love, appears as no less constitutive of the joy of love (*dilectum caritatis*) than the moment of union. Because the Son eternally reciprocates the Father's love, the contradiction between willing to be and willing to give oneself away is overcome: the "longing" of eros is always already transformed into the joy of union and is a necessary element of this joy.

Any speech about desire or need in God must, of course, be purified with respect to discourse about human eros. When we claim that there is in the divine Trinitarian relations the analogical archetype of what created, embodied spirits experience as longing for love, we in no way intend to undermine divine perfection. In the very moment in which we affirm that the Father, in giving himself totally to the Son, "longs for" the Son's receptive answer, we must eliminate our anthropomorphic temptation to reduce this affirmation to our created experience and measure of what it means. In the simple act of God's eternity, there is no time, no succession, no before and after. We wish instead to illuminate how the human experience of eros, understood in its original beauty and purity (Song of Songs), is the finite experience that most perfectly foreshadows the overcoming—realized preeminently in God—of the opposition between beatitude and desire, between "health" and "sickness" (Song 2:5, 5:8b).

It is in this respect not accidental that the oxymoronic topos of the "blissful wound" of love is common to both mystical literature and love

23. Richard of St. Victor, *On the Trinity*, 130.

poetry.[24] Nowhere else do we find a token of the transfiguration of the "passion of desire" (eros) into an experience simultaneously painful and blissful. The poverty that the piercing experience of "falling in love" makes one suffer is suffered as a cause of pain only because, in our fallen condition, it is usually accompanied by one's fear of not being reciprocated—or, more generally, of not finding in the beloved the balsam able to heal the wound that he or she has opened in one's heart. It is, in contrast, a rather common experience that, in a mature relationship of reciprocity, the intensity of one's longing is per se constitutive of one's joy together with, and not in opposition to, the fruition of ever new union.[25]

Active Passion

In seeing that eros contributes essentially to the joy of love, we also begin to see how its neediness is intrinsically generous. Let us now consider further how the element of passive desire is in the act of love no less generous than the kenotic aspect. If there is a quality distinctive of erotic love, it is intense *pathos*, as Gregory of Nyssa observed.[26] Eros is *agape epitetamene*, love full of tension.[27] Regardless of whether it is spiritual or carnal, eros reveals not only the nature of receptivity but also the intensity of the lov-

24. See especially Gregory of Nyssa, *Homilies on the Song of Songs* 12 (Migne, *PG* 44.1029), where the doctor of *epektasis* (endless desire) speaks impressively about the "beautiful and sweet wound" of the soul's ever-greater longing for the divine bridegroom.

25. The permanent and fluid alternation between distance and closeness is—once again, not accidentally—a leitmotiv of the Song of Songs. Consider, e.g., the mysterious final verse (8:14), in which the bride seems to urge the bridegroom to go back to the mountains of spices from which he came.

26. The nuptial analogy, by virtue of the *pathos* belonging essentially to self-giving love, is also key in responding to another central question in today's theological debate, namely, the question of how to reconcile the traditional (and metaphysically necessary) tenet of divine immutability with the biblical doctrine of God's vulnerability and loving engagement with man in the history of the covenant. Only a serious consideration of the erotic dimension of the act of love can fully account for the analogy of "suffering" in God and render justice to the language of Scripture concerning divine passions. On the question of divine suffering in the contemporary debate, see Hans Urs von Balthasar, *Theo-drama: Theological Dramatic Theory*, vol. 5, *The Last Act*, trans. Graham Harrison (San Francisco: Ignatius Press, 1994), 212–68.

27. Cf. Gregory of Nyssa, *Homilies on the Song of Songs* (Migne, *PG* 44.1048C). Cf. Jean Daniélou, *Platonisme et théologie mystique: Essai sur la doctrine spirituelle de Saint Grégoire de Nysse* (Paris: Aubier, 1944), 218.

er's desire for union. Richard of St. Victor identified this with unprecedented clarity in his work *On the Four Degrees of Violent Love*: "You know well enough that it is one thing to speak about love and another about its perfection; one thing to speak about love itself and another about the violence of it."[28] This element of intense passion, which Richard calls violence, is far from being insignificant or just a "romantic" accident. Rather, it points to one of the main reasons why the nuptial analogy is so crucial in biblical revelation: nowhere as in nuptial love do we experience the transformation of desire into a generous gift, through which the lovers give each other joy. A bridegroom never gives *simply* himself to the bride. He gives himself and his desire for union, and the intensity of this desire substantially affects his power to give joy to the beloved. It is hardly deniable that the joy a lover gives to the beloved is proportional to the intensity of the passion of desire that "endows," as it were, the free act of giving. The reason for this is evident: through the expression of his passion, the lover makes the beloved aware of her power to give him joy through her "yes." He gives her the capacity to be all the more a giver. But it is not only that she is able to give him joy, for his passion also grants joy to her. We know from an *agraphon* of the Lord quoted by Paul that "it is more blessed to give than to receive" (Acts 20:35); in other words, there is more joy in giving than in receiving. Therefore, when the lover through his passionate desire enables the beloved to give more, it is because giving is a source of greater joy that he also bestows this joy upon the beloved. Passion in a relation of free and stable reciprocity becomes itself a further gift within the gift: one gives *more* the more one desires (Jn 19:28, 19:34). The lover becomes a source of "quenching water" precisely through the "bleeding" of one's wound (Jn 19:34).

The poetic imagery of the Song of Songs, through its apparently awkward metaphors, explores more deeply than any other scriptural text this paradoxical transformation of yearning desire into inebriating, seducing, and delighting gift. Those bodily organs that are in the semantic field of sensual pleasure mainly receptive—mouth, lips, hands, nose, belly,

28. Richard of St. Victor, *On the Four Degrees of Violent Love*, in *On Love: A Selection of Works of Hugh, Adam, Achard, Richard, and Godfrey of St. Victor*, Victorine Texts in Translation 2, ed. Hugh Feiss (Hyde Park, NY: New City Press, 2012), sec. 1, para. 3, 275.

cheeks[29]—become in the "circle" of nuptial love givers; that is to say, they bestow at a different, "interpersonal" level those same delightful goods (food, drinks, fragrance, oils) that in the premetaphorical sphere they instead receive.[30] For the lover, the beloved's mouth, which at a "lower" level merely receives food, itself becomes "food": "Your lips distil nectar, my bride; / honey and milk are under your tongue" (Song 4:11). Hands, in their very grasping movement toward the beloved, distil liquid myrrh with its drawing scent (5:2). The nose, which is a symbol of the receptive search, becomes itself rich in promising fragrance (7:8); the belly, archetype of hungry emptiness, becomes a heap of wheat (7:2). These metaphors convey far more than a euphemistic reference to sexual pleasure. They sing that admirable "communication of idioms" between giving and receiving that is the most remarkable feature of nuptial love in its inseparably spiritual and embodied reality. For the authentic lover, the other's yearning desire for one's own gift is a gift of the highest kind: it becomes a source of joy.

In describing the circular conversion of giving and receiving in love, we must not forget that the movement of love remains intrinsically ordered. There is a hierarchy in this marvelous "alchemy" that transforms passion into powerful action: desire, or eros, becomes an active gift only in unity with and dependence on the free gift of self that the receptive passion of desire endows with further generosity.

We must further qualify our treatment of eros in light of the filial relation. One could make the case that the paradoxical transformation of

29. Particularly curious is the poem's apparently awkward insistence on the attractive power of cheeks, but this image, too, illustrates the transformation of receptive organs into donative ones. Cheeks veil the jaw, the chewing part of the mouth. In the symbolism of the Song, it is precisely the fact that they are the most "consuming" organs in the premetaphorical sphere that makes them an important symbol of desire, of the other person's hunger.

30. We find multiple examples of this in the text of the Song: "O that you would kiss me with the kisses of your mouth! / For your love is better than wine" (1:2); "Your lips distil nectar, my bride; honey and milk are under your tongue" (4:11); "Your mouth is lovely. / Your cheeks are like halves of a pomegranate / behind your veil" (4:3, repeated in 6:7); "His cheeks are like beds of spices, / yielding fragrance" (5:13); "I arose to open to my beloved, / and my hands dripped with myrrh, / my fingers with liquid myrrh" (5:5); "His lips are lilies, / distilling liquid myrrh" (5:13); "Your navel is a rounded bowl / that never lacks mixed wine. / Your belly is a heap of wheat, / encircled with lilies" (7:2); "The scent of your breath [is] like apples" (7:8). See also Song 1:2, 1:4b, 2:3, 2:5, 4:3b, 4:10b, 4:11, 4:13c, 5:1, 6:7a, 6:11d, 6:16f, 7:2, 7:9, 7:12–13, 8:2.

desire into gift is no less true of the "begging" child in relation to his parents than it is in the nuptial relation.[31] What is distinctive of nuptial love, however, is the fact that the gift that the lover desires is total union with the person of the beloved; that is, the lover desires the beloved herself, and not her gifts or "inheritance." For the bridegroom of the Song, the "inheritance," the "Promised Land," the "garden of Eden" is the bride herself.[32] St. Bernard, commenting on the Song of Songs, points out that whereas the child loves and honors the father also because he is his heir and receives everything from him, for the bride, love itself, given and received, is the only prize yearned for.[33] Despite the fact that this opposition between son and bride becomes problematic when we transfer the idea to divine Trinitarian communion, Bernard's intuition that there is an exclusivity and purity in nuptial love not found in the filial relation helps us to see better how important the nuptial analogy can be in accounting for the form of the Trinitarian act of love as one that entails a total gift of self.

By considering the transformation of desire into gift of self, we come to better understand our initial claim: the act of love is not generous *and* erotic, but generous *as* erotic. It is generous only as a unity of free self-giving and desire. In this sense, it is again Dionysius who gives us the most

31. Charles Péguy so insightfully pointed this out in his *The Portal of the Mystery of Hope*. See on this my article "'The Mystery of Mysteries': On Péguy's Vision of Hope," *Communio: International Catholic Review* 41, no. 4 (Winter 2014): 804–42.

32. Song 4:12–5:1. Significantly, some of the classic symbols of the "sweetness" of the Promised Land become in the Song metaphors that indicate not so much the bridegroom's love for the bride but vice versa: "Your lips distil nectar, my bride; / honey and milk are under your tongue (4:11); cf. Song 5:1: "I come to my garden, my sister, my bride, / I gather my myrrh with my spice, / I eat my honeycomb with my honey, / I drink my wine with my milk."

33. "Love is a great reality; but there are degrees to it. The bride stands at the highest. Children love their father, but they are thinking of their inheritance, and as long as they have any fear of losing it, they honor more than they love the one from whom they expect to inherit. I suspect the love which seems to be founded on some hope of gain. It is weak, for if the hope is removed it may be extinguished, or at least diminished. It is not pure, as it desires some return. Pure love has no self-interest. Pure love does not gain strength through expectation, nor is it weakened by distrust. This is the love of the bride, for this is the bride—with all that means. Love is the being and the hope of a bride. She is full of it, and the bridegroom is contented with it. He asks nothing else, and she has nothing else to give. That is why he is the bridegroom and she the bride; this love is the property only of the couple. No-one else can share it, not even a son." Bernard of Clairvaux, *On the Song of Songs IV*, trans. Irene Edmonds (Kalamazoo, MI: Cistercian, 1980), 83.2.5.

perfect definition of nuptial love: *erotike agathotes*, "erotic goodness," or "good eros."[34] This oxymoron keeps together the elements of ecstatic giving and drawing desire, showing their unity in the simplicity of the act without collapsing them into each other.

Turning our attention back to the Johannine narrative of Jesus's death on the cross, we see that the two climactic moments of the narrative symbolically reflect this twofold dimension of the act of love: self-emptying and drawing. On the one hand, Jesus's final act of pouring forth the Spirit (*paredoken to pneuma*, Jn 19:30) follows closely the solemn "I thirst" (19:28). On the other, water and blood pour forth out of his pierced side (19:34). In each case, a symbol of self-emptying and total giving is associated with a symbol of intense yearning: thirst in the former case and the pierced heart in the latter. Through the association of these symbols, John invites us to contemplate the glory of God as an ineffable unity of passionate yearning and free self-emptying, both expressed through the concrete body of Jesus. In the supreme hour of the uplifting of the Son of Man (12:32), what is ultimate finally becomes visible: God's generous thirst for union with the Church is manifested, and, *in and through* this thirst, the Father's eternal love for the Son is visibly mirrored (15:9).

Another important Johannine symbol of the twofold essence of nuptial love is the pouring out of precious oil. As others have pointed out, Mary's act of anointing Jesus's feet with fragrant nard alludes most likely to the analogous action performed by the bride of the Song. St. John recounts, "Mary took a pound of costly ointment of pure nard and anointed the feet of Jesus and wiped his feet with her hair; and the house was filled with the fragrance of the ointment" (12:3). We are recalled to the bride's song: "While the king was on his couch, / my nard gave forth its fragrance" (Song 1:12).[35] The Johannine symbol, merging the generous and humble character of the act—Mary anoints Jesus's feet and wipes them with her hair—with the erotic overtones entailed in the allusion to the Song of Songs, unites dynamically the moment of "thoughtless"

34. *DN* 4.13.712A.

35. "Oil poured out" (*ekkenothen*) is also, according to the Song, the name of the beloved king himself: "Your anointing oils are fragrant, / your name is oil poured out; / therefore the maidens love you" (1:3).

giving away (the nard is very costly) with the moment of drawing desire, which is proper to the act of nuptial love.[36] As the Song makes clear, the "outpouring" is an act of giving that by its very nature draws the beloved to the giver *through* the strong fragrance that the oil poured out emanates. The symbolism thus conveys with unparalleled precision the circular structure of the act of love: divine eros is a circle.[37]

Having considered the witness to "good eros" in Scripture, we now make a final, crucial step: this twofold description of the act of nuptial love also allows for a deeper appreciation of the Eucharist as the most perfect, unsurpassable manifestation in the history of divine *nuptial love*. In the Eucharist, even more radically than on the cross, we see in act the display of God's nuptial love in its twofold character: the self-abasement of the Word that the Eucharist entails is both a means of total self-giving (body, soul, and divinity) and an act of supreme self-concealment, through which God makes the efficaciousness of his action dependent on the active faith of the receiver.[38] This is the paradox of the Eucharist: nowhere does God give himself totally over to his creature as he does in and through the Eucharist. Only through it does the believer receive a real, unifying share in the body, soul, and divine life of the Lord. Yet nowhere is the Lord more concealed and thereby dependent on the beloved's response of loving faith than in the Eucharist. The merging of the highest hypostatic freedom, that of the divine Logos, with the most passive and inert symbols in the ladder of being, bread and wine, expresses at an inimitable degree of perfection the unity in distinction between action and passion proper to the form of nuptial love.

At this point, we have all the elements needed to draw the bold conclusion aimed at from the beginning: nuptial love images divine life not in spite of but, in the sense specified above, thanks to its embodied character. The body is a principle of difference between human lovers that simultaneously enables fruitful union; thus it plays an indispensable role in

36. Mary's act of anointing and wiping Jesus's feet is highly ambiguous: On the one hand, it seems to express worship, a spirit of service, and adoring respect. On the other, it does have a certain audacious and sensuous character, made all the more evident by the highly probable allusion to Song 7:5: "A king is held captive in the tresses." Cf. Winsor, *King Is Bound*.

37. Cf. *DN* 4.17.

38. The eucharistic unity of self-giving and self-concealment is superbly captured in the medieval hymn, attributed to Thomas Aquinas, *Adoro te devote, latens Deitas*.

man's imaging analogously the personal unity in abiding difference proper to divine Trinitarian life. The body also serves constantly to remind the human person of his dependence on another in order to be himself, thus educating man to the true meaning of difference—bearing another within one's own identity. Further, the male and female body mediates erotic desire and allows human beings to give and receive one another reciprocally, and in so doing it participates essentially in the unity of giving and receiving, activity and passivity, that belongs to love.[39]

"Full Joy": Fruitfulness as Condition of Unity

We have discussed the suitability of the nuptial analogy between divine Trinitarian life and human nuptial love as regards difference between the lover and beloved, their unity through reciprocal gift, and the circular structure of love realized in the transformation of erotic desire into gift.[40] The fifth essential characteristic of nuptial love remains to be addressed in its relation to Trinitarian communion. Let us, then, consider fruitfulness and therefore the role of the Holy Spirit as bond between the Father and the Son.

The rich imagery of the Song of Songs again has much to teach us, despite appearances to the contrary. One of the most disconcerting features of the Song is that no explicit mention is made of the openness of

39. Dionysius's reflections on matter also help us see how the body represents analogically, and in a privileged way, the "passively active" (receptive) dimension of the divine act of love. He once again glimpses something extremely profound when he insists, consistently with the logic of his doctrine of dissimilar symbolism, that there is a sense in which nonbeing—understood Neoplatonically as "pure matter" or shapeless darkness—not only participates in the Good and the Beautiful but also *is* a name of the Good, because the divine Cause is elevated by way of overeminence beyond any graspable form: "And yet reason (*o logos*) will dare to say even this: that even non-being participates in the Beautiful and the Good; it actually is the Beautiful and the Good, when one celebrates God as super-essential by way of removal of all things" (*DN* 4.7.704B). "And if one may venture to say so, even non-being desires that Good who is elevated beyond any being, and aspires to be in the Good" (*DN* 4.3.697A). For his doctrine of dissimilar symbolism, see Dionysius the Areopagite, *The Celestial Hierarchy* 2.

40. The title alludes to that full joy (*pepleromene chara*), which according to the fourth gospel is the fruit of agape received and reciprocated through one's obedience to the new commandment of love (Jn 15:10–12) and through one's confident petition (Jn 16:23–24). The disciple's response of enduring faith and love brings about the "perfect joy," the joy of Jesus himself (Jn 15:11), which is the joy of fruitfulness (Jn 16:20–22).

the lovers' bond to fruitfulness. Yet we claim that fruitfulness is present in the Song—if not in the form of children, then in a more fundamental or prior sense. Nothing so much as *nuptial eros*, rightly understood, allows the spirit to surpass through existential experience the irresistible temptation to oppose giving and receiving in terms of greater or lesser dignity and active power. This temptation is overcome because in the circle of love, both one's desirous receptivity and free giving give joy to the other. Now, we suggest that in the Song this joy, which would not exist without the actual reciprocal and desirous gift of the spouses, "impersonates" that almost hypostatic "third," which *is the fruit* of the reciprocal gift and which alone allows the union to be what it wants to be: total.

If we read the Song as a coherent whole, we notice readily how the bride suffers a climactic transformation through the development of the drama. At the beginning, she seems to be more passive and shy. We find her longing for the king, waiting for his coming, hiding in the clefts of the rock. At the end, she has become the terrible queen, irresistible as an "army with banners" (6:4, 6:10, 7:1), who alone is able to keep the king captive in her tresses (7:5).[41] In the prelude and in the first poem, the bride longed for the wine of her king's love (1:2); she looked for the choicest fruits of the banquet of the king, whose attractiveness was a banner over her (2:4). The woman seemed to perceive herself more as receiver than as giver:

> O that you would kiss me with the kisses of your mouth!
> For your love is better than wine,
> your anointing oils are fragrant,
> your name is oil poured out.
>
> (Song 1:2–3)

In chapter 4, however, the same goods that the bride yearned to receive from her beloved have become the goods that the bridegroom desires to receive from her, who is now described as his garden (4:12).

41. After the second run in the night (Song 5:2–8), the transformation of the bride becomes even more striking. In Song 6–7, the *Shulammite* is celebrated as a terrible queen. The final identification of the bride with a palm tree (7:7) recalls the apple tree of 2:3, which was identified with the bridegroom. Through this inclusion between beginning and end, the process of inversion of roles is brought to a climactic fulfillment. The one who ascends and climbs is now the beloved bridegroom, whose characteristic movement of drawing near was in the beginning of the Song a descending movement.

How sweet is your love, my sister, my bride!
how much better is your love than wine,
and the fragrance of your oils than any spice!
(Song 4:10; cf. 1:2–3)

The bride seems now to be more eager to give than to receive:

Let my beloved come to his garden,
and eat its choicest fruits.
(Song 4:16)[42]

We suggest that this order, this progressive transformation of the bride from receiver into giver, from "very dark," humble "vinedresser" (1:5–6) into terrible, resplendent queen (7:1), is not accidental. It is the fruit of the lived "circle" of love given and received. In fact, the choicest fruits that she offers back to the bridegroom are the fruit of his love in her. Precisely in receiving the bride becomes a powerful giver, thanks to the exuberant joy that she gives him through her very reciprocation.

It is through the analogy of joy, even before that of the child, that we become able to appreciate the role of the Holy Spirit, the Comforter, as both unifying bond and overflowing fruit—or, better, as bond precisely *qua* fruit.[43] In fact, it is only through this "overflowing joy" that the receiver, the Son, can receive not simply the Father's substance but also the idiomatic character uniquely proper to him: to be the giver. Conversely, it is only through this same joy, which the Holy Spirit hypostatically is, that the Father can receive from the Son the latter's proper hypostatic quality: to be the receiver. The objection could be raised that the Son, in the *actio passiva* of receiving the Father's being, is already appropriating the idiom of the Father: to be giver. The Father is Father only through the Son, no less than vice versa. A crucial distinction must be made, however, between the sense in which the Son participates in the constitution of the Father as Father and the sense in which he participates in the procession of the Holy Spirit. In the first instance, the Son "gives" to the Father only and exactly

42. Cf. Song 6:1–2, 6:11.

43. It is obvious that in the case of human love joy is not hypostatic. But as the spontaneous fruit of love reciprocated, joy possesses, in a genuinely analogous sense, the character of a third, which is simultaneously the mutual abiding of the two in each other and more than the sum of them.

that which he is simultaneously receiving from the Father: the relation Father-Son itself, or, from a different perspective, his procession from the Father. There is complete identity, in this case, between what the Father gives and what the Son gives back to the Father. It thus becomes clear how the claim that the Son actually gives the Father something of his own is inconsistent; there is nothing "new" that the Son's "yes" to the Father adds to the Father's initiative. In other words, the Son does not properly receive any power of initiating/beginning, which is the idiom of the Father. The idiomatic difference remains here a source of mere opposition. Different, however, is what happens with the procession of the Holy Spirit *a Patre Filioque*. Of course, the Spirit proceeds *principaliter a Patre*, because the Son is born from the Father. And yet the Spirit is a genuinely new third, who, not unlike the joy that the spouses give each other through their reciprocal gift, is not simply identical with the Father's act of generation but is fruit of both this act and the Son's reception. Considering the Holy Spirit in this way, we perhaps grasp a first reason for the inseparability between union and fruitfulness. The desire for fruitfulness is intrinsic to the desire for total union and not parallel to it, because without fruitfulness, the union, the exchange, cannot be total.

In light of both this intrinsic relation between union and fruitfulness and of the logic of the communication of idioms, a careful reading of the Song of Songs offers the best response to a romantic reduction of love to closed intimacy. Through such a reading, we discovered the analogy of joy that binds the lovers in reciprocal giving and receiving. There is a real sense in which it is only through this "third," the fruit of reciprocal gift, that the miracle the lovers yearn for—a union that is truly total—can take place. This is because only such a third allows each one to share in everything that belongs to the other, even the exclusively personal idioms. The fruitful and therefore true union is not tragic, because it does not dissolve the lovers into each other but rather reveals and glorifies the goodness of their difference.[44]

Our consideration of fruitfulness also brings us to see why, in the on-

44. We can speak therefore, again through a paradox, of "communication of the incommunicable." The personal idiom remains incommunicable as to its origin, but it is also truly communicated in the play of love, thanks to and through the third.

tological structure of nuptial love, respect for the difference given in *taxis* is not against a complete equality between the lovers but is, rather, constitutive of it. In the logic proper to the "nuptial mystery," difference, unity, and fruitfulness are not merely juxtaposed elements. There is a strictly necessary co-implication among them.

The necessity of fruitfulness to genuine nuptial love draws us into a final argument, which is once again centered on the concept of goodness as generosity: not only can there be no truly generous gift without eros, but also there can be no truly generous gift without fruitfulness. This claim is the intrinsic conclusion of all that has been said up to this point. Without fruitfulness, the total gift of self would deny itself as gift, because—precisely in remaining faithful to itself as an intrinsically erotic act of giving—it would ultimately lose its generous character in its erotic one. Even in God the first lover needs the beloved's reception in order to be himself, that is, the giver. This means, however, that the first lover cannot be truly generous, because he cannot give more than what is actually necessary for him to give in order to be himself. The element of grace, of gratuitous generosity, that is inherent to the gift as an act of freedom would in this way be emptied from within. This is why the bridegroom must be paradoxically able to give more than himself in order to be truly generous, in order to give gratuitously.[45]

Without fruitfulness, faithfulness to the gift and freedom in giving end up in tension. The opposition between fidelity and freedom, or between need and generosity, can ultimately be overcome only through self-transcendence of the gift in fruitfulness: the free, generous character of the gift requires its unforeseen, fruitful overflowing through the beloved's reception in order to remain itself, that is, generous and full of grace. Only through its fruit can the spouses' reciprocal gift of self be what it actually

45. Another way of saying the same thing, translating all of this into the temporal language of human love, is that if the content of one's total gift of self were *only* the faithfulness to what one has given through the vow/promise, then one would never be able to give more than what is expected of him; i.e., one could never give more than what is *right and just*. This limitation would frustrate the inherently generous character of the gift, which is by definition an unforeseen grace, something given *as not due*. One cannot give more than all of oneself, yet in the nuptial vow this is precisely what one has promised to give. This is perhaps also a reason why fruitfulness is required from within the nature of the nuptial gift if it is to be truly generous.

is, a giving both natural and generous, a response to the urging of eros and at the same time a gift that bears the character of an irreducible freedom.

The Tragedy of Stavrogin: Freedom as Self-Denial versus Freedom as Fruitfulness

In recognizing the opposition into which love's dynamic falls when fruitfulness is omitted, we arrive at what is perhaps the argument's most important conclusion: when the nuptial gift is not given truly, potential lovers become caught in the tragic opposition between nature and freedom, or between dependence on an objective good and the creativity of free choice. Such opposition, according to which freedom demands the denial of objective meaning and which is the distinctive mark of our post-Christian and postmodern culture, can in the end be overcome only through an understanding of being that takes seriously the Trinitarian logic of the nuptial analogy. Nowhere have I found the tragic but also "diabolically" fascinating logic of liberal nihilism more profoundly expressed than in F. Dostoevsky's character Prince Stavrogin, the terrible yet magnetic protagonist of *Demons*. Stavrogin is a man who bears within himself the call to the highest perfection. His strength of will goes beyond any ordinary limit; his self-control is almost supernatural. One might even say that in him Dostoevsky portrays a freedom capable of detachment and self-denial that even in the greatest saints is hardly visible. Not accidentally, his name bears within itself a reference to the cross (*stauros* means "cross"), and Dostoevsky clearly suggests a parallel between Christ and the prince.[46] The prince, however, is not an *alter Christus*. He is, rather, a tragic parody of him; he is the Antichrist. His immensely powerful freedom is not put in service of the good, because he never finds an ideal

46. Memorable, e.g., is the scene in which the prince, resembling Jesus in Jn 18:22, is able to bear the humiliation of being slapped in the face in front of everybody by Shatov—without responding to the offense: "It seems to me," comments the narrator, "that if there were such a man, for example, as would seize a red-hot bar of iron and clutch it in his hand, with the purpose of measuring his strength of mind, and in the course of ten seconds would be overcoming the intolerable pain and would finally overcome it, this man, it seems to me, would endure something like what was experienced now ... by Nikolai Vsevolodovich." Fyodor Dostoevsky, *Demons*, trans. Richard Pevear and Larissa Volokhonsky (New York: Everyman's Library, 2000), 205.

capable of drawing the full devotion of his heart.[47] In this way, the prince becomes a sort of living hypostasis of a freedom that is almost absolute yet at the same time is tragic, bored, glacially cold, and deprived of any real love. Instead of affirming himself through dependence on an objective good, Stavrogin finds real pleasure only in the exercise of self-denial. This is why he is drawn with the same degree of attraction toward the most heroic and disinterested sacrifice for a neighbor as he is toward the lowest and most self-humiliating actions: in both he can feel the still life-giving, inebriating taste of his freedom.[48] He reflects:

> Every extremely shameful, immeasurably humiliating, mean, and, above all, ridiculous position I have happened to get into in my life has always aroused in me, along with boundless wrath, an unbelievable pleasure. Exactly the same as in moments of crime, or in moments threatening to life. If I was stealing something, I would feel, while committing the theft, intoxication from the awareness of the depth of my meanness. It was not meanness that I loved (here my reason was completely sound), but I liked the intoxication from the tormenting awareness of my baseness.... When I was slapped ..., it was there as well, in spite of the terrible wrath.[49]

Here, Stavrogin himself reveals the sense in which he is a figure of the Antichrist, that is, someone who looks like Christ in some respects and yet is the opposite of him in some others. He gives himself over to destruction but does so without love and only for the sake of an empty freedom.

What we see in Stavrogin, then, is the perverted, diabolical beauty of a freedom that is identified with pure denial. As Divo Barsotti observes, there is in absolute denial, even denial of one's own good, a mysterious, diabolical attractiveness that depends on the dimension of *gratuity* that *randomness* seems to entail. In other words, the very idea of "losing oneself," of transgressing the law, can exercise a fascination on the soul that does not simply depend on one's attachment to a partial good; rather, it arises from the sense of limitless freedom that a readiness to lose oneself seems

47. "I've tested my strength everywhere.... This testing for myself, and for show, proved it to be boundless.... But what to apply my strength to—that I have never seen." Dostoevsky, *Demons*, 675.

48. Dostoevsky, *Demons*, 254.

49. Dostoevsky, *Demons*, 692–93.

to entail. Why does the capacity for freedom through the loss of oneself so fascinate the soul? This is something that the classical (Greek) philosophy of goodness perhaps did not explore. Considering Stavrogin against the background of our Trinitarian reflections, we can suggest an answer: absolute denial mesmerizes the soul because it is the only possible (diabolical) surrogate of the self-transcendent freedom that coincides with the ultimate form of the good: fruitful, self-giving love.[50] In other words, in going consciously and "why-lessly" against one's own good, what one is truly affirming is one's thirst for freedom, for self-transcendence. But this can happen, because one implicitly presupposes that receptive obedience to a good imposed by somebody else entails the mortification of precisely such a desire for freedom and self-transcendence—which is contrary to what the fruitful character of love shows to be true.

In short, what seems to lay behind the tragedy of Prince Stavrogin is precisely a heretic understanding of Christ's human and divine freedom in terms of pure self-denial. As a matter of fact, the freedom that is self-transcendence, when cast purely in terms of self-denial, is felt to be inescapably opposed to nature and, therefore, to desire and dependence. But in the logic of nuptial love, the opposite is true. It is precisely the unity of desire and self-giving that allows for true self-expansion and transcendence, and this in fruitfulness. There is, objectively embedded in us, a desire for creative freedom that belongs to the very nature of the human person—this is undeniably true. Yet this desire cannot be satisfied by way of man's denial of his erotic and dependent nature. On the contrary, it is precisely one's faithfulness to the natural call to love, conceived as a unity of receiving and giving, that enables man to transcend himself in fruitfulness. The analogy of nuptial love allows us to see how man becomes, through fidelity to his highest calling revealed in Christ's revelation of God's love, an ever more beautiful image of the fruitful love that God is.

50. Kirillov unconsciously unmasks this hidden origin of the prince's perverted behavior, using once again an evangelical term: "I thought you yourself were seeking a burden?" / "I'm seeking a *burden*?"—replies Stavrogin—"Yes." Dostoevsky, *Demons*, 289, emphasis added. The prince's attraction for self-denigrating actions is the perverted parody of the love of the cross.

III

Modern Economy, Work, and the Human Family

7

Discerning the Signs of Our Times

Gaudium et spes, Contraception, and Some Cultural Implications for Marriage and the Family as Natural Communities

DAVID S. CRAWFORD

The Family and "Anxious Questions"

"Though mankind is struck with wonder at its own discoveries and its power, it often raises anxious questions about the current trend of the world, about the place and role of man in the universe, about the meaning of his individual and collective strivings, and about the ultimate destiny of reality and humanity."[1] This passage from *Gaudium et spes* captures a central aim of the Second Vatican Council. The Council Fathers sought both to engage a modern world in awe of "its own discoveries and power" and to discern and respond to its "anxious questions." If the first line of the Pastoral Constitution begins with *gaudium et spes* ("joy and hope"), this essential affirmation of the gospel immediately precedes its equally important counterweight: "the griefs and anxieties of the men of this age."[2] So while offering an open and positive appraisal of modernity's accomplishments, the constitution also sought to address "problems of special urgency" or "particularly urgent needs ... which go to the roots

1. Second Vatican Council, *Gaudium et spes (GS)*, "Pastoral Constitution on the Church in the Modern World," December 7, 1965, no. 33.

2. *GS*, no. 1.

of the human race."[3] Significantly, the first of these "urgent needs" to be considered was the situation of marriage and the family in the modern world.[4] The result was a profound deepening of the Church's traditional doctrine.

The priority given to the family reflects several cultural developments and emerging issues that preceded the Council: the changing role and place of women in society, the normalization of divorce, growing hedonistic tendencies, increased acceptance of "free love," and so forth.[5] Many of these developments had already been extensively addressed, most significantly thirty-five years earlier by Pius XI in *Casti connubii* (1930). The immediate background for the Council Fathers, however, included the recent advent of the anovulant pill and fears of global population growth that had brought mounting pressure on the Church's traditional teaching on birth control.[6] The pill presented an especially thorny doctrinal problem. Many thought it might constitute a morally acceptable form of birth control, notwithstanding the fact that Pius XII had already condemned it only a few years earlier.[7] The reasoning in favor of its moral acceptability was invited by an impoverished understanding of the nature of the evil of contraception, which seemed to many to be reducible to the physical corruption of the marital act itself, as occurs for example with barrier methods. A related argument claimed that the pill merely extends natural cycles of infertility.[8] From this point of view, it might be legitimate for the same

3. *GS*, no. 46.

4. *GS*, no. 47.

5. *GS*, no. 47.

6. For a contemporary expression of the apparent urgency, see Felix F. Cardegna, SJ, "Contraception, the Pill, and Responsible Parenthood," *Theological Studies* 65 (1964): 611–36.

7. Pius XII, "Address to the Seventh International Hematological Congress in Rome," September 12, 1958, *The Pope Speaks* 6, no. 4 (1960): 392–400, at 395.

8. The argument rested on an ambiguity in the underlying reasons for the Church's teaching. Previous contraceptive means relied on some sort attack on the integrity of the act itself, such as in barrier methods or onanism. If the effect of the pill is simply to extend natural infertility, rather than to interfere in the physical act itself, then perhaps it would not be an immoral form of birth control. The position was most famously argued in L. Janssens, "Moral conjugale et progestogenènes," *Ephemerides theologicae Lovanienses* 39 (1963): 787–826. See also Felix F. Cardegna, SJ, "Contraception, the Pill, and Responsible Parenthood," *Theological Studies*, 65 (1964): 611–36; Robert Blair Kaiser, *The Encyclical That Never Was: The Story of the Commission on Population, Family and Birth, 1964–1966* (London: Sheed and Ward, 1985, 1987). By defining contraception in terms of intention (*HV*, no. 14), *Humanae vitae* rules

reasons as—or even as an aid to—the "rhythm method," which Pius XII had approved. In the end, the issue was not resolved at the Council but was deferred for further study by the famous "Papal Commission on Population, Family, and Birth" and for final resolution by the pope, which occurred in Paul VI's *Humanae vitae* (1968). The Council Fathers did grant that "modern conditions" could produce difficulties for married love and fruitfulness but also deplored recommendations of "dishonorable solutions" and reminded the faithful that "a true contradiction cannot exist between the divine laws pertaining to the transmission of life and those pertaining to the fostering of authentic conjugal love."[9] Hence the question of the pill and birth control must be seen as an important part of the mix of issues confronting the Church at the time of the Council and as part of the larger context of her attempt to engage modernity and address its "anxious questions."

Our Issues?

My thesis is that the Church's perennial teaching regarding birth control, as reaffirmed by both *Casti connubii* and *Humanae vitae*, is crucially necessary for sustaining an anthropologically adequate sense of the family, such as the one so richly developed by *Gaudium et spes*. Before discussing why and how the teaching can be so profoundly important, we should address an obvious objection. It may seem that some of the issues raised by the Council Fathers—including the question of the pill and birth control—are no longer relevant. Being half a century removed, *their* issues are no longer *our* issues. For one thing, their issues seem a bit exhausted. Although no one today is unclear as to whether the pill is a form of contraception condemned by the Church, the broader teaching itself remains as widely known as it is ignored. The consequent tendency to want

out "physicalist" reasoning of this sort in relation to the meaning of contraception, though it does not speak directly to the question of whether choosing as one's moral object what amounts to a physical corruption of the act (such as through condom use) might not constitute a different or further type of disorder. See also my "Benedict XVI and the Structure of the Moral Act: On the Condoms Controversy," *Communio: International Catholic Review* 38, no. 4 (2011).

9. *GS*, no. 51.

simply to set such issues aside is perhaps understandable, and the issue is rarely addressed from the pulpit or—we might hazard a guess—in the confessional.

Yet the issues revolving around marriage and sexuality generally seem all but inescapable. Consider the large role they have played thus far in the current pontificate. The two recent synods on the family, with all the atmospherics surrounding them, are evidence of this inescapability. Both in their preparation and during their debates, the discussion continually threatened to veer toward a reexamination of the whole Catholic teaching concerning sexual and conjugal ethics. Controversy over these sorts of issues (and one might argue that the teaching of *Humanae vitae* lies at their center) has only continued to haunt the reception of Pope Francis's Post-Synodal Apostolic Exhortation *Amoris laetitia*.[10]

Complicating this "inescapability" is the fact that such issues are difficult to contain. Even the Church's teaching on contraception cannot be confined in its implications to a discrete and marginal teaching or even to a minor branch of ethics. A reexamination of the Church's teaching in this area inevitably brings with it a reexamination of the whole of the Church's fundamental moral, anthropological, and ecclesial doctrines. This fact was recognized early on by those involved in the debate over birth control around the time of the Council.[11] Discussion quickly tended, for example, in the direction of proportionalism, a theory that would radically reshape the Church's fundamental ethical doctrine.[12] It also became clear that such a trajectory threatened the very basis of the Church's ecclesiology, as well as her theological and philosophical anthropologies.

10. See, e.g., the recent initiative "Catholic Scholars' Statement on the Ethics of Using Contraceptives," signed by approximately a hundred scholars and presented to a meeting hosted by the United Nations in New York on September 20, 2016, http://www.wijngaardsinstitute.com/statement-ethics-using-contraceptives/.

11. See Kaiser, *Encyclical That Never Was*, 74, regarding an early meeting of the Papal Commission. Ultimately, the issues in fundamental moral theology were addressed by St. John Paul II in *Veritatis splendor*, "The Splendor of Truth," August 6, 1993. The inevitability of the broader implications can also be seen in the preparatory documents for the 2015 Synod on the Family.

12. See Kaiser, *Encyclical That Never Was*, 54, discussing E. Schillebeeckx's essentially proto-proportionalist theory as expounded by the author in 1963. This is, in other words, an immediate threat to the Catholic teaching on "moral absolutes."

Her ecclesiology was challenged because questions were immediately raised regarding the teaching authority of the Church in relation to morality and natural law. Many also wondered at the implications of saying that the Church's teaching might have been in serious error for nearly two millennia, given that the teaching in question had profoundly shaped the lives and motivated the actions of millions of couples and families over the course of history.[13] The Church's theological and philosophical anthropologies were challenged because a reevaluation of the teaching on contraception implied a reevaluation of the meaning of the body and of human person's basic relationship with creation.

The difficulty with issues that surround sexuality is aggravated by the profound moral and metaphysical gulf between the Church and main currents of modernity. This fact lends even greater support to the objection that the questions of the Council Fathers are no longer relevant for us today. The challenges of that time have been replaced by seemingly more radical ones. Rather than questions concerning the pill or women's place in the workforce, we are confronted with, for example, a rapidly accelerating devaluation of the natural pattern of male and female and a growing acceptance of biotechnological means of conceiving children. Such issues were barely on the horizon for the Church at the time of the Council. Given that we now face what seem like much more serious issues, why revisit the earlier concerns of the Council Fathers?

These more radical challenges are only intensifications of earlier ones. The implications of earlier issues make such radicalization inevitable. Once the anthropological and doctrinal fabric begins to unravel, it is difficult to prevent its complete disintegration. In fact, not only is there a gulf between the Church's teachings and modern assumptions, but also it is increasingly clear that these indicate a deep and violent contradiction. As the Council Fathers saw, the "urgent problems" implied by the modern world "go to the roots of the human race." Modernity, therefore, *must* reject the Church's moral proposals if it is to retain essential aspects of its self-understanding. If modernity generally seeks to liberate the individu-

13. That the teaching has been universal and consistent for nearly two millennia is shown by John T. Noonan, *Contraception: A History of Its Treatment by the Catholic Theologians and Canonists* (Cambridge, MA: Harvard University Press, 1965, 1986), 6.

al from the givenness of natural order, particularly as that order pertains to the body, the Church's sacramental understanding of reality situates the body organically and symbolically within the relations of the person to his or her communities, origins, and ultimate destiny. The clash seems inevitable.

If our issues are those of the Council Fathers only intensified, then perhaps a glance back will help us "discern the signs" of *our own* times by allowing us to sketch out an underlying logic that remains as challenging today as it was at the time of the Council.

Natural Communities

In attempting to fortify and deepen the Church's doctrine on marriage and the family, *Gaudium et spes* reemphasized the perennial teaching that—even if they are profoundly shaped by culture, time, and place—their origin lay not in humanity's own constructive powers but in God's creative act. "God himself is the author of matrimony," the Council Fathers tell us.[14] So while marriage in its initiation (*matrimonium in fieri*) depends on the free consent of the spouses, the continuation and essence of the bond (*matrimonium in facto esse*) lies beyond human choice. Not only marriage's permanence, but also its fundamental meaning and natural structure are therefore gifts. "Christ the Lord abundantly blessed this many-faceted love, welling up as it does from the fountain of divine love and structured as it is on the model of His union with the Church."[15] Something similar can be said of the familial community: "Thus the Christian family, which springs from marriage as a reflection of the loving covenant uniting Christ and the Church, and as a participation in the covenant, will manifest to all men the Savior's living presence in the world, and the genuine nature of the Church."[16] The marital and familial communities are, like the Church herself, paradigmatic examples of creaturely, natural communities.

14. *GS*, no. 48.

15. *GS*, no. 48.

16. Hence the Council Fathers in *Lumen gentium* (*LG*) also characterize the family as the "domestic Church" (*LG*, no. 11). See also *Familiaris consortio* (*FC*), no. 49; *Letter to Families*, nos. 3, 13, 19 (1994).

By "natural communities," I mean human communities with certain crucial characteristics. First, a natural community's structure and meaning precede the free acts of its members. It therefore exhibits a "given" character. Like marriage, it depends on human freedom, yet its origin and structure lie in substantial ways prior to and beyond that freedom. This means that the members of a natural community both do and do not give themselves the community. They freely enter into it (e.g., the bride and bridegroom in giving consent), or they carry out the acts that correspond to its flourishing (e.g., spouses or parents and children live out an existing marital or familial community), but in each case the basic structure and nature of the community is given.

More importantly, however, a natural community's structure and meaning are inscribed in human nature; its "form" therefore is apparent in the members prior—ontologically, but also often chronologically—to membership. Natural communities are, of course, profoundly shaped by culture and history, and in this way they are also "given." But culture cultivates what is given more radically in human nature itself, even as it also develops and informs that nature.

Not only does the community lie both within and beyond the freedom of its members, but also this priority *enables* and *informs* its members' free actions. A natural community partly constitutes the possibility, form, and structure of those actions. Its already given structure and meaning inform their instantiation, and their instantiation always bears the stamp of that structure and meaning.

Finally, although a natural community is not simply different from its members, it is not reducible to them, either. It is not an association entered into for the strictly individual interests of each of its members. For the same reason, neither can it be instrumentalized to some good outside or beyond it or its members. Rather, a natural community exhibits a certain ontological weight. Because it possesses a given form, with a given structure and interior order, it is a genuine whole (and not simply a "heap"). As a whole, it is integrally good, as well as being good for its members and for larger communities. And this in turn means that its order and meaning must be integral, with its members—its "parts"—integrally related to each other in nonexchangeable ways. Moreover, it is integrated not only in terms of the nonexchangeable relations of its members, but also in terms of the meaning and structure that inform the kind of community that it is.[17]

The Natural Family

The marital and familial communities are paradigmatic examples of "creaturely and natural communities." It is crucial to recognize that these communities are both given in creation and naturally structure the individual human being. We are all born of a mother and a father, who are the source of our lives and give to us innumerable personal characteristics. We can neither give ourselves our mothers and fathers, nor can we choose new, "more desirable" ones. When we are born, we bear both a likeness to and an aptness for those who give us life. The infant is apt for the mother, and indeed cannot survive without her or at least a surrogate, just as the mother is apt for the infant. Yet we find as we grow and our needs deepen

17. A couple of qualifications are in order. First, my point is not that there are two kinds of communities, natural and nonnatural, and that marriage and family have been wrongly categorized on the nonnatural side. Rather, the problem to be addressed here is our tendency in modernity to *view* natural communities, such as the marital and familial communities, in a positivistic way. I would in fact argue that all human communities, insofar as they really *are* communities, will exhibit at least some of the characteristics set forth. So we might say that all communities are to that extent "natural," although just as clearly some types of communities will fulfill these criteria more completely or unambiguously than others because some will be tied more directly to what is given in human nature. So a business partnership can be thought of as a mere association of some sort, rather than a natural community in the truest and fullest sense, even if, e.g., much that makes a business partnership to be what it is may be located in human nature. We may question, then, whether in principle *any* community can ever *really* be nonnatural and still be genuinely human. Hence we may question whether the positivistic approach can *ever* adequately reflect what is true in reality. Nevertheless, as will become clear, the marital and familial communities (as well as some others we could think of, such as the Church) are natural in a paradigmatic sense. Second, it should be clear that by using the term "natural" I do not mean to make the theological distinction between "nature" and "grace" or what is supernatural. The marital and familial communities that are our focus are both theologically "natural" (in the sense that they are primitively part of God's creative act) and graced (as having been brought to sacramental fulfillment or as constituting a state of life or a way of being in the Church, as is the case with the family as "domestic Church"; *LG*, no. 11). Again, my purpose is to make a contrast with modernity's positivistic tendencies rather than with God's gifts over and beyond mere creation. For a more complete discussion of natural communities, see my "Gay Marriage, Public Reason, and the Common Good," *Communio: International Catholic Review* 41 (2014): 380–437.

that it is precisely the relations we bear, inscribed in our flesh, that allow us to develop and mature at a personal level. The primordial fact of being a son or daughter to a particular mother and father reveals a humanly weighty truth. It shows us both our origins and our destiny, our own mortality and the weight of being.

Just as the child's nature points back to the gift of his or her origin in the parents, so too the natural relationship between man and woman points to the child. The child is already implicit in the kind of community man and woman constitute, in the kind of acts that are proper to it, and in the specific type of free consent they give to each other in marriage. The man-woman couple, in other words, already has the larger family community inscribed within it. The community of man and woman, its natural ordination toward the larger community of the family, is already visibly and bodily inscribed in the natures of man and woman.[18]

Moreover, the natural and given orders of marriage and the family do not stand in opposition to our freedom, but in fact make freedom possible. For example, there simply are no sexual acts whatsoever without the sexual body, and the sexual body is only sexual as male or female. But male and female are obviously and visibly correlative. Therefore sexual acts can only exist because of the given correlation of the male and female bodies. Our acts of freedom cannot make that order but can only take it up, even when our sexual acts seem outwardly to deny its personal or fully human relevance, as is the case with homosexual acts. Without presupposing as radically fundamental the "binary" order of man and woman, sexual acts of any kind whatsoever simply could not be at all. Of course, this obvious and unavoidable truth does not of itself prove that acts outwardly denying the human and personal meaning of sexual correspondence are morally wrong. Much more would need to be said, beginning with what we mean by "morally wrong." But it does cast suspicion on them when we

18. This attention to the body in its visibility is central to John Paul II's teaching in his "Catechesis on Human Love," in John Paul II, *Man and Woman He Created Them: A Theology of the Body*, trans. Michael Waldstein (Boston: Pauline Books and Media, 2006), 203. See also Karol Wojtyła, "The Anthropological Vision of *Humanae Vitae*," trans. and intro. William May, *Nova et Vetera* 7, no. 3 (2009): 731–50; David S. Crawford, "Benedict XVI and the Structure of the Moral Act: On the Condoms Controversy," *Communio: International Catholic Review* 38, no. 4 (Winter 2011): 561*ff.*

recognize the depth of our communal ties made visible in the body. What this unavoidable truth does show is that we cannot deny this bodily order of male and female its primordial relevance, even for the possibility of actions that seemingly defy its human importance. Acts that seem to deny this correlation of the sexes do not in fact escape it, but can only be parasitic on it.[19] This is a reason for what I called earlier the "inescapability" of the issues swirling around sexuality, marriage, and the family.

Because our individual acts cannot help but to take up the order that allows them to be in the first place, they also cannot help but to be symbolic instantiations of the meaning and structure of the community that allows them to be.[20] Sexual acts of any kind whatsoever must reflect (either by congruity or incongruity) the communal meaning (nuptial and familial) inscribed in our bodies. Acts that in some way deviate from that meaning, such as homosexual or contracepted acts, then become a kind defacement of the body's inherent symbolic meaning.

That the Council Fathers understood marriage, the family, and sexual acts in this organic, creaturely, and natural way is evident from the text. We can see it, for example, in their insistence that marriage and the family derive from God's creative act, that the spouses enter into the marital relationship rather than construct it, that children flow naturally from it, and that children are the fruit and gift of conjugal love. We can see it in the integral sense of the marital and familial communities and the nonexchangeable nature of the relations that constitute that community. We can see it in the depiction of the marital and familial communities as wholes, not simply reducible to their members or to their various parts or qualities. Finally, we can also see it in the Pastoral Constitution's most characteristic teaching regarding marriage, its mediation between procreation and conjugal love.

The legacy prior to the Council saw a certain tension between love and procreation. Emphasis on love tended to be seen as a diminishment

19. For a fuller discussion of this point, see my "Liberal Androgyny: 'Gay Marriage' and the Meaning of Sexuality in Our Time," *Communio: Catholic International Review* 33, no. 2 (2006): 239–65.

20. Cf. Wojtyła, "Anthropological Vision of *Humanae Vitae*," 743; Crawford, "Benedict XVI and the Structure of the Moral Act."

of the importance of the procreative end, while emphasis on the procreative end appeared to deny the centrality of love.[21] The period following the Council saw this dualism continue in a new form. Some argued that the Council Fathers had elevated love to an end parallel to procreation. If marriage now has two ends, they may come into conflict. Where such a conflict might occur, a couple would have to choose between them. Naturally, in such situations, love would win over the merely "biological" end of procreation.[22]

Such an interpretation runs contrary to the Council Fathers' purpose, as is verified by their "reminder" that there can be no real contradiction between procreation and authentic conjugal love. Helpful here is scholarship on the development of *Gaudium et spes*'s passages on marriage and the family by Archbishop F. Gil Hellín, who was for many years subsecretary of the Pontifical Council for the Family. According to Hellín, the passages of the Pastoral Constitution discussing marriage exhibit a distinctive manner of reference regarding the nuptial bond, signaling a conceptualization quite different from the fragmented one implied by competing ends. The Council Fathers characteristically refer to marriage as the "conjugal covenant" (*foedus coniugale*) or "conjugal community" (*communitas coniugalis*), a formula that emerged deliberately over the course of the text's numerous redactions. The Council Fathers then characterize the conjugal covenant or community as itself constituted by "conjugal love" (*amor coniugalis*) and "institution" (*institutum*).[23] According to Hellín, this formulation indicates that the conjugal community or covenant is essentially the combined elements of institution and love. In

21. See Gil Hellín, "El lugar propio del amor conyugal en la estructura del matrimonio según la *Gaudium et spes*," *Annales Valentinos* 6, no. 11 (1980): 1–35. William E. May penned an unpublished English translation: "The Proper Place of Conjugal Love in the Structure of Marriage according to *Gaudium et Spes*," Christendom Awake, accessed November 14, 2017, http://www.christendom-awake.org.

22. See, e.g., Bernard Häring, "The Inseparability of the Unitive-Procreative Functions of the Marital Act," in *Contraception: Authority and Dissent*, ed. C. Curran (New York: Herder and Herder, 1969). See also Kaiser, *Encyclical That Never Was*, reporting on Schillebeeckx's early thesis of "a ladder of values in marriage, with love at the top and biology at the bottom. 'Since the biological value is secondary, or lower,' he said, 'its exclusion can be justified by reason of the highest value'" (54).

23. Hellín, "Proper Place of Love in the Structure of Marriage," esp. 38*ff.*

effect, he tells us, the Council Fathers decided to define marriage as the "institution of conjugal love."[24] They mean to say, therefore, that love is not the end but a crucial element of the substantial *form* of marriage. It follows, then, that procreation is the final cause of marriage, while conjugal love (when objectified by the bond and institution) is its formal cause. This also means that marriage offers the *form* of love to spouses, that is, the form to which they are called to *con*form. This conformity takes a lifetime and is in itself the objective perfection of love (*caritatis perfectionem*) to which all of the faithful are called,[25] but specified by the spouses' married state of life.[26] The graces of matrimony "can lead the spouses to God with powerful effect and can aid and strengthen them in the sublime office of being a father or a mother."[27]

If we follow Hellín's logic, we can see the rich way it allows us to think about the organic wholeness of the communities of marriage and the family and their interrelationship. The act of marriage *in fieri*, the consent that makes marriage, is essentially a mutual act of giving (and more deeply *being given by God*). It is the foundational act of conjugal love, a love that the Council Fathers tell us "is caught up into divine love and is governed and enriched by Christ's redeeming power and the saving activity of the Church."[28] The bond and the institution that result are the objective and indissoluble oneness of the spouses. Even if the spouses' affection for each other fades, this bond, as the ontological objectification of their mutual belonging, as what we might call "objective love" formally and juridically maintained by the institution, highlights their personal failure like a scarlet streak in snow, and calls them back to subjective conformity. If love, then, is the form of marriage and procreation

24. Hellín, "Proper Place of Love in the Structure of Marriage," 2, 38*ff*.

25. The Council describes this in terms of man's "common vocation to perfection," without which there is no salvation. *LG*, nos. 14, 32; see also nos. 11, 40. Thomas Aquinas, *Summa theologiae* II-II, q. 184, a. 3.

26. *Familiaris consortio*, 11: "Christian revelation recognizes two specific ways of realizing the vocation of the human person, in its entirety, to love: marriage and virginity or celibacy. Either one is, in its own proper form, an actuation of the most profound truth of man, of his being created in the image of God"; Hans Urs von Balthasar, *The Christian State of Life*, trans. M. F. McCarthy (San Francisco: Ignatius Press, 1983): 224–49.

27. *GS*, no. 48.

28. *GS*, no. 48.

its end, we can see the relation between them as an organic (hylemorphic) oneness, just as form and finality are principles of the oneness of a single being. Procreation is therefore the objective end of conjugal love, and the two cannot be seen as parallel or extrinsically related. In this way, genuine conjugal love and procreation cannot possibly find themselves in opposition or competition, because they are related organically as form and finality.

Interestingly, it remains perfectly possible according to this logic to think of both procreation and love as ends of marriage, but now in a more nuanced way. The procreative end is the end that strictly speaking transcends the marriage bond as such. The child, as marriage's fruit, stands nevertheless outside the marriage, and will one day enter into his or her own union with another from entirely outside the family circle. If the familial community flows naturally from the marital community, it also radically transcends it. Love, on the other hand, is an end in the sense that the perfection of the form of something is an integral or intrinsic end. It is the immanent good of marriage as such. If love is the objective form of marriage, constantly calling the spouses to conform to its objective demand, both love and fruitfulness are in fact ends, but ends that are intrinsically or organically related and inseparable.

Modernity and Christianity

Gaudium et spes exhibits both an engagement with and the influence of some of modernity's signal accomplishments. In offering a Christian humanism, the Council Fathers prioritize the person. This perspective in its turn allows them to appropriate fully—while radically deepening—a well-rounded view of conjugal love's role and place, even if they continue to insist that "marriage and conjugal love are by their nature ordained toward the begetting and educating children." If the text offers a deep development of the meaning of conjugal love, doing so in no way implies that that love is turned in on itself. Significantly, the text centers the marital and familial communities in Christ, who is himself placed at the conceptual center of the Pastoral Constitution. Each of these doctrinal developments are fundamental to, and therefore deeply influenced and indeed enabled by, the Council Fathers' engagement with the achievements of modernity. Furthermore, it is undeniable that modernity as we know it could emerge only from the matrix of Christianity, with the latter's emphasis on the dignity of the person in his or her free response to God and with its respect for the integrity and relative autonomy of nature within God's creation. It is no accident, then, that modernity develops only in the Christian West. If modernity is in important ways *post*-Christian, it is nevertheless post-*Christian*. That is, if modernity's instincts largely tend toward doubt and atheism, this fact cannot nullify its appropriation of basic conceptual categories whose ancestry is inalienably, and whose basic structures remain, Christian. We can see this in modernity's characteristic ways of understanding, for example, history, the person, and freedom.

Yet the cultivating dominion of the first parents over the garden easily slips into modernity's characteristically violent domination of nature. So, despite modernity's Christian background and the ways modernity has influenced the development of doctrine, the Council Fathers' teaching on marriage and the family clearly faces some heavy cultural headwinds. Not only contemporary thought but also modern thought in its origins seem particularly hostile to her understanding of natural order. Creaturely order and relative autonomy[29] give way to the dialectic of pure heteronomy and autonomy. Modernity's tendency toward positivism and empiricism, its tendency to understand knowledge in productive rather than contemplative terms, its moralizing separation of fact and value (such that the moral and the charitable are purely will centered and no longer structuring elements of the created order), all militate against the idea of marriage and family as natural communities. Each of these developments is antagonistic to the metaphysics or symbolic ontology (the sacramental sense of reality as a whole) that could make sense of natural communities.[30]

29. *GS*, no. 36.

30. Cf. Joseph Cardinal Ratzinger, "Difficulties Confronting the Faith in Europe Today," *Communio: International Catholic Review* 38 (Winter 2011): 728–37, 734. See also Angelo Scola, *The Nuptial Mystery*, trans. M. Borras (Grand Rapids, MI: Eerdmans, 2005): 224–25, 346–47. The antagonism in part stems from modernity's reductive view of "symbol." See Alexander Schmemann, *For the Life of the World* (Crestwood: St. Vladimir's Seminary Press, 1998 [1963]), 128*ff*.; David L. Schindler, "Liturgy, Nuptiality, and the Integrity

Here we rejoin the question of birth control. The question was a difficult and important one at the time of the Council. Contraceptive practices were hardly unique to the cultural situation addressed by the Council Fathers. Yet if the ancients were well acquainted with them, their significance for modern culture seems particularly profound. The question faced by the Council Fathers, then, must be placed within this broader sweep of modernity.

The Denatured Family

There are of course innumerable examples we might point to for evidence of the difficulty contraception presents to the intelligibility of marriage and the family as natural communities, but the scope of this essay allows us to point to only one. The late "group process" historian Rudolph Binion offers such an example. He sought to study the implications of the widespread use of contraceptives and the consequent drop in fertility in France and America following the two revolutions.[31] He related this decreased fertility—which preceded similar drops in the rest of Europe by nearly a century—to the revolutions themselves: the political autonomy represented by the revolutions was mirrored in the home and within the spousal relationship. The political spirit of freedom and self-governance in effect meant a renegotiation of the relations of husband and wife. At the heart of this domestic revolution, women sought to take "control of their family life, and in particular their own bodies, inasmuch as they refused to accept unrestrained childbearing."[32] Significantly, while birth control methods had long been associated with illicit sexual activity, after the revolutions they were invited into the marriage bed itself.[33] This development implied deeper social and cultural change than is often appreciated.

---

of Cosmic Order: Symbolic Ontology and Feminism," *Communio: International Catholic Review* 28 (2001).

31. Rudolph Binion, *Past Impersonal: Group Process in Human History* (DeKalb: Northern Illinois University Press, 2005), 14–45.

32. Binion, *Past Impersonal*, 39.

33. Binion, *Past Impersonal*, 32–45.

The penetration of this revolutionary spirit into the home marked the start of a major upheaval and turnabout in relations between the sexes which has since spread throughout the West and, intensifying from year to year, has tended not only to undermine the time-honored male primacy in the public sphere, but also to break down all the long-established differences between the sexes in the domestic and professional walks of life—in dress, in hairstyle, in ornaments, even in ways of making love.[34]

There are other profound cultural implications. For example, the introduction of contraceptive practices into marriage introduces the phenomenon of the "generation gap," caused by lowered fertility. If having fewer children both increases the age differences between parents and children and intensifies the intimacy of the familial relations, these relations can also become "explosive."[35] The result, Binion observes, is a magnification of differences in generational expectations and outlooks.[36] This in turn lends itself to intergenerational tensions, which in their turn accelerate the sort of progressive corrosion of traditions we see in modern societies.

More interesting, however, are the effects of the growing acceptance of birth control in the rest of Europe, which began in the last decades of the nineteenth century, and which he attributes to both the increase in women's autonomy and the pressures of population growth. Here, too, through the acceptance of contraceptive practices within marriage, wives "claimed their bodies as their own to use or enjoy as they pleased and not as organic machines for reproducing as long as they could."[37] But this widespread acceptance of contraceptive practices in respectable homes comes with a certain personal cost. Binion sees this acceptance as giving rise to the dominant late nineteenth- and early twentieth-century literary themes of marital and familial dysfunction and hypocrisy (e.g., Ibsen's *The Wild Duck* [1884] and Strindberg's *The Ghost Sonata* [1907]). Citing numerous examples, Binion concludes that "By the 1890s, any ambitious fiction that probed domestic life, as most fiction then did, was apt to present it as a pernicious mistake, and the more pernicious the deeper the probing had gone."[38] Con-

34. Binion, *Past Impersonal*, 44.
35. Binion, *Past Impersonal*, 28.
36. Binion, *Past Impersonal*, 28.
37. Binion, *Past Impersonal*, 30.
38. Binion, *Past Impersonal*, 14.

sider the development of what by now have become stock literary figures: the "strong woman" or independent wife (e.g., Ibsen's *A Doll House* [1879]), the clinging neurotic mother (e.g., Ibsen's *Ghosts* [1882]), the domineering or dissipated father (e.g., *Ghosts*; Dostoyevsky's *The Brothers Karamazov* [1879/80]), the unfeeling or dimwitted husband (e.g., Flaubert's *Madame Bovary* [1857]), the parents and children separated by an infinite gulf (e.g., Turgenev's *Fathers and Sons* [1861], Shaw's *Misalliance* [1910], and Strindberg's *The Pelican* [1907]), the children who seek only escape (e.g., Butler's *The Way of All Flesh* [1884]), even in death (e.g., *The Pelican*), and so forth.[39] The literary critique of marriage and family seems unremitting.

But what is its cause? Binion proposes an interesting explanation. "Marital contraception crashed a huge moral barrier," and the "generation that first infringed it in Europe beginning in the 1870s paid the penalty in the classic form of a guilt crisis clearly inscribed in the creative literature of the time."[40] If the connections he draws between political revolution and contraception and between contraception and the literary critique of the family are thought-provoking, this explanation seems suspect. Not only does he at times appear to project current attitudes and conceptual categories on previous centuries,[41] but also his attempt to psychologize "the generation that first infringed" the ancient taboo seems both simplistic and reductive. In effect, he supposes that the "guilt complex" is a passing phenomenon, constituting a growing pain in the natural progression of history toward individual liberation.

Perhaps, however, a more satisfying conclusion may be drawn from the historical connections themselves. The widespread acceptance of contraceptive practices into respectable married life can only bring with it a conceptual division between sexual union and the having of children. Under such circumstances, the child no longer appears to be quite necessary or naturally related to human love. As a result, the need for and meaning of marriage are obscured, and indeed many of the literary works

39. Binion, *Past Impersonal*, 14–31.

40. Binion, *Past Impersonal*, 29, 43.

41. At times, his discussion presupposes an understanding of history as the progressive liberation from political-social and bodily-physical conditions, leading finally to our more enlightened selves. This tendency was famously criticized by Herbert Butterfield in his *The Whig Interpretation of History* (New York: W. W. Norton, 1965).

cited by Binion express liberation precisely in the form of independence and promiscuity.[42] The literary critique of the family, then, may simply have drawn out the implications of this development: postrevolutionary marriage and family eventually come to seem like bourgeois impositions, as though civil society had decided to regulate free love with a distorting, inhibiting, and finally inhuman structure, designed to contain and define personality. Rather than seeing the marital and familial communities as creaturely and natural, the revolutions inaugurate a growing sense that they are non-natural or even *un*natural impositions.

This leaves marriage and sexuality with a bit of an identity crisis. The common historical narrative tells us of a shift in the nineteenth century from a sexual ethic rooted in the priority of procreation to one founded on the ideal of romantic love.[43] The rise of sexology and then psychoanalysis during that century and the next also deemphasizes sexuality's relation to the child and focuses instead on the question of physiological or psychological normality.[44] The effect is an increasingly subjectivist view of sexuality, and with it the loss of the givenness of form and order. In effect, it is a loss of the grounds for thinking of the man-woman relationship according to the logic of a natural community. The free-love counterpart of the imposed and unnatural marriage of nineteenth-century literature is in effect a rejection of form, the form that allows us to think of a community as an integral whole. What is left is only what now seem like arbitrary relations, imposed artificially for some end outside of those relations themselves. The heroes of this narrative are those individuals with sufficient strength of will to break free from given forms into the formless and ephemeral spontaneity of free love.

It is no accident therefore that sexology and then psychoanalysis

42. As Elizabeth Anscombe put it: "Christianity taught that men ought to be as chaste as pagans thought honest women ought to be; the contraceptive morality teaches that women need to be as little chaste as pagans thought men need be." "Contraception and Chastity," in *Faith in a Hard Ground: Essays on Religion, Philosophy and Ethics*, ed. M. Geach and L. Gormally (Charlottesville, VA: Imprint Academic, 2008), 170–91, at 171.

43. See, e.g., Jonathan Ned Katz, *The Invention of Heterosexuality* (New York: Penguin, 1995); John D'Emilio and Estelle B. Freedman, *Intimate Matters: A History of Sexuality in America*, 2nd ed. (Chicago: University of Chicago Press, 1988).

44. See, generally, Michel Foucault, *The History of Sexuality*, vol. 1, *An Introduction* (Vintage Books, 1978); Katz, *Invention of Heterosexuality*.

dealt mainly with questions of sexual deviancy, including homosexuality, in the second half of the nineteenth century. The loss of the direct link between sexual union and procreation, now obscured by the widening acceptance of birth control, generates the need to understand sexuality on new grounds. New disciplines must therefore attempt to sort things out, and of course these disciplines will take shape within the new model of the positive and empirical sciences. Yet without an adequate metaphysics, and without the ability to see the marital and familial communities as natural, it becomes difficult to say why, for example, a sexual relationship must be between a man and a woman.[45] If so, then thinkers such as Michael Foucault or Judith Butler, or cultural phenomena such the "trans" or "LGBTQ" movements, are nothing more than the intensification or further radicalization of this very logic.

Important here is that the literary assault on the family is an assault on the family as an unnatural and imposed institution. The wide use of contraception profoundly strengthens modernity's modern tendency toward a positivistic and legalistic understanding of human communities, such as marriage and the family. It confirms the basis for the angst expressed in that literature that the marital and familial communities are bourgeois impositions on nature, which itself is conceived as a formless remainder reducible to individual acts of will. What the calculated diminution of fertility following the revolutions and leading to the European literary attack on the family may show, then, is how contraception both logically flows out of but also radicalizes an undercurrent of modern thought already present in the Enlightenment's characteristic ways of conceived individuality, independence, and liberty.

We might assume that the historical events that Binion describes are but eddies in the wider and deeper currents of modernity. But there is something inherently deep and undeniable about the body and its inherent and symbolic meanings, and insofar as the widespread use of contraception constitutes a cultural rethinking of those meanings, it too has

45. Elizabeth Anscombe argued that the acceptance of contraception—i.e., the denial of the idea that the sexual act is necessarily connected to bearing children—leaves us unable to explain much else about sexuality, including why sexual acts ought to be confined to marriage (or even why there would be such a thing as marriage) and why sexual acts between those of the same sex should not be considered good. "Contraception and Chastity," 172.

profound significance. If modern thought, in both its ontological-cosmological and political-legal-ethical aspects, seeks to prioritize progressive liberation from natural and given order, then the body will certainly at some point present a central difficulty. For the body offers an "inescapable" meaning; it seems to speak perennially about the meaning of our lives and our actions. If for a time we can suppress it, the body continues to stand as a witness. The "psychology" of the situation, then, is not confined to one generation's elimination of what is ultimately a baseless taboo, as Binion's thesis supposes. Rather, birth control's implicit goal of liberation must constantly resist nature and the evidence of the body, since the obscurity it introduces is always incomplete. The perennial nature of this tension can be seen even more strongly today. We have traveled much further down the road in our attempts at denying the body's meaning. But the "inescapability" of that meaning is evidenced not only by the violence of the nineteenth-century literary critique but also by the vitriolic, scorched-earth quality of our contemporary debates.

The Papal Commission

So when the Council Fathers both reaffirmed the natural communities of marriage and family and took up birth control in light of the pill, they addressed issues that had been festering for a long time and had already profoundly shaped perceptions of the meaning of man and woman, sexuality, marriage, and the family. Yet the pill represents a watershed. If we give credence to Binion's "group process" argument, then perhaps we could also say that distancing the act of contraception from the sexual act itself, as the pill does, minimizes the occasion for guilt. It might make contraception seem as innocuous as allergy medicine or, for that matter, as natural as normal cycles of infertility. But the more important point is simultaneously subtler and more fundamental: as a decisive development of modern technology, the pill does not simply obstruct an act, wherein the obstruction continues to bear a perverse witness to the act in its integrity. Rather, it constitutes an important step toward the modern dream of radically dominating and reordering nature, now applied in a decisive way to the human subject itself, or more precisely, the woman *herself*.

We can see this by referring back to the immediate aftermath of the Council. I have already mentioned the famous papal commission, established by John XXIII and extended and expanded by Paul VI, which began meeting in 1963.[46] The majority of the commission, which advised overturning the traditional doctrine, attempted to answer the question of what makes contraception morally illicit. It offered its conclusions in a report to Paul VI (the "Majority Report").[47] Its outlook is typically modern and moralizing: contraceptive practices are morally neutral but they can be used in immoral ways, for example, when a couple acts selfishly or hedonistically. But they can also be used in generous, loving ways, ordered to responsible parenthood.[48] For its part, "responsible parenthood" is depicted in terms of control and choice with regard to childbearing. What matters is not the individual act but rather the "generous fecundity" of a couple's married life as a whole (the "totality doctrine").

To support this description of "responsible parenthood," the majority has recourse inter alia to a certain theology of history, rooted in Genesis. "The dominion of God is exercised through man, who can use nature for his own perfection according to the dictates of right reason."[49] From here, the report tells us that contemporary man "feels that he is more conformed to his rational nature, created by God with liberty and responsibility, when he uses his skill to intervene in the biological processes of nature so that he can achieve the ends of the institution of matrimony in the conditions of actual life, than if he would abandon himself to chance."[50] The majority's discussion of the duty "to humanize and to bring to greater perfection for the life of man what is given in nature"[51] becomes ambig-

46. See *GS*, no. 51n14.

47. The "Majority Report" is collected in Robert G. Hoyt, ed., *The Birth Control Debate* (Kansas City, MO: National Catholic Reporter, 1968), under the title "'On Responsible Parenthood': The Final Report" (79–101) along with several other documents, including the "Minority Report," which Hoyt titles "'The State of the Question': A Conservative View" (25–61), and a response to the Minority Report, titled "The Question Is Not Closed: The Liberals Reply" (63–77). References in what follows to the "majority" or the "Majority Report" are to the argument, as presented in both "On Responsible Parenthood" and "The Question Is Not Closed," without distinguishing between them.

48. Hoyt, *Birth Control Debate*, 84–85.

49. Hoyt, *Birth Control Debate*, 63–77, 69.

50. Hoyt, *Birth Control Debate*, 69.

51. Hoyt, *Birth Control Debate*, 89. Or again: "to put under human control what is given by physical nature" (79).

uous when it is specified in terms of "man's tremendous progress in control of matter by technical means," which is said to "correspond perfectly to the divine decrees,"[52] and by the majority's repeated reduction of the body's generative powers to "biological" or "physiological processes."[53]

It is part of the very human vocation to bring order to man's material conditions, the majority declares, and modern technology has allowed the imposition of this order on an unprecedented scale. More specifically, humanity's domination of nature has been turned onto the human subject itself. If the body's generative powers are presented reductively as "biological processes," humanity can bring technological rationality to these functions for the sake of a more fully human life. These "biological processes" are inherently subpersonal and therefore must be "humanized" by the application of modern technology. In effect, the majority seems to think that the human body needs to be humanized. Its view of the body is as dualistic as it is mechanistic.

Far from constituting a crisis for Christianity, then, modernity's progressive technological mastery of nature, including the body, is its fullest expression. If this domination brings "joy and hope," there is little indication from the majority that it might also evoke "anxious questions."[54]

From *Praxis* to *Poiesis*

The anthropological outlook implicit in this view gives rise to the majority's ethical judgment. "Responsible parenthood" is the rational choice of when to have children and how many to have, aided by technological ordering of bodily processes and functions. Chastity is understood, ac-

52. Hoyt, *Birth Control Debate*, 79.

53. Hoyt, *Birth Control Debate*, 70, 71, 73, 90; see also, e.g., B. Häring, "The Inseparability of the Unitive-Procreative Functions of the Marital Act," in *Contraception: Authority and Dissent*, ed. Charles Curran (New York: Herder and Herder, 1969), 176–92.

54. This sanguine view of modernity was common among theologians of the time. Schillebeeckx, e.g., has written of modernity's elimination of medieval traces of the pagan sense of nature's sacredness. By descralizing nature, modernity supposedly opened the way for man's free construction in his approach to God in holiness. *World and Church*, trans. N. D. Smith (New York: Sheed and Ward, 1971), 101. See the criticism of Henri de Lubac, *A Brief Catechesis on Nature and Grace*, trans. B. Richard Arnandez, FSC (San Francisco: Ignatius Press, 1984), 191–234.

cording to the majority's "totality doctrine," as a general orientation within the marriage as a whole toward a "prudent and generous fecundity."[55] The ethical question comes down, in other words, to the proper use of "technical means." Reflected here by implication are the essential ingredients of the modern and Enlightenment ontological-ethical outlook, highlighted by a basic rejection of moral order and charity as already symbolically present in the structures of God's creation.[56]

Consider the contrast with classical ethics. Appetites rooted in bodily affections certainly need to be brought into rational order. This habitual ordering is what we call virtue. But for the classical tradition, virtue is the ordering of the appetites themselves. This is the central point of classical ethics. The ethical task, we might say, is the effort to discover the truth interior to appetite. What do we really desire? What desire underlies all desires? Certainly for the ancients, the rational nature of man and woman dictates what is good or perfective for the human animal. But the body, particularly in its sexual dimorphism, is evidence for reason to deliberate about what is true. For Christianity, this starting point is refined and mediated by the doctrine of creation. If I am first and foremost God's creature, then the visible structures of the body certainly inform the meaning of desire. They are sacred evidence of its inner truth.

But the majority authors assume that unwanted fertility is first a *technological* problem. Ethics only comes into the picture after the fact, as it were, as a matter of the moral use or application of technology. The ethical problem is shifted from the rational and habitual ordering of appetite—what is given by nature—to the generous or ungenerous use of technology, which renders that intrinsic ordination unnecessary.[57] The majority in effect converts what had always been a question of virtue into a question of technique, *praxis* into *poiesis*/*techne*.

55. Hoyt, *Birth Control Debate*, 89.

56. See Ratzinger, "Difficulties Confronting the Faith in Europe Today," 728–37; Benedict XVI, "The Listening Heart: Reflections on the Foundations of Law," Address to the German Bundestag, Reichstag Building, Berlin, September 22, 2011; Hans Jonas, *The Phenomenon of Life: Toward a Philosophical Biology* (Evanston, IL: Northwestern University Press, 1966), 195*ff*.

57. Cf. Martin Rhonheimer, "Contraception, Sexual Behavior, and Natural Law: Philosophical Foundations of the Norm of '*Humanae Vitae*,'" *Linacre Quarterly* 56, no. 2 (1989): 20–57, at 43.

Humanae vitae

Humanae vitae rejected the majority report's recommendations. It defined contraception as "all acts that attempt (*intendat*) to impede procreation."[58] By defining contraceptive acts in terms of intention, it answered lingering questions as to whether the pill constituted an illicit form of contraception within Church teaching. It showed that the traditional teaching on birth control was not confined to the obvious physical obstruction of the act itself, present in other types of contraception. But to define an evil act is not to say *why* it is evil. For this, *Humanae vitae* famously put forward its "inseparability doctrine": contraception is evil because it separates what should never be separated, the unitive and procreative meanings of the conjugal act.[59] Put more strongly, to separate these "significations" is to destroy the act's conjugality. To act against one of these significations is to act against the whole and, at a deeper level, to act against both. What is wrong with contraceptive acts, then, is not only that they violate the procreative meaning but also that they are no longer truly or fully unitive.

This teaching runs far more radically against the Majority Report's position than is typically recognized. In fact, it presupposes the organic and metaphysical unity of the marital and familial communities as natural in the manner described above and intended by the Council Fathers. Of course, it might be objected that the majority has in fact, through the "totality doctrine," simply transferred the unitive and procreative meanings to the level of the marriage as a whole, as opposed to *Humanae vitae*'s insistence on the centrality of individual acts, and has thereby preserved the organic and symbolic wholeness of a natural community. But this objection hardly escapes the critique, since it is only through the technological domination of the body that the "totality" is made possible. In that sense, the totality doctrine itself, as conceived by the majority, is only a product of the prior reduction of the body to the functional interrelationship of its parts. This in effect is to read the body's symbolic order

58. *HV*, no. 14, trans. J. Smith, in *Humanae Vitae: A Generation Later* (Washington, DC: Catholic University of America Press, 1991), 272–95.

59. *HV*, no. 12.

out of the idea of the marital community, in favor of a higher "spiritual" reality that has been, in effect, abstracted from it. In other words, the majority's position tends in the direction of neutering the entire symbolic or sacramental logic of the faith.

I do not mean to claim that the majority did not seek to present marriage and family as God's creations or as natural communities. But the majority does take the decisive step of reducing the body to its biological functions,[60] and in doing so, it treats the body as needing humanization through technological domination. The effect is to go a long distance toward draining the body and its acts of their fully human and symbolic significance. So even though the majority would never have dreamed of calling marriage or the family unnatural impositions of civil society, its view of the body follows a logic that suggests similar conclusions.

The Technological Family

The dangers implicit in the Majority Report's position are greater than is often appreciated. If the majority implicitly reduces the body to the functional interrelations of its parts, and conceives its counterpart, the

60. The reductive character of speaking of the body in this manner was laid bare by Karol Wojtyła: "The expression 'order of nature' cannot be confused with nor identified with the expression 'biological order,' as the latter, even though also signifying the order of nature, denotes it only inasmuch as it is accessible for the empirical-descriptive methods of natural sciences … Confusing the order of existence with the 'biological order' in this way, or rather obscuring the former with the latter—which, together with all the empiricism [*sic*], seems to loom greatly over the mentality of modern man, especially the modern intellect—causes particular difficulties in understanding Catholic sexual ethics on the basis of its very presuppositions.… The sexual drive has its objective greatness precisely because of this link with the divine work of creation, a greatness that almost completely disappears in the field of vision of a mentality influenced by the 'biological order' alone. In relation to that order, the sexual drive is only a sum of functions, which from the biological point of view undoubtedly tend to a biological end, to reproduction. So, since man is the master of nature, should he not mold these functions—even in an artificial way, with the help of an appropriate technique—in a way that he deems fitting, that suits him? The 'biological order,' as a work of the human mind separating some elements of this order from what really exists, has man as its immediate author … The case is different with the 'order of nature.' It constitutes a group of cosmic relations that occur among beings that really exist. It is thus the order of existence, and the whole order present in existence finds its basis in the one who is the unceasing source of this existence, in God the Creator." *Love and Responsibility*, trans. G. Ignatik (Boston: Pauline Books and Media, 2013 [1960]): 39–41.

fully human and personal domain of freedom and reason, as the ability to dominate those functions, then the majority's underlying logic would seem to lend itself to a complete technological mediation of procreation. This danger is a primary theme of *Donum vitae*, which views the normalization of assisted reproductive technologies (ARTs), such as in vitro fertilization (IVF), as the logical outcome of the normalization of contraception. If we can nullify the procreative meaning of particular conjugal acts by means of contraception, then why can we not also nullify procreation's natural origins in conjugal union? ARTs are simply the logical extension of treating the procreative powers of the human body in a mechanistic or functionalist way. If the procreative powers of the human organism can be replaced by technological means, then these means are treated as essentially equivalent to the natural conception of children. Whatever qualitative differences may arise will revolve around subjective wants (people's preferences, aesthetic or otherwise) or functionality (which manner of conceiving children works best in a given situation). But the mechanistic treatment of the body implies that natural conception of children can in principle be replaced by ARTs without genuine loss.

Yet, as *Donum vitae* warns, if the unitary integrity of the conjugal act is destroyed by the denial of its procreative meaning, then it is also true that a nonunitive act (e.g., the use of IVF) is only procreative in a corrupted way because it conceives the child mechanistically, according to the logic of production.[61] The teachings of *Humanae vitae* on contraception and *Donum vitae* on ARTs are only flipsides of the same coin.[62]

A similar logic is present in the acceptance of "gay marriage," which typically depends on the idea that (1) marriage and procreation are not essentially related to each other and (2) even if they are related, the possibility of legal and technological means places homosexuals in a functionally equivalent position to husband and wife.[63] In this context it begins to make sense to speak of "gender" as "assigned," or to wonder whether that "assignment" might have been mistaken. This is why the "gay mar-

61. *Donum vitae*, II, B, 4.

62. Pius XII had years earlier already seen this logical connection. See "Address to Seventh International Hematological Congress," September 12, 1958.

63. See, e.g., *Perry v. Schwarzenegger*, 704 F.Supp.2d 921, at 997 (2010).

riage" movement, already somewhat passé, has so quickly given way to the "trans" movement.

The technologically mediated familial relations implied by the normalization of ARTs make the familial relations themselves appear in the end to be something we simply produce by means of rational and free interventions in mechanical processes. The family is thereby understood as a human product, with all the normal values and disvalues we attach to other products. This result plays into the essentially bourgeois outlook of contemporary culture, an outlook impressed into the flesh and blood of familial relations. Modern contraceptives and ARTs treat childbearing according to the model of a consumer or lifestyle decision, as though what had been a paramount civic good—the survival of society from generation to generation—can now be secured as a beneficial externality of private consumer choice.

Discerning the Signs of the Times: *Amoris laetitia*

What has been said thus far offers a framework for discerning the signs of our own times, which grow ever more complicated. To this end, *Amoris laetitia* offers a strong reaffirmation of *Humanae vitae*'s central teaching:

> conjugal union is ordered to procreation "by its very nature." The child who is born "does not come from outside as something added on to the mutual love of the spouses, but springs from the very heart of that mutual giving, as its fruit and fulfillment." He or she does not appear at the end of a process, but is present from the beginning of love as an essential feature, one that cannot be denied without disfiguring that love itself. From the outset, love refuses every impulse to close in on itself. Hence *no genital act* of husband and wife can refuse this meaning; even when for various reasons it may not always in fact beget new life.[64]

Francis has also rejected technologies that separate procreation from "the sexual relationship between man and woman," as well as the equation of same-sex relationships with marriage.[65] He has railed against the imposition of "gender ideology" on developing countries and is clearly

64. Pope Francis, *Amoris laetitia* (*AL*), "On Love in the Family," March 19, 2016, no. 80 (italics added).

65. *AL*, nos. 52, 56, 251.

scandalized by Western culture's forgetfulness of the unique, primordial, and irreplaceable relationship of man and woman in marriage and parenthood.[66] Just as importantly and profoundly, he has put his finger on what is perhaps the central issue of our times: our technological culture's dehumanizing implications.[67] If the argument up to now has been near the mark, it is the logic of this culture that has become manifest in the recent disintegration of the marital and familial communities.

Still, at times, we may feel we are teetering on a knife's edge. While most of the discussion surrounding the 2014 and 2015 synods leading up to *Amoris laetitia* centered on the issue of communion for divorced and civilly remarried Catholics, and on the "accompaniment" of those in other sorts of "irregular relationships," other important and related matters were not far in the background. The teaching of *Humanae vitae* was among these, and the preparatory documents were dangerously ambiguous with regard to the central logic of Paul VI's great encyclical.[68] These ambiguities would seem to reveal an appetite among some Synod Fathers to rethink the teaching on contraception, perhaps in a way reflecting the Majority Report's arguments half a century earlier.

Take, for example, the *Instrumentum laboris* for the 2015 Synod. In a passage ostensibly reaffirming the teaching *Humanae vitae*, the *Instrumentum* spoke of "the unitive and procreative character *of marriage*."[69] *Humanae vitae*, on the other hand, had spoken of the unitive and procreative meanings *of the conjugal act*. Although this may seem a subtle differ-

66. E.g., "Address of His Holiness Pope Francis to the Polish Bishops," Apostolic Journey of His Holiness Pope Francis to Poland on the Occasion of the XXXI World Youth Day, Krakow, Poland, July 17–21, 2016, http://www.vatican.va. One would also want to consider the Holy Father's striking criticisms of the logic of technological domination of nature, as applied to the whole of the created order. See *Laudato si'*, "On Care for Our Common Home," May 24, 2015, no. 106*ff*.

67. See, e.g., *Laudato si'*, no. 115.

68. See David S. Crawford and Stephan Kampowski, "The Integrity of Moral Deliberation: On Paragraph 137 of the *Instrumentum Laboris*," *Communio: International Catholic Review*, 42, no. 2 (Summer 2015); "An Appeal: Recalling the Teaching of *Humanae Vitae* (and *Veritatis Splendor*)," *First Things*, September 10, 2015, https://www.firstthings.com/web-exclusives/2015/09/an-appeal.

69. XIV Ordinary General Assembly of Bishops, *Instrumentum laboris*, "The Vocation and Mission of the Family in the Church and the Contemporary World," June 23, 2015, no. 45 (emphasis added).

ence, it is in fact crucial. It is not simply wrong to say that marriage itself bears inseparable unitive and procreative meanings. Yet *Humanae vitae*'s connecting these to the conjugal act was intended to fortify a precise point. The inseparability of these meanings in the conjugal act, set forth in paragraph 12, is clearly intended to reinforce the teaching of paragraph 11, namely, that "each and every marriage act must be open to the transmission of life."[70] By placing the inseparability of the unitive and procreative meanings in "marriage," rather than in the conjugal act itself, the *Instrumentum* in fact implies that while the totality of married life must be open to life, this does not necessarily pertain to particular marital acts. This passage, in other words, would imply a reversion to the reductively moralizing approach of the Majority Report. It would imply a return to the report's doctrine of totality, as rejected by *Humanae vitae*, along with the implicit materialization and nonsacramental view of the body, a body that must be "humanized" by technological reason.

Fortunately, both the majority of the Synod Fathers in the *Relatio Finalis*[71] and the Holy Father in *Amoris laetitia* rejected this dangerously ambiguous language. Yet the text of *Amoris laetitia* is nothing if it is not by turns both beautiful and frustratingly inscrutable. The striking clarity of the passage quoted above is perhaps hobbled by a possible reading of a later passage of the Exhortation, which undermines the objectivity of moral truths by treating them as "general rules" that may be inapplicable in particular circumstances (no. 304). This passage might be construed as saying that, while the reaffirmation of the earlier passage presents a "general rule" or "ideal," objective moral truths (moral absolutes) are not necessarily applicable in concrete, individual situations. Hence, it might be inferred, the actual "chaste" solution—the truly "responsible" one—might be the use of contraception. In effect, then, the teaching could be interpreted to mean

70. "Necessarium esse, ut quilibet matrimonii usus ad vitam humanum procreandam per se destinatus permaneat," *HV*, no. 11. The translation used is that of M. A. Calegari, SJ, in *Humanae Vitae: Encyclical Letter of His Holiness Pope Paul VI* (San Francisco: Ignatius Press, 1998), 15.

71. *The Vocation and Mission of the Family in the Church and in the Contemporary World: Final Report of the Synod of Bishops to the Holy Father, Francis,* October 24, 2015, http://www.vatican.va/roman_curia/synod/documents/rc_synod_doc_20151026_relazione-finale-xiv-assemblea_en.html.

that, if particular hardships make the "general rule" inapplicable, then the correct and even virtuous action, the one "approved" by God, is resort to contraception. To put it another way, the effect would be to teach that while the "general rule" may offer a guiding ideal, technological domination of the body's generative "functions" would be the morally correct and therefore virtuous course of action in many or perhaps most concrete situations. Yet the authors of the Majority Report would have conceded as much. In effect, the Church would cast a nod and wink at practices that embody the report's anthropology.[72]

Conclusion

The Council Fathers sought to offer a vision of the marital and familial communities that would put the integral relationship between conjugal love and its fruitfulness on display. As natural communities, marriage and the family are rooted both in freedom and the givenness of creation. They are something that we are invited into, rather than something we simply give ourselves. The actions proper to husbands, wives, parents, and children can themselves only take up the order inscribed in those communities and remain a full manifestation of their organic meaning.

Contraception, on the other hand, implies a displacement of the symbolic order inscribed in the body and marriage and family as natural communities with an alternative anthropology. In this way, the actions of the body would be drained of their ontological weight as symbolic instantiations of marital and familial communities. If *Amoris laetitia* were construed as authorizing this effective displacement, it would constitute a dangerous, albeit tacit, drift into the inhuman and formless anonymity of the interchangeable functionalities of the new world order, so clearly denounced elsewhere by the Holy Father.[73]

72. *AL*, no. 303, would also undermine *Humanae vitae*'s teaching. There, the exhortation appears to attribute to conscience a capacity for authorizing exemptions in cases where an actor is aware of his own inability to live according to a moral truth, even telling us that God may "approve" such an exemption.

73. See, e.g., Kerri Lenartowick, "Pope Francis Rejects Throw-Away Culture," Catholic News Agency, September 22, 2013, http://www.catholicnewsagency.com/news/pope-francis-rejects-throw-away-culture/.

8

In Dialogue with the World

The Church and the Evanescence of the Family

MARGARET HARPER MCCARTHY

Introduction

In the wake of the fiftieth anniversary of *Gaudium et spes,* the question that is once again in dispute is the nature of the Church's "openness to the world." This question has long been debated by commentators on the text who, shortly after its publication, expressed no lack of criticism about the naiveté of the "openness" that was so much in the air at the time of the Council.[1] For some today, this concern has gained so much traction—particularly under the influence of Joseph Ratzinger/Benedict XVI—that the Church seems to be going through something of a reversal or "about-face" of the Council's position.

Foremost among those who make this charge is Lieven Boeve.[2] According to Boeve, the openness to the world that so marked the Second Vatican Council in general—and *Gaudium et spes* in particular—meant that the Church was stepping out from its "ghetto" beyond the ebb and flow of worldly time so as to be more immersed in it. This suggested that

1. See Charles Moeller, "History of the Constitution," in *Commentary on the Documents of Vatican II*, vol. 5 (Montreal: Palm Publishers, 1969), 62; see also Joseph Ratzinger, *Theological Highlights of Vatican II*, trans. Thomas Rausch (New York: Paulist, 2009), 212–44.

2. Lieven Boeve, "Conversation and Cognitive Dissonance: Evaluating the Theological-Ecclesial Program of Joseph P. Ratzinger/Benedict XVI," *Horizons* 40 (December 2013): 242–54; Boeve, "Europe in Crisis: A Question of Belief or Unbelief? Perspectives from the Vatican," *Modern Theology* 23, no. 2 (April 2007): 205–27.

the Church was finally becoming incarnate, and that it, by implication, was allowing itself to learn from the world and even be shaped by it. "Openness" meant that the Church had come to grips with the more dynamic, or dialogical, conception of truth taught by *Dei verbum*, and had become willing to undergo a conversion by confessing its sin of hubris and the presumption that it alone possessed the truth and had nothing to gain from the world.[3] As for the world itself, such "openness" meant that the Church's mission was to become "incarnate," and no longer marked by the previous "dualism" that "makes the human turn away from the all-too-human to face its eternal destiny."[4]

According to Boeve, however, the original openness that once characterized the spirit of the Council is now all but a faint memory, thanks especially to the decades-long prominence of Joseph Ratzinger/Benedict XVI. Under the pressure of this persisting influence, old lines have been redrawn both *ad extra*—for example, in the selective dialogue with pre-Reformation bodies (i.e., the Orthodox) and integralists (i.e., Lefevrites)—as well as *ad intra*, with the crippling of dialogue itself through the condemnations of divergent theologians, the publication of catechisms and compendia (that rigidly fix doctrines in place), the negation of the authority of episcopal conferences, and the prohibition of discussions on controversial issues, such as women's ordination. Above all, the "return to the ghetto" is most evident in the Church's intransigent insistence on "anachronistic" positions concerning issues of sexual relations and biomedical ethics. These, say Boeve, are the "highly symbolic identity markers of this opposition," and it is here where one can see, most of all, the Church turning away from the world so as to once again ascend proudly back to an unchanging perfection.[5] Notwithstanding Ratzinger's involvement with the drafting of *Dei verbum*, and his endorsement of a more comprehensive view of revelation as "event," Boeve suspects that behind this "opposition to the world" lies a "neo-platonic framework" and an ahistorical, propositional idea of truth.[6] According to

3. Boeve, "Conversation and Cognitive Dissonance," 249–53.

4. Boeve, "Conversation and Cognitive Dissonance," 247.

5. Boeve, "Conversation and Cognitive Dissonance," 250.

6. Boeve, "Conversation and Cognitive Dissonance," 247–52. See Ratzinger, "Revelation Itself," in *Commentary on the Documents of Vatican II*, vol. 3 (Montreal: Palm Publishers, 1968), 170–73.

Boeve, the Church has once again begun to close her door on the world.

This essay takes up Boeve's charge by looking at the deepest reasons for why the Church is open to the world, and shows how these reasons help to correct both the understanding of the Church that was prevalent prior to the Council and the dominant view that has since characterized the postconciliar period. I then consider what is meant by "the world" in its most theological sense and attempt to offer an account that is at once thoroughly "worldly" while still being open to God. Here I show that what Boeve criticizes as an other-worldly tendency is, in fact, the most worldly view of all, however much it may demand the conversion of the world. Finally, I propose with Boeve that the family be taken as the privileged point of contact for seeing the relation between the Church and the world. Noting modernity's commitments to an abstract conception of man, however, particularly in its denial of basic human bonds, I conclude, contrary to Boeve, that the Church's "intransigence" on questions related to the family are where the Church's commitments to the reality of the world are most evident, however much it be a "sign that will be opposed" (Lk 2:34).

Openness to the World

There is no doubt that the Second Vatican Council wanted to meet the world in a fresh new way. Admonishing the "prophets of doom who are always forecasting disaster, as though the end of the world were at hand," John XXIII famously called the Church to "look to the present, to the new conditions and new forms of life introduced into the modern world, which have opened new avenues to the Catholic apostolate," noting that the "Church has not watched inertly the marvelous progress of the discoveries of human genius, and has not been backward in evaluating them rightly."[7] *Gaudium et spes*, which can be said to express the most fundamental intentions of the Council, would serve as the "counter syllabus" of an official reconciliation with a world that for the recent past had been met only with "declarations of war."[8] This new approach to

7. John XXIII, "The Opening Speech to the II Vatican Council," October 11, 1962.

8. Moeller, "History of the Constitution," 8. Cf. Joseph Ratzinger, *Principles of Catho-*

the world is noteworthy above all in its engagement with atheist humanism to which the Pastoral Constitution was in large part meant to be an answer.[9] In early deliberations on the document, the view held by many Council Fathers that atheism should be met with a simple condemnation was vigorously countered by the prevailing majority, who suggested, instead, starting from its more positive core of a confident and optimistic humanism.[10] As a result, the final text endeavored to show that theism and humanism are not at odds, but rather that they coincide in Christ, in whom "the mystery of man takes on light."[11] In this way the document showed that the Christian God, far from being an alienating projection, is rather "the God who empties himself of what belongs to him in order to lead man to what is most his own."[12] By implication, the Church, as well, cannot be viewed as an alienating force in the world but is the very condition by which the world comes into its own.

But there were many questions during the drafting of the pastoral constitution over the excessive optimism about the world to which the Church was "now" open. There were, for example, reservations over the downplaying of sin, which did not seem to penetrate the structure of the constitution's anthropology regardless of how many emendations were made.[13] What is more, though, there was a question about the precise nature of the relation between man (i.e., the world) and Christ (i.e., the Church). This question concerns the extent to which the Christological conclusion of *Gaudium et spes* 22 bears on its overall doctrine of man. There was a risk, Ratzinger thought, of making Christology a mere "crowning conclusion" juxtaposed to a "rational philosophical picture of man." As he wrote in his commentary on the document, "the text …

lic Theology: Building Stones for a Fundamental Theology, trans. Sr. Mary Frances McCarthy (San Francisco: Ignatius Press, 1987).

9. In Moeller's commentary on the Pastoral Constitution, he writes that with regard to atheism "it was considered that the schema as a whole would itself constitute an answer." "History of the Constitution," 62.

10. See J. Ratzinger, "The Dignity of the Human Person," in *Commentary on the Documents of Vatican II*, 5:143–47.

11. *GS*, no. 22.

12. Ratzinger, "Dignity of the Human Person," 146.

13. Ratzinger, "Dignity of the Human Person," 123–24. Cf. Moeller, "History of the Constitution," 62–64.

prompted the question why exactly the reasonable and perfectly free human being described in the first articles was suddenly burdened with the story of Christ. The latter might well appear to be a rather unintelligible addition to a picture that was already quite complete in itself."[14] This problem, he added, was the "real reason for the protest against the 'optimism'" of the constitution, not the lack of a more "pessimistic" account of sin.[15] It was this ambiguity about the relation between man and Christ that Ratzinger feared would lend itself to an unfortunate postconciliar form of optimism that would significantly depart from the intentions of the Council—and indeed this has been the direction that history has largely taken.

The "optimism" and "openness" of the postconciliar period has tended, thought Ratzinger, to unconditionally identify Christ (and the Church) with the world, conferring upon human history a sacral aura that drives mankind onward.[16] "The feeling that, in reality, there were no longer any walls between Church and world, that every 'dualism,' body-soul, Church-world, grace-nature and, in the last analysis, even God-world, was evil—this feeling became more and more a force that gave direction to the whole."[17] Regardless of the original intent of the conciliar documents, this identification of the Church with the world seemed to be the inevitable goal of a course set at the Council, whose own "evolution" had begun with "more closed" dogmatic statements (e.g., *Lumen gentium*) and ended with "more open" ones (e.g., *Gaudium et spes*).[18] This was the tearing down of "walls" that was so longed for at the outset of the Council. I speak here of a theology of secularization, one in which Christianity is now identified with the world and with the hopeful, progressive forces of a natural order understood "not as something already existing, but rather only as an entity to be created."[19]

14. Ratzinger, "Dignity of the Human Person," 119–20.
15. Ratzinger, "Dignity of the Human Person," 120.
16. Ratzinger, *Theological Highlights,* 227
17. Ratzinger, *Principles of Catholic Theology*, 383.
18. Ratzinger, *Principles of Catholic Theology*, 378, 390.
19. Ratzinger, "The Christian and the Modern World," in *Dogma and Preaching: Applying Christian Doctrine to Daily Life*, trans. Michael J. Miller and Matthew J. O'Connell (San Francisco: Ignatius Press, 2011), 164.

It is difficult not to notice how this unchecked and uncritical movement of "openness towards the world" has tended to make the Church obsolete, altering it into something that is "mythological" or, at best, into a source of religious motivation for worldly programs already in place.[20] Less obvious, however, is how much this movement has risked making *the world* obsolete, whereby, in accordance with its own logic of progress, the world has each of its moments programmed for obsolescence in its desire to pursue each and every new "update." For all its attempts to embrace the world and its history, postconciliar theology has become caught in what must ultimately be said to be a profoundly negative view. Such a view lays the vertical Neoplatonic escape from the world on its side, reorienting this flight from reality toward the horizontal "progress" of a world now understood purely historically and as an infinitely open temporality. Even the rather unorthodox American feminist Camille Paglia has said that such a secular idea of history could only have been invented by men, because they are always trying to escape the world![21]

In light of this trajectory, it must be asked why the Church should be open to the world and in what manner. I note here, along with Nicholas Healy, that "what is [so often] missing from ... reports of the new 'appreciation,' 'dialogue,' and 'reconciliation' is a reflection on *why* the Church is interested in the world" in the first place. If the Church is "now" open to the world, continues Healy, it is because of the growing awareness of the centrality and universality of Christ and his Church.[22]

This increased awareness is the theme of a book written by Hans Urs von Balthasar in the period leading up to the Council, one bearing a title reflecting much of the spirit of the time: *Razing the Bastions*.[23] Without denying that the universal horizon of the Church "can be demonstrably traced to the earliest Christian sources," Balthasar writes that in the Middle Ages, the Church

20. Ratzinger recounts the tendencies toward radicalization that judged the once progressive as "reactionary, bourgeois, and even mythical." See *Principles of Catholic Theology*, 386.

21. Camille Paglia, *Sexual Personae* (New Haven, CT: Yale University Press, 1990), 11.

22. See Nicholas J. Healy Jr., "Eucharistic Ecclesiology and Eschatology: On the Church's Relation to the World," chap. 4, this volume.

23. Hans Urs von Balthasar, *Razing the Bastions* (San Francisco: Ignatius Press, 1993).

had a very summary relationship to the non-Christian world—pagans, Jews, heretics, schismatics—even as late as the period of the missionary mendicant orders. At the level of consciousness humanity possessed at that period, an awareness of ultimate solidarity and fellowship in destiny could not yet exist, and one cannot presuppose such an awareness without anachronism.[24]

The ultimate reason for this "bastion-like" ecclesiology, according to Balthasar, was the dominant formulation of predestination that ever since St. Augustine had seemed to place an unbridgeable moat between the Church and the world.

In the Middle Ages, and still in the Baroque period, the former attitude [of the privileged person] was the essential one; the latter [that of the responsible person] followed as a possible derivative at best. Things could not be otherwise as long as the Augustinian view of predestination—two classes of men from the very outset, one chosen and the other rejected—was seriously taken as basic. One cannot say that the medieval Christian felt himself, fundamentally, and in his very identity as a Christian, responsible for the non-Christian.[25]

It was in view of this fault line between Christian and non-Christian that Balthasar proposed a "razing of the bastions" of the most radical kind. This meant a deepening of the terms of limited election to find in it not a barrier from the nonelect so much as a responsibility toward them.[26] But even more radically, it meant rethinking the theology of predestination in light of its original context in the doctrine of creation and showing

24. Balthasar, *Razing the Bastions*, 31, 61.

25. Balthasar, *Razing the Bastions*, 58–59.

26. "Augustine and the Middle Ages read and understood Romans, chapter nine, and they trembled before the mystery. We read it too, but we find the solution for what makes us tremble in chapters ten and eleven, which the Middle Ages did not yet perceive in their terribly extensive, exorbitantly demanding, universal significance. The parable of the two brothers, the one rejected and the other chosen, becomes transparent in this reference to the intended truth about the chosen and the rejected people. But now these two stand alternately for one another in a unique dialectic that cannot be illuminated by any other example, a dialectic that is the essence of the Christian theology of history: the chosen people is rejected because of its guilt, so that the non-people which was not chosen may be brought into election; and in its turn this non-people is chosen so that the fist promise to the chosen people may reach its fullness, so that Israel may become spiritual and as such, that is, as universal, as 'Israel as a whole, may be saved." Balthasar, *Razing the Bastions,* 59. The rethinking of "election" as a "mission" also stands at the heart of Ratzinger's "true universalism." Cf. *The Meaning of Christian Brotherhood* (San Francisco: Ignatius Press, 1988), 75–84.

how the reason for the world as such bears with it, at the most radical level, a profound "bridge" between Christ, his Church, and the world.[27]

Such Christocentrism can be detected in many of the texts of the Second Vatican Council. The very announcement of the Council appeals to the universal plan of salvation by the God who "wishes all men to be saved" through the "universal sacrament of salvation": the Church.[28] But it was not only a matter of the Church having a universal mission, bearing the *lumen gentium* ("light of nations"), but also that it had this by virtue of the fact that it was linked to the very beginning, to the "plan," and therefore to "the whole of man's history" as its "center" and "purpose."[29]

27. We note that this rethinking of the theology of predestination is the culmination of preconciliar debates concerning the place and unity of Christ and Creation. On these debates, see my "Predestination to the Glorious Liberty of the Sons and Daughters of God in Jesus Christ: Putting Predestination in Its Place," in *Sufficit gratia tua: Miscellanea in onore del Card. Angelo Scola, Arcivescovo di Milano, in occasione del 70° genetliaco* (Venice: Marcianum Press, 2012), 342–45; and "Vatican II and the Church's 'Openness to the World': Casting a Wider Net through the Still 'Narrow Gate,'" *Communio: International Catholic Review* 39 (Spring-Summer 2012): 250–51.

28. "The Church's anxiety to promote and defend truth springs from her conviction that without the assistance of the whole of revealed doctrine man is quite incapable of attaining to that complete and steadfast unanimity which is associated with genuine peace and eternal salvation. For such is God's plan. He wishes all men to be saved and to come to the knowledge of the truth. Unhappily, however, the entire Christian family has not as yet fully and perfectly attained to this visible unity in the truth. But the Catholic Church considers it her duty to work actively for the fulfillment of that great mystery of unity for which Christ prayed so earnestly to His heavenly Father on the eve of His great sacrifice. The knowledge that she is so intimately associated with that prayer is for her an occasion of ineffable peace and joy. And why should she not rejoice sincerely when she sees Christ's prayer extending its salvific and ever increasing efficacy even over those who are not of her fold?" John XXIII, "Address at the Opening of Vatican Council II," October 11, 1962. See also the following text from *Ad gentes* (*AG*): "Divinely sent to the nations of the world to be unto them 'a universal sacrament of salvation,' the Church, driven by the inner necessity of her own catholicity, and obeying the mandate of her Founder (cf. Mk 16:16), strives ever to proclaim the Gospel to all men" (*AG*, no. 1). *Lumen gentium* (*LG*) also had this universal extent in view: "Christ is the Light of nations. Because this is so, this Sacred Synod gathered together in the Holy Spirit eagerly desires, by proclaiming the Gospel to every creature, to bring the light of Christ to all men, a light brightly visible on the countenance of the Church" (*LG*, no. 1).

29. "Missionary activity is nothing else and nothing less than an epiphany, or a manifesting of God's decree, and its fulfillment in the world and in world history, in the course in which God, by means of mission, manifestly works out the history of salvation" (*AG*, no. 9). "The Church … likewise holds that in her most benign Lord and Master can be found the key, the focal point and the goal of man, as well as of all human history. She also maintains that beneath all that changes there are many realities which do not change and which have

If there was any doubt that this was the nature of the Church's openness to the world, Pope Paul VI recalled the Council Fathers to it at the beginning of the second session:

> From what point, dear brethren, do we set out? . . . What is the road we intend to follow? What is the goal we propose to ourselves? These three very simple and at the same time very important questions have, as we well know, only one answer, namely that here at this very hour we should proclaim Christ to ourselves and to the world around us; Christ our beginning, Christ our life and guide, Christ our hope and our end. . . . Let no other light be shed on this Council, but Christ the light of the world![30]

However much the Council succeeded in conveying this, it was this Christocentric intuition that animated the Council's openness to the world.[31] If the Church was "raising its bastions," it was because of a growing awareness of its role as the fulfilling answer to the "restlessness" of the world's deepest longings and pursuits.[32] It was not, therefore, a mere latecomer hoping to peacefully coexist with the world and play some small role in the promotion of man's historical projects. This newer form of "ghettoization," as Ratzinger calls it, ironically assumes a "pre-theological" concept of the world, one that brings the Church in too late with its "belated embrace."[33] On the contrary, the Church's "openness" to the world is founded princi-

their ultimate foundation in Christ, who is the same yesterday, and today, and forever. Hence under the light of Christ, the image of the unseen God, the firstborn of every creature, the council wishes to speak to all men in order to shed light on the mystery of man and to cooperate in finding the solution to the outstanding problems of our time" (*GS*, no. 10). See also de Lubac's discussion of the early pagan scandal over Christianity's novelty in time: *Catholicism: A Study of Dogma in Relation to the Corporate Destiny of Mankind*, trans. Lancelot Sheppard (London: Burns, Oates and Washbourne, 1950), 126–27, 146.

30. "Address at the Opening of the Second Session of Vatican Council II," September 29, 1963.

31. Ratzinger, who was critical about the lack of unity in *Gaudium et spes*, would still say about the Christological statement in article 22: "for the first time in an official document of the magisterium, a new type of completely Christocentric theology appears. On the basis of Christ this dares to present theology as anthropology and only becomes radically theological by including man in discourse about God by way of Christ, thus manifesting the deepest unity of theology." "Dignity of the Human Person," 159.

32. The famous Christological text of *Gaudium et spes* 22 follows the text from the opening to Augustine's *Confessions*: "Thou hast made us for Thyself, O Lord, and our hearts are restless till they rest in Thee."

33. Ratzinger, *Principles of Catholic Theology*, 379, 390.

pally on the deep openness of the world to Christ, an openness established at the very founding of creation itself.

The World

With regard to the concern about the flight from the world that has often accompanied the question of the Church's openness, it should be noted how locating the Church's relation to the world in creation radically gives worldliness its due. The doctrine of creation identifies worldly being as the manifestation of divine goodness but does so while recognizing that the world, at the same time, is the result of an utterly gratuitous act. Because there is no need in God, nor anything in the world that preexists its creation (i.e., creation *ex nihilo*), nothing is a "given," or simply "there" as a self-constituting foundation or a *causa sui.*[34] The paradox of creation's goodness and integrity while being simultaneously dependent on the gratuity of God's act cannot be overlooked here.[35] The God of Christianity (and Judaism before it) is a "Thou" and not a "One" to be approached only when every worldly difference, individuality, and personality (including the family) is ultimately left behind.[36] As Robert Spaemann observes:

> The particular individual [prior to Christianity] is of no significance in comparison with the universal idea, a nothing that exists only to realize and implement the real thing, which is the idea. In Plato's *Republic* only the lower classes have individual fulfillment of some kind—marriage, possessions, enjoyment, etc.—as

34. Kenneth Schmitz examines this difference between the "gift" and the "given" in its modern significance in *The Gift: Creation* (Milwaukee: Marquette University Press, 1982), 34–44.

35. This paradox is the thesis of Schmitz's book. (See note 34 above.)

36. Balthasar writes: "Plotinus [removes] the 'One' which knows no opposite term above the 'spirit' that has its life in the tension between thinking and being thought, between loving and being loved, between 'I' and 'Thou.' The 'One,' source of all love and insight, cannot itself be a loving 'Thou' … the divine absolute, which cannot cease to be the object and the goal of all of man's religious striving, disappears into the realm of that which cannot be uttered, that which lacks a 'Thou': it is that which is loved, that to which all goodness must be attributed, but since it remains severed impersonally from all dialogue between 'I' and 'Thou,' it can be attained only by the one who leaves his personal being as a limitation behind him and penetrates through to that which is devoid of contraries." "Movement towards God," in *Explorations in Theology*, vol. 3, *Creator Spirit*, trans. Brian McNeil (San Francisco: Ignatius Press, 1993), 26.

the goal of their existence. Their share in truth is to let themselves be ruled by those who have put individuality behind them and have only the universal in view, those with no personal ties, family, or possessions.[37]

It is precisely in the Christian tradition, where the world is a gift (*donum*) and not a "given" (*datum*), that we find the most profound recognition of the world's goodness and integrity.[38] The latter of these characteristics became something of an obsession to the later Catholic philosophical tradition.[39] Christianity, in other words, is utterly defined by a disposition of openness to the world of the most radical kind.

But contrary to the usual opposition between an "optimism" of the world and a "pessimism" in which "world" is synonymous with sin, we can see that the very foundation of worldly optimism is that God gives the world a ground of inner integrity that is wholly its own. This remains "good" even as this gift includes the possibility of the world's opposition to its Giver and to the vital ground upon which it continually depends.[40] In giving the world to itself, in other words, God takes a risk, or as Kenneth Schmitz writes:

[God] … freely determines to create a creature of a certain sort with integrity and freely determines to respect that integrity. In creating creatures who have freedom, he even determines to respect the capacity to flaw the original gift. The German word, *Opfer*, catches both meanings, for the creator's love is both an offering and, potentially, a victim.[41]

Given the nature of the gift of the world to itself, it is precisely from within the deepest roots of a Christian optimism that all serious questions as to

37. Robert Spaemann, *Persons: The Difference Between 'Someone' and 'Something,'* trans. Oliver O'Donovan (Oxford: Oxford University Press, 2006), 19.

38. Cf. Schmitz's discussion on the direct relation between the absolute dependence of creatures owing to their being created and their ontological integrity in *The Gift*, 71–84.

39. Cf. Balthasar's history of the concept of nature in Catholic theology in *The Theology of Karl Barth* (San Francisco: Ignatius Press, 1992), 267–325.

40. In his reflection on the idea of the "world," Hans Urs von Balthasar writes: "since freedom is the very essence of love, God cannot and will not withhold such freedom from the chief beings in the world, and this in turn means that, from all eternity, he designs the world in such a way that it includes the eventual misuse of freedom in the form of human (and angelic) sin." *The Final Act, Theo-Drama: Theological Dramatic Theory*, vol. 5 (San Francisco: Ignatius Press, 1998), 99.

41. Schmitz, *The Gift*, 96–97.

the Church's "openness" require discernment about what the world truly is and what it is not: a decision over whether the world is *donum* or mere *datum*, the latter of which carries the biblical sense of "a decision in favor of this world alone and *against* what is godly and eternal" (cf. Rom 12:2).[42] Returning to the deep reasons for optimism about the world requires us to abandon all shallow optimisms precisely for the sake of the world.

We must add here a note on history, which also receives greater ontological status from the doctrine of creation. In creating the world, the Eternal creates time, including that moment in time in which he joined himself to us through the hypostatic union. "In Jesus Christ, the Logos is no longer the realm of ideas, values and laws which governs and gives meaning to history, but is himself history," says Balthasar in his meditation on the *Theology of History*.[43] The conciliar document on revelation would express this by recourse to the category of "event," insisting as it does in the unity of "words and deeds."[44] By virtue of creation, the incarnation, and the resurrection, history has a thoroughly positive meaning, for its contingent facts now bear the eternal (i.e., the *Logos*) and carry the imperishable in its perishable moments. To look at it from the other side, history is the domain to which the Eternal God has entrusted himself freely, although not, of course, out of need, as the French poet Charles Péguy has so richly described:

> [Jesus Christ] has pronounced, carnally and in time, eternal words …
> It is to us, the weak, that he was given,
> He depends on us, weak and carnal,
> To bring to life and to nourish and to keep alive in time
> These words pronounced alive in time.
> … To nourish with our blood, with our flesh, with our heart
> The words which, without us, would collapse fleshless.
> To grant, (it's incredible), to grant to the eternal words,

42. Ratzinger, *Dogma and Preaching*, 169.

43. Balthasar, *A Theology of History* (New York: Sheed and Ward, 1963), 18. With this statement, Balthasar points to the novelty of Christianity against the backdrop of pre- and post-Christian philosophies that subordinate history in one way or another to the necessary, universal, and abstract (6–7).

44. *Dei verbum*, no. 2. Ratzinger drew special attention to this point in his commentary of the Dogmatic Constitution "Revelation Itself," 172.

In addition, like a second eternity,
A temporal and carnal eternity, an eternity of flesh and of blood,
Nourishment, an eternity of body,
A worldly eternity.[45]

[The Church] promises to eternity
    A time
To the spirit
    A flesh.
To Jesus
    A Church.
To God himself
    A creation (his creation, the creation)[46]

It is hard to imagine a more radical word on the positivity of the world and its history than in this "strange reversal, insane reversal," which leads us all the way back to the nature of God himself.[47] But again, just as the world has in itself the capacity to become a "this world," so too can its history become a mere sequence of moments with no *Logos* in it—a mere "to-morrow, and to-morrow, and to-morrow," a moving forward with no turning back.[48] In other words, worldly time can become "progress," a movement forward with no other criterion for judgment other than what is simply today. This view of history often accompanies a shallow optimism about the world that is unaware of both the "ambivalence of all external human progress" and how profoundly and paradoxically negative its outlook is, since every "today" will always be trumped by its "tomorrow."[49] Given the distinctive

45. Charles Péguy, *Portal of the Mystery of Hope*, trans. David L. Schindler (New York: Continuum, 1996), 55.

46. Péguy, *Portal of the Mystery of Hope*, 61.

47. Péguy, *Portal of the Mystery of Hope*, 61. Referring to Balthasar's thinking about the "positivity of difference" in God, we note that the very reason for the nonnecessity of the world for God is at the same time the reason for the world, and therefore its positivity as created and historical. See *The Final Act*, 68–102.

48. Shakespeare, *Macbeth*, act 5, scene 5, line 19. Péguy's image of the virtue of hope is a "little girl" who "leads the way" for her "older sisters," "Faith" and "Charity." Yet even as little "Hope" forges bravely ahead, she never strays from her point of departure, from her origin, which is the "great grace" that enables her to be hopeful. See *Portal of the Mystery of Hope*, 7.

49. Ratzinger, *Theological Highlights*, 227. Ratzinger elsewhere refers to the negative relation of history with the "utopianism . . . that believes that, hitherto, everything has been done badly and only now will begin to be done properly." *Principles of Catholic Theology*, 373.

Christian account of the world's *exitus*, the *reditus* of history, beginning as it does with the incarnation, will not be an escape in any direction.

Returning to the question of the Church's "openness to the world," we note that if this is rooted in the mystery hidden before all ages in the "God who creates all things" (Eph 3:8–9), then this turning is not a matter of a "bland and shallow humanism" that is anxious about being on top of the times.[50] Evaluating what had come of the "razing of the bastions" that had been so desired before the Council, Balthasar writes, "those who seek mitigations in everything and express delight at the 'progress' and the growing 'maturity' as each barrier falls do not understand what the Fathers were concerned with." What the Council Fathers intended, he continues, "was to direct into the secular world through the Church … the mysterious ray of Trinitarian and crucified love, wholly and completely."[51] It is because of what the Church possesses and wants to direct into the world that the Church is open to the world. It is only on account of this gift by which the mystery of man and his world truly becomes clear. But it is for this same reason, together with the world's own mysterious tendency toward becoming a "this world," that the Church's encounter with the world will never be a matter of "pure harmony," as Benedict XVI cautioned.[52] She will always be, in her very openness, a "sign that will be opposed" (Lk 2:34), a witness, and even a martyr.

The Family

We now turn to the specific question of the family. A Christian theological perspective asserts that the future of humanity passes by way of the family. The question about the family was one of the privileged points of

---

On this "lack of an attitude of critical reserve toward forces that have left their imprint on the modern world," see also *Principles of Catholic Theology*, 350.

50. Hans Urs von Balthasar, *The Moment of Christian Witness* (San Francisco: Ignatius Press, 1994), 126.

51. Balthasar, *Moment of Christian Witness*, 125. On this point, Ratzinger speaks of the task "to permeate the one world of all men with the spirit of Jesus Christ." See *Dogma and Preaching*, 179.

52. Benedict XVI, "Address to the Roman Curia offering Them His Christmas Greetings," December 22, 2005.

contact between the Church and the world at the time of the Council.[53] It was (and is) one of the "urgent problems" highlighted by the pastoral constitution.[54] Today, however, some allege that the growing tension between the Church and the world at this "point" is not because the problem has become more urgent "on the world's side," so to speak, but because the Church has turned away from the world by refusing to adapt to changing situations and circumstances. In light of the foregoing, this view, however "worldly" it may appear to the majority of people today, commits itself to what is, in the end, an utterly unworldly outlook that lacks any genuine realism. Moreover, it is a view that commits itself to a profoundly ahistorical, and even antihistorical, outlook that requires constant detachment from the past by way of "progress." To be "open" to the world, in this sense, would not only do no favors for the world but also render the Church obsolete: being *of* the world, the Church could not also be *in* it.

Because the Church is rooted in the mystery of a choice made "before the foundation of the world" (1 Pt 1:20), she is deeply committed (i.e., "open") to the worldliness of the world and therefore to the humanity of man, whose origins lie with the familial bonds in which man receives himself as an embodied being. But this very openness involves a realism as to the ambivalence that characterizes the free creature in the temporal order, caught as he is between his filial *capax* and the temptation to become a man of "this world," one "all wrapped up in himself."[55] It is for these reasons that the Church in its encounter with the world must help to make more clear what it is that makes the world more itself and what it is that does not. This requires, in part, a proper reading of the "signs of the times."[56]

Turning to our question, we note, along with the French political philosopher Pierre Manent, that one the most striking "signs" of the modern view that directly impinges on the question of the family is its commit-

53. *GS*, nos. 47–52.

54. *GS*, no. 46.

55. Pope Paul VI, "Address of Pope Paul VI during the Last General Meeting of the Second Vatican Council," December 7, 1965.

56. *GS*, no. 4.

ment to abstraction: to an "individual," in a "state of nature," who appears out of nowhere.[57] John Locke founded his new political order on the basis of just such an abstraction. It was freedom *from* the relation one was born into, and therefore not chosen, that was the condition for the autonomy of the new citizen. Audaciously, Locke turned to Genesis for his authority. Adam, he said, was the ideal man because he had been "created" and not born. Never having been in the "defective" and "imperfect state," he was "capable from the first instant of being able to provide for his own support and preservation and govern his action."[58] According to some, Locke's new theory of education had the express purpose of overcoming the "defect" of those who had been born, so as to make them more attune to the new liberal society, founded as it was on self-constituting agents and the contractual relations appropriate to them.[59] James Block, in his work on education in the liberal tradition, notes that parents were to look to "the idyll of an earlier Eden, a land where children form themselves out of their own ribs, becoming individuals self-conceived in the primordial land of the self-made." Following Locke's advice, parents were to raise their children as though they had not been born and to treat them, therefore, not as heirs, but as future citizens capable of adult liberal behavior.[60] In his own distinct way, Rousseau thought the same about the child as did his forbearers. His Émile has a tutor set between him and his parents so as to protect him early on from their corrupting influences; chiefly, the "temp-

57. Pierre Manent, *An Intellectual History of Liberalism*, trans. Rebecca Balinski (Princeton, NJ: Princeton University Press, 1994), 36.

58. John Locke, *The Second Treatise on Government*, VI, sec. 56.

59. See James E. Block, *The Crucible of Consent: American Child Rearing and the Growing of Liberal Society* (Cambridge, MA: Harvard University Press, 2012), 21.

60. Block, *Crucible of Consent*, ix. The contemporary English sociologist Anthony Giddens, who considered the family to be the new avant-garde of the project of democratization (i.e., as putting its intimate relations at the service of the democratization), has said the following regarding parents and their children: "Can a relationship between a parent and young child be democratic? It can, and should be, in exactly the same sense as is true of a democratic political order. It is a right of the child, in other words, to be treated as a putative equal of the adult. Actions which cannot be negotiated directly with a child, because he or she is too young to grasp what is entailed, should be capable of counterfactual justification. The presumption is that agreement could be reached, and trust sustained, if the child were sufficiently autonomous to be able to deploy arguments on an equal basis to the adult." *Transformation of Intimacy: Sexuality, Love, and Eroticism in Modern Society* (Cambridge: Polity Press, 1992), 191–92.

tation" to become dependent on them.[61] Rousseau's "bible" was *Robinson Crusoe*, the story of the orphaned child who became learned in the art of self-sufficiency.[62] Émile, states Rousseau's American translator, "cares no more for his father than his dog."[63] In like manner, Nietzsche came no closer to seeing the positivity of the dependence of childhood than his liberal counterparts, even though he upheld the "child" as representing the epitome of man. For Nietzsche, the child was always a "starting over." The child "casts off" the values with which he has been encumbered by tradition so as to now "create" new ones.[64]

But theory is one thing, political reality another. In a striking observation on an American nation that came to exist precisely as a "starting over," the famous French observer Alexis de Tocqueville noted how much the new political theories devised in the old world had been put into practice in the new:

> In democratic peoples, new families constantly issued from nothing, others constantly fall into it and all those who stay on change face; the fabric of time is torn at every moment and the trace of generations is effaced. You easily forget those who have preceded you, and you have no idea of those who will follow you.[65]

The "new world" was not only geographically new, it was also the very embodiment of the new abstract anthropology and of an "Adam" without origin and without history—a "prodigal son."[66]

The choice for a fictitious "natural" man, abstracted as he is from his social nature and from "those who have preceded him and those who will

61. The early intervention of the tutor is meant to prevent any disturbance to the child's "remaining in place," which is his being sufficient to himself in a blissful, presocial "state of nature." He does this by keep the child at arm's length from others, especially his parents, so that any disproportionate desire be stirred up in the child and he be lead to depend on him or her. See Jean-Jacques Rousseau, *Emile; Or, On Education*, trans. Allan Bloom (New York: Basic Books, 1979), 41, 83–84.

62. Rousseau, *Emile*, 184–200.

63. See Bloom's introduction in Rousseau, *Emile,* 15.

64. Friedrich Nietzsche, *Thus Spoke Zarathustra: A Book for All and None*, in *The Portable Nietzsche*, ed. and trans. Walter Kaufmann (New York: Penguin Books, 1976), 137–39.

65. Alexis de Tocqueville, *Democracy in America*, trans. Harvey C. Mansfield and Delba Winthrop (Chicago: University of Chicago Press, 2000), 483.

66. Jay Fleigleman suggests the "prodigal son" as the metaphor for the ideal citizen in his study on early America. See *Prodigals and Pilgrims: The American Revolution against Patriarchal Authority, 1750–1800* (Cambridge: Cambridge University Press, 1982).

follow," is a choice for an open future with nothing in the way. As Alan Bloom said, modern men are "open ended" for "lack of a binding past," and they "can be anything they want to be," even if (he adds sarcastically), "they have no particular reason to want to be anything in particular."[67] The choice for an abstraction is thus a choice for a construct. "There is in liberal politics," says Manent, "something deliberate and experimental that implies a conscious and 'constructed' plan," one that concerns ourselves above all else.[68] To put it in terms used by Cardinal Ratzinger, it is the choice for the *verum quia faciendum*, that is, for a "truth" as feasibility, centered on action and the future.[69]

What should be clear, however, is how this construction is contrary to man's social nature, above all where it is expressed in and through sexually differentiated bodies in which we find ourselves *always already* in relations that define us (i.e., "constitutive" relations).[70] To begin with, we are *born*, and thereby owe our existence to our parents, inheriting from them not only their property, wealth, language, and the like, but also *our very being*. Then, being one of two sexes, we find ourselves *always already* poised toward the opposite sex. To be male or female is to be already in relation to the other, which is why marriage, even though it requires consent, is not simply a voluntary or consensual arrangement. Finally, we are *always already* potentially mothers or fathers in our relations with the opposite sex. All of this situates our freedom, from the beginning, in an embodied reality beyond our choosing. Ratzinger, looking at the bodily way in which we come into the world, notes what this means for the kind of freedom we actually have.

67. Alan Bloom, *The Closing of the American Mind: How Higher Education Has Failed Democracy and Impoverished the Souls of Today's Students* (New York: Simon and Schuster, 1987), 87.

68. Manent, *Intellectual History of Liberalism*, xvi. In this spirit, Giddens writes: "the more we reflexively 'make ourselves' as persons, the more the very category of what a 'person' or 'human being' is comes to the fore." *Modernity and Self-Identity* (Cambridge: Polity Press, 1991), 217.

69. Joseph Ratzinger, *Introduction to Christianity*, trans. J. R. Foster (San Francisco: Ignatius Press, 2004), 57–66.

70. The term is largely attributed to David L. Schindler. See his "The Embodied Person as Gift and the Cultural Task in America: *Status Quaestionis*," *Communio: International Catholic Review* 35 (2008): 397–431.

> [The child in the mother's womb] is the very example which brings out the basic figure of human freedom and makes clear what is typically human about it ... The being of another person is so closely interwoven with the being of this person ... [that] to be oneself in this way is to be radically from and through another.... We must now add that even once the child is born and the outer form of its being-from and with changes, it remains just as dependent on, and at the mercy of, a being-for ... The child in the mother's womb is simply a very graphic depiction of the essence of human existence in general.[71]

But it is precisely this fact of being "radically from and through" that is problematic for us, especially today. It is here that we see how much the abstract construct of "man" that is so dominant is also counterfactual and the fruit of a deep resistance to the way things actually appear. Ratzinger continues:

> this being-with compels the being of the other—that is, the mother—to become a being-for, which contradicts her own desire to be an independent self and is thus experienced as the antithesis of her own freedom.... Let us say it even more precisely: man quite spontaneously takes for granted the being-for of others in the form of today's network of service systems, yet if he had his way he would prefer not to be forced to participate in such a "from" and "for," but would like to become wholly independent, and to be able to do and not to do just what he pleased. The radical demand for freedom, which has proved itself more and more clearly to be the outcome of the historical course of the Enlightenment, especially of the line inaugurated by Rousseau, and which today largely shapes the public mentality, prefers to have neither a whence nor a whither, to be neither from nor for, but to be wholly at liberty. In other words, *it regards what is actually the fundamental figure of human existence itself as an attack on freedom* which assails it before any individual has a chance to live and act. The radical cry for freedom demands man's liberation from his very essence as man, so that he may become the "new man." In the new society, the dependencies which restrict the I and the necessity of self-giving would no longer have the right to exist.[72]

To be clear, it is not only the unborn child who happens to be an impediment to the abstract freedom of his or her parents, but also, more gen-

71. Joseph Ratzinger, "Truth and Freedom," *Communio: International Catholic Review* 23 (Spring 1996): 27.

72. Ratzinger, "Truth and Freedom," 27–28.

erally, "the fundamental figure of human existence itself" that no longer has a right to exist. That "figure"—with its "whence" and "whither"—is an attack on our freedom. This is why we are "at war with all that gives us birth," including that which is born: nature itself.[73] It is we ourselves, *as we actually are*, who are not allowed to exist.[74]

Why, though, do we find this abstract, counterfactual account of ourselves so attractive and self-evident, and why do we consent so readily (and obediently!) to it? There is no need for studies to show us how dramatically the three constitutive relations are, or can be, to account for why we go to such lengths to place them under our control. It would be safe to say that a large percentage of the violence perpetrated by human beings takes place within the space of the man-woman, father-mother, and child relations. Sartre was thus not entirely wrong when he said famously that the "other is hell." The other does objectify me, and it is especially the body that proves fatal for freedom by making me visible to the other's objectifying gaze.[75] The story is as old as original sin, whose first effects were played out precisely in the space between man, woman, and child. But here too we have a clue as to the reasons for this ancient effect. When the serpent restates the command that the man and woman are not to eat from every tree of the garden, he presents a caricature of God—a parsimonious Master—by insinuating that the goodness of God, the Father, is a thing to be doubted. The original sin of man and woman according to the biblical account, then, is that they believed the caricature and dis-

73. This is Manent's paraphrase of Hobbes's *bellum omnium contra omnes* in *Intellectual History of Liberalism,* 40. On the suspicion of fatherhood in modernity, see M. J. Le Guillou, *Le mystère du père: Foi des apôtres, gnoses actuelles* (Paris: Fayard, 1973), 156.

74. Commenting on Hobbes, Leo Strauss shows how much the "war" has nature itself as its target: "Man can guarantee the actualization of wisdom, since wisdom is identical with free construction. But wisdom cannot be free construction if the universe is intelligible. Man can guarantee the actualization of wisdom, not in spite of, but because of, the fact that the universe is unintelligible. *Man can be sovereign only because there is no cosmic support for his humanity*. He can be sovereign only because he is absolutely a stranger in the universe. He can be sovereign only because he is forced to be sovereign. Since the universe is unintelligible and since control of nature does not require understanding of nature, there are no knowable limits to his conquest of nature" (emphasis added). *Natural Right and History* (Chicago: University of Chicago Press, 1950), 174–75.

75. Jean-Paul Sartre, "The Look," in *Being and Nothingness,* trans. H. E. Barnes (New York: Philosophical Library), 252–302.

trusted God by ultimately taking things into their own hands.[76] From then on, the human drama is forever marked by the same distrust and a defensive "protection" from both "vertical" and "horizontal" relations.

However ancient the story of the fall may be, what is clear from the biblical account is that it is wholly *secondary*, an aberration. In the beginning, it was *not* good to be alone. It is here where modernity distinguishes itself, for according to it we are by definition alone nonspeaking, apolitical, unborn (and, today, androgynous and sterile) individuals, for whom "it is good to be alone."[77] It is the invention of a new "natural," which is really a construct.[78] The other, by definition, is our "hell," which is why relations between men and women are becoming increasingly reconfigured along contractual, consensual lines.[79] This adds a layer of protection from the "attack" of our parents, the opposite sex, and our children (both

76. J. P. Batut offers this interpretation of original sin in his comparison with the temptation of Jesus in the desert. See "The Chastity of Jesus and the 'Refusal to Grasp,'" *Communio* 24 (1997): 5–13.

77. David Crawford discusses the androgynous character of liberalism in "Recognizing the Roots of Society in the Family, Foundation of Justice," *Communio* 34 (2007): 379–412, and more recently in "Mechanism, Public Reason, and the Anthropology of Orientation," in *Humanum* (Fall 2012): 17–37. I also note here that the individualism of early liberalism is not remedied by the newer relationalism. The formerly private familial relationships are now being fully transformed on democratic, consensual terms into redefinable, renegotiable and ever terminable "pure relations." They are the new vanguard of the (still individualistic) liberal project. See esp. Anthony Giddens, "Intimacy as Democracy," in *Transformation of Intimacy*, 184–204.

78. Judith Butler, following Foucault, claims that the idea of a "state of nature" is really the effect (i.e., "construct") of a highly successful stratagem of power that hides the real origin behind the appearance of a "prior" or "given." Cf. *Gender Trouble* (New York: Routledge, 1990), 3. While Butler herself does not limit her etiology to the moderns, her postmodern preoccupation with power may find in the moderns a justifiable cause for her claim, especially where the "state of nature" is concerned.

79. In his *Second Treatise*, Locke does recognize a paternal authority over children to which they did not consent (cf. "Paternal Power," chap. 6). In light of his general aim to argue for the essential equality of human beings bound to each other by consent alone, however, he relativizes that authority as much as possible, rendering it merely practical and temporary, so as to order and shape it according to the more essential, consensual bonds. Fleigleman discusses the effect of this re-situation and reconfiguration of familial bonds on early American thinking about child-rearing, where the overarching concern was about parental "tyranny" thwarting the goal of raising independent and self-sufficient individuals. See *Prodigals and Pilgrims*, 9–35. He notes, too, the enthusiasm of early Americans about marriage for the express reason that, in contrast to the paternal-filial bond, it was a voluntary, contractual union. See *Prodigals and Pilgrims*, 123–53.

those living, and yet to be conceived), since now we cannot even think that they might define us.

But there is something newer still, a new "layer of protection" made available by today's "plastic sexuality."[80] By disassociating sex from the claims the opposite sex has over us, we can protect ourselves from the entangling complications of children and, in turn, from any and all forms of "compulsory heterosexuality."[81] Finally, so as to complete the circle, this disassociation from sex further protects us from the claims of those whose carnal embrace we have always relied upon for our existence. These new unions, which are, in principle, incapable of generating children, destroy the structure of kinship that has always existed by reintroducing children to sex through the "deliberate construction" of assisted reproductive technologies.[82] These free future children from the first constitutive bond by separating them from their mothers or fathers (or both), leaving them, as de Tocqueville describes it, with no "trace of generations."[83] The fabric of time, having been all but eliminated, now emerges historyless in a progressive incarnation in which every "tomorrow" becomes detached from any "yesterday." Man's "war with all that gives him birth" can thus be definitively "won," however counterintuitive this may seem.[84] It is the last

80. The term is Anthony Giddens's: "Plastic sexuality is decentred sexuality, freed from the needs of reproduction. It has its origins in the tendency, initiated somewhere in the late eighteenth century, strictly to limit family size; but it becomes further developed later as the result of the spread of modern contraception and new reproductive technologies. Plastic sexuality can be molded as a trait of personality and thus is intrinsically bound up with the self." *Transformation of Intimacy*, 2.

81. The term comes from A. Rich's essay "Compulsory Heterosexuality and Lesbian Existence," *Signs: Journal of Women in Culture and Society* 5, no. 4 (Summer 1980): 631–60.

82. Giddens, *Modernity and Self-Identity*, 220. Butler, e.g., although wary of allying new gender "performances" to marriage and the family, is enthusiastic about ART because of its challenge to heterosexual reproduction and the whole structure of kinship (and culture) established by these carnal bonds. See her *Undoing Gender* (New York: Routledge, 2004), 11, 26, 102–30.

83. Alexis de Tocqueville, *Democracy in America*, trans. Harvey C. Mansfield and Delba Winthrop (Chicago: University of Chicago Press, 2000), 483.

84. The radical feminist Shulamith Firestone augured the use of artificial reproductive technology well before its invention, suggesting that it would bring about the final break of the child from his dependence on his parents. "The reproduction of the species by one sex for the benefit of both would be replaced by (at least the option of) artificial reproduction: children would be born to both sexes equally, or independently of either, however one chooses to look at it; the dependence of the child on the mother (and vice versa) would give

nail in the coffin of the "fundamental figure of existence" that the new anthropology persistently seeks to destroy.

It should be clear in this brief consideration of the "signs of the times" that "the very notion of being [and] of what being human really means" is being called into question, particularly insofar as it is embodied and caught up in the "whence and whither" of history.[85] As Benedict XVI said, in his famous Christmas address to the curia:

> Man and woman as created realities, as the nature of the human being, no longer exist. Man calls his nature into question. From now on he is merely spirit and will. The manipulation of nature, which we deplore today where our environment is concerned, now becomes man's fundamental choice where he himself is concerned. From now on there is only the abstract human being, who chooses for himself what his nature is to be.[86]

In other words, what was perhaps not so clear fifty years ago—namely, how much the very idea of a created order had been called into question by modernity—is how much the "new age of human history" (*GS*, no. 54) rests on a deep resistance to the world's own worldliness and history. As a result, the rediscovery of the Church's deepest openness to the world, as discussed at the time of the Council, must now include a concern that the world not close the door *on its very self.* This is a far greater concern than the one over any residual (and unfortunate) pre–Vatican II exclusivism.

Conclusion

So what must be done? It is already something to take seriously the "signs of the times" and to see how counterfactual they have become, built as they are on the almost buried "fundamental figure of existence." But this also requires that we challenge the idea of the inevitability of the current situation. "History," as Guardini says, "does not run on its own: it is *run*

way to a greatly shortened dependence on a small group of others in general and any remaining inferiority to adults in physical strength would be compensated for culturally.... The tyranny of the biological family would be broken." *The Dialectic of Sex* (New York: William Morrow, 1970), 11.

85. Benedict XVI, "Address to the Roman Curia," December 22, 2012.

86. Benedict XVI, "Address to the Roman Curia," December 22, 2012.

… [and] can also be run badly," even to the point of running right out of the world itself.[87] We human beings are responsible for this "situation" and can be invited out of it. Indeed we must be if we are not to lose altogether our grip on the world in the flight from it.

There are, I suggest, two dimensions to this invitation. The first is to attend to the dissatisfaction that the majority opinion already does and will continue to produce insofar as it is counterfactual. Having been undomesticated, we can expect the world to feel unhomelike and for this feeling to become progressively worse.[88] Even this will be a resource. As the Canadian philosopher George Grant put it: "any intimations of authentic deprival are precious, because they are the ways through which intimations of good, unthinkable in the public terms, may yet appear to us."[89] The second is to direct into the world the mysterious ray of Trinitarian and crucified love by way of Christian witness.[90] Witnesses to that "ray" will display the goodness of a humanity caught up and redeemed in its "whence and whither" and will radiate to a world rightly obsessed with its own freedom, a more convincing way to be free *inside* the world.

Now, at the end, we return to the very beginning, both to the problem and its redress. As for the problem, the *Compendium of the Social Doctrine*

87. Romano Guardini, *The End of the Modern World* (Wilmington, DE: ISI Books, 1998), 209.

88. Using the expression of Heidegger, David L. Schindler explains how the ontology of modernity perpetuates the "un-homelike" structure of our culture: "Homelessness … consists of an abstract and mechanistic pattern of being, thinking, acting, and producing that makes human beings rootless in a world stripped of its intrinsic creaturely order." "Homelessness and the Modern Condition," *Communio: International Catholic Review* 27 (2000): 415.

89. "The affirmation stands: how can we think deprivation unless the good which we lack is somehow remembered? To reverse the platitude, we are never more sure that air is good for animals than when we are gasping for breath. Some men who have thought deeply seem to deny this affirmation: but I have never found any who, in my understanding of them, have been able, through the length and breadth of their thought, to make the language of good secondary to freedom … if we make the affirmation that the language of good is inescapable under most circumstances, do we not have to think its content? The language of good is not then a dead language, but one that must, even in its present disintegration, be re-collected, even as we publicly let our freedom become ever more increasingly the pure will to will." George Grant, "A Platitude," in *Technology and Empire* (Toronto: House of Anansi, 1969), 141.

90. Cf. note 51 above.

of the Church suggests that the narrative of original sin offers to us the permanent pattern of temptation:

> Disobedience to God means hiding from his loving countenance and seeking to control one's life and action in the world. Breaking the relation of communion with God causes a rupture in the internal unity of the human person, in the relations of communion between man and woman and of the harmonious relations between mankind and other creatures. It is in this original estrangement that are to be sought the deepest roots of all the evils.[91]

Here we find the full account of what *Gaudium et spes* means when it says that *creatura sine creatore evanescit*.[92] As for the redress, Pope Francis has told us that it will be precisely an opening up to the "Thou" of God that will open us to the human world—to the constitutive relations of the family—and to "our common home" of the whole created order. It will be, in other words, because of the presence of that "ray" in and through the Church—our new home—that we will be open to the world and be at home in it . . . and not evanesce.[93]

91. *Compendium of the Social Doctrine of the Church* (Washington, DC: USCCB Publishing, 2004), 14.

92. *GS*, no., 36.

93. Francis, *Laudato Si,* no. 119.

9

Gaudium et spes Fifty Years Later

On Human Work and the Economy

ANDREW V. ABELA

Introduction

This essay addresses the question of what twenty-first-century economic life would look like if we took seriously the anthropology of gift proposed by *Gaudium et spes* (*GS*).[1] Let us begin by recalling two foundational points about human anthropology highlighted by the pastoral constitution. First, "only in the mystery of the incarnate Word does the mystery of man take on light" (no. 22), and second, "man ... cannot fully find himself except through a sincere gift of himself" (no. 24). One could be excused, having read only *Gaudium et spes*, of thinking that these do not necessarily apply to economics. It is often assumed that modern economics is generally "neutral" with respect to such religious claims as to man's ontological truth, and for its part, the pastoral constitution does not explicitly apply the language of an anthropology of gift to its section on economic concerns (nos. 63–67). Particularly in light of *Caritas in veritate*,

1. Inspiration for this essay was drawn primarily from two organized discussions exploring various ideas relevant to this topic. The first was a discussion series on economics between the faculty of the John Paul II Institute of Marriage and Family and the Busch School of Business and Economics at the Catholic University of America. This discussion series, titled "*Communio* Economics," was formative in the ideas presented in this essay. Another was a series of debates between philosopher Russell Hittinger, a leading authority on Catholic social doctrine, and Frédéric Sautet, an Austrian economist and Catholic convert. This debate is now pending publication by the Catholic University of America Press.

however, I think it is safe to assume that the intention of the Council was to address the whole of man and to apply these statements to economic life as well. *Gaudium et Spes* 46 makes clear that the "particularly urgent needs characterizing the present age" are only to be approached from the foundation of "the dignity of the human person" as established by Part I of the constitution. I say more on this below, but let us first assess how these principles inform other statements of *Gaudium et spes* that more directly address the economic situation of man in the modern world.

The importance of human work, which is obviously significant for any economic consideration, is another theme addressed by the Council document:

> When man develops the earth by the work of his hands or with the aid of technical means, in order that it might bear fruit and become a dwelling worthy of the whole human family and when he consciously takes part in the life of social groups, he carries out the design of God manifested at the beginning of time, that he should *subdue the earth, perfect creation and develop himself.* At the same time he obeys the commandment of Christ that he *place himself at the service of his brethren.*[2]

Gaudium et spes has already made it clear that every "design" of God is primarily directed at restoring the image of God in man; thus the intention of the above text is to say that, through work, man places himself at the service of his brethren and, by giving himself, comes to image his Creator.[3] This point helps illuminate a later text emphasizing the centrality of the human person in all aspects of economic life:

> In the economic and social realms, too, the dignity and complete vocation of the human person and the welfare of society as a whole are to be respected and promoted. For man is the source, the center, and the purpose of all economic and social life.[4]

Man is "the source, the center, and the purpose of all economic and social life," precisely because, through work, man discovers the mystery of his

2. *GS*, no. 57. Emphasis added.

3. See *GS*, no. 12. The constitution also states that every "authentic" use of human freedom is "an exceptional sign of the divine image within man" (*GS*, no. 17). The scope of this claim goes far beyond the activity of man in his acts of religious devotion and clearly encompasses the entirety of man's economic life as well.

4. *GS*, no. 63.

dignity as one made in the image of God. Note that both texts thus stand to be understood in light of paragraphs 22 and 24, which ground the dignity of the human person wholly on the revelation of Jesus Christ: "Only in the mystery of the Incarnate Word does the mystery of man take on light" (no. 22). Through work, man undertakes something of a "sincere gift of himself," and in doing so, receives himself as a mystery that can only be understood by the light of the Incarnate Word.

Taking this essential anthropological principle as its starting point, I propose several key implications of the Council's understanding of man for economic life. The obvious place to look for some of these more practical economic considerations is Part II of *Gaudium et spes*, which is the section on "particularly urgent needs characterizing the present age" (no. 46). Chapter 3 of this section, titled "Economic and Social Life," is clearly pertinent, but it is also important to look broadly at other chapters in Part II so as to get a greater sense of the whole. In particular, Chapter 1, "Fostering the Nobility of Marriage and the Family"; Chapter 2, "The Proper Development of Culture"; and Chapter 4, "The Life of the Political Community" and all have great economic significance, and this essay draws tacitly and sometimes explicitly on the ideas contained therein.

Complications and Root Issues

The biggest challenge to developing such implications lies in the conflict between a genuine theological anthropology and the liberal individualism that lies at the heart of the modern economy. Contemporary economic theory is perhaps the foremost exemplar of liberal, utilitarian theory, and, as a consequence, economic life has largely come to be seen in liberal, utilitarian terms. Liberal economies tend to assess human beings solely in terms of their use and productivity, and thus often promote economic systems in which individuals are redefined merely as "entities" rather than "persons." One of the reasons it has become so difficult to promote a theological anthropology in economics is because of the great disparity between an individualistic and utilitarian worldview and one that is theological informed. One can observe this divide every day in modern economic life and it is particularly evident the more one moves away from small businesses and communities. Family businesses and other such small entrepreneurial start-ups tend to be quite humane, in part because the dignity of the people one interacts with on a day-to-day basis in such institutions is immediately apparent. But as soon as these small businesses grow and are sold to millions of shareholders, they become increasingly beholden to utilitarian and individualistic concerns.

One particular company I observed during my time as a consultant in the business world changed as it went public. After the transition, an employee tried to give a suffering coworker some extra time off as an act of compassion but was told by a supervisor that because the company was now public, it was beholden to the interests of its shareholders. Such a gesture would no longer be possible. It is remarkable how often the utilitarian and individualist interests of a liberal economy get in the way of such basic expressions of human compassion.

Research has consistently suggested that the more students study economics, the more selfish and greedy they become.[5] Although economics is often presented in purely theoretical terms, it invariably affects our perception of how human beings live and act. Economists generally believe that economic theories are just useful approximations; they are not, I argue, sufficiently attune to the manner of how these theories in fact present a way a person *should* behave.

A theological anthropology would have businesses run in ways that serve the common good. In classical terms, the common good refers to the pursuit of perfection and human fulfillment, and to the greater truth that encompasses the whole of the community. Even though the pursuit of individual goods is indispensable to the achievement of the common good, the common good is never reducible to the particular goods pursued by individuals, nor can it be construed merely as the sum total of goods secured by an economy.[6] Unfortunately, the description of the common good found in *Gaudium et spes* is somewhat ambiguous on this

5. See, e.g., Long Wang, Deepak Malhotra, and J. Keith Murnighan, "Economics Education and Greed," *Academy of Management Learning and Education* 10, no. 4 (2011): 643–60, and Ariel Rubinstein, "A Sceptic's Comment on the Study of Economics," *Economic Journal* 116 (March 2006): C1–C9.

6. See David S. Crawford, "Gay Marriage, Public Reason, and the Common Good," *Communio: International Catholic Review* 41, no. 2 (2014): 384–408.

point. The text defines the common good as "the sum of those conditions of social life which allow social groups and their individual members relatively thorough and ready access to their own fulfillment" (no. 26). This passage seems to offer a liberal conception of the common good as merely an aggregate of goods, rather than as something inseparable from the community in question. Such a conception would risk fragmenting society into a multiplicity of individual economic interests and obscuring how these interests are integrated and unified by a greater whole.

Given that the language of liberal individualism has all but completely eroded the way we perceive those "goods" that an economy is meant to secure, it is difficult not to despair over the state of modern economic life. But although economic reform is undoubtedly an enormous challenge, the text of *Gaudium et spes* provides some prospect of future transformation. With a view to this end, I offer seven suggestions or imperatives for developing a more humane theory of economics that reflects the anthropological concerns of *Gaudium et spes.* Although each imperative could be the topic of an entire dissertation, I instead use them to provide something of landscape so as to highlight certain contours of an economic model informed by theological and anthological principles.

Possible Solutions

The first economic imperative necessitated by the anthropological viewpoint of *Gaudium et spes* is the need to recognize the role of the family in economic flourishing. As the pastoral constitution observes, "The well-being of the individual person and of human and Christian society is intimately linked with the healthy condition of that community produced by marriage and family" (no. 47). The passage goes on to consider the challenges to married love and how marriage is "too often profaned by excessive self-love [and] the worship of pleasure." Then it continues: "Moreover, *serious disturbances are caused in families by modern economic conditions*, by influences at once social and psychological, and by the demands of civil society" (no. 47).[7] Poor economic circumstances, in other words, invariably have a negative effect on family life.

7. Emphasis added.

Now, *Gaudium et spes* does not explicitly state that the causal chain between families and economies also runs in the other direction, that is, that healthy families also help produce healthy economic lives for people and societies. But this is a point that both David Schindler and the late Stratford Caldecott have worked to demonstrate: that good family policy necessarily lies at the center of good economic policy.[8] One must be cautious in asserting such connections. There always lies a danger of instrumentalizing marriage for the sake of work and construing the family as a mere means to greater efficiency and economic productivity. But this is not the claim here. The observation is that if families are unhealthy, everything else about social life will suffer, including the economic life of the family. This correlation is extensively demonstrated by research that shows how rare material poverty is in intact, never-divorced families in which the husband and wife are married and stay together. In the United States, there is a 12 percent chance that a child of married parents who reaches the age of six will have experienced at least one year of material poverty. But if the parents are unmarried, the chance of having experienced a year of poverty by age six rises to 68 percent. Meanwhile, 81 percent of children in unmarried households who reach adulthood experience at least one year of poverty, as opposed to 22 percent of children in married households.[9] The difference is enormous.

The Heritage Foundation has done an interesting exercise on this topic to demonstrate that poverty is not simply an external issue affecting single-parent households, but that resolving single-parent situations could also be key to reducing poverty. Noting that as much as 80 percent of long-term child poverty occurs in households of unmarried parents, the foundation tried to calculate what would happen if the unmarried parents of children living in poverty were married. What they found was that if they *were* married, then two-thirds of families would no longer live

8. See Doug Bandow and David Schindler, eds., *Wealth, Poverty, and Human Destiny* (Wilmington, DE: ISI Books, 2003).

9. Mark R. Rank and Thomas A. Hirschl, "The Economic Risk of Childhood in America: Estimating the Probability of Poverty across the Formative Years," *Journal of Marriage and Family* 61, no. 4 (1999): 1064. See also Robert I. Lerman, *How Do Marriage, Cohabitation, and Single Parenthood Affect the Material Hardships of Families with Children?* (Washington, DC: Urban Institute, July 1, 2002), 20.

in poverty. Corroborating evidence has shown that the standard of living in unmarried family situations is substantially raised by moving into a married state, and some studies have suggested that child poverty could be reduced by as much as 30 percent if the number of children with married parents was restored to its pre-1970s levels.[10] Other research has indicated that, even while allowing for variables, married men earn 27 percent more than single men, with the explanation being that men generally work harder and attain higher degrees of financial success when they have others who depend on them.[11]

Once again, this research should not make us eager to instrumentalize marriage or the family for economic purposes. But it does illustrate the fact that an economic theory that ignores marriage, or that fails to make marriage central, is doomed from the start to have an unrealistic view of

10. Robert E. Rector, *Increasing Marriage Will Dramatically Reduce Child Poverty*, Center for Data Analysis Report 03-06 (Washington, DC: Heritage Foundation, May 20, 2003). See also Robert I. Lerman, *Married and Unmarried Parenthood and Economic Well-Being: A Dynamic Analysis of a Recent Cohort* (Washington, DC: Urban Institute, July 1, 2002): "moving into a married state raises living standards by about 65 percent relative to single parents living with no other adult, over 50 percent relative to single parents living with at least another adult, and 20 percent relative to cohabitation" (32). See also Paul R. Amato and Rebecca A. Maynard, "Decreasing Nonmarital Births and Strengthening Marriage to Reduce Poverty," *Next Generation of Antipoverty Policies* 17, no. 2 (2007): "in 2000, 15.6 percent of all children were poor. The poverty rate was substantially lower (8.2 percent) for children living with married parents than for all other children (31.2 percent)" (128). Amato and Maynard estimate that "if the share of children with married parents in 2000 [67.8] were the same as it was in 1970 (85.2 percent)," then there would be a 20 to 29 percent decline in child poverty (128–30); variation depends on which of their three statistical methods is adopted.

11. See Mark Western, Belinda Hewitt, and Janeen Baxter, "Marriage and Money: Variations across the Earnings Distribution," *Australian Journal of Labour Economics* 8 (2005): 163–79: "The final model includes human capital, job characteristics and family status variables; after adjusting for all variables married men earn around 14 per cent more than single men" (177). For the effects of fatherhood on generally economic welfare, see Alexandra Killewalda, "A Reconsideration of the Fatherhood Premium: Marriage, Coresidence, Biology, and Fathers' Wages," *American Sociological Review* 78, no. 1 (2013): 96–116: "Married men who become residential fathers receive wage gains of around 4 percent, above and beyond the marriage premium of 7 percent" (111), and "at least some of the fatherhood premium is due to productivity-related differences in men's behavior" (112). See also Shelly Lundberg and Elaina Rose, "The Effects of Sons and Daughters on Men's Labor Supply and Wages," *Review of Economics and Statistics* 84, no. 2 (2002): 251–68: although the role of children is typically ignored in studies of male labor supply and wage determination, fatherhood has quantitatively and statistically significant effects on both outcomes" (264); "men work more hours and earn more per hour after becoming fathers" (258).

humanity. The institution of marriage is a preeminent good of human society precisely because it is the supreme expression of an anthropology of gift that expresses the truth of the human person as naturally oriented to the giving of himself to another in love. *Gaudium et spes* points to the central role that marriage plays in economic flourishing precisely because a genuine economy can only serve this "common good" of all men. The "intimate partnership of married life" can therefore be said to have a "very decisive bearing on the ... peace and prosperity of the family itself and of human society as whole," precisely because marriage provides the anthropological foundation to human flourishing of which the economic life is one expression.[12] Hence the first imperative for the imagining of economics according to a theological anthropology of gift is that one must recognize the centrality of the family to economic health and prosperity.

Our second economic imperative is borrowed directly from Pope Benedict's *Caritas in veritate*, which speaks of the need to make "gratuitousness" a part of everyday economic activities.[13] Although the language of *Gaudium et spes* once again results in a certain degree of ambiguity, Benedict makes it clear that the labor of economic gratuitousness has its ground in the dignity and mission of the human person, whose full truth resides in the making of a sincere gift of himself. The first part of paragraph 57, quoted above, says that when we work, we image the Creator by giving ourselves to others. But the text continues by saying:

> When man gives himself to the various disciplines of philosophy, history and of mathematical and natural science, and when he cultivates the arts, he can do very much to elevate the human family to a more sublime understanding of *truth, goodness, and beauty*.[14]

12. *GS*, no. 48.

13. Pope Benedict XVI, *Caritas in veritate* (*CV*), 2009: "The great challenge before us, accentuated by the problems of development in this global era and made even more urgent by the economic and financial crisis, is to demonstrate, in thinking and behaviour, not only that traditional principles of social ethics like transparency, honesty and responsibility cannot be ignored or attenuated, but also that in *commercial relationships* the *principle of gratuitousness* and the logic of gift as an expression of fraternity can and must *find their place within normal economic activity*. This is a human demand at the present time, but it is also demanded by economic logic. It is a demand both of charity and of truth" (no. 36).

14. *GS*, no. 57. Emphasis added.

The distinction, while perhaps not intended, is unfortunate, for the text seems to suggest that when you work, you serve others, but when you do philosophy, theology, or some other meaningful academic discipline, *then* you serve truth, beauty, and goodness. It is as if the passage were suggesting that the charity and giving of oneself in work involves only labor, whereas philosophy and theology are disciplines that allow one to think about truth, goodness, and meaningful things. This could unfortunately reinforce the common assumption that the workplace is distinct from a place of contemplation, which is widely assumed today, and that money and labor are only the means by which one has opportunity to do other things in pursuit of truth, beauty, and goodness. But in fact, as Benedict suggests, man's economic life and his contemplative life occur together. Specifically, Benedict emphasizes the need to make room for "gratuitousness" in our economic lives, precisely because such a principle enables economic activity to fulfill its mission of being an expression of the common good.[15] He writes that the economic sphere is neither "ethically neutral, nor inherently inhuman," because what is authentically human is not conducted "outside" or "after" it. Instead, economic life is "part and parcel of human activity ... precisely because *it is human*," which is why it ought to be in turn "structured and governed in an ethical manner."[16] The second imperative of a reimagined economy is thus the demand for economics to approach its activity as an expression of the whole of man and not as something exterior or extrinsic to man's spiritual nature.

The third imperative is perhaps more contentious, for it concerns the necessity of market economies, and *Gaudium et* spes explicitly demands that markets assume a subordinate role in man's economic life. The Council does not explicitly disparage markets, and the pastoral constitution does refer to "an inventive spirit, an eagerness to create and to expand enterprises ... [that] must be promoted" (no. 64). This clearly represents some manner of approval for market economies, for which John Paul II also gives a qualified endorsement in *Centesimus annus*.[17] But there is a

15. See *CV*, no. 7.

16. *CV*, no. 36. Emphasis added.

17. John Paul II, *Centesimus annus,* 1991: "It would appear that, on the level of individual nations and of international relations, the *free market* is the most efficient instrument for

danger when looking at market economies, one that Adrian Walker has put quite nicely: "While claiming to leave freedom open to the objective good of the person, liberal economics surreptitiously weights it in the direction of self-interest understood as financial gain."[18] A market economy, in other words, invariably imparts its own set of values and beliefs on human nature and, in particular, imposes presuppositions concerning the nature of freedom, happiness, and the meaning of economic life. The market economy pretends, like all of liberalism, to be neutral, but in fact it always has a strong leaning toward utilitarianism, one that values financial gain above all else. The Hittinger-Sautet debate is helpful in illuminating the existence of this leaning in its evaluation of the Austrian economic situation. The debate suggests that the market order, while important, is an instrument that Austrian economics has made an error in elevating by essentially making it the guiding principle of society at large.

The conclusions reached at this debate lend support to further insights made by two other leading Austrian economists, Friedrich Hayek and Ludwig von Mises. Their insights concern the impossibility of central planning and what is known as the "economic calculation problem." Effective central planning, they argue, is impossible, because a society without markets cannot determine prices, since prices are by definition subjective and are only determinable through the outworking of markets. One cannot objectively assess the price of a thing simply by looking at it, measuring it, or studying it—an "objective" price is a meaningless idea.[19]

---

utilizing resources and effectively responding to needs" (no. 34); "can it perhaps be said that, after the failure of Communism, capitalism is ... the model which ought to be proposed to the countries of the Third World which are searching for the path to true economic and civil progress?" (no. 42) "The answer is obviously complex. If by 'capitalism' is meant an economic system which recognizes the fundamental and positive role of business, the market, private property and the resulting responsibility for the means of production, as well as free human creativity in the economic sector, then the answer is certainly in the affirmative, even though it would perhaps be more appropriate to speak of a 'business economy,' 'market economy' or simply 'free economy'" (no. 42). For further remarks and qualifications, see generally sections 19, 33–35, and 39–43.

18. Adrian Walker, "The Poverty of Liberal Economics," in *Wealth, Poverty, and Human Destiny*, ed. Doug Bandow and David L. Schindler (Wilmington, DE: ISI Books, 2003), 30.

19. See Ludwig von Mises, "Economic Calculation in the Socialist Commonwealth," trans. S. Alder, in *Collectivist Economic Planning*, ed. F. A. Hayek (London: George Rout-

Prices, then, are set by markets, and without prices, one cannot decide how to feed, clothe, or house people efficiently. One cannot, for example, make a purely objective decision on whether it is better to make a house out of wood, brick, or stainless steel. Although one could make a choice on aesthetical grounds, or one based on an understanding of the nature of such materials, without a market, there is no way to determine whether one type of material or another is more economically viable for a society to use. Only a market can determine whether there is enough of a given material or whether it is economically more sensible to use one material over another. Without markets to determine the prices of various options, it becomes impossible to answer such questions. That is why, throughout history and across cultures and geographic regions, there have always been markets in one form or another to put prices on things and to allow people to determine what things are worth. This is also why socialist economies invariably collapse. Despite the famous observation of British Prime Minister Margaret Thatcher that socialism fails because eventually it runs out of other people's money, in fact, socialist economies collapse because their central planners make poor decisions in terms of allocating scarce resources.[20]

Gaudium et spes recognizes the rightful autonomy of economic systems when it states that such activity should be carried out "according to its own methods and laws," and in this way the text acknowledges the importance and need of realities such as markets.[21] But a "rightful autonomy" is never one that leaves God behind, nor does it dispense of the need for human persons to image their Creator.[22] The constitution, therefore, recognizes and understands the subordinate role of markets to the truth of the dignity of the human person when it states that the "fundamental

ledge and Sons, 1935; reprint, Clifton, NJ: Augustus M. Kelley, 1975), 87–130. See also Friedrich Hayek, "The Nature and History of the Problem" and "The Present State of the Debate," in *Collectivist Economic Planning*, 1–40, 201–43.

20. Margaret Thatcher, interview with Llew Gardner, *Thames TV This Week*. Aired February 5, 1976, on ITV. Thatcher's exact words were: "Socialist governments traditionally do make a financial mess. They always run out of other people's money. It's quite a characteristic of them."

21. *GS*, no. 64.

22. *GS*, no. 41.

finality of [economic] production is not the mere increase of products nor profit or control but rather the service ... of the whole of man."[23] Interestingly, this suggests that there is a way of conceiving the allocation of resources and the assigning of prices in market economies as not simply the arbitrary means of achieving purely monetary or economic ends. Markets, in other words, can be genuine expressions of the way in which human persons give themselves to one another (and to God) within a concrete order of material things. The moral demands that accompany this obligation are not extrinsic to economic activities, but their very core and center. Thus the imperative need to recognize the importance of markets while at the same time acknowledging their subordinate role as expressions of an anthropology of gift.

The fourth imperative is that we must bring a Catholic understanding of property to bear on modern economics. According to *Gaudium et spes*, "Private property or some ownership of external goods confers on everyone a sphere wholly necessary for the autonomy of the person and the family, and it should be regarded as an extension of human freedom" (no. 71). It is a nuanced and insightful sentence, making the point that private property is necessary for living out our personhood and natural autonomy. Property, in other words, is not mine because it belongs to me, as it is typically construed by contemporary and classical views of private property. Rather, property is mine because it is part of living out my personhood and is an extension of my innate dignity as a human being.

Based on this relation of property to personhood, *Gaudium et spes* also presents obligations for how to use property, drawing from Aquinas's important distinction between the ownership and use of property:

> God intended the earth with everything contained in it for the use of all human beings and peoples.... man should regard the external things that he legitimately possesses not only as his own but also as common in the sense that they should be able to benefit not only him but also others.[24]

Here the universal destination of created goods is being affirmed, suggesting a key insight that complements the earlier point about the subordina-

23. *GS*, no. 64.
24. *GS*, no. 69.

tion of markets. Even though prices are always only subjective measures, prices alone never tell the full story of the thing being bought and sold. The price of a thing does not describe the "worth" of a thing in human terms. In fact, sometimes there is a significant disparity between the price of a thing and its human worth. In terms of price, a $100,000 car arguably costs far more than its worth as a human thing, whereas, thankfully, a walk in the woods costs far less than its worth in human terms.

The imperative, then, for an economy based on a theological anthropology is that we bring to it a more *human* sense of the meaning of property. Although markets are important, and prices play an indispensable role in any economy, they should not override the inherent, human-oriented worth of created goods. As *Gaudium et spes* goes on to say, "by its very nature private property has a social quality which is based on the law of the common destination of earthly goods."[25] This statement should not be read outside of the broader logic of the Council document, which insists that economic activities, such as the possession of private property, never operate independently from the need to manifest the truth and dignity of the human person as expressed by an anthropology of gift. The "social quality" of property, in other words, is not simply a consequence of its being a commodity in an order of economic exchange. Property derives its "nature" from the premise of economic life itself, which lies ultimately in the gift-character and hence "social" nature of man. This is why the Council insists that the obligation to charitably give one's property to the poor is not merely an ancillary consequence of economic or material abundance. The insinuation is that there is something in the nature of property itself oriented to its belonging "to everyone," and that through the sharing and giving of earthly goods, property participates in and helps achieve man's ultimate mission.[26]

The fifth imperative is that we must come to recognize economics as a normative theory in terms of defining human ends. The chief conceit of modern economists is that they believe economics to be a purely prescriptive theory. It is commonly asserted that economics contains no preconceived notions and that it is merely a neutral means for bringing

25. *GS*, no. 74.
26. See *GS*, no. 69.

about whatever ends man desires. But this is a typically liberal conceit, for, in fact, whether intentionally or not, economics dictates various kinds of normative content, particularly as it concerns the purpose and direction of human life. In general, it tends to privilege material over spiritual goods and choice over goodness.[27]

Gaudium et spes, in contrast, makes no pretense of being not normative. For example, it talks about how "the active sharing of all in the administration and profits of these enterprises in ways to be properly determined is to be promoted" (no. 68) and how investments should be "directed toward procuring employment and sufficient income for the people both now and in the future" (no. 70). The constitution promotes a vision of economics in which the finality of human existence is taken seriously and treated as the explicit end to which man's economic activities are aimed.

The sixth imperative is that we must take seriously the principle of subsidiarity. *Gaudium et spes* talks about how "the political community exists ... for the sake of the common good, in which it finds its full justification and significance" (no. 74).[28] The text goes on to add:

> Rulers must be careful not to hamper the development of family, social or cultural groups, nor that of intermediate bodies or organizations, and not to deprive them of opportunities for legitimate and constructive activity; they should willingly seek rather to promote the orderly pursuit of such activity.[29]

This kind of language often emerges in Catholic social doctrine, and much has been written about the importance of subsidiarity. But what always accompanies this principle is a normative request for how it is be implemented and administered. Usually, the default assumption is that the state should be responsible, and that there should be law and regulation to ensure it is appropriately applied. This is precisely how *Gaudium et spes* expresses the need for more regulation:

27. The question of the role of normative content in economic theory is a complex one. A helpful text on the question is Andrew Yuengert, *The Boundaries of Technique: Ordering Positive and Normative Concerns in Economic Research* (New York: Lexington Books, 2004).

28. Note once again the ambiguity as to what conception of the "common good" is being put forward here.

29. *GS*, no. 75.

The complex circumstances of our day make it necessary for public authority to intervene more often in social, economic and cultural matters in order to bring about favorable conditions which will give more effective help to citizens and groups in their free pursuit of man's total well-being.[30]

By and large, modern societies have followed *Gaudium et spes* on this point and have widely accepted state intervention over their economies. But this intervention brings serious risks and consequences.

The theory of regulatory capture presents one of the clearest articulations of the risks associated with state-controlled regulation. This theory states that regulations, over time, invariably benefit those who are regulated more than the supposed beneficiaries of the regulation. It suggests that because those who are regulated tend to be much more powerful and easier to coordinate, and because they tend to be fewer in number, they are therefore able to more easily manipulate regulatory systems to serve their interests.[31] Take, for example, the business of regulating of utilities. Electric companies typically must follow specific laws created by a government board that regulate, among other things, the prices they are allowed to charge. Now, the average individual spends little time thinking about the price of electricity: once a month he simply assesses his cost, writes a check, and transfers funds to the company. Contrast this with how much time economists and lobbyists for utility companies spend thinking about the price of electricity. For them, it is a full-time job. These companies employ professional lobbyists to try to influence regulation, and they are often more successful than your average private citizen on account of their position and single-minded purpose.

Additionally, most industries are now so complicated that the regu-

30. *GS*, no. 75.

31. See the seminal articles by Nobel Laureate George J. Stigler, "The Theory of Economic Regulation," *Bell Journal of Economics and Management Science* 2, no. 1 (1971): 3–21, and Samuel P. Huntington, "The Marasmus of the ICC: The Commission, The Railroads, and the Public Interest," *Yale Law Journal* 61, no. 4 (1952): 467–509. See also developments by Marver H. Bernstein, *Regulating Business by Independent Commission* (Princeton, NJ: Princeton University Press, 1955); idem, "Independent Regulatory Agencies: A Perspective on Their Reform," *Annals of the American Academy of Political and Social Science* 14 (1972); and Michael E. Levine and Jennifer L. Forrence, "Regulatory Capture, Public Interest, and the Public Agenda: Toward a Synthesis," *Journal of Law, Economics, and Organization* 6 (1990): 167–98.

lators themselves often have to have worked in the industry to have the requisite expertise for regulating it. Many are even hired back by industries they were once charged with regulating them. The result is a torturous and conflicting process in which regulation appears to be serving the principle of subsidiarity, but is actually contributing to the creation of a situation in which large corporations and the state forge an unspoken alliance, one aimed at maximizing the amount of money they can extract from people. Once politics becomes a tool for the extraction of wealth by a small elite, society is in dire trouble, for the political and human ends of such a society will become increasingly subordinate and subject to the designs of this wealthy class. In the United States, it would seem as though we are close to a point where politics has become such a tool, if we have not in fact crossed that line already. Despite our ceaseless appeal for state intervention and regulation, this has only perpetuated a system in which large, multinational corporations benefit and dominate. We remain quite far from implementing any principle of genuine subsidiarity.

To take seriously the principle of subsidiarity requires that we look past the mere pretense of state oversight and evaluate whether it in fact contributes to the growth, common good, and well-being of a community. Take, for example, the attempt by the European Union (EU) to accommodate for the many diverse harvesting practices used by European farmers by standardizing the practice of washing eggs. In 2008, the EU passed a law permitting the sale and distribution of washed eggs. Such a law would have otherwise strengthened local economies and promoted the economic well-being of communities had it not also legislated the specific machine required to meet regulatory standards. As it turns out, this machine costs €20,000, well beyond the budget of most small farmers, who are now no longer able to sell eggs washed by any other method. However much it may have been the original intent of the European legislature to protect small farmers and businesses interested in buying local goods, the intervention has in fact had the opposite effect, and the only obvious benefactor of this law has been the manufacturer of the specific egg-washing machine. Genuine subsidiarity must always be measured by the concrete goods it secures for the local communities, businesses, and families that it claims to help.

The seventh and last imperative would require a whole essay to itself and can thus only be mentioned here in the most cursory of ways. Primarily, it involves the largely forgotten medieval teaching concerning the practice of *usury*, which, of course, is not something that can simply be appropriated by implausibly or naïvely turning back the clock of history. Rather, what is demanded is a reappropriation of the genuine medieval insight that inanimate matter by itself is unfruitful. What this implies is the corresponding ethic that it is immoral to demand payment for a loan of something that does not contribute to the creation of material wealth.[32]

Conclusion

This brief sketch of the possibilities for economic reform will hardly make one hopeful, particularly given that unless one is a lobbyist or the leader of some political party, there is little one can do to effect systematic change in what is an immense and highly entrenched system. But the chief aim of a pastoral constitution is not to enact sweeping socioeconomic or political changes, but rather to help inform those called to live and work in the world. The laity are charged with the responsibility of transforming the character of modern economic life, and this is a task that cannot wait for the implementation of some overarching political strategy. It must begin right away and in a manner worthy of the truth of God and the human person as revealed by Jesus Christ. By way of conclusion, therefore, I offer some practical suggestions as to how to live out each of these imperatives in one's day-to-day life, with the hope that by doing so it might become clearer how economic activities can be themselves genuine expressions of an anthropology of gift.

The foremost expression of a theologically informed economic life is the priority it gives to fostering the growth of holy families. This includes, among other things, avoiding any behaviors, patterns, or actions that would instrumentalize marriage and subordinate the family to oth-

32. See Thomas Aquinas, *Summa theologiae* II-II, q. 78, drawing on Aristotle, *Politics* 1.3, 1.10–11, and *Nicomachean Ethics* 5.5; Louis de Bonald, "Money," in *The True and Only Wealth of Nations* (Ann Arbor, MI: Sapientia, 2006); and Bernard Dempsey, SJ, *Interest and Usury* (London: Dennis Dobson, 1948).

er interests, be they personal, social, or economic. The gift character of the family, and of all its members, must be upheld above all else, and the economic decisions of a family must therefore always seek to preserve a God-centered selflessness that flows from its anthropological foundation. The most basic way in which a family can accomplish this is by making economic decisions that do not always focus on the best deal or the cheapest possible thing. A theologically informed economic life prioritizes the local over the multinational, regardless of which is cheaper, on account that it recognizes the gift of the family to the concrete here-and-now rather than to some abstract economic system. The gratuitousness of the family toward local economic life should also be expressed through charity as well as by the pursuit of vocations that seek to contribute to what is true, good, and beautiful about human society and persons. Ways need to be found to work with neighbors, friends, and other families to solve local problems, and the demand for state oversight and subsidiarity—which is in many cases the beginning of the problem and often causes a loss of awareness for what is local—should be limited. Although the responsible economic support of our families necessarily comes first, this should (as much as possible) never be at the expense of our capacity to contribute meaningfully in a way that discloses and unfolds the dignity and truth of the human person in our day-to-day encounters.

Nonetheless, an economic life informed by an understanding of the gift character of man must also avoid talking about markets and economies in overly negative terms. Although ordinary individuals have little effect on global market economies and, as a result, often experience feelings of powerlessness, ambivalence, and resentment toward those economic realities, an anthropologically informed economic outlook cannot pretend that such markets are evil. Markets play a subordinate but nonetheless necessary role in the fostering of human life, and we should not disparage markets simply because some of their features are unjust. It is a good thing to buy and accumulate property because it brings autonomy, stability, and the possibility of leisure to family life. Similarly, it is good and responsible to save money, to invest in worthwhile enterprises, and to generously contribute to socioeconomic and political projects. Market economies are genuinely good not simply because they provide opportunity for the performance of abstractly moral and upright acts, but also because of the subordinate role they play in upholding the truth of the human person by reinforcing the universal destination of earthly goods. Economic life is not a morality-free zone, and faithful Catholics can never become pure *homo economicus*, or the "economic man," even if to do so would be advantageous in certain situations. Regardless of whether one is going to make less money in a transaction or lose value on one's investment, the price or cost of a thing can never be the ultimate criterion. The *human* value of economic realities must always take precedent, meaning that economic decisions should always look more favorably on those companies or dealings that honor a vigorous ethic. Such points may seem obvious, but it often goes unnoticed how everyday economic actions are accompanied by moral implications that in turn affect the meaning of the human person and the meaning of society at large.

Although few readers of this essay will be money lenders—thus making an injunction against charging usurious interest somewhat impertinent—many will nonetheless be money borrowers, and it is therefore important to highlight the other side of the financial transaction. The practical principle here is straightforward: avoid borrowing money that requires interest to be paid, except in circumstances in which money is saved or earned for some genuinely *human* purpose. It is acceptable, in other words, to borrow money for school if doing so will help secure a better job or true vocation. Likewise, it is acceptable to borrow money to buy a house if buying a house saves on the cost of rent and promotes the building of a *home*. But it is not acceptable to borrow money for school if you are merely pursuing personal interests, nor is it acceptable to run up the balance of a credit card for the purposes of acquiring property or experiences that are esteemed solely for their material or social worth, such as with a luxury car, dream house, or an extravagant vacation. Let me be clear: education, houses, cars, and vacations are all goods that human beings rightly pursue, but they are only *human* goods to the extent that they are pursued according to the subordination of economic realities to human values, rather than the other way around. If you want to study for personal growth, then do so part-time and take classes on a pay-as-you-go basis. If you want to buy a car or a house, then make sure that such an acquisition is practically in your means and is being done in pursuit of a value that is greater than oneself. However much these brief practical suggestions may risk the appearance of unsolicited advice, they are nonetheless helpful for communicating the main point of this essay in a simple way. It is only an economics informed by an adequate anthropology—such as that advanced by *Gaudium et spes*—that makes life more human and societies more sustainable.

10

Redeeming Work

On *Technē* as an Encounter between God, Man, and the World

D. C. SCHINDLER

Introduction

In his commentary on *Gaudium et spes*, which he wrote shortly after the Second Vatican Council, then-cardinal Ratzinger makes a comment in passing that initially stands out as enigmatic: discussing the way "dominion" figures in man's imaging of God, he refers to "the significance of work" as "the fundamental question of the whole Constitution."[1] For Ratzinger, apparently, the relationship between the Church and the modern world, which is the theme of *Gaudium et spes*, turns on the meaning of work. The reason this observation is enigmatic is not only that he makes it on the way to addressing other matters and does not pause to explain how or why this is the case, as one would naturally expect him to do after positing such a strong statement. It is also enigmatic because, although the question of work is raised in different contexts, it does not stand out in any obvious sense as a central theme in *Gaudium et spes*, as the organizing principle of the various other themes that the document treats. While there is certainly some comment on work—above all in paragraphs 67 and 68 in chapter 3, "Economic and Social Life"—*Gaudium et spes* does not seem to give this discussion special weight in comparison with other

1. *Commentary on the Documents of Vatican II*, vol. 5, *Pastoral Constitution on the Church in the Modern World*, ed. Herbert Vorgrimler (New York: Herder and Herder, 1969), 122.

sections, and it does not say anything especially new with respect to the Catholic social teaching developed in the well-known encyclicals prior to Vatican II.[2] In these two paragraphs, the document insists on the importance of recognizing the dignity of work, which rests on the dignity of the human person, and explains that the economic systems by which human work is organized and regulated must protect and cultivate this dignity, both by providing employment and sufficiently remunerating it in accordance with the just demands of human nature. Perhaps more profoundly, the document identifies a theological dimension of work by indicating how work is a way of bringing creation to perfection (the "work" of creation) and a way of sharing in Christ's redemptive activity, which has traditionally been identified as a "work." Even if we grant the continued importance of these discussions, however, their significance does not yet explain why Ratzinger would identify work as the "fundamental question of the whole Constitution," especially considering the obvious importance of some of the other questions *Gaudium et spes* addresses.

It would be difficult to divine precisely what Ratzinger may have had in mind when he made the remark, and in any event, our interest here is not so much his view as it is the subject matter itself. A strong argument can in fact be made for the centrality of the question of work in *Gaudium et spes*, and making this argument brings to light dimensions of the question of work that call for further development. There are at least three points that one can offer to compose such an argument, each of which opening a task of its own that would take us far beyond the limits of the present context. There is value, nonetheless, in stating them simply. First, it is generally recognized that one of the great contributions of *Gaudium et spes* (and this becomes especially clear in John Paul II's pontificate) is its rediscovery of the central significance of anthropology in the Church's engagement with the world: it is precisely *through* revealing man to himself that Christ reveals the meaning of the world more broadly, since creation is in fact groaning for the revelation of the sons of God. This desire to understand man, the embodied creature that God created in some

2. E.g., Leo XIII, *Rerum novarum*, Encyclical on Capital and Labor, May 15, 1891; Pius XI, *Quadragesimo anno*, Encyclical on Reconstruction of the Social Order, May 15, 1931; John XXIII, *Mater et magistra*, Encyclical on Christianity and Social Progress, May 15, 1961.

sense for his own sake and unsurpassably ennobled by taking on the flesh of human nature, leads in a natural way to posing the question of work. Work is not only unique to man among all created beings—neither animals nor angels work in the proper sense of the term—but also part of the twofold commandment that man received from God at his creation.[3] The commandments to marry and procreate ("Be fruitful and multiply," Gn 1:28) and to transform the world through work (to "subdue" the earth and to "till" and "keep" the garden, Gn 1:28, 2:15) represent the divine mission that defines human existence. John Paul II famously developed a theology of the body, which we typically associate above all with the reality of human love in marriage, but the theme of work was also of special interest to the late pope, and there is good reason to think of this theme as "part 2" of a theology of the body.[4] Like marriage, work is an activity that is essentially connected with our embodied existence, and in a way similar to marriage; it concerns a specifically bodily fruitfulness, though in this case it is a cultivation and promotion of the fruitfulness of the world in itself. In sum, the elevation of the importance of anthropology gives the question of work a fundamental weight.

This leads to the second point. If marriage represents man's imaging of God *ad intra*—that is, as John Paul II proposed, the *communio personarum* of marriage and the family reflects and makes concrete in a specific way the Trinitarian relations of the divine persons that "constitute," as it were, the very essence of God[5]—we might say that work represents man's imaging of God *ad extra*: in his work, man images the extraordinary mystery of God's bringing about something genuinely other than himself that is nonetheless good—very good. Christ's entry *into* the world in order to accomplish the "work" of redemption is not a replacement of creation but a transformation that nevertheless, and however surprisingly,

3. "*Work is one of the characteristics that distinguish* man from the rest of creatures, whose activity for sustaining their lives cannot be called work." John Paul II, *Laborem exercens*, Encyclical on Human Work, September 14, 1981, opening blessing.

4. Though he is not writing from a Catholic perspective, Herbert Applebaum includes John Paul II as one of the most significant theorists of work in the twentieth century. See his *The Concept of Work: Ancient, Medieval, and Modern* (Albany: State University of New York Press, 1992), 503–12.

5. See the general audience of November 14, 1979, in John Paul II, *The Theology of the Body: Human Love in the Divine Plan* (Boston: Daughters of St. Paul, 1997), 45–48.

restores creation to its original meaning. In a sense, from God's perspective, redemption is an extension of the original gift: "My Father is working still," Jesus said, "and I am working" (Jn 5:17). The question of human work plays itself out, we might say, *between* the work of the Father and the work of the Son. In work, man both affirms the world and transforms it. Now, this twofold activity of affirmation and transformation lies, according to *Gaudium et spes*, right at the heart of the Church's mission. In this respect, we may look at the Church's assumption, judgment, and interpretation of human work as a paradigm of her mission more generally.

The third point arguing for the centrality of the question of work in *Gaudium et spes* is that the constitution is about the Church's engagement not with the world *tout court* but more specifically with the *modern* world. Culturally speaking, there are few aspects of human existence in which the changes of modernity have had a more direct impact than in work. In his well-known book *Leisure: The Basis of Culture*, Josef Pieper defines the ethos of modernity effectively as the replacement of a sense of the world as gift—a gift that invites praise, thanksgiving, and celebration, all essentially contemplative activities—with the "workaday world," the world of "total work," in which the value of all things arises exclusively from the human effort put into them.[6] If Pieper's assessment is true, then the question of work offers a privileged way into the problem of modernity. To reflect on the meaning of work brings us face to face with the question of the modern transformation of existence; it sets into relief the difference between the classical and contemporary worldviews, and it requires us to assess the implications of this difference. What is especially interesting in approaching the problem of modernity specifically under the aspect of work is that those issues that might otherwise appear to be abstract, proper to professional philosophers and theologians, reveal themselves to be extremely concrete and relevant to every one of us to the extent that we work, that is, to the extent that we are human and so carry out the mission implanted in our nature from the beginning.

It is just this point that demands our attention. One of the characteristic features of modernity is the tendency to reduce matters to their

6. Josef Pieper, *Leisure: The Basis of Culture*, trans. Alexander Dru (San Francisco: Ignatius Press, 2009).

practical implications, to judge ultimately by utilitarian criteria: the ethos of modernity leads us in our consideration of a theme to ask not what something is but instead what we can do with it, to ask after strategies and tactics rather than seek a deeper understanding. If this is true, it entails that we tend to pose the question of work in the modern world primarily from a modern perspective: instead of asking most fundamentally about the meaning of work, we concern ourselves more with questions about its practice, its conditions, its distribution or availability, its proper organization and regulation, and so forth. Those on the political left emphasize what are conceived as "social justice" issues, namely, worker exploitation, poverty, unemployment, and, at a deeper level, more structural questions concerning the organization of economic systems. On the right, there is perhaps a desire to understand work as a special opportunity to learn and exercise virtue, and an emphasis on work as a means to make a contribution to society. Both sides give a certain priority to the justice of wages, whether in the name of equality or with a view to the proper integration of work into the healthy life of a family. Both sides, though perhaps on somewhat different grounds, emphasize the opportunities for charity that work represents. Yet despite the many aspects of the question of work that these political opposites address, both remain within the pragmatic horizon characteristic of modernity.

All these aspects are clearly important, requiring careful thought and prayerful attention; all of them, moreover, have received significant treatment in the tradition of Catholic social teaching and make an appearance in *Gaudium et spes*. Even so, it is crucial to see that none of them concerns the meaning of work in itself. The reason this is important comes to light in a special way when we return to the point indicated above: work is a fundamental human reality, representing the proper place of man's engagement with the world. If Christ entered into this reality, assuming it as his own, then to think of the question of work exclusively in terms of the issues mentioned—the primarily ethical problems of social justice and virtue—is to reduce Christ's work of redemption ultimately to a moral message. To think, in other words, that the issue of work holds interest for the Church only to the extent that it touches on some moral question is to concede implicitly that the grace of redemption, the communication of which is the Church's raison d'être, does not reach to the inner reality of man and the world, does not penetrate to the core of human existence in the world, but remains instead a kind of overlay of subjective intentionality or, at most, a mere external regulation. If work is a symbol of human praxis, of man's life *in* the world, then to concede this superficiality with respect to work is to concede it in principle with respect to all other human activities, cultural institutions, and values. It is to take for granted an essential divide between the religious life of the Church and the secular logic of the world in itself, which is precisely the move that gave rise to the crisis the Second Vatican Council was convened to address. This divide implies a competition between worldly autonomy and Christian—that is, ecclesial, sacramental—form, which makes all the problems of the Church's relation to the modern world *essentially* insoluble. All of this is at stake in the apparently simple question concerning the meaning of work, and once we see this implication, Ratzinger's initially enigmatic observation becomes quite compelling.

The Meaning of Work in the Modern World

What does it mean, then, to ask the question of the meaning of work in itself? It means, first, recognizing that work does in fact have a meaning in itself, that there is an intelligible essence of work that expresses itself in the various activities that go by the name. It is by virtue of such an essence that we may think of work as a reality—an essential expression of human existence, a way of being in the world—that has significance already in itself, in relative abstraction from questions of productivity, the justice of wages, working conditions, and so forth.[7] It is only by recognizing its intrinsic meaning that we are able to affirm work as a place of encounter between man and the world, and *therefore* between man and God, because it is only thus that we affirm work as a fundamental expression of man's imaging God in the charge he was given to have dominion over all things (Gn 1:28): God, after all, did not issue this command because he

7. "Intrinsic goods"—i.e., goods that arise inside of a "practice"—as distinct from the products of an activity, are close to what I am calling the intrinsic meaning of work, but a difference still remains. On the intrinsic goods of work, see chapter 8 of Russell Muirhead, *Just Work* (Cambridge, MA: Harvard University Press, 2007).

needed someone to till the garden and was otherwise occupied. No, with this command God gave man a capacity to share, however distantly, in his creation of the world, which means that work is not first of all a function of extrinsic need or utility but is most essentially a gift. Part of the gift that God gives to man in creating him is the very possibility of participating in the work of creation. If being is a gift that is a task (*Auf-gabe*), work is a task that is a gift (*Auf-gabe*).

In the reflections that follow, I make and elaborate two basic claims: first, that, according to its inner logic and original essence, work has the form of an encounter between man and world that opens up *naturally* to God; second, that the dominant modern sense of work represents an elimination of just this encounter and natural movement in work, so that the Church's engagement with the world requires a recovery of the premodern notion of work. Only according to this richer notion of work can work serve as a symbol of the Church-world relation. To give substance to this proposal, I point briefly to arguments regarding the general modern approach to work offered by Matthew Crawford, above all in his book *Shop Class as Soulcraft*.[8] Then, again briefly, I describe an alternative approach drawn from Plato's reflections on the meaning of *technē*, which lies, we might say, at the philosophical core of work.

Crawford's book is essentially a plea on behalf of the value—that is, the goodness and beauty—of manual labor in a world that has tended to privilege "white-collar" professions. Crawford began his professional life working in a public policy think tank after receiving a PhD in political philosophy, until the emptiness of that work drove him to return to his first love: motorcycles. He now runs a garage in Virginia (though, truth be told, the extraordinary success of his first book landed him the position of senior fellow at the Institute for Advanced Studies in Culture at the University of Virginia). His argument, in a nutshell, is that the various revolutions that have occurred in the sphere of work in the modern era—the Industrial Revolution, the revolution of the modern economy, the Taylorist revolution (i.e., the institution of mass production), and the many renewals of the technological revolution—have resulted in a grow-

8. Matthew B. Crawford, *Shop Class as Soulcraft: An Inquiry into the Value of Work* (New York: Penguin, 2009).

ing separation between "thinking" and "doing" in the organization of work. Human intelligence has increasingly come to bear on work primarily in the form of engineering, planning, management, marketing, sales, advertising, and perhaps at the limit customer service (though admittedly we may be stretching the word "intelligence" here beyond its natural scope). What we have, in all these cases, is intelligence directed not in an actual way to some real thing produced, some tangible good, but rather principally to the various *means* of production and distribution. As a discrete object of human activity, the means thus acquire a kind of entitative status in themselves, involving increasingly sophisticated and institutionalized relations that are required to justify their own existence as much as to facilitate the production of some real good outside themselves. This is the well-known phenomenon of "bureaucracy." The abstraction of the means gives rise to a system of activities that run parallel to the actual work of production and thus lack intrinsic involvement in this work—a phenomenon that finds itself almost effortlessly parodied in popular culture.[9] In short, the "thinkers" are not in any real sense "doers"; they are not involved in an intrinsically human way in the hands-on making of good things.

On the flip side, by virtue of the separation of means and ends, the human agency of the "doers" is compromised in a fundamental way: there is essentially no need for those in production to *understand* what they are doing, because management has taken care of that. The worker does not work with a conception of the whole of the reality he is meant to produce. While it has been recognized that some general sense of what goes on in other departments can foster a sense of cooperation and of being "part of a team" and thus increase productivity, in reality efficiency is impaired the more broadly one's attention and responsibility are stretched. The ideal is for each worker to have absolute focus and absolute responsibility for one part of the process separated out from all the rest. But this separation inevitably entails an increasing impoverishment of the content of his work. As Hegel observed in the early nineteenth century, such work is *designed* to be replaced by machines, because it is itself little more than a human,

9. We might consider, e.g., the television show *The Office*, or the comic strip *Dilbert*.

and hence inevitably imperfect, imitation of mechanical activity.[10] It is crucial to see that even if individuals doing such work never lose their jobs at the factory, they are nevertheless already, at the deepest level, unemployed, because they have ceased to be workers in the genuine sense of the term: authors and originating sources of a *work*, a relatively complete thing recognized as good. The Greek word *ergon*, from which the English word "work" ultimately derives, also means a deed accomplished or a feat normally involving prowess, skill, and greatness of soul. Measured against this rich definition of "work," the "doers" who lack an understanding of the whole no longer fill the economic role of producer or maker; instead, they are effectively merchants like everyone else, though what they sell is not any particular thing but only their labor. As a commodity, work ceases to be recognized as an activity possessing actual content, an expression of one's person, and a real relationship that one has with some actual thing in the world; instead, it has become abstract power, a certain quantity of time and energy that can be indifferently applied to anything at all, according to the directives of whoever owns the power. In this respect, even though "doing" is opposed to the "thinking" that has been reduced to a reified, empty means, such as we see in bureaucratized management, in another respect, it comes to follow a similar pattern: "doing," too, tends to be increasingly separated from content and reified as a mere means in itself—in this case, "man power."

I call the phenomenon just described, taken in its entirety, the "technologizing" of work and suggest that this captures the specifically modern form that work has come to represent. While this word is not one Crawford himself uses and would in another context require some argument to justify its fittingness, what I mean here by "technology" is a separation of means from ends, followed by a rationalizing or organizing of the means, in abstraction from the ends, for the sake of greater efficiency or productivity.[11] To technologize work is to think of it not as some

10. See Georg W. F. Hegel, *Elements of the Philosophy of Right*, ed. Allen W. Wood, trans. H. B. Nisbet (Cambridge: Cambridge University Press, 1991), sec. 198, 232–33.

11. Crawford takes pains to show that he does not intend a romantic critique of all things modern, a root-and-branch dismissal of technology: after all, he is presenting motorcycle maintenance as a paradigm of work. In the present essay, however, I use the word "technology" in a specific sense, distinct from *technē*, to designate not human artifice in general

concrete activity (carpentry, sailing, practicing medicine) but above all as optimized, productive "power." I contrast technology with ancient *technē* on this score in just a moment, but first I want to make a final observation about the technologization of work, point to one of its implications, and explain what Crawford proposes in response. We might say that the technologizing of work represents a "division of labor" in the most radical sense. It is not only a breaking apart of work activities into their smallest and most manageable components but also simultaneously, and at a deeper level, a division that cuts through every instance of labor itself. As technologized, work no longer represents a concentrated engagement of the whole man, body and soul, in a fruit-bearing activity that immerses him in the world. It is now a labor that sets him *on* the world and, in separating thinking from doing, in a certain sense separates his soul from his body—which, incidentally, is the classical definition of death. It is a division of labor from human meaning, because it is a division of labor from the created things of the world that are objectively meaningful.

One of the more profound and far-reaching consequences of this radical division of labor is the cutting loose of the economy from its roots in nature, which would provide organic limits and keep the production, exchange, and consumption of goods anchored in local communities.[12] As Crawford points out, the more the components of work are separated from each other, the more otherwise natural realities and human activities are turned into commodities, the value of which is necessarily, by its own inner logic, determined by the market. This is, specifically, the *global* market, because the economy, once severed from nature and human meaning, is no longer restrained and ordered by anything outside itself; there can no longer be anything outside the economy to define it and give it a logic of service in relation to something that exceeds it. In this case, the economy can only define and regulate itself, which means that it cannot but encompass the globe. The law of optimization will thus inherently require the outsourcing of different components of work and

but only that sort characterized by the abstraction of means from ends in the manner I have been discussing.

12. The classic work on this theme is Karl Polanyi, *The Great Transformation: The Political and Economic Origins of Our Time*, 2nd ed. (Boston: Beacon Press, 2001).

the mobilization of the workforce. The further the process of technologization develops, the greater and more substantial becomes the machinery—both literal and metaphorical—that is interposed between man and the world. Instead of mediating an encounter between man and world that would transform both in different ways, work becomes an imposition—in both directions. The medium becomes opaque, and man loses the basic reference point in nature by which he can orient himself and so bear the genuine fruit of culture. In this case, the provision of work to otherwise destitute regions of the world represents a mitigation of poverty only in the crudest sense of the term; at a deeper level, in relation to the quality of human existence, outsourcing is actually an exportation of poverty. By sending abroad the fragmentation of the human person and of man and world—both of which amount to the separation of man and meaning—the provision of technologized work condemns laborers to a partial existence, a permanent deprivation.

Crawford responds to this crisis by extolling the virtues of manual labor—the ability to make or fix things with one's own hands—which he points out is the sort of work that will never go "offshore."[13] These virtues all stem from the fairly straightforward observation that, in doing this work, one is directly confronted with a reality that presents its own set of criteria for the engagement, its own standards of completion and fittingness: *I* don't decide when my faucet has stopped leaking; *it* decides, and its coming to this decision demands my fully attentive and obedient cooperation. The objective reality, the intrinsic nature of the thing, calls me out of myself in my interaction with it and requires the subordination of my will. If we understand this properly and pay attention to our experience of it, we discover that such subordination is not an affront to our freedom but rather a deepening of it and a granting of genuine substance to our agency. "To be master of your own stuff," Crawford says, "entails also being mastered by it."[14] What does this mean? It means, I believe, that our will becomes more genuinely free the more its "power" is drawn from the reality of the world in which it is involved, rather than artificially multiplied through the separation from the world that tech-

13. Crawford, *Shop Class*, 3.
14. Crawford, *Shop Class*, 57.

nology constantly invents new ways to facilitate. As real capacity, human agency acquires a nuanced and textured shape, a breadth and depth, a maturity, and an intrinsic wisdom through which man extends himself into the world and the world extends itself into man. This extension entails an essentially receptive moment, which involves a trusting consent to something that is in some respect greater than my will. The respect in which it is greater is that *it*—this reality I seek to master—sets the terms most directly; it provides the determination, the form, to which my will must *con*form. Only once it does—"once" here meaning not the flash of a single moment but the fruit of a long and patient labor, in which a real, natural development occurs—do I find my agency more capacious than it was before. The previously opaque and foreign reality is now relatively transparent—though not because it has finally yielded, defenseless, to the force of my will power. Instead, it has become in a certain respect internal to my will in all its substantial reality.

Platonic *Technē*

Crawford's reflections on the reality of work, profound as they are, are not altogether new. In fact, his contrast between genuine manual labor and the perversion of work just described echoes in remarkable ways an ancient dispute—namely, that depicted by Plato between philosophy and Sophistry. In the context of this dispute, Plato reflects on the proper meaning of *technē*—art, skill, or craft, or, in other words, the practical wisdom ordered to making—which represents, we might say, the essence of work. It is worthwhile to recall the basic features of Plato's notion of *technē* in relation to our present discussion for three reasons. First, consulting Plato as regards the question of work helps to clarify what we might call the essential difference between ancient *technē* and modern technology, which in turn illuminates further the impact of modernity on the meaning of work, as we have been exploring it here. Second, connecting Crawford to Plato gives a metaphysical weight to Crawford's more directly cultural and anthropological reflections and roots those reflections more deeply in the philosophical tradition. Third, connecting Plato conversely to Crawford shows that the contrast between an ancient and a modern concept of work is not a crudely chronological matter (i.e., "old is good, new is bad") but concerns above all a difference in mode of being, which is relevant to any historical period.

The principal context in which Plato discusses the meaning of *technē* is his debate with the Sophists, the itinerant teachers who sold their lessons. They invariably found eager buyers insofar as their lessons consisted of instruction in skills and techniques through which one could become successful, particularly in terms of wealth and political power. Sophistry represents for Plato something like a "technologizing" of human communication, in the sense of the term we have proposed: it is, first, the rationalizing of means—in this case, persuasive speech and the art of argumentation—that have been abstracted from any real relation to an end or to particular content; second, it is an interpretation of these means as *entirely* practical, that is, the simple production of results in a manner that leaves the theoretical or substantial content of those results up to the agent in any particular case. The novelty of Sophistry lay in the fact that it made efficiency a principal goal, and it was attractive because of its discovery of the power of purifying means, both in the sense of rationalizing them, excising inefficiencies so that they can be harnessed and controlled, and in the sense of cleansing them of content and so rendering them neutral. In a word, Sophistry represented in a decisive and symbolic way the absolutizing of instrumentality.

There is a clear analogy between the Sophistical notion of rhetoric and the modern notion of work: work is, in the modern sense, a mere instrument whose value depends on what it produces—whether that be in the obvious sense of the quantity of change effected in the world, the things produced, and the profit generated, or in the more subtle sense of the virtue acquired, the good things accomplished, the support given to one's family, the contribution made to society, the glory rendered to God, and so forth.[15] Plato's critique of Sophistry, insofar as it illuminates the

15. Although these are all consequences of work as distinct from dimensions of the essence of work in itself, there are significant differences in their relation to that essence. Virtue, e.g., can be intrinsic to work understood as a praxis, which brings it much closer to the inner essence of work than, say, the reward of a wage. Nevertheless, the point upon which I am insisting is the good *itself* of work, which remains distinct, even if in some cases inseparable, from any of its consequences.

meaning of *technē*, which lies at the heart of work, may thus be taken as a critique of the modern concept of work—or at least this is what I am proposing. We have space in the present context only to present three basic points in Plato's conception of *technē*, though it should be evident how these resonate with the rest of our reflections thus far.

First, Plato explains in the *Republic* that a *technē*, any *technē*, is by its inner logic ordered to the good of that upon which it is set or to which it is directed, as distinct from the good of the practitioner, the good of the art itself, or any other external purpose.[16] None of these is excluded in principle, but, understood correctly, they prove to be secondary fruits resulting from the pursuit of the proper good. Thus the art of medicine is directed not to itself but to the body; in other words, it does not heal medicine but, through the use of medicine, heals human beings. The *technē* thus has an essentially self-transcending or other-referential character. The achievement of its proper good, human health, may entail a host of further goods in a natural and spontaneous way: the doctor, for example, may become rich, learn the true meaning of service, or come to understand better the deep mystery of human suffering; he may make discoveries that improve the practice, or he may make a contribution to the well-being of his community. At least some of these outcomes might deepen, and improve the quality of, the doctor's practice of his art. But none of these, strictly speaking, is the proper purpose of the *technē* of medicine, and that *technē* becomes distorted when we forget this. It is a simple point, but the world would be a profoundly different place if it were understood and acknowledged.

Second, a *technē* is a kind of knowledge and as such is rooted in the truth of its object. As Plato shows in the *Gorgias*, one cannot speak well about something unless one understands it.[17] He makes this point in response to the Sophists, who think of language in a purely instrumentalist sense; for them, one can learn techniques of effective writing and speaking that can be applied subsequently to anything. If this is the case, however, it means that language is not of its very essence a matter of truth. For Plato, by contrast, a word is, by definition, a medium through which

16. See Plato, *Republic* 341c–342e.

17. The argument we are discussing occurs in *Gorgias* 453a–461b.

the truth makes itself manifest.[18] Analogously to language, he observes, every *technē*, by its very essence, is inescapably a matter of truth. Medicine is not ordered to merely feeling good, to the merely subjective conviction that one is healthy, or to the effecting of an outward *appearance* of well-being. Instead, it is ordered to *being* healthy, to health in its truth. One cannot practice medicine unless one knows what health really is. In sum, for Plato, every *technē* is both rooted in the truth of reality and ordered to its good; in other words, *technē* concerns the goodness of the truth of its particular matter, and the truth of its goodness. At the outset, I referred to the need to recover a contemplative dimension of work: that dimension arises precisely to the extent that *technē* is rooted in the truth and ordered to the goodness of a thing in itself.[19]

Now, truth and goodness converge in beauty. The third point regarding Plato's conception of *technē* comes from the *Phaedrus*, a dialogue essentially about beauty, the love it engenders, and the proper use of language in its regard. The specific point concerns the proper scope of the knowledge entailed in a *technē*. There is in this, I believe, a deep connection with the theme of beauty, though there is no room here to bring it to light. Be that as it may, the *Phaedrus* at one point picks up the thread from the discussion in the *Gorgias* we just described, and carries it a step further into the very theme we started with. To paraphrase the discussion: Socrates affirms the claim we just made, namely, that *technē* presupposes knowledge of the truth of its object, but then he asks further, What do we need to know in order to know the truth of a thing?[20] To specify the question, he takes the medical art once again as an example: What do we need to know in order to know the truth of human health? Though he does not explain his answer to this question—in fact, rather than offer an argument, he appeals to the authority of Hippocrates, the father of medi-

18. On the relation between language and truth in Plato, see the insightful explanation of Julius Stenzel, "Das Problem der Willensfreiheit im Platonismus," in *Studien zur Entwicklung der platonischen Dialektik von Sokrates zu Aristoteles* (Stuttgart: B. G. Teubner, 1961), 171–87.

19. This aspect of the argument is developed more fully in an earlier version of this essay, "Work as Contemplation: On the Platonic Notion of *Technē*," *Communio: International Catholic Review* 42, no. 4 (Winter 2015): 594–617.

20. Plato, *Phaedrus* 269d and following.

cine—it is not too difficult to adduce reasons: in order to know the truth of health, he says, we need to know the nature of the cosmos as a whole.[21] Drawing on Plato's discussions elsewhere, we might add: to know this, we have to know the nature of the first cause of the cosmos, the nature of God himself.

Plato's claim that a particular *technē* requires knowledge of the whole stands out in an especially vivid way in the example of medicine (even more so when we consider the state of things today). It seems, however, that something analogous might be said about every *technē*—and so every genuine kind of work—precisely insofar as it is a *technē*, ordered to the goodness of the truth and the truth of the goodness—or, in a word, to the genuine beauty—of its particular reality. Let us consider, for example, the *technē* of housebuilding and imagine someone who comes to this work out of a genuine love of houses. What does he have to know in order to build a proper house? What sort of questions would naturally enter into his field of interest? For one, there are the questions of materials. What is quality in this case, why is plaster and brick better than wallboard, what is the best wood, and where does it come from? What is the source of this wood, how did the trees grow, and what is the climate and history of the region? What is the history of the company that harvested and cut the timber? On another level, he would also have to know what a house is for. What constitutes human flourishing, and how do the layout, design, and shape of the rooms in their relation to each other and to the whole contribute to this flourishing (the prominence of hospitality, e.g., would yield a different design compared to the privileging of storage)? And then there is the great question of style. What is the relation between usefulness and beauty? What *is* beauty? What is the evolution of styles throughout history, and how do different styles reflect different worldviews, different convictions about the meaning of life, different understandings of the nature of God? What I want to point out in this example is that the *particular* reality of that upon which one works—a house, in this case—opens up beyond itself, ultimately to the whole world and to God, if it is affirmed and pursued through a genuine

21. For a longer discussion of this point, see D. C. Schindler, "The Healthy and the Holy," *Communio: International Catholic Review* 41, no. 3 (Fall 2014): 544–63.

love—and this is because love is connected to beauty, the goodness of the truth and the truth of the goodness of a thing.

In this, we find a rather obvious analogy with a good love relationship. As opposed to disordered relationships, which are ruled by empty desire and insecurity and which withdraw us from our family, friends, and outside interests, a genuine love opens up in a natural way to others, and it does so *through* its very particularity. There is in love not only a spontaneous movement of hospitality—a genuine love makes room in itself for what is other, both in the sense of children and in the broader sense of family, community, and so forth—but also, as a fruit of this love, a deepening of one's interest in the world and one's relation to God. Something similar can be said for work in the proper sense: there are kinds of work that shut out the world, sometimes quite dramatically, and I venture to say that these are almost invariably saturated with technologies (either in the literal sense or in the more expanded sense of bureaucratic and functionary mediations), fragmented into commodifiable pieces, and instrumentalized in relation to wholly extrinsic ends: the "division of labor." By contrast, in real work, the activity itself opens up the world; one encounters the meaning of things in a simple and yet profound way. As Crawford describes regarding his work on motorcycles, which is evidently for him a labor of love, even what might be an extremely precise and narrowly focused occupation can connect one with a broader community. It does so by naturally posing the question of human excellence, whether or not the worker is explicitly conscious of all this:

> I try to be a good motorcycle mechanic. This effort connects me to others, in particular to those who exemplify good motorcycling, because it is they who can best judge how well I have realized the functional goods I am aiming at. I wouldn't even know what those goods *are* if I didn't spend time with people who ride at a much higher level than I, and are therefore more discerning of what is good in a motorcycle. So my work situates me in a particular community. The narrow mechanical things I concern myself with are inscribed within a larger circle of meaning; they are in the service of an activity that *we* recognize as part of a life well lived. This common recognition, which needn't be spoken, is the basis for a friendship that orients by concrete images of excellence.
>
> My point, finally, isn't to recommend motorcycling in particular, nor to ideal-

ize the life of a mechanic. It is rather to suggest that if we follow the traces of our own actions to their source, they intimate some understanding of the good life.[22]

We can go a step further, beyond Crawford, by pointing out that anytime there is an encounter with the world in its basic meaning, an intrinsic encounter with other human beings, a creation of community, or a discovery of the question of the meaning of life, there is—however unconscious it may be—an encounter with God, the source and absolute exemplar of all goodness, truth, and beauty, and of the love in which these are received, affirmed, and cultivated.

Conclusion

To conclude, let us turn back to the question of the role of work as a central theme in *Gaudium et spes*. The document is concerned with the Church's encounter with the modern world, and Ratzinger pointed to work as the fundamental question of the constitution, which suggests that work represents a privileged place of this encounter and that the form it takes bears on the meaning of both the Church and the world. While one might interpret this emphasis on work as an elevation of the various questions of "social justice" in the conventional understanding of the term and so a relativizing of properly theological themes, our reflection on the meaning of work *in itself* suggests a different way to understand it. If work is a matter of the intrinsic goodness, truth, and beauty of the world as created, and if the transformative activity of work, engaged in as a *technē* rather than as a technology, opens up that world beyond itself to the meaning of human existence and ultimately to God's own purposes, then work brings into contact the inner essence of the world and the inner essence of the Church. To put it another way, it reveals that one does not need to abandon the center of the Church in order to enter into the heart of the world.[23] Recognizing this casts a new light on some old questions regarding the autonomy of the "secular" world, the relation between nature and grace, and so forth, all of which are acknowledged

22. Crawford, *Shop Class*, 196–97.

23. David L. Schindler, *Heart of the World, Center of the Church:* Communio *Ecclesiology, Liberalism, and Liberation* (Grand Rapids, MI: Eerdmans, 1996).

to be central concerns of *Gaudium et spes*. Perhaps work is, after all, the fundamental question of the whole constitution.

In the end, it should not be surprising that the question of work should figure so centrally in the anthropological and Christocentric refocusing of the mind of the Church in the Vatican II documents, since, along with the primordial sacrament of marriage, work is the original task God gave to man at the very origin. Taken as a whole, this task is the commission to be fruitful both *inside* the human relation of the family and *out beyond* the family *in* the world, and through man's cultivation to enable the world to open up from its own innermost core to God, just as it flourishes in the goodness of its own truth. We thus come to understand why Christ—who took on the human condition in his act of redemption, and in doing so both restored creation to its original integrity and elevated it infinitely beyond itself to share in the intimate exchange of Trinitarian love—not only performed the great work of his sacrificial death *for* us but also, for long years and in a quiet, hidden way, first lived alongside us and, we might say, did our work *with* us: "He worked with human hands, He thought with a human mind, acted by human choice and loved with a human heart."[24]

24. *GS*, no. 22.

BIBLIOGRAPHY

Amato, Paul R., and Rebecca A. Maynard. "Decreasing Nonmarital Births and Strengthening Marriage to Reduce Poverty." *Next Generation of Antipoverty Policies* 17, no. 2 (2007): 117–41.

Andresen, Carl. "Zur Entstehung und Geschichte des trinitarischen Personbegriffes." *Zeitschrift für die neutestamentliche Wissenschaft* 52, no. 1–2 (1961): 1–39.

Applebaum, Herbert. *The Concept of Work: Ancient, Medieval, and Modern.* Albany: State University of New York, 1992.

Balthasar, Hans Urs von. *The Glory of the Lord: A Theological Aesthetics*. 7 vols. Translated by Erasmo Leiva-Merikakis. San Francisco: Ignatius Press, 1982.

———. *The Christian State of Life*. Translated by M. F. McCarthy. San Francisco: Ignatius Press, 1983.

———. *Theo-drama: Theological Dramatic Theory*. 5 vols. Translated by Graham Harrison. San Francisco: Ignatius Press, 1990–92.

———. *Explorations in Theology*. 5 vols. Translated by A. V. Littledale. San Francisco: Ignatius Press, 1991.

———. *Unless You Become Like This Child*. Translated by Erasmo Leiva-Merikakis. San Francisco: Ignatius Press, 1991.

———. *The Theology of Karl Barth*. San Francisco: Ignatius Press, 1992.

———. *Razing the Bastions*. San Francisco: Ignatius Press, 1993.

———. *The Moment of Christian Witness*. San Francisco: Ignatius Press, 1994.

———. *A Theology of History*. San Francisco: Ignatius Press, 1994.

———. *Tragedy under Grace: Reinhold Schneider on the Experience of the West*. San Francisco: Ignatius Press, 1997.

———. *Theo-logic: Theological Logical Theory*. 3 vols. Translated by Adrian J. Walker. San Francisco: Ignatius Press, 2004.

Bandow, Doug, and David L. Schindler, eds. *Wealth, Poverty, and Human Destiny*. Wilmington, DE: Intercollegiate Studies Institute, 2003.

Barsotti, Divo. *La rivelazione dell'amore*. Bologna: Edizioni Dehoniane, 1955.

Batut, J. P. "The Chastity of Jesus and the 'Refusal to Grasp.'" *Communio: International Catholic Review* 24 (1997): 5–13.

Bibliography

Baum, Gregory, and Donald Campion. *De Ecclesia in Mundo Huius Temporis: The Pastoral Constitution on the Church in the Modern World*. New York: Paulist, 1967.

Berman, Morris. *The Re-Enchantment of the World*. Ithaca, NY: Cornell University Press, 1981.Bernstein, Marver H. *Regulating Business by Independent Commission*. Princeton, NJ: Princeton University Press, 1955.

———. "Independent Regulatory Agencies: A Perspective on Their Reform." *Annals of the American Academy of Political and Social Science* 400 (1972): 14–26.

Bieler, Martin. *Freiheit als Gabe: Ein schöpfungstheologischer Entwurf*. Freiburg: Herder, 1991.

Binion, Rudolph. *Past Impersonal: Group Process in Human History*. DeKalb: Northern Illinois University Press, 2005.

Block, James E. *The Crucible of Consent: American Child Rearing and the Growing of Liberal Society*. Cambridge, MA: Harvard University Press, 2012.

Bloom, Alan. *The Closing of the American Mind: How Higher Education Has Failed Democracy and Impoverished the Souls of Today's Students*. New York: Simon and Schuster, 1987.

Boeve, Lieven. "Europe in Crisis: A Question of Belief or Unbelief? Perspectives from the Vatican." *Modern Theology* 23, no. 2 (April 2007): 205–27.

———. "Conversation and Cognitive Dissonance: Evaluating the Theological-Ecclesial Program of Joseph P. Ratzinger/Benedict XVI." *Horizons* 40 (December 2013): 242–54.

Bonino, Serge-Thomas, ed. *Surnaturel: A Controversy at the Heart of Twentieth-Century Thomistic Thought*. Translated by Robert Williams. Ave Maria, FL: Sapientia Press, 2009.

Bordoni, Marcello. *Gesù di Nazaret: Signore e Cristo; Saggio di Cristologia sistematica*. Rome: Herder-PUL, 1982–86.

Braine, David. "The Debate between Henri de Lubac and His Critics." *Nova et Vetera* 6 (2008): 543–90.

Bruaire, Claude. *L'être et l'esprit*. Paris: PUF, 1983.

Bulgakov, Sergei. *The Lamb of God*. Translated by Boris Jakim. Grand Rapids, MI: Eerdmans, 2008.

Butler, Judith. *Gender Trouble*. New York: Routledge, 1990.

———. *Undoing Gender*. New York: Routledge, 2004.

Butterfield, Herbert. *The Whig Interpretation of History*. New York: W. W. Norton, 1965.

Cardegna, Felix F. "Contraception, the Pill, and Responsible Parenthood." *Theological Studies* 65 (1964): 611–36.

Carpenter, Humphrey, ed. *The Letters of J. R. R. Tolkien*. Boston: Houghton Mifflin, 2000.

Cernera, Anthony J., ed. *Vatican II: The Continuing Agenda*. Fairfield, CT: Sacred Heart University Press, 1997.

Chibici-Revneanu, Nicole. *Die Herrlichkeit des Verherrlichten: Das Verständnis der doxa im Johannesevangelium*. Tübingen: Mohr Siebeck, 2007.

Coda, Piero. "L'uomo nel mistero di Cristo e della Trinità: L'antropologia della *Gaudium et spes*." *Lateranum* 54 (1988): 164–94.

———. "Antropologia teologica e agire umano nel mondo nella *Gaudium et spes*." *Lateranum* 55 (1989): 176–207.

Colombo, Giuseppe. *La ragione teológica*. Milan: Glossa, 1995.

Congar, Yves M.-J., and Michel Peuchmaurd, eds. *L'Église dans le monde de ce temps: Constitution pastorale "Gaudium et spes."* 3 vols. Paris: Éditions du Cerf, 1967.

Crawford, David S. "Liberal Androgyny: 'Gay Marriage' and the Meaning of Sexuality in Our Time." *Communio: Catholic International Review* 33, no. 2 (2006): 239–65.

———. "Recognizing the Roots of Society in the Family, Foundation of Justice." *Communio: International Catholic Review* (2007): 379–412.

———. "Benedict XVI and the Structure of the Moral Act: On the Condoms Controversy." *Communio: International Catholic Review* 38, no. 4 (2011): 548–82.

———. "Mechanism, Public Reason, and the Anthropology of Orientation." *Humanum: Issues in Family, Culture & Science* (Fall 2012): http://humanumreview.com/articles/mechanism-public-reason-and-the-anthropology-of-orientation.

———. "Gay Marriage, Public Reason, and the Common Good." *Communio: International Catholic Review* 41 (2014): 380–437.

———. "An Appeal: Recalling the Teaching of *Humanae Vitae* (and *Veritatis Splendor*)." *First Things*. September 10, 2015, https://www.firstthings.com/web-exclusives/2015/09/an-appeal.

———. "*Evangelium vitae*, the Rhetoric of Freedom, and *Roe v. Wade*'s Totalitarian Implications." *Nova et Vetera* 13, no. 4 (2015): 1209–28.

Crawford, David S., and Stephan Kampowski. "The Integrity of Moral Deliberation: On Paragraph 137 of the *Instrumentum Laboris*." *Communio: International Catholic Review* 42, no. 2 (Summer 2015).

Crawford, Matthew B. *Shop Class as Soulcraft: An Inquiry into the Value of Work*. New York: Penguin, 2009.

Curran, Charles, ed. *Contraception: Authority and Dissent*. New York: Herder and Herder, 1969.

Daniélou, Jean. *Platonisme et théologie mystique: Essai sur la doctrine spirituelle de Saint Grégoire de Nysse*. Paris: Aubier, 1944.

Davis, Ellen F. *Proverbs, Ecclesiastes, and the Song of Songs*. Westminster Bible Companion. Louisville, KY: Westminster John Knox Press, 2000.

De Andia, Ysabel. *Henosis: L'union à Dieu chez Denys l'Aréopagite*. New York: E. J. Brill, 1996.

———. "*Eros* and *Agape*: The Divine Passion of Love." *Communio: International Catholic Review* 24, no. 1 (Spring 1997): 29–50.

Bibliography

De Bonald, Louis. *The True and Only Wealth of Nations*. Ann Arbor, MI: Sapientia, 2006.

De Lubac, Henri. *Athéisme et le sens de l'homme: Une double requête de Gaudium et spes*. Paris: Cerf, 1968.

———. *The Church: Paradox and Mystery*. Translated by James R. Dunne. Staten Island: Alba House, 1969.

———. *A Brief Catechesis on Nature and Grace*. Translated by Richard Arnandez. San Francisco: Ignatius Press, 1984.

———. *Entretien autour de Vatican II: Souvenirs et reflections*. Paris: Cerf, 1985.

———. *The Splendor of the Church*. Translated by Michael Mason. San Francisco: Ignatius Press, 1986.

———. *Catholicism: Christ and the Common Destiny of Man*. Translated by Lancelot C. Sheppard and Elizabeth Englund. San Francisco: Ignatius Press, 1988.

———. *At the Service of the Church: Henri de Lubac Reflects on the Circumstances That Occasioned His Writings*. Translated by Anne Elizabeth Englund. San Francisco: Ignatius Press, 1993.

———. *The Discovery of God*. Translated by Alexander Dru. Grand Rapids, MI: Eerdmans, 1996.

———. *The Mystery of the Supernatural*. Translated by Rosemary Sheed. Grand Rapids, MI: Eerdmans, 1998.

———. *Corpus Mysticum: The Eucharist and the Church in the Middle Ages*. Translated by Gemma Simmonds, Richard Price, and Christopher Stephens. Edited by Laurence Paul Hemming and Susan Frank Parsons. Notre Dame, IN: University of Notre Dame Press, 2006.

———. *Carnets du Concile*. 2 vols. Paris: Cerf, 2007.

D'Emilio, John, and Estelle B. Freedman. *Intimate Matters: A History of Sexuality in America*. Chicago: University of Chicago Press, 1988.

Dempsey, Bernard. *Interest and Usury*. London: Dennis Dobson, 1948.

Desmond, William. *Hegel's God: A Counterfeit Double?* Burlington, VT: Ashgate, 2003.

De Tocqueville, Alexis. *Democracy in America*. Translated by Harvey C. Mansfield and Delba Winthrop. Chicago: University of Chicago Press, 2000.

Dostoevsky, Fyodor. *Demons*. Translated by Richard Pevear and Larissa Volokhonsky. New York: Everyman's Library, 2000.

Durand, Jean-Dominique, ed. *Henri de Lubac: La rencontre au coeur de l'Église*. Paris: Cerf, 2006.

Fagan, Patrick, Kirk Johnson, Lauren Noyes, and Robert Rector. *Increasing Marriage Will Dramatically Reduce Child Poverty*. Washington, DC: Heritage Foundation, May 20, 2003.

Faggioli, Massimo, and Andrea Vicini, eds. *The Legacy of Vatican II*. Mahwah, NJ: Paulist, 2015.

Feingold, Lawrence. *The Natural Desire to See God According to St. Thomas Aquinas and His Interpreters*. Ave Maria, FL: Sapientia Press, 2010.

Firestone, Shulamith. *The Dialectic of Sex*. New York: William Morrow, 1970.

Fisichella, Rino, ed. *Il Concilio Vaticano II: Recezione e attualità alla luce del Giubileo*. Cinisello Balsamo: Paoline, 2000.

Flannery, Austin, ed. *Vatican Council II: The Conciliar and Post Conciliar Documents*. Northport, NY: Costello, 1975.

Fleigleman, Jay. *Prodigals and Pilgrims: The American Revolution against Patriarchal Authority, 1750–1800*. Cambridge: Cambridge University Press, 1982.

Foucault, Michel. *The History of Sexuality*. New York: Vintage, 1978.

Gaillardetz, Richard R., and Catherine E. Clifford. *Keys to the Council: Unlocking the Teaching of Vatican II*. Collegeville, MN: Liturgical, 2012.

Geach, M., and L. Gormally, eds. *Faith in a Hard Ground: Essays on Religion, Philosophy and Ethics*. Charlottesville, VA: Imprint Academic, 2008.

Giddens, Anthony. *Transformation of Intimacy: Sexuality, Love, and Eroticism in Modern Society*. Cambridge: Polity Press, 1992.

Gilson, Étienne. *Being and Some Philosophers*. Toronto: Pontifical Institute of Mediaeval Studies, 1952.

Giussani, Luigi. *The Religious Sense*. Translated by John Zucchi. Montreal: McGill-Queen's University Press, 1997.

———. *At the Origin of the Christian Claim*. Translated by Viviane Hewitt. Montreal: McGill-Queen's University Press, 1998.

Grant, George. *Technology and Empire*. Toronto: House of Anansi, 1969.

Guardini, Romano. *The End of the Modern World*. Wilmington, DE: Intercollegiate Studies Institute, 1998.

Habermas, Jürgen. "Modernity's Consciousness of Time and Its Need for Self-Reassurance." In *The Philosophical Discourse of Modernity: Twelve Lectures*. Cambridge: Polity Press, 1987.

Hayek, Friedrich, ed. *Collectivist Economic Planning*. London: George Routledge and Sons, 1935.

Healy, Nicholas J. "Henri de Lubac on Nature and Grace: A Note on Some Recent Contributions to the Debate." *Communio: International Catholic Review* 35 (2008): 535–64.

Hegel, Georg W. F. *Elements of the Philosophy of Right*. Edited by Allen W. Wood. Translated by H. B. Nisbet. Cambridge: Cambridge University Press, 1991.

Hellín, Gil. "El lugar propio del amor conyugal en la estructura del matrimonio según la *Gaudium et spes*." *Annales Valentinos* 6, no. 11 (1980): 1–35.

Hoyt, Robert G., ed. *The Birth Control Debate*. Kansas City, MO: National Catholic Reporter, 1968.

Huntington, Samuel P. "The Marasmus of the ICC: The Commission, The Railroads, and the Public Interest." *Yale Law Journal* 61 (1952): 467–509.

Hütter, Reinhard. *Dust Bound for Heaven: Explorations in the Theology of Thomas Aquinas.* Grand Rapids, MI: Eerdmans, 2012.

Janssens, L. "Moral conjugale et progestogenènes." *Ephemerides theologicae Lovanienses* 39 (1963): 787–826.

John Paul II. *Man and Woman He Created Them: A Theology of the Body.* Translated by Michael Waldstein. Boston: Pauline Books and Media, 2006.

Jonas, Hans. "Gnosticism and Modern Nihilism." *Social Research* 19, no. 4 (December 1952): 430–52.

———. *The Gnostic Religion.* Boston: Beacon Press, 2001.

———. *The Phenomenon of Life.* Evanston, IL: Northwestern University Press, 2001.

Kaiser, Robert Blair. *The Encyclical That Never Was: The Story of the Commission on Population, Family and Birth, 1964–1966.* London: Sheed and Ward, 1985, 1987.

Katz, Jonathan Ned. *The Invention of Heterosexuality.* New York: Penguin, 1995.

Keel, Othmar. *The Song of Songs: A Continental Commentary.* Minneapolis: Fortress Press, 1994.

Killewalda, Alexandra. "A Reconsideration of the Fatherhood Premium: Marriage, Coresidence, Biology, and Fathers' Wages." *American Sociological Review* 78, no. 1 (2013): 96–116.

Ladaria, Luis. *Jesus Christ, Salvation of All.* Translated by María Cristina Herrera and María Isabel Reyna. Miami: Convivium Press, 2008.

Latourelle, René, ed. *Vatican II: Assessment and Perspectives: Twenty-Five Years After (1962–1987).* Mahwah, NJ: Paulist, 1988.

Le Guillou, M. J. *Le mystère du père: Foi des apôtres, gnoses actuelles.* Paris: Fayard, 1973.

Lerman, Robert I. *How Do Marriage, Cohabitation, and Single Parenthood Affect the Material Hardships of Families with Children?* Washington, DC: Urban Institute, July 1, 2002.

———. *Married and Unmarried Parenthood and Economic Well-Being: A Dynamic Analysis of a Recent Cohort.* Washington, DC: Urban Institute, July 1, 2002.

Levine, Michael E., and Jennifer L. Forrence. "Regulatory Capture, Public Interest, and the Public Agenda: Toward a Synthesis." *Journal of Law, Economics, and Organization* 6 (1990): 167–98.

Long, Steven. "Obediential Potency, Human Knowledge, and the Natural Desire for the Vision of God." *International Philosophical Quarterly* 37 (1997): 45–63.

———. *Natura Pura: On the Recovery of Nature in the Doctrine of Grace.* New York: Fordham University Press, 2010.

López, Antonio. "Vatican II's Catholicity: A Christological Perspective on Truth, History, and the Human Person." *Communio: International Catholic Review* 39 (2012): 82–117.

———. "God Opens His Love to Man: The Family as the Human Path to Communion with God." *Anthropotes* 31, no. 1 (2015): 125–62.

Louth, Andrew. *Maximus the Confessor*. London: Routledge, 1996.

Lundberg, Shelly, and Elaina Rose. "The Effects of Sons and Daughters on Men's Labor Supply and Wages." *Review of Economics and Statistics* 84, no. 2 (2002): 251–68.

Malloy, Christopher J. "De Lubac on Natural Desire: Difficulties and Antitheses." *Nova et Vetera* 9 (2011).

Manent, Pierre. *An Intellectual History of Liberalism*. Translated by Rebecca Balinski. Princeton, NJ: Princeton University Press, 1994.

Marengo, G., J. Prades López, and G. Richi Alberti, eds. *Sufficit gratia tua: Miscellanea in onore del Card. Angelo Scola, Arcivescovo di Milano, in occasione del 70°genetliaco*. Venice: Marcianum Press, 2012.

Martin, Jennifer Newsome. *Hans Urs von Balthasar and the Critical Appropriation of Russian Religious Thought*. Notre Dame, IN: University of Notre Dame Press, 2015.

Martinez, Raul Berzosa. *La teología del sobrenatural en los escritos de Henri de Lubac: Estudio historico-teologico (1931–1980)*. Burgos: Aldecoa, 1991.

McCarthy, Margaret H. "Vatican II and the Church's 'Openness to the World': Casting a Wider Net through the Still 'Narrow Gate.'" *Communio: International Catholic Review* 39 (Spring-Summer 2012): 227–68.

McWhirter, Jocelyn. *The Bridegroom Messiah and the People of God: Marriage in the Fourth Gospel.* New York: Cambridge University Press, 2006.

Merton, Robert. *Science, Technology, and Society in Seventeenth-Century England.* New York: Howard Fertig, 1970.

Milbank, John. *The Suspended Middle: Henri de Lubac and the Debate Concerning the Supernatural.* Grand Rapids, MI: Eerdmans, 2005.

Monod, Jacques. *Chance and Necessity*. New York: Vintage, 1972.

Montagnes, Bernard. *The Doctrine of the Analogy of Being According to Thomas Aquinas*. Milwaukee: Marquette University Press, 2004.

Morgan-Wynne, John E. *The Cross in the Johannine Writings*. Eugene, OR: Pickwick Publications, 2011.

Mortensen, John R. *Understanding St. Thomas on Analogy*. Boca Raton, FL: CreateSpace, 2007.

Muirhead, Russell. *Just Work.* Cambridge, MA: Harvard University Press, 2007.

Murphy, Roland E. *The Song of Songs: A Commentary on the Book of Canticles or the Song of Songs.* Minneapolis: Fortress Press, 1990.

Newman, John Henry. *The Arians of the Fourth Century*. London: Longmans, Green, 1890.

Nielsen, Jesper Tang. "The Narrative Structures of Glory and Glorification in the Fourth Gospel." *New Testament Studies* 56, no. 3 (2010): 343–66.

Nietzsche, Friedrich. *The Portable Nietzsche*. Edited and translated by Walter Kaufmann. New York: Penguin, 1976.

Noonan, John T. *Contraception: A History of Its Treatment by the Catholic Theologians and Canonists*. Cambridge, MA: Harvard University Press, 1965, 1986.

Oakes, Edward T. "The *Surnaturel* Controversy: A Survey and a Response." *Nova et Vetera* 9 (2011): 626–56.

O'Malley, John W. *What Happened at Vatican II*. Cambridge, MA: Belknap Press, 2008.

Ouellet, Marc. *Divine Likeness: Toward a Trinitarian Anthropology of the Family*. Translated by Philip Milligan and Linda M. Cicone. Grand Rapids, MI: Eerdmans, 2006.

———. *Mystery and Sacrament of Love: A Theology of Marriage and the Family for the New Evangelization*. Translated by Michelle K. Borras and Adrian J. Walker. Grand Rapids, MI: Eerdmans, 2015.

Paglia, Camille. *Sexual Personae*. New Haven, CT: Yale University Press, 1990.

Péguy, Charles. *Portal of the Mystery of Hope*. Translated by David L. Schindler. New York: Continuum, 1996.

Pellettier, Anne-Marie. Lectures *du Cantique des cantiques: De l'énigme du sens aux figures du lecteur.* Rome: Editrice Pontificio Istituto Biblico, 1989.

———. *Cantico dei Cantici: Nuova versione, introduzione e commento di Gianni Barbiero.* Milan: Paoline, 2004.

Pieper, Josef. *Leisure: The Basis of Culture*. Translated by Alexander Dru. San Francisco: Ignatius Press, 2009.

Pinckaers, Servais. "The Natural Desire to See God." Translated by Aaron Riches. *Nova et Vetera* 8 (2010): 627–46

Polanyi, Karl. *The Great Transformation: The Political and Economic Origins of Our Time*. Boston: Beacon Press, 2001.

Prosperi, Paolo. *Al di là della parola: Apofatismo e personalismo nel pensiero di Vladimir Losskij.* Rome: Città Nuova, 2014.

———. "'The Mystery of Mysteries': On Péguy's Vision of Hope." *Communio: International Catholic Review* 41, no. 4 (Winter 2014): 804–42.

Rahner, Hugo. *Greek Myths and Christian Mystery*. Translated by B. Battershaw. New York: Harper and Row, 1963.

Rank, Mark R., and Thomas A. Hirschl. "The Economic Risk of Childhood in America: Estimating the Probability of Poverty Across the Formative Years." *Journal of Marriage and Family* 61, no. 4 (1999): 1058–67.

Ratzinger, Joseph. *Behold the Pierced One: An Approach to a Spiritual Christology*. Translated by Graham Harrison. San Francisco: Ignatius Press, 1986.

———. *Principles of Catholic Theology: Building Stones for a Fundamental Theology*. San Francisco: Ignatius Press, 1987.

———. *Church, Ecumenism and Politics: New Essays in Ecclesiology*. New York: Crossroad, 1988.

———. *The Meaning of Christian Brotherhood*. San Francisco: Ignatius Press, 1988.

———. *A New Song for the Lord*. New York: Crossroad, 1996.

———. *Called to Communion: Understanding the Church Today*. Translated by Adrian Walker. San Francisco: Ignatius Press, 1996.

———. *Introduction to Christianity*. San Francisco: Ignatius Press, 2004.

———. *Jesus of Nazareth: From the Baptism in the Jordan to the Transfiguration*. Translated by Adrian J. Walker. New York: Doubleday, 2007.

———. *Theological Highlights of Vatican II*. Translated by Thomas Rausch. New York: Paulist, 2009.

———. "Difficulties Confronting the Faith in Europe Today." *Communio: International Catholic Review* 38 (Winter 2011): 728–38.

———. *Dogma and Preaching: Applying Christian Doctrine to Daily Life*. Translated by Michael J. Miller and Matthew J. O'Connell. San Francisco: Ignatius Press, 2011.

Renaud, Bernard. *Je suis un Dieu jaloux: Évolution sémantique et signification théologique de qine'ah*. Paris: Cerf, 1963.

Rhonheimer, Martin. "Contraception, Sexual Behavior, and Natural Law: Philosophical Foundations of the Norm of '*Humanae Vitae*.'" *Linacre Quarterly* 56, no. 2 (1989): 20–57.

Rich, A. "Compulsory Heterosexuality and Lesbian Existence." *Signs: Journal of Women in Culture and Society* 5, no. 4 (Summer 1980): 631–60.

Richard, Lucien, Daniel T. Harrington, and John W. O'Malley, eds. *Vatican II: The Unfinished Agenda; A Look to the Future*. New York: Paulist, 1987.

Ricoeur, Paul. *The Symbolism of Evil*. New York: Harper and Row, 1967.

Rousseau, Jean-Jacques. *Emile; Or, On Education*. Translated by Allan Bloom. New York: Basic Books, 1979.

Rubinstein, Ariel. "A Sceptic's Comment on the Study of Economics." *Economic Journal* 116 (March 2006): C1–C9.

Sartre, Jean-Paul. *Being and Nothingness*. Translated by H. E. Barnes. New York: Philosophical Library.

Scheeben, Matthias J. *The Mysteries of Christianity*. Translated by Cyril Vollert. London: B. Herder, 1946.

Schillebeeckx, Edward. *World and Church*. Translated by N. D. Smith. New York: Sheed and Ward, 1971.

Schiller, Friedrich. "Die Götter Griechenlands." In *Sämtliche Werke*. Edited by Gerhard Fricke and Herbert Göpfert. Munich: Hanser, 1962.

Schindler, David C. "The Healthy and the Holy." *Communio: International Catholic Review* 41, no. 3 (Fall 2014): 544–63.

———. "Work as Contemplation: On the Platonic Notion of *Technē*." *Communio: International Catholic Review* 42, no. 4 (Winter 2015): 594–617.

———. *Freedom from Reality: On the Diabolical Character of Modern Liberty*. Notre Dame, IN: University of Notre Dame Press, 2017.

Schindler, David L. *Heart of the World, Center of the Church: Communio Ecclesiology, Liberalism, and Liberation*. Grand Rapids, MI: Eerdmans, 1996.

———. "Homelessness and the Modern Condition." *Communio: International Catholic Review* (2000): 411–30.

———. "Liturgy, Nuptiality, and the Integrity of Cosmic Order: Symbolic Ontology and Feminism." *Communio: International Catholic Review* 28 (2001): 1–31.

———. "The Embodied Person as Gift and the Cultural Task in America: *Status Quaestionis*." *Communio: International Catholic Review* 35 (2008): 397–431.

———. *Ordering Love: Liberal Societies and the Memory of God*. Grand Rapids, MI: Eerdmans, 2009.

Schindler, David L., and Nicholas J. Healy. *Freedom, Truth, and Human Dignity: The Second Vatican Council's Declaration on Religious Freedom*. Grand Rapids, MI: Eerdmans, 2015.

Schmemann, Alexander. *For the Life of the World*. Yonkers, NY: St. Vladimir's Seminary Press, 1998.

Schmitz, Kenneth L. *The Gift: Creation*. Milwaukee: Marquette University Press, 1982.

———. *At the Center of the Human Drama: The Philosophical Anthropology of Karol Wojtyła/Pope John Paul II*. Washington, DC: Catholic University of America Press, 1993.

———. *The Texture of Being: Essays in First Philosophy*. Edited by Paul O'Herron. Washington, DC: Catholic University of America Press, 2007.

Schnackenburg, Rudolf. *The Gospel According to St. John*. Translated by Kevin Smyth. London: Burns and Oates, 1980.

Scola, Angelo, Gilfredo Marengo, and Javier Prades López. *La persona umana: Antropologia teologica*. Milan: Jaca Books, 2000.

———. *The Nuptial Mystery*. Translated by Michelle K. Borras. Grand Rapids, MI: Eerdmans, 2005.

Segbroeck, Frans Van, Christopher M. Tuckett, Gilbert van Belle, and Joseph Verheyden, eds. *The Four Gospels 1992: Festschrift Frans Neirynck*. Leuven: Leuven University Press, 1992.

Smith, D. Moody. *The Theology of the Gospel of John*. Cambridge: Cambridge University Press, 1995.

Smith, Janet E. *Vitae, a Generation Later*. Washington, DC: Catholic University of America Press, 1991.

Spaemann, Robert. *Persons: The Difference Between "Someone" and "Something."* Translated by Oliver O'Donovan. Oxford: Oxford University Press, 2006.

Stenzel, Julius. "Das Problem der Willensfreiheit im Platonismus." In *Studien zur Entwicklung der platonischen Dialektik von Sokrates zu Aristoteles*. Stuttgart: B. G. Teubner, 1961.

Stigler, George J. "The Theory of Economic Regulation." *Bell Journal of Economics and Management Science* 2, no. 1 (1971): 3–21.

Strauss, Leo. *Natural Right and History*. Chicago: University of Chicago Press, 1950.

Sullivan, Maureen. *The Road to Vatican II: Key Changes in Theology*. New York: Paulist, 2007.

Taylor, Charles. *A Secular Age*. Cambridge, MA: Harvard University Press, 2007.

Thüsing, Wilhelm. *Die Erhöhung und Verherrliching Jesu im Johannesevangelium*. Münster: Aschendorff, 1979.

Tournay, Raymond Jacques. *Word of God, Song of Love: A Commentary on the Song of Songs*. New York: Paulist, 1988.

Varghese, Johns. *The Imagery of Love in the Gospel of John*. Rome: Gregorian and Biblical Press, 2009.

Vonier, Abbot. *A Key to the Doctrine of the Eucharist*. Bethesda, MD: Zaccheus, 2003.

Vorgrimler, Herbert, ed. *Commentary on the Documents of Vatican II*. Translated by Walter M. Abbott. New York: Crossroad, 1989.

Wang, Long, Deepak Malhotra, and J. Keith Murnighan. "Economics Education and Greed." *Academy of Management Learning and Education* 10, no. 4 (2011): 643–60.

Weber, Max. *The Protestant Ethic and the Spirit of Capitalism*. Translated by Talcott Parsons. New York: Scribner, 1958.

———. "Science as a Vocation." In *The Vocation Lectures*. Edited by J. G. Burke. Berkeley: University of California Press, 2004.

Western, Mark, Belinda Hewitt, and Janeen Baxter. "Marriage and Money: Variations across the Earnings Distribution." *Australian Journal of Labour Economics* 8 (2005): 163–79.

White, Thomas Joseph. "Imperfect Happiness and the Final End of Man: Thomas Aquinas and the Paradigm of Nature-Grace Orthodoxy." *The Thomist* 78 (2014): 247–89.

Winsor, Ann Roberts. *A King Is Bound in the Tresses: Allusions to the Song of Songs in the Fourth Gospel*. New York: Peter Lang, 1999.

Wojtyła, Karol. *Sources of Renewal: The Implementation of Vatican II*. Translated by P. S. Falla. San Francisco: Harper and Row, 1979.

———. *Person and Community: Selected Essays*. Translated by Theresa Sandok. New York: Peter Lang, 1993.

———. *Persona e atto*. Translated by Giuseppe Girgenti and Patrycja Mikulska. Milan: Bompiani, 2001.

———. "The Anthropological Vision of *Humanae Vitae*." Translated by William May. *Nova et Vetera* 7, no. 3 (2009): 731–50.

———. *Love and Responsibility*. Translated by G. Ignatik. Boston: Pauline Books and Media, 2013.

Yuengert, Andrew. *The Boundaries of Technique: Ordering Positive and Normative Concerns in Economic Research*. New York: Lexington Books, 2004.

CONTRIBUTORS

ANDREW V. ABELA is the university provost and founding dean of the School of Business and Economics at the Catholic University of America in Washington, DC. He is a widely published essayist in the field of marketing and Catholic social teaching, and has recently coedited a book titled *A Catechism for Business: Tough Ethical Questions and Insights from Catholic Teaching* (2014).

DAVID S. CRAWFORD is an associate dean for academic affairs and associate professor of moral theology and family law at the Pontifical John Paul II Institute for Studies on Marriage and Family at the Catholic University of America. He is the author of *Marriage and the Sequela Christi* (2004) and of numerous essays on issues pertaining to marriage, family, and the human person.

NICHOLAS J. HEALY JR. is an associate professor of philosophy and culture at the Pontifical John Paul II Institute for Studies on Marriage and Family at the Catholic University of America and editor of the North American edition of *Communio: International Catholic Review*. He has most recently coauthored a book titled *Freedom, Truth, and Human Dignity: The Second Vatican Council's Declaration on Religious Freedom* (2015).

MATTHEW LEVERING is the James N. and Mary D. Perry Jr. Chair of Theology at Mundelein Seminary at the University of Saint Mary of the Lake in Mundelein, Illinois. He is coeditor of *Nova et Vetera* and the *International Journal of Systematic Theology* and author of numerous books, including *Engaging the Doctrine of the Holy Spirit: Love and Gift in the Trinity and the Church* (2016) and *Proofs of God: Classical Arguments from Tertullian to Barth* (2016). With Matthew Lamb, he edited *Vatican II: Renewal within Tradition* (2008) and *The Reception of Vatican II* (2017).

ANTONIO LÓPEZ, FSCB, is a priest of the Fraternity of St. Charles Borromeo as well as provost/dean and associate professor of theology at the Pontifical John Paul II Institute for Studies on Marriage and Family at the Catholic University of

America. He is the author of *Gift and the Unity of Being* (2013), *Rinascere: La memoria di Dio in una cultura tecnologica* (2015), and *Spirit's Gift: The Metaphysical Insight of Claude Bruaire* (2006), and the chief editor of the *English Critical Edition of the Works of Karol Wojtyła/John Paul II.*

MARGARET HARPER MCCARTHY is an assistant professor of theological anthropology at the Pontifical John Paul II Institute for Studies on Marriage and Family at the Catholic University of America. She is the editor of the quarterly review *Humanum: Issues in Family, Culture, and Science* and editor of the recent book *Torn Asunder: Children, the Myth of the Good Divorce, and the Recovery of Origins* (2017).

PAULO PROSPERI, FSCB, is a priest of the Fraternity of St. Charles Borromeo and assistant professor of patrology and systematic theology at the Pontifical John Paul II Institute for Studies on Marriage and Family at the Catholic University of America. His published works include essays on the subject of typological exegesis and the witness of Church Fathers in *Communio: International Catholic Review.*

D. C. SCHINDLER is an associate professor of metaphysics and anthropology at the Pontifical John Paul II Institute for Studies on Marriage and Family at the Catholic University of America. He is an editor of the North American edition of *Communio: International Catholic Review*; author, most recently, of *Freedom From Reality: The Diabolical Character of Modern Liberty* (2017) and *The Catholicity of Reason* (2013); and coeditor of *A Robert Spaemann Reader* (2015).

DAVID L. SCHINDLER is dean emeritus and Gagnon Professor of Fundamental Theology at the Pontifical John Paul II Institute for Studies on Marriage and Family at the Catholic University of America. He is editor of the series "*Ressourcement:* Retrieval and Renewal in Catholic Thought," published by Eerdmans, and editor-in-chief of the North American edition of *Communio: International Catholic Review*. His published books include *Freedom, Truth, and Human Dignity: The Second Vatican Council's Declaration on Religious Freedom* (2015) (coauthored with Nicholas J. Healy), *Ordering Love: Liberal Societies and the Memory of God* (2011), and *Heart of the World, Center of the Church: Communio Ecclesiology, Liberalism and Liberation* (1996).

ADRIAN J. WALKER is a visiting associate professor at the School of Theology and Religious Studies at the Catholic University of America and a fellow of the Institute for Human Ecology. He also serves as editor for *Communio: International Catholic Review* and is the translator of numerous works by such authors as Hans Urs von Balthasar, Adrienne von Speyr, and Joseph Ratzinger/Benedict XVI.

INDEX OF NAMES

Index of Names

INDEX OF SUBJECTS